ヘルシング

ヘルシング

HELLSING

DELUXE EDITION 2

by

KOHTA HIRANO

平野耕太

translation

DUANE JOHNSON

lettering and retouch

WILBERT LACUNA

and STUDIO CUTIE

DARK HORSE MANGA

president and publisher
MIKE RICHARDSON

US editor
CHRIS WARNER

assistant editor
KONNER KNUDSEN

collection designer
SKYLER WEISSENFLUH

digital art technician
ADAM PRUETT

This volume collects material previously published in *Hellsing* volumes 5, 6, 7, and 8.

Dark Horse Manga
A division of Dark Horse Comics LLC
10956 SE Main Street, Milwaukie OR 97222

DarkHorse.com

Represented in the EU by Authorised Rep Compliance Ltd.
Ground Floor, 71 Lower Baggot Street, Dublin, D02 P593, Ireland
ARCCompliance.com

To find a comics shop near you, visit FindYourComic.store.

First edition: November 2020
ISBN 978-1-50672-001-2

9 10
Printed in China

Library of Congress Cataloging-in-Publication Data

Names: Hirano, Kohta, author, artist. | Johnson, Duane, 1976- translator.
Title: Hellsing / Kouta Hirano ; translation, Duane Johnson.
Other titles: Herushingu. English
Description: Deluxe edition. | Milwaukie, OR : Dark Horse Manga, 2020- | v. 1: "This volume collects material previously published in Hellsing volumes 1, 2, 3, and 4" | Summary: "The international sensation returns in deluxe hardcover editions. The shadowy Hellsing Organization fights back against the supernatural horrors that prey upon humanity. And Hellsing's secret weapon, a vampire lord of terrifying power, must stand against an undead army that marches beneath the banner of the swastika!"-- Provided by publisher.
Identifiers: LCCN 2020002768 | ISBN 9781506715537 (v. 1 ; hardcover)
Subjects: LCSH: Graphic novels.
Classification: LCC PN6790.J33 H5648613 2020 | DDC 741.5/952--dc23
LC record available at https://lccn.loc.gov/2020002768

CONTENTS

28 FLASH POINT 007
29 D 4 015
30 D 5 037
31 D 6 055
32 D 7 079
33 D 8 103
34 D 9 127
35 XANADO 143
36 FINAL FANTASY 1 159
37 FINAL FANTASY 2 183
38 FINAL FANTASY 3 20
39 FINAL FANTASY 4 22
40 FINAL FANTASY 5 239
41 THE SCREAMER 257
42 AUBIRD FORCE 269
43 GUN BULLET 293
44 BALLOON FIGHT 309
45 SOLDIER OF FORTUNE 1 333
46 SOLDIER OF FORTUNE 2 349
47 SOLDIER OF FORTUNE 3 365
48 SOLDIER OF FORTUNE 4 383
49 SOLDIER OF FORTUNE 5 399
50 SOLDIER OF FORTUNE 6 41
51 LAST MISSION 427
52 GET AWAY 44
53 YAKSA 463
54 THE MAN I LOVE 48
55 OGRE BATTLE 489
56 ANGEKUS 52
57 WIZARDRY 1 539
58 WIZARDRY 2 565
59 WIZARDRY 3 579
60 WIZARDRY 4 599
61 WIZARDRY 5 625

ヘルシング

HELLSING

ヘルシング

平野耕太

ORDER 28

FLASH POINT

SO THIS IS WHERE YOU'VE BEEN, MASTER.
カッカッカッカッカッ
KATZ KATZ KATZ KATZ KATZ
WE'VE LOOKED ALL OVER.
MISS INTEGRA WISHES TO SEE YOU.
MAS-TER?
?
カッカッカッ
KATZ KATZ KATZ

HE'S HAVING A KIP...
SO IT WOULD SEEM.
THAT'S DOWNRIGHT CREEPY! NO WAY AM I WAKING HIM UP.
SNOOZE
EVEN SO...
THIS STATE OF AFFAIRS HERE...
SCOOP
HE'S EATEN HIS FILL AND NOW SLEEPS HIS FILL.
ALMOST LIKE SOME "SAVAGE BEAST."
PLIP
NO DOUBT HE HAS SENSED SOMETHING. SOMETHING.
THE SCENT OF CONFLICT, OR SOME SUCH.
SCENT?

AH!! HE JUST GRINNED.
I SEE YOU GRINNING, MASTER.
SO IT WOULD SEEM.
…… ……
IT'S LIKE HE'S THINKING ABOUT WHAT HE'LL DO FOR FUN TOMORROW.
LIKE... ...A SLEEPING CHILD....
PERHAPS... HE IS IN THE MIDST OF A DREAM.
TWITCH
WHOA!
A DREAM!!
KA
KAAA
THAT REMINDS ME, WALTER.
I HAD THIS WEIRD DREAM WHEN WE WENT TO SOUTH AMERICA, SEE.
AH-HAH.
THERE WAS THIS ODD SPIRIT THING, YOU SEE.
IT SAID IT WAS HARKONNEN OR SOMETHING.

ALUCARD.
WAKE UP. ALUCARD.
SSSP
BUDDA BUDDA BUDDA BUDDA
WHAT ARE YOU?
GOGOGOGOGOGOGO
BEEP BEEP BEEP BEEP BEEP
THIS AIN'T HADAKA NO TAISHO-WILLIS.
I'M YOUR GUN.
THE SPIRIT OF THE JACKAL-WILLIS.
GO GO GO

BANNG
BANNG
ドキューン
ドキューン
S-STOP! STOP THAT-WILLIS!
LISTEN!! PLEASE, LISTEN TO WHAT I'VE GOT TO SAY-WILLIS!
ギュルルルルルルルルル
GRRRRR
WHAT IS THIS PLACE?
I'M LEAVING.
THIS'S THE SPACE OF THE JACKAL SPIRIT, MY DIMENSION.
IT'S CALLED "WILLIS SPACE" -WILLIS.
ゴゴゴゴゴゴゴ
GOGOGOGOGOGOGO
YOU'RE NEVER GETTIN' OUTTA HERE AGAIN -WILLIS.
NAKATOMI PLAZA
IN HERE YOU'LL TAKE PART IN SUBTLE MOVIES THAT NO ONE CAN DECIDE IF THEY'RE GOOD OR BAD FOR THE REST OF YOUR LIFE -WILLIS.
ブリブリブリブリ
BRRRRRRRR
HUH...?!
YOU AND ME'RE GONNA GO ALL OVER THE PLACE IN NAKATOMI PLAZA...
USE A KATANA TO SAVE A FAT GANGSTER WITH TESSHO GENDA'S VOICE FROM TAKIN' IT UP THE ASS...
AND WE'RE ONNA BLOW E CRAP OUTTA N ASTEROID WITH STEVE USCEMI AND SWEEP THE GOLDEN ASPBERRY AWARDS. -WILLIS
WHAT'S THE DIFFERENCE BETWEEN STEVE BUSCEMI'S FACE AND GAMON KAWAI'S FACE?

BSHH
SPAKKK
THAT ONE'S AN IMPOSTER.
AND THAT WAS A CLOSE CALL.
!!
BTOOM BTOOM BTOOM
VWAA
AH!! WHAT'S GENERAL DE GAULLE DOING THERE?!
WHAT?!
SERAS AND INTEGRA ARE WAITING.
GREETINGS, I'M CHRISTOPHER WALKEN.
I'M TOM BERENGER.
I'm Maximilian Schell.
Let's just kill them all.
THE ODESSA FILE!!
GET LOST!
TOGETHER WE ARE THE DOGS OF WAR. DEATH.
GO HOME.
GREETINGS, I'M THE "EMPEROR."
WHO ARE YOU?!
GREETINGS, I'M THE CORE OF PART 4.
THIS DOESN'T MAKE ANY SENSE!!
GO GO GO GO GO

HOLY SHITE!
HE'LL HAVE WOKEN UP, THEN.
DID YOU HAVE SOME SORT OF BAD DREAM?
ALU-CARD?
NO.
IT'S NOTHING.
HMPH.
ORDER 28 / END

ORDER 29

VOOONE.
TWOOO.
THREEE.
RADAR CONTROL, CHECK. PROPULSION SYSTEM CONTROL, CHECK.
23% OF ENEMY PROVISIONS ARE USABLE BY US.
GOOD.
VAT ABOUT THE GHOULS?
VE LOCKED THEM UP IN THE SHIP'S HOLD.
THEY VOULD ONLY BE A NUISANCE NOW.
カッカッカッ
KATZ KATZ KATZ
VAT OF LIEUTEN-ANT RIP VAN?
GOOD.
SHE'S TAKING A NAP.

A NAP? ON DECK?
ON A BRIGHT, SUNNY, UNPLEASANT DAY LIKE THIS?
... ...I ENVY HER.
IT'S SURE THAT VE VILL NEVER AGAIN BE ABLE TO BATHE IN SUNLIGHT.
VAT VE'VE GAINED IS A GREAT THING. VE VERE FEEBLE OLD MEN AFTER ALL.
BUT VAT VE'VE LOST IS ALSO GREAT.
QUITE GREAT.
VE CAN'T EVEN FEED PIGEONS IN THE PARK ON SUNDAYS, OUR DAYS OFF, ANYMORE.
VE'RE MONSTERS.
VE'RE NOW NUMBERED AMONG THE MONSTERS.
BUT BEFORE THEM, VE MUST LOOK LIKE MERE ROOKIES.
THEY ARE THE VERE-VOLVES.
THE VARMONGERS.

ORDER 29 D④

TICK
TICK
TICK
TICK
TICK
カチ
カチカチ
カチカチ

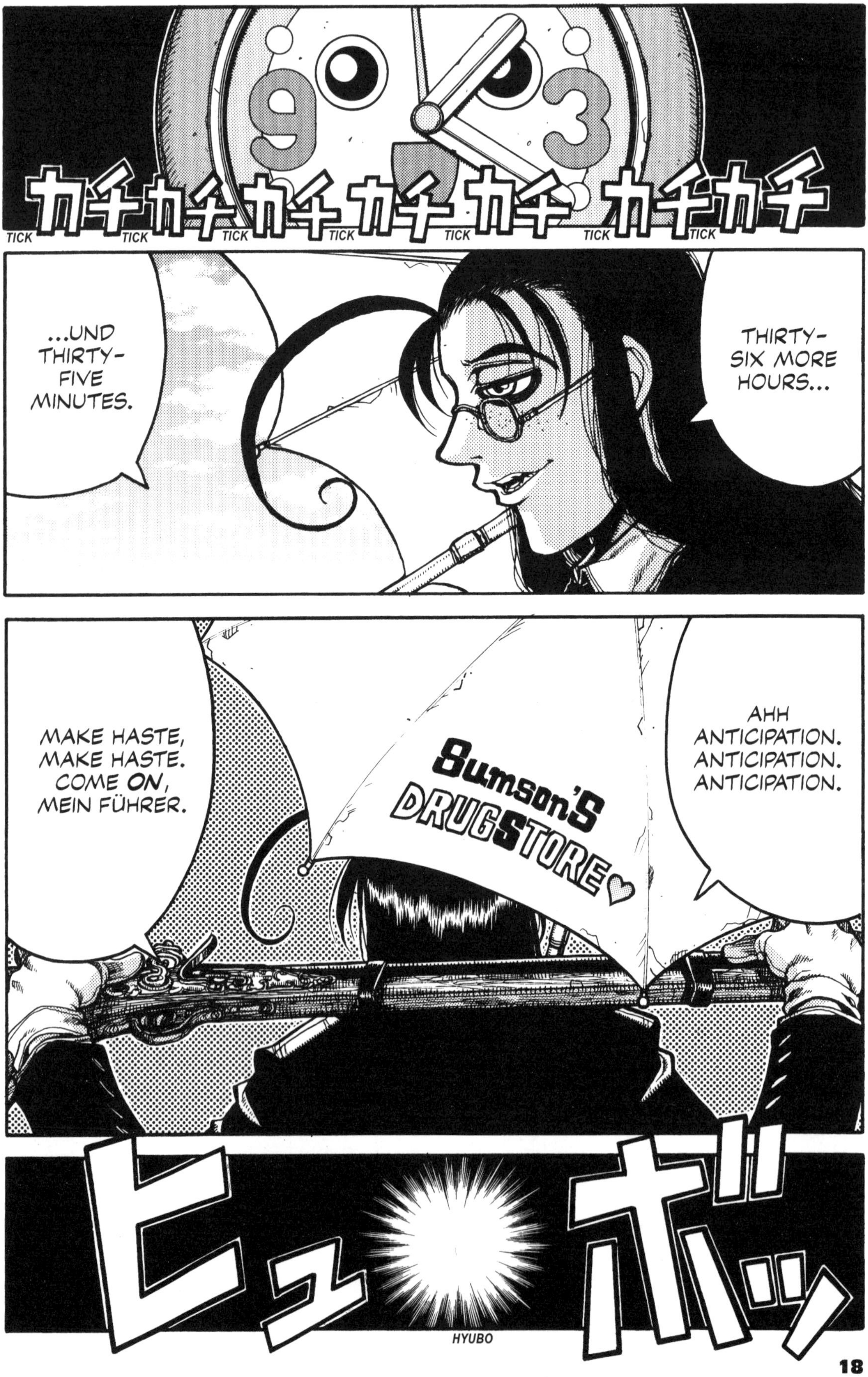

カチカチカチカチカチ カチカチ
TICK TICK TICK TICK TICK TICK TICK
THIRTY-SIX MORE HOURS...
...UND THIRTY-FIVE MINUTES.
AHH ANTICIPATION. ANTICIPATION. ANTICIPATION.
Sumson'S DRUGSTORE
MAKE HASTE, MAKE HASTE. COME ON, MEIN FÜHRER.
ヒュ ボッ
HYUBO

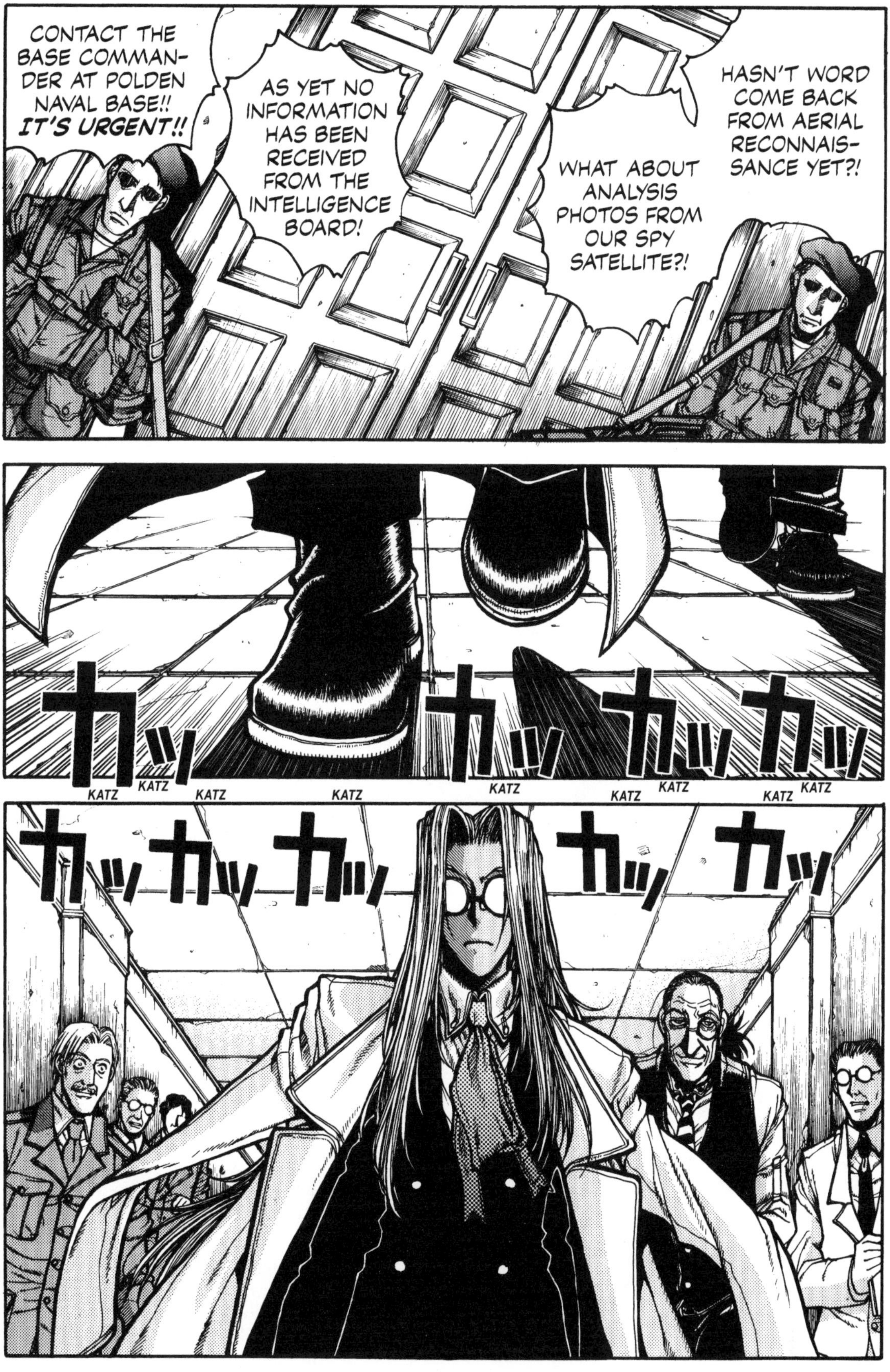
HASN'T WORD COME BACK FROM AERIAL RECONNAISSANCE YET?!
WHAT ABOUT ANALYSIS PHOTOS FROM OUR SPY SATELLITE?!
AS YET NO INFORMATION HAS BEEN RECEIVED FROM THE INTELLIGENCE BOARD!
CONTACT THE BASE COMMANDER AT POLDEN NAVAL BASE!! *IT'S URGENT!!*
カッ カッ カッ カッ
KATZ KATZ KATZ KATZ KATZ KATZ KATZ KATZ KATZ
カッ カッ カッ カッ カッ

GCHAK
!!
!
HEAD-QUARTERS
BRITISH NATIONAL SECURITY SPECIAL GUIDANCE DIVISION

HELLSING...
...IS HERE ON HER MAJESTY'S SECRET SERVICE.
カッ
KATZ
THERE YOU ARE.
SIR INTEGRA.
BRITISH ROYAL NAVY VICE-ADMIRAL SIR SHELBY M. PENWOOD

POINT
ADMIRAL!! DON'T TELL ME YOU INTEND TO SEEK HELP FROM THAT LOT!!
THIS IS A MATTER OF NATIONAL SECURITY!
WOULD YOU PERMIT THE INVOLVEMENT OF A SUSPICIOUS GROUP LIKE THEM?!
THIS FALLS WELL UNDER THE JURISDICTION OF OUR NAVY.
IT'S NO BUSINESS OF PEOPLE LIKE YOU.
NOW CLEAR OFF!!
KATZ
KATZ
KATZ
DMP
!!
WHA!
...
...
WHA?!

SPOP
SNIP
I WOULD'T MIND LEAVING...
...BUT ARE YOU SURE YOU WOULDN'T?
PLEASE... WORK WITH US ON THIS, SIR HELLSING.
THAT'S ENOUGH.
EXCUSE ME?!
...
...
WHAT IS THE PRESENT SITUATION, ADMIRAL?

EIGHTEEN HOURS AGO, COMMUNICA-TIONS WERE LOST WITH OUR NEWLY BUILT ROYAL NAVY AIRCRAFT CARRIER HMS EAGLE...
...ON MANEUVERS IN THE ATLANTIC, AFTER IT HAD BROADCAST A REPORT OF CONTACT WITH A HELICOPTER OF UNKNOWN ORIGIN.
PRESENTLY IT IS SITTING IDLE AT A POINT 300KM AWAY FROM ROLLINGTON.
ORIGINALLY THIS WAS OUR OWN PROBLEM TO DEAL WITH.
HOWEVER, HERE ARE SATELLITE PHOTOS THAT WERE SENT TO US SEVERAL HOURS AGO.
HAVE A LOOK.
FLAPA
!!
...
...!!
CATEGOR-ICALLY THIS IS NO LONGER OUR PROBLEM.
IT'S AN ACT OF MADNESS.

MILLENNIUM.
THE LETZTES BATAILLON.
ABSOLUTELY
RIDICULOUS!!
WHAM

IT'S A SHIP'S MUTINY, OR A RIOT!
VAMPIRES?
HA!
ADMIRAL!! I CAN'T BELIEVE YOU'RE SERIOUS ABOUT THIS!!
VAMPIRES? NAZI REMNANTS? THIS LITTLE JOKE IS WEARING THIN!!
WE HAVEN'T THE TIME TO PLAY OCCULT GAMES WITH YOU!!
I DON'T KNOW JUST HOW MUCH CONFIDENCE HER MAJESTY HAS IN YOU...
...BUT YOU'RE SADLY MISTAKEN IF YOU THINK YOUR PRIVILEGES WILL GET YOU ANYTHING HERE.
WE WOULD HAVE YOU REMAIN A FLY ON THE WALL.
VERY WELL THEN.
LET ME SEE JUST HOW SKILLED YOU ARE.

SINCE THE INCIDENT BEGAN, WE HAVE TRIED SEVERAL TIMES TO OPEN COMMUNICATIONS...
...BUT NO RESPONSE HAS BEEN FORTHCOMING WHATSOEVER.
GO OVER THE SITUATION.
YES, SIR!
... ...!!
WE'VE DISPATCHED SEVERAL RECONNAISSANCE PLANES...
...BUT ONCE AGAIN, NO REACTION.
IT SEEMS TO BE ABANDONED... RATHER... A GHOST SHIP.
!
BUT NO, OUR LATEST INTELLIGENCE INDICATES ONE PERSON ON DECK...
...BENEATH A PARASOL.

PRESENTLY, TWO SAS* SQUADS ARE ON AP-PROACH...
...VIA HELICOPTER TO ASSESS AND TAKE CONTROL OF THE SITUATION.
KYUN
KYUN
KYUN
*NOTE: BRITISH "SPECIAL AIR SERVICE."
THEY SHOULD REACH THE TARGET BEFORE LONG.
WHISPER
ボソッ
I PITY THOSE MEN.
WHAT WAS THAT?!
ADMIRAL, LET ME JUST SAY THIS.
WHAT?
THEY'RE ALL DEAD.
YOU'VE DONE NOTHING MORE THAN PRODUCE THIRTY PIECES OF MEAT.

ギュバババババ
BADDA
BADDA
BADDA
VISUAL CONFIRMATION OF HMS EAGLE!! WE'LL BE THERE IN A FEW MINUTES.
RIGHT!! IS EVERYONE READY?
READY FOR DROP!!
BADDA
BADDA
AT THE SAME TIME A TEAM ARRIVES AT THE FORE DECK...
...WE IN B TEAM WILL DEPLOY AND RAPPEL DOWN TO THE AFT DECK!!
TAKE CARE, MEN. WE DON'T KNOW WHAT'S GOING ON.

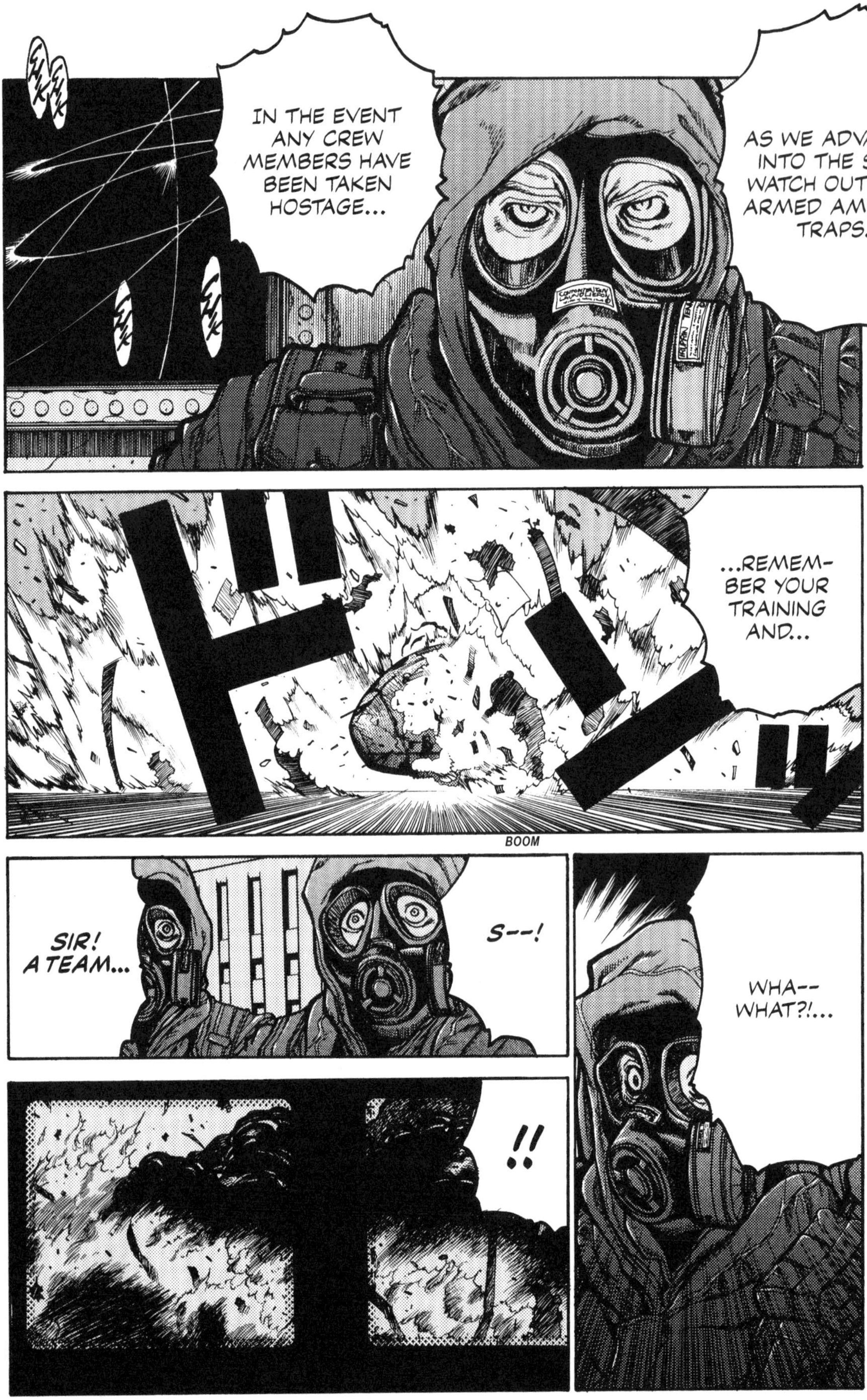

IN THE EVENT ANY CREW MEMBERS HAVE BEEN TAKEN HOSTAGE...
AS WE ADVANCE INTO THE SHIP, WATCH OUT FOR ARMED AMBUSH TRAPS.
...REMEMBER YOUR TRAINING AND...
BOOM
S--!
SIR! A TEAM...
WHA-- WHAT?!...
!!

WHEEOOOOOO
ヒュウウウウウ
ウウ ウウウウ
?!
S--!
SIR!!
BKOK
バガッ
キュルルルル
SHUSHUSHUSHU
ビュバッ
BYOOO
WHA...
WHAT THE HELL...
キュルルルル
SHUSHUSHU

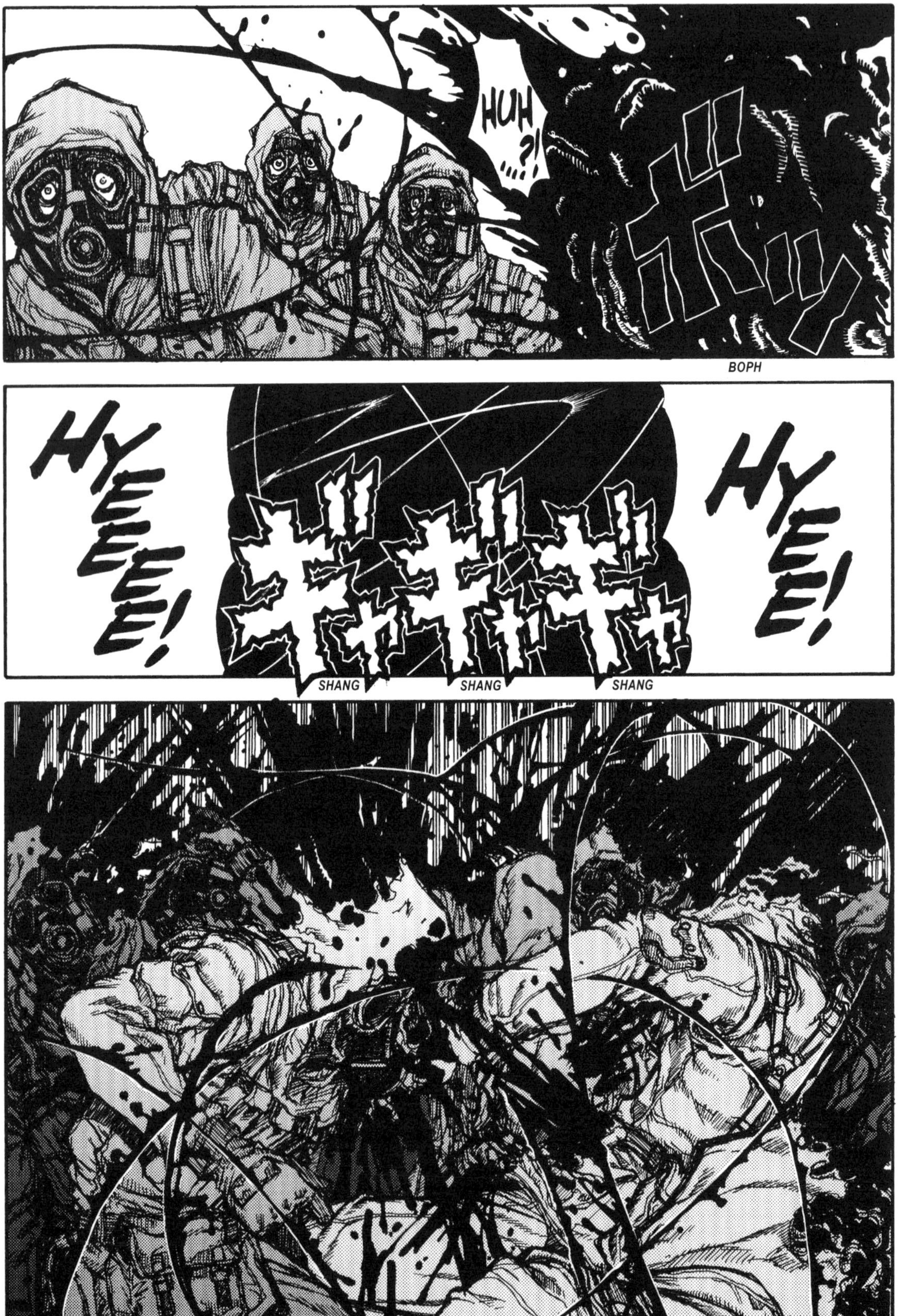
HUH ?! ...?!
BOPH
HYEEE!
HYEEEEE!
SHANG
SHANG
SHANG

ビチッ
SPAP
A...
AIIEEE!
キュッ ギュッ
SHNG
SHNG
BDOOM
ドガッ

ゴゴゴゴゴゴゴゴゴゴゴ
ROARRRRRRR
MY VARHEAD VILL...
...PUNISH ALL VITHOUT DISTINCTION.
カチ
カチ
TICK TICK
カチ
カチ
TICK TICK
EXACTLY THIRTY-SIX HOURS LEFT TO GO.
VAT A TRAGEDY. VAT A COMEDY.

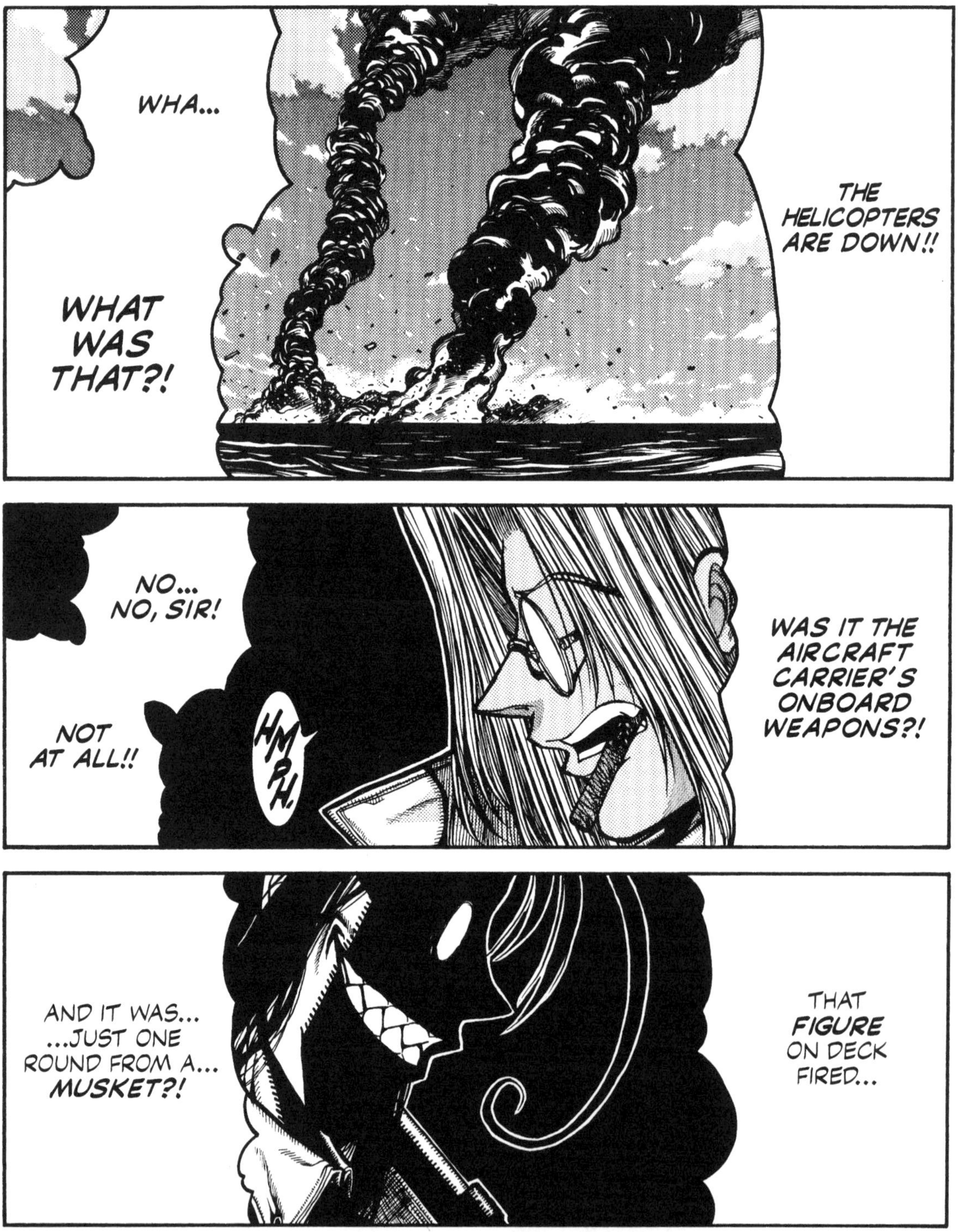
THE HELICOPTERS ARE DOWN!!
WHA...
WHAT WAS THAT?!
WAS IT THE AIRCRAFT CARRIER'S ONBOARD WEAPONS?!
HMPH.
NO... NO, SIR!
NOT AT ALL!!
THAT FIGURE ON DECK FIRED...
AND IT WAS... ...JUST ONE ROUND FROM A... MUSKET?!

ORDER 29 / END

ORDER 30

*NOTE: DER FREISCHÜTZ = "THE MAGIC BULLET MARKSMAN."

ORDER 30

D⑤

THE SAS TEAMS... WERE THERE ANY SURVIVORS?!
SOMETHING THIS INSANE... CAN'T BE!
WHAT ABOUT THE RECONNAIS-SANCE REPORT...?
THERE'S A TERRIBLE BLAZE ON THE OCEAN SURFACE. THAT'S ALL...
GET IN TOUCH WITH AIRBORNE COMMAND
CALL UP 2ND SQUAD'S CHIEF!
HOW COULD SOMETHING LIKE THIS HAPPEN?!
ISN'T THERE SOME MISTAKE?! RECONFIRM IT...
THIS IS A FARCE.
WH...?
WHAT WAS THAT?!
I MERELY STATED THAT THIS IS A FARCE.
GTAK
WH...
WHERE DO YOU INTEND TO GO, SIR INTEGRA?
I CANNOT CONTINUE OUR LITTLE SOCIAL.
AS LONG AS YOU PROLONG THIS ESCAPADE, NOTHING CHANGES. TIME CONTINUES TO BLEED AWAY.

WE PERCEIVE THIS CHAIN OF EVENTS TO BE THE WORK OF VAMPIRES...
...AND **WE** SHALL TAKE ACTION THE WAY WE CHARACTER-ISTICALLY DO.
WHA...
WHAT DO YOU MEAN?!
FINE, OFF WITH YOU THEN!!
SIR PENWOOD, I HAVE SAID MY PIECE.
AD--!
ADMIRAL!!
YES, OF COURSE I UNDER-STAND, INTEGRA.
WE RECOGNIZE HELLSING'S *PREROGA-TIVE*!!

JA.
...
...
KATZ KATZ KATZ
BATAM
WHAT DO YOU THINK?
WELL!
IT IS A GOOD DECOY, AND AN OBVIOUS ONE.
THE MORE TIME IT CONSUMES, THE BETTER IT SERVES THEM.
KATZ
KATZ
KATZ
KATZ
BUT NEITHER CAN WE IGNORE IT.
TREATING IT AS A MERE GHOST SHIP WOULD BE TOO DANGEROUS.
KATZ
KATZ
KATZ

IT'S OUT OF THE QUESTION FOR US TO DEAL WITH IT PERSONALLY.
YET, WE CANNOT DISREGARD IT.
KATZ
IF WE APPROACH IT, WE'RE ATTACKED.
THIS IS A TYPICAL BATTLE OF THREAT AND BESIEGEMENT.
KATZ
I SUPPOSE THE OCEAN IS THE CASTLE WALL, WITH AN INFINITELY WIDE MOAT.
KATZ
KATZ
AND THOSE "MAGIC BULLETS."
THERE'S NOTHING THAT CAN GET CLOSE IN THE FACE OF THOSE.
KATZ
HOWEVER, THEY HAVE NO MEANS OF ESCAPE.
TO VAMPIRES, THE SEA IS THE SAME AS THE PITS OF HELL'S CAULDRON.
BUT IT'S THE SAME CASE FOR US.
IF THEY MANAGE TO ESCAPE THE EAGLE, THAT IS WHERE THEY WOULD FALL TO.
KATZ
KATZ
KATZ
YES!
QUITE RIGHT.

HOW ARE WE GOING TO SEND...
...ALUCARD OR SERAS INTO THAT MARITIME STEEL STRONGHOLD?
KATZ
A HEAVY WARSHIP.
NON.
IT WOULD REQUIRE TOO MUCH TIME.
AND THEY WILL NOT LET THEIR CAPTURED SHIP REMAIN IDLE INDEFINITELY.

A SMALL HIGH-SPEED BOAT.
NON.
THERE ARE LARGE ANTI-AIRCRAFT CANNONS AND THE CIWS* CLUSTER.
I DON'T THINK IT COULD STAND UP AGAINST A STORM OF BULLETS.
*NOTE: CLOSE-IN WEAPONS SYSTEM
AN AIRCRAFT.
DESCENT FROM DIRECTLY OVERHEAD.
NON.
AGAINST THE ONBOARD *SAM...
...AN OVERHEAD APPROACH IS BEYOND OUR MEANS.
*NOTE: SURFACE TO AIR MISSILES
PERHAPS THE USE OF AN AIRCRAFT ACCOMPANIED BY...
...COPIOUS AMOUNTS OF DECOY CHAFF.
NON.
EVEN IF WE FOOL THE MISSILES...
...THE "MAGIC BULLETS" REMAIN.

TO CONCLUDE...
ZOOO
IN THE FACE OF MISSILES AND A HAIL OF BULLETS...
...AS WELL AS THE MAGIC BULLETS...
...WE HAVE TO FIND A WAY TO GET ME ONTO THE DECK OF AN AIRCRAFT CARRIER AT SEA.
THOSE ARE THE RULES.
ZROOO

NOT EXACTLY A REASONABLE DEMAND.
NO, WAIT.
PERHAPS THERE IS A WAY.
ONLY ONE TYPE OF PLANE WOULD FACILITATE SUCH RECKLESSNESS.
BROAAAAAAR

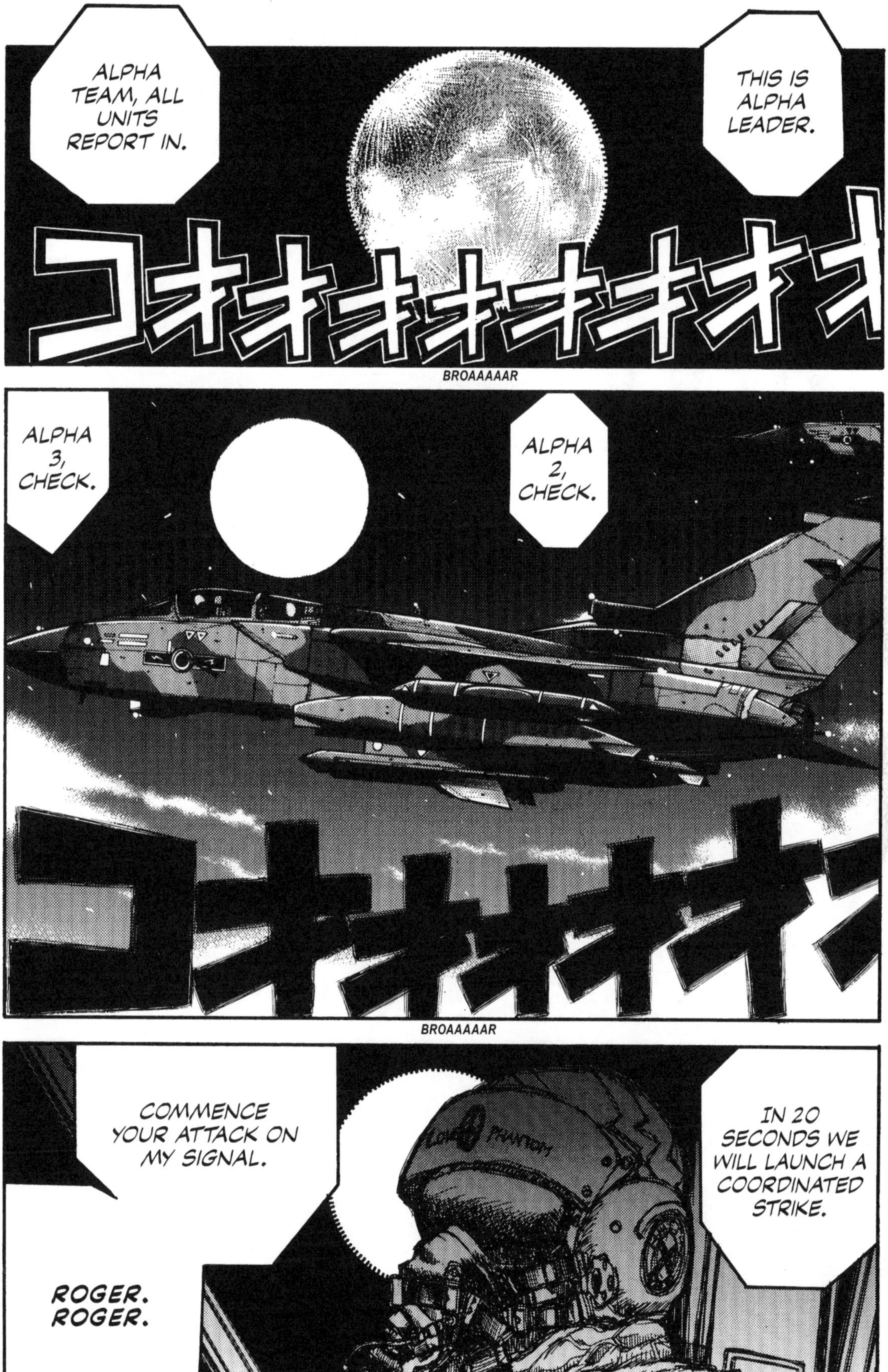
THIS IS ALPHA LEADER.
ALPHA TEAM, ALL UNITS REPORT IN.
BROAAAAAR
ALPHA 2, CHECK.
ALPHA 3, CHECK.
BROAAAAAR
IN 20 SECONDS WE WILL LAUNCH A COORDINATED STRIKE.
COMMENCE YOUR ATTACK ON MY SIGNAL.
ROGER. ROGER.

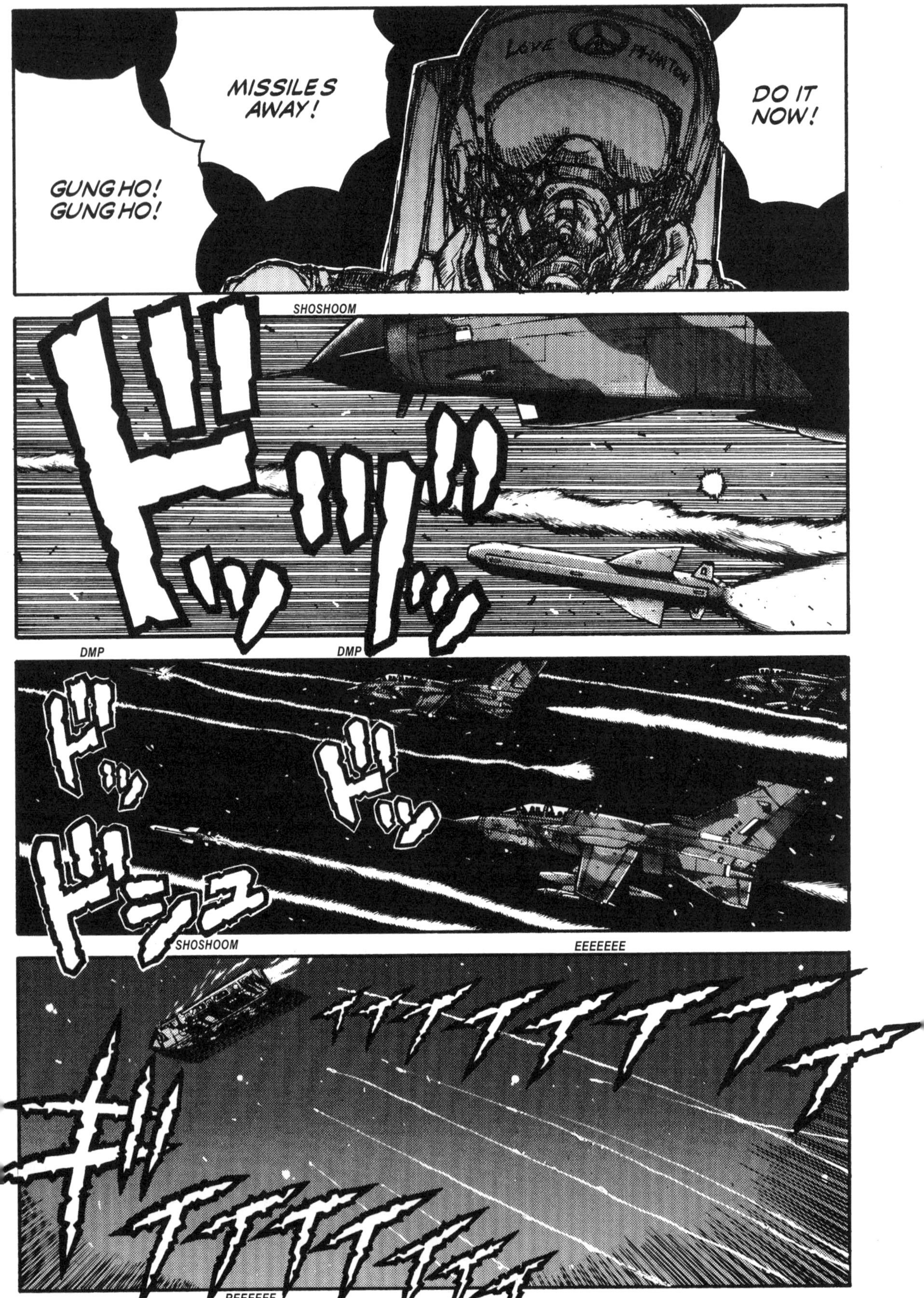
DO IT NOW!
MISSILES AWAY!
GUNG HO! GUNG HO!
SHOSHOOM
DMP
DMP
SHOSHOOM
EEEEEEE
REEEEEE

BKOOM
BDOM
BOMPH
BOOOOM
SHPAAA

THE MISSILES... ...?!
WHA--!
THEY SELF-DESTRUCTED?!
IMPOSSIBLE!
NO! THEY WERE TAKEN OUT!
ALL UNITS!! FORM UP AND--
KREEEEE
G--! GWAHH!
WHAT'S WRONG?!
WHAT'S WRONG, ALPHA2?!
GREEE
GREEE
GREEE
DOOM
LOVE
A-AL-ALPHA 2 JUST...
WHAT HAPPENED, ALPHA 3?!
ALPHA 3! ALPHA 3!
RESPOND!!

!!
バチャ
BLUCH
ボッ
BOPH
フヒュウゥ
KYOOOO

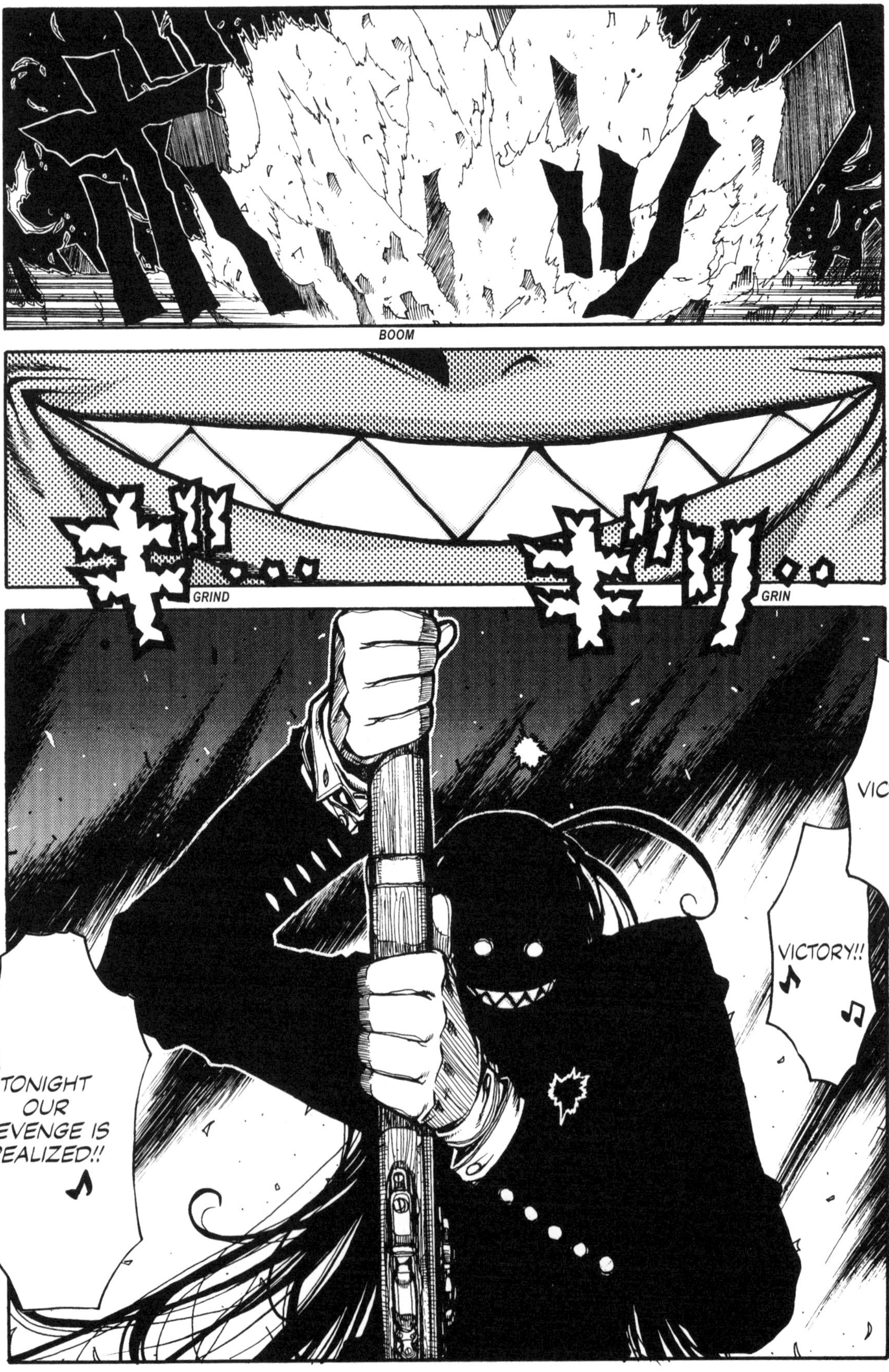
BOOM
GRIND
GRIN
VICTORY!!
VICTORY!!
TONIGHT OUR REVENGE IS REALIZED!!

SHUDDER
AWAH..
THUMP
VAT ?! ...
VAT IST ...?
VAT... IST THIS?
A
IT'S HIM!!
IT'S HIM!!
HE IST COMING!!

ROYAL AIRFORCE
BOMPH
ORDER 30 / END

ORDER 31

THE EXP 14L-E, AN EXPERIMENTAL STRATOSPHERIC MODEL.
IT'S ONE OF THE TWO SR-71 RECONNAISSANCE JETS RETIRED FROM SERVICE A FEW YEARS AGO...
...BY THE U.S. MILITARY AND SOLD TO OUR RAF'S R&D DEPARTMENT.
ALTHOUGH ONLY THE EXTERIOR IS AS IT WAS WITH THE AMERICANS,
THE INTERIOR HAS BEEN SO ALTERED THAT YOU COULD ACCURATELY SAY IT'S A DIFFERENT PLANE.
TO BEGIN WITH, THE RECONNAISSANCE MODELS ARE TWO-SEATERS.
BUT NOT THIS ONE.
THE RECONNAISSANCE FACILITIES ARE GONE, AND IT'S BEEN RETAILORED AS A ONE-SEATER.
IT'S DESIGNED TO BREAK HIGH-ALTITUDE AND HIGH-SPEED RECORDS.
AN AIRPLANE FOR PERSONAL USE.
AND SO, I'LL ASK YOU ONCE MORE.
JUST WHO IN HELL ARE YOU LOT?
THE HELLSING AGENCY... ...YOU SAID?

ORDER 31 D6

VE HAF A RADAR BLIP!! IT'S INBOUND!!
AGAIN? THE FOOLS, COME TO BE MADE SCRAPS OF SEAWEED ONCE MORE.
NEIN! THIS ONE... AH...!
SPEED, MACH 2.8!! ALTITUDE... 85,000?!
VAT?! IMPOSSIBLE.
85,000 YOU SAID?!
IT'S A RECON-NAISSANCE PLANE.
UN SR-71.
?
YOU DON'T KNOW? THEY'VE BEEN IN MAGAZINES MANY TIMES.
IT VAS BORN DURING THE COLD VAR, UN ARTISTICALLY STYLED RECON-NAISSANCE PLANE.
BUT THIS IST THE FIRST I'VE HEARD OF BRITAIN HAVING ANY.
HAHA! VY DON'T VE KNOCK IT OUT OF THE SKY?
VE CAN'T.

THIS SHIP'S ANTIAIRCRAFT MISSILES VOULD DO NOTHING.
IT'S A MONSTER VHICH FLIES THROUGH THE STRATOSPHERE FASTER THAN MACH 3.
HE IST COMING!!
LIEUTENANT!! VAT IST?! VAT'S HAPPENING?!
EXACTLY WHO IST COMING?!
LIEUTENANT!!
RIP
IST
ING!!

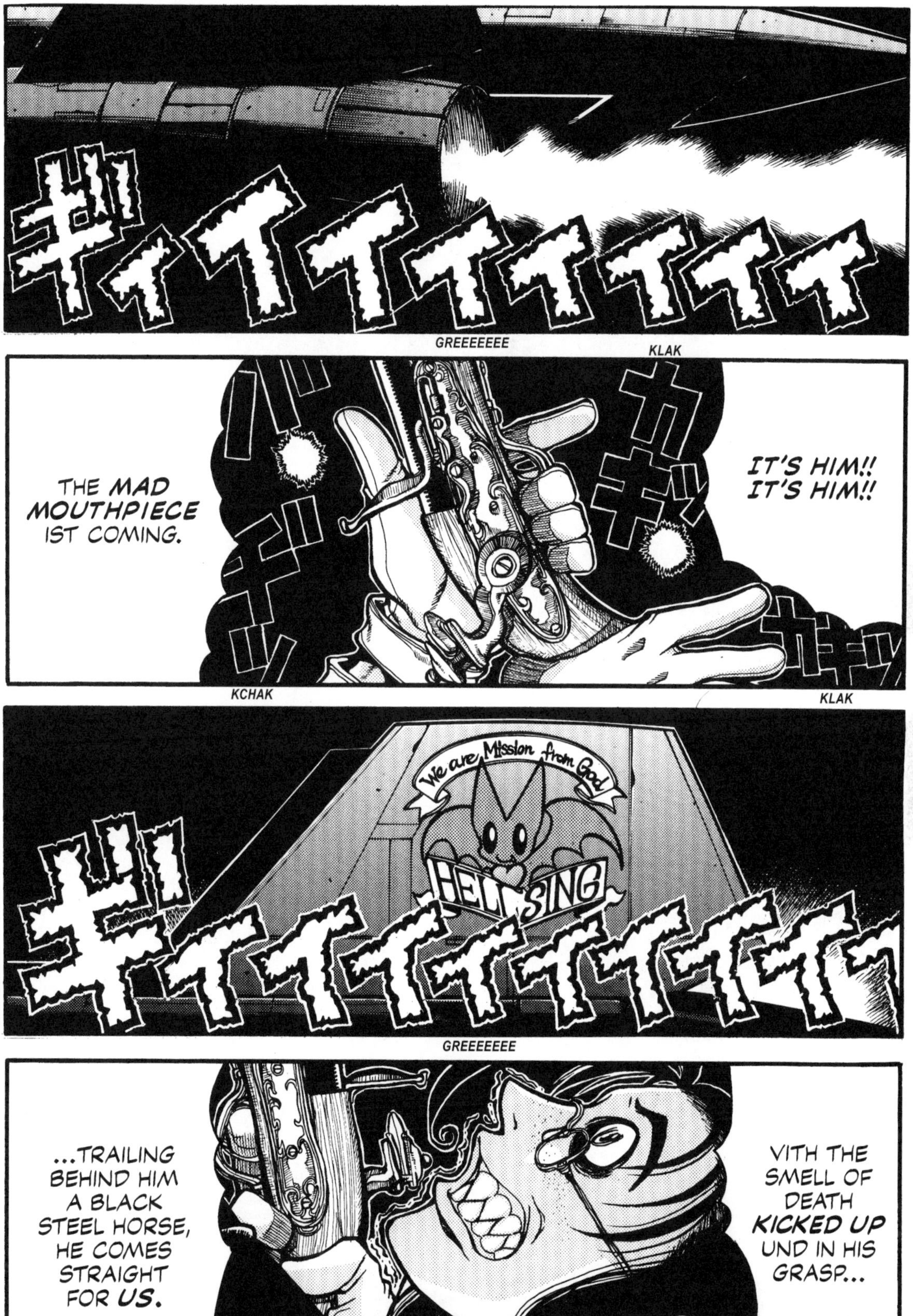
GREEEEEEE
KLAK
IT'S HIM!! IT'S HIM!!
THE MAD MOUTHPIECE IST COMING.
KCHAK
KLAK
We are Mission from God
HELLSING
GREEEEEEE
VITH THE SMELL OF DEATH KICKED UP UND IN HIS GRASP...
...TRAILING BEHIND HIM A BLACK STEEL HORSE, HE COMES STRAIGHT FOR US.

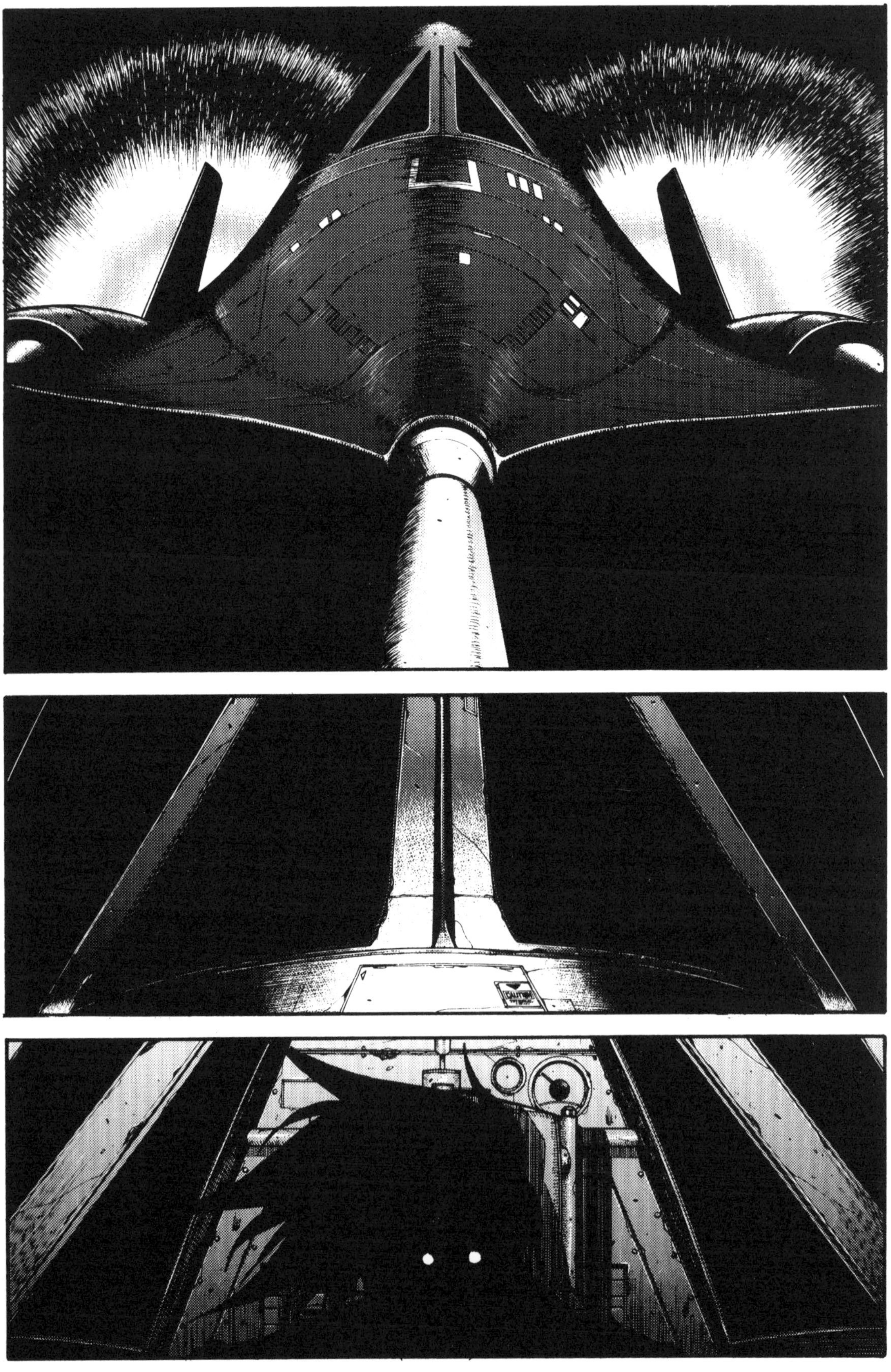
CAUTION

LEEEEEER
コオオオ オオオオオ
ROAAAAAR
TAKE HEED. FOR IF THOU PRESUMETH TO FLIRT WITH SPIRITS...
...THOU SHALT JOIN THEM.

AIRFORCE
ROOOOO
ROOOOO

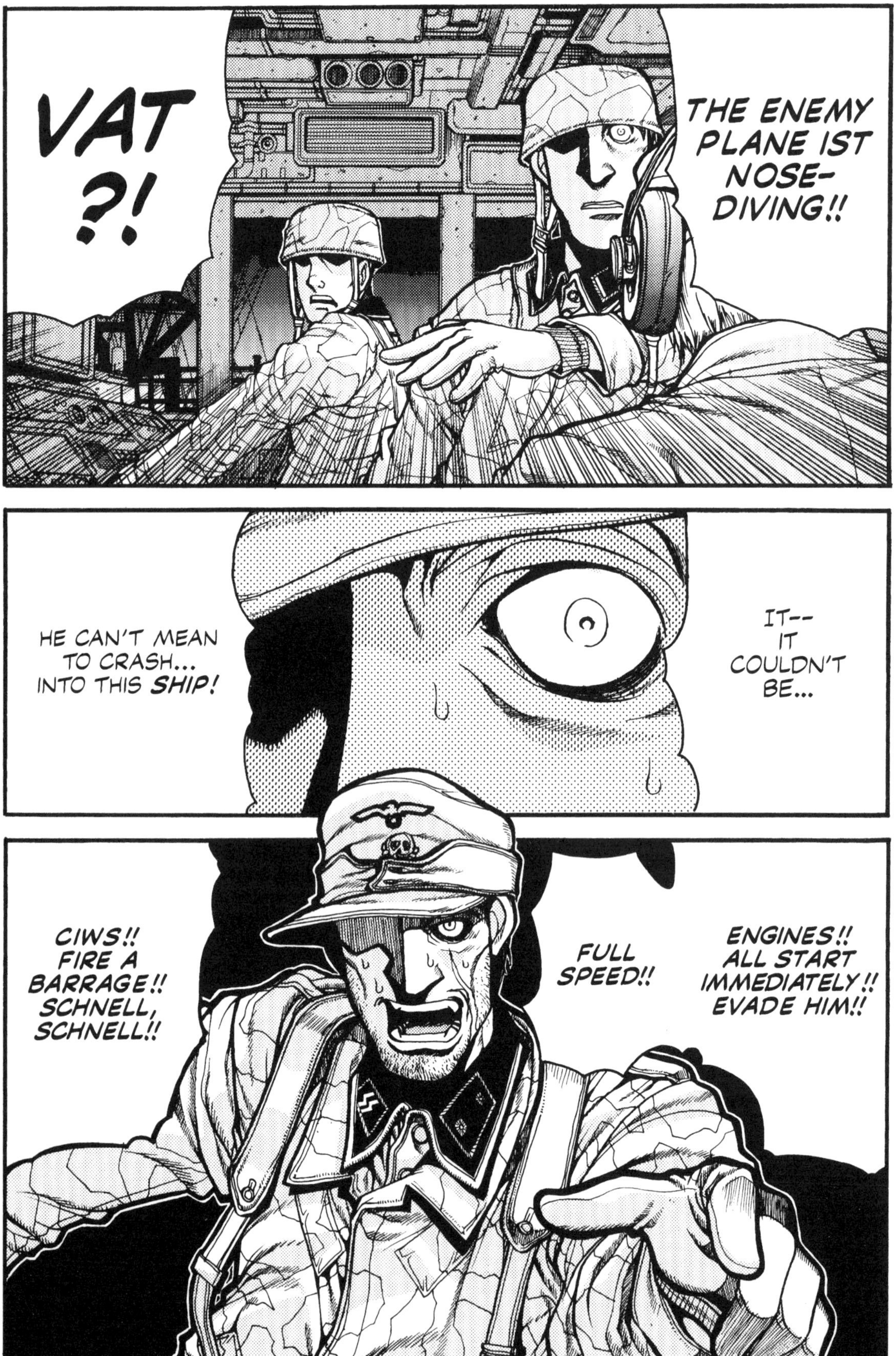
VAT ?!
THE ENEMY PLANE IST NOSE-DIVING!!
IT-- IT COULDN'T BE...
HE CAN'T MEAN TO CRASH... INTO THIS SHIP!
ENGINES!! ALL START IMMEDIATELY!! EVADE HIM!!
FULL SPEED!!
CIWS!! FIRE A BARRAGE!! SCHNELL, SCHNELL!!

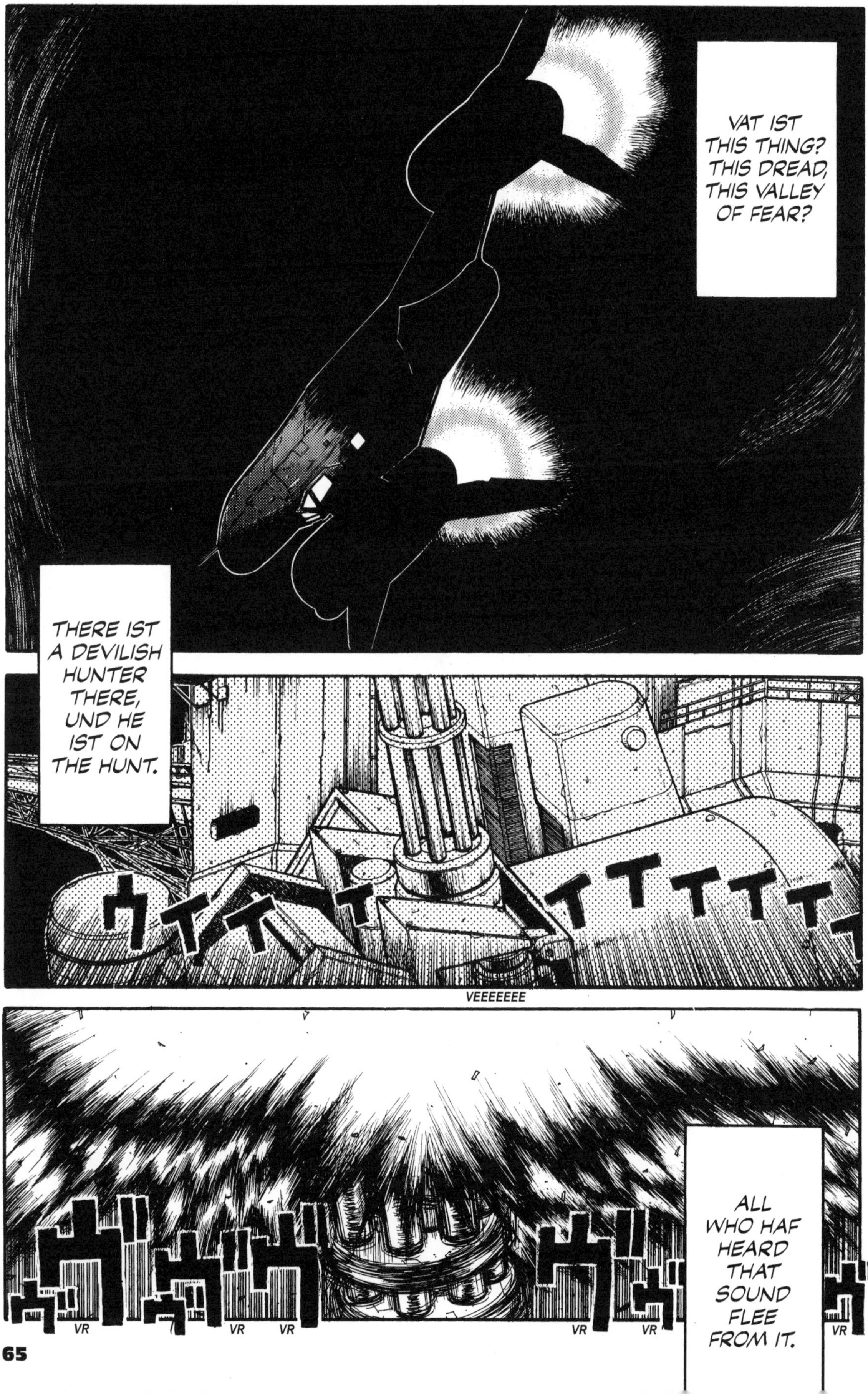
VAT IST THIS THING? THIS DREAD, THIS VALLEY OF FEAR?
THERE IST A DEVILISH HUNTER THERE, UND HE IST ON THE HUNT.
VEEEEEEE
ALL WHO HAF HEARD THAT SOUND FLEE FROM IT.
VR VR VR VR VR VR

AS A HUNTER, VAT IS THERE TO FEAR?
DOES FEAR **EXIST** VITHIN THE HEART OF THE HUNTER?
BUT THOSE WHO TEST GOD DO SO IN SIN.

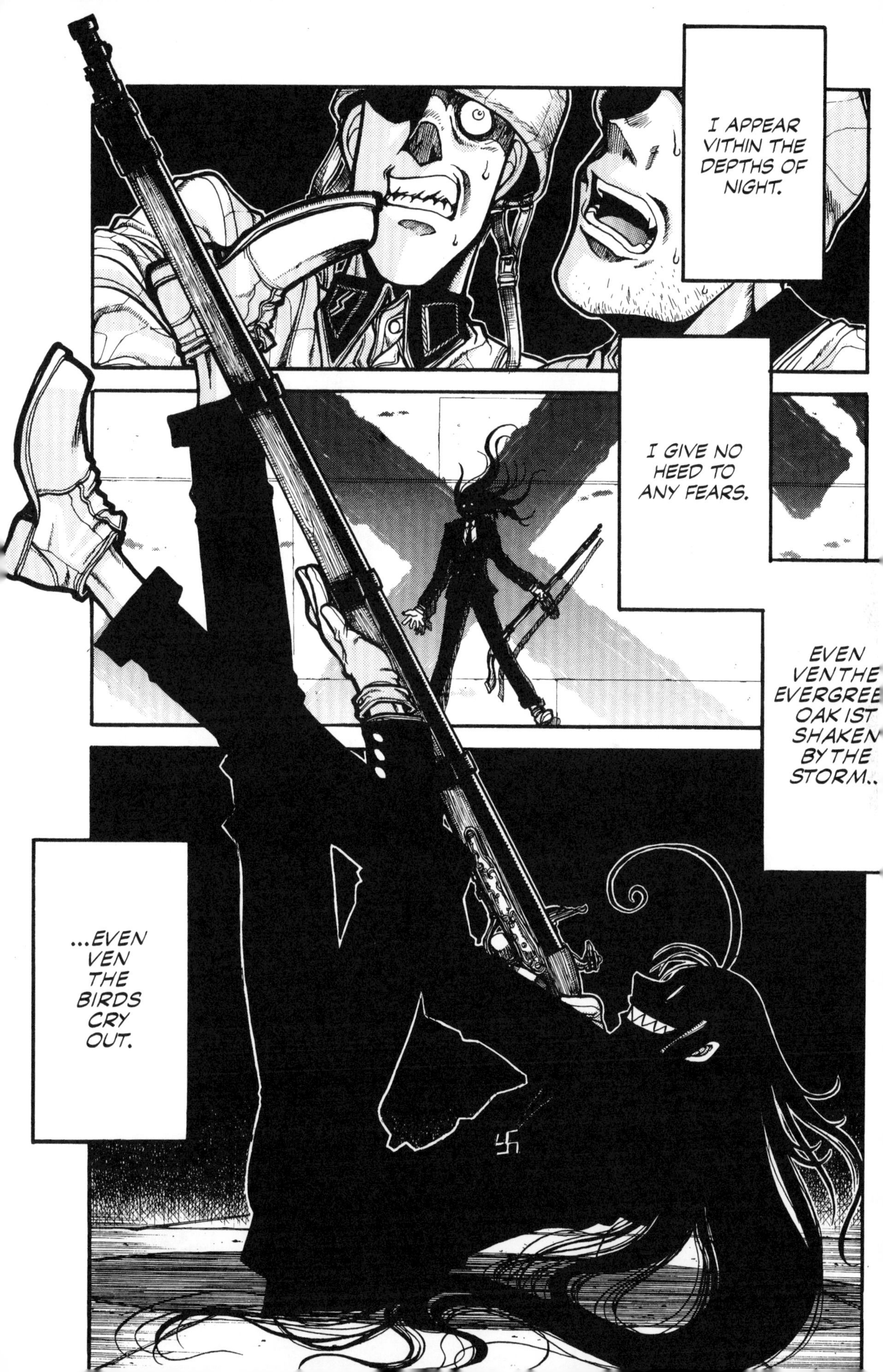
I APPEAR VITHIN THE DEPTHS OF NIGHT.
I GIVE NO HEED TO ANY FEARS.
EVEN VEN THE EVERGREE OAK IST SHAKEN BY THE STORM..
...EVEN VEN THE BIRDS CRY OUT.

I AM VORRIED. I AM VORRIED.
I AM VORRIED. I AM VORRIED.
SHPAA
HERE ST NO NEED TO URRY SO.
GI GI GI GI GI GI
DON'T GO. DON'T GO.

THE MOON-BEAMS ARE STILL SURE.
THE MOON-LIGHT MAKES IT YET LIKE TWILIGHT.
TUNK
KRAK KRAK KRAK
GI GI GI
BWEE BWEE BWEE BWEE
BEFORE LONG THAT LIGHT TOO VILL FADE.

WHUPH
BDAM
BDAM

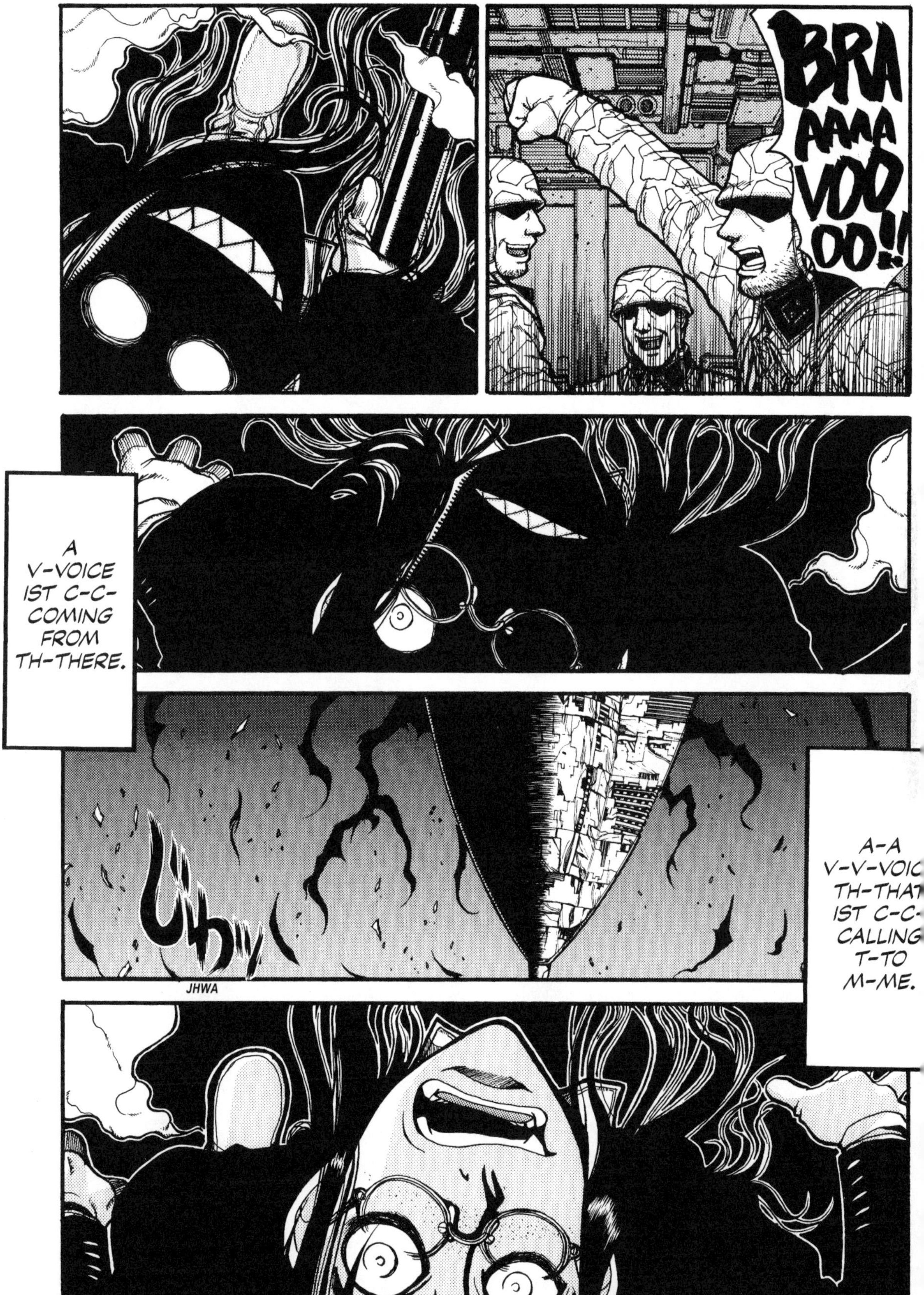
BRAAAAVOOOO!!
A V-VOICE IST C-C-COMING FROM TH-THERE.
A-A V-V-VOIC TH-THAT IST C-C-CALLING T-TO M-ME.
JHWA

BAKI
BAKI
BAKI
BAKI
BAKI
CONTROL ART RESTRICTION SYSTEM.
CROMWELL
LEVEL 3, LEVEL 2, LEVEL 1.
RELEASED.

BEFORE LONG, I GUESS THE LIGHT OF THE SUN SHALL BE LOST TOO.

FATE HAS DRIVEN YOU.

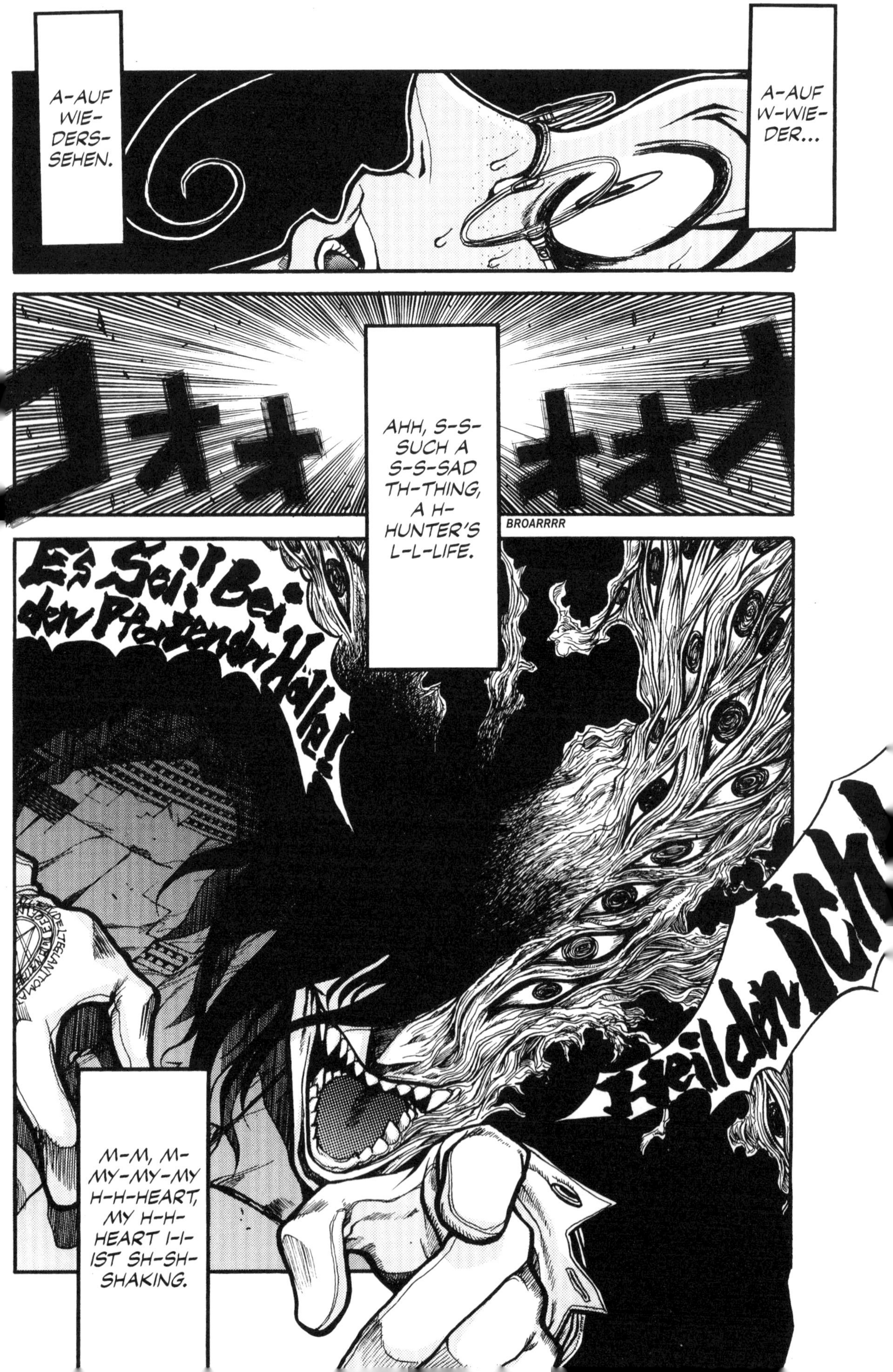
A-AUF W-WIE-DER...
A-AUF WIE-DERS-SEHEN.
AHH, S-S-SUCH A S-S-SAD TH-THING, A H-HUNTER'S L-L-LIFE.
BROARRRR
Es Sei! Bei den Pforten der Hölle!
M-M, M-MY-MY-MY H-H-HEART, MY H-H-HEART I-I-IST SH-SH-SHAKING.

BWOOM

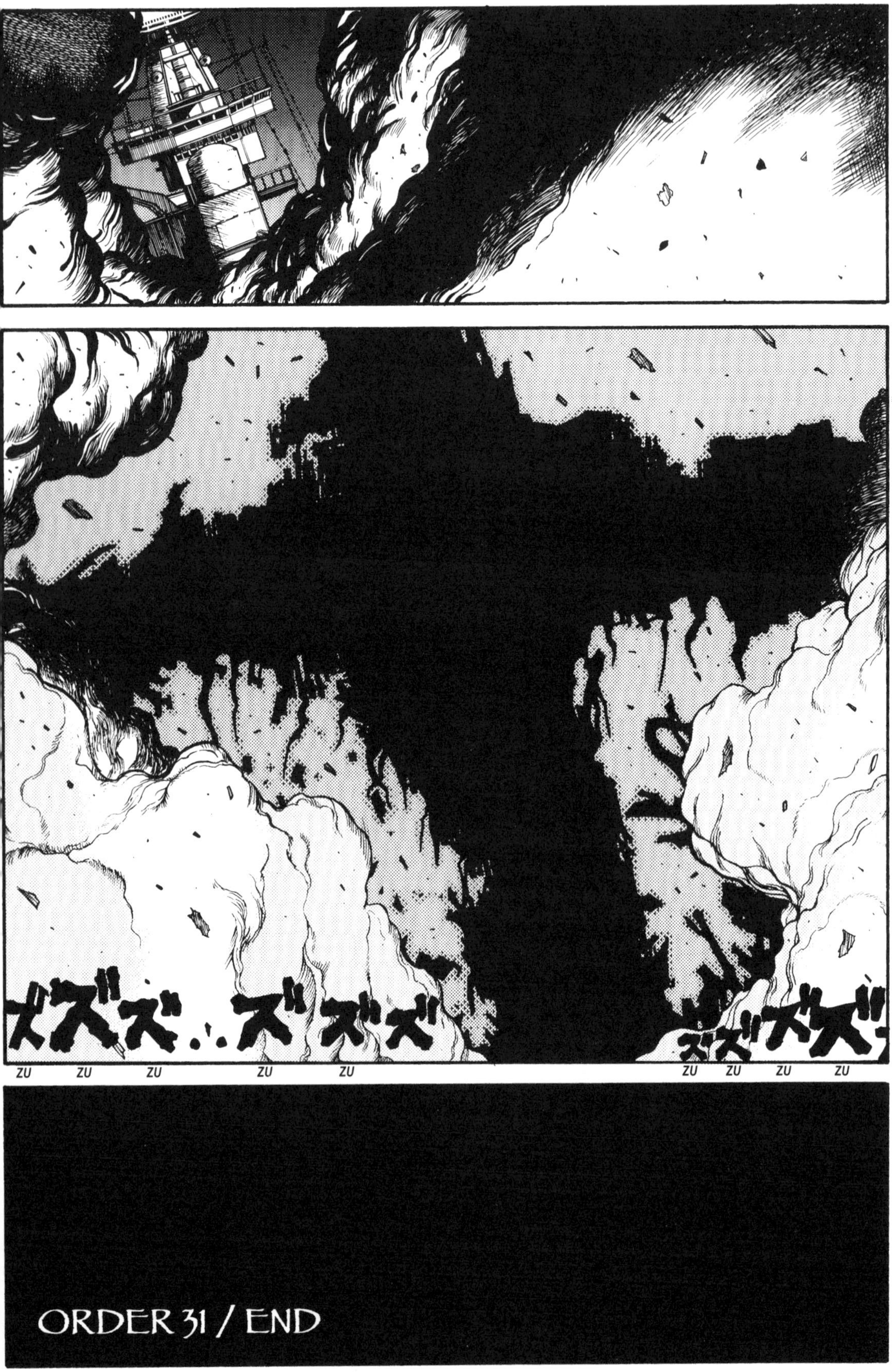
ズズズ...ズズズ
ZU ZU ZU ZU ZU
ズズズズ
ZU ZU ZU ZU
ORDER 31 / END

ORDER 32

AAAAAA
GHAAAA
AHAAA
SHUNK
GLUSH
We are Missoin from God
HELLSING

ROARRRR
AH...
AHHHH!
......!
!

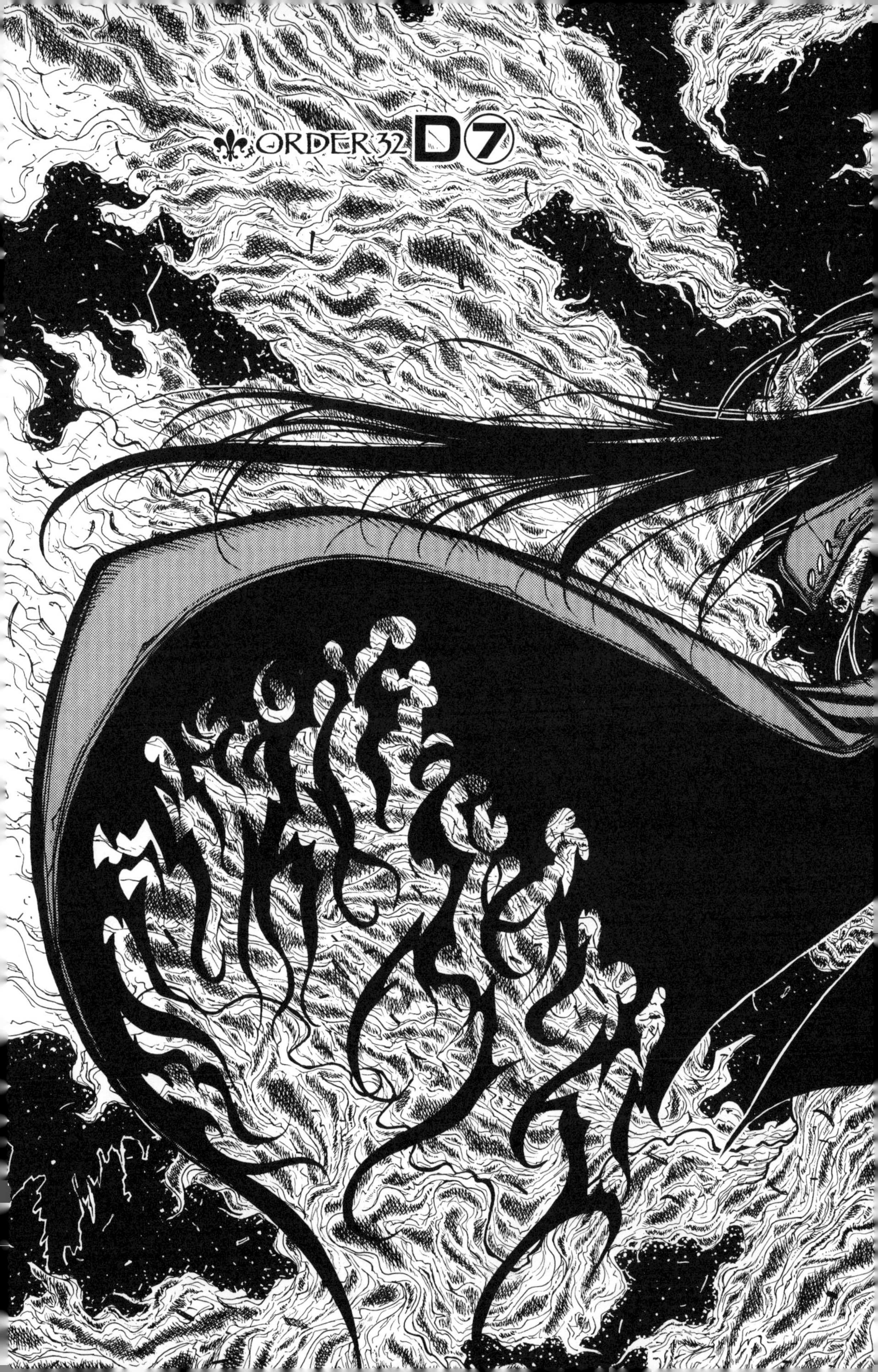
ORDER 32 D7

オォオォォォオオォ
ROARRRRRRR

"A MAGNIFICENT ABILITY, LIEUTENANT RIP VAN.
"NO DOUBT THE "MAGIC BULLETS" OF THE LEGENDARY DEMONIC HUNTER."
"J-JAWOHL!
"HERR MAJOR!!"
VYOO

"DER FREISCHÜTZ, EH?
"CERTAINLY THIS IST THE SAME AS THE DEVIL'S OWN DEED."
ROARRRRRR
"BUT IT VOULD BE BEST IF YOU KEPT SOMETHING IN MIND, LIEUTENANT.
"J...JA?"
SHOOOM

オオオオオオオオオオ
ROARRRRRRR
"DO YOU KNOW THE FINALE OF DER FREISCHÜTZ, LIEUTENANT?
"AT THE END OF THE OPERA, CASPAR IST TAKEN TO HELL BY THE HUNTER DEMON KING, ZAMIEL...
"...WHOM HE HAD DALLIED VITH. THEN CASPAR'S CORPSE IST CAST INTO THE VOLF'S GLEN.
"FOR IF THOU PRESUMETH TO FLIRT VITH SPIRITS, THOU SHALT JOIN THEM.
"TAKE HEED, LIEUTENANT.

TREMBLE TREMBLE TREMBLE TREMBLE TREMBLE

!!
BLOW
AH...
HEE!
BUDDA
BUDDA
BUDDA
BUDDA
BUDDA
BUDDA
BUDDA
LIEUTENANT!!

SHFF
AHH...
AH
AH...
SHOOM
orsicht!
FWOOSH
BADOOM
SHOOM

PULL YOURSELF TOGETHER, LIEUTENANT!!
I THOUGHT YOU VERE A VEREVOLF! LIEUTENANT!!
DASH
IT ISN'T MUCH LONGER UNTIL THE TIME OF HERR MAJOR'S ORDERS!!
UNTIL THEN!!
SOMEHOW VE MUST... ...!!
!!
...FREAKS!!
PRODUCTS OF MADNESS!!

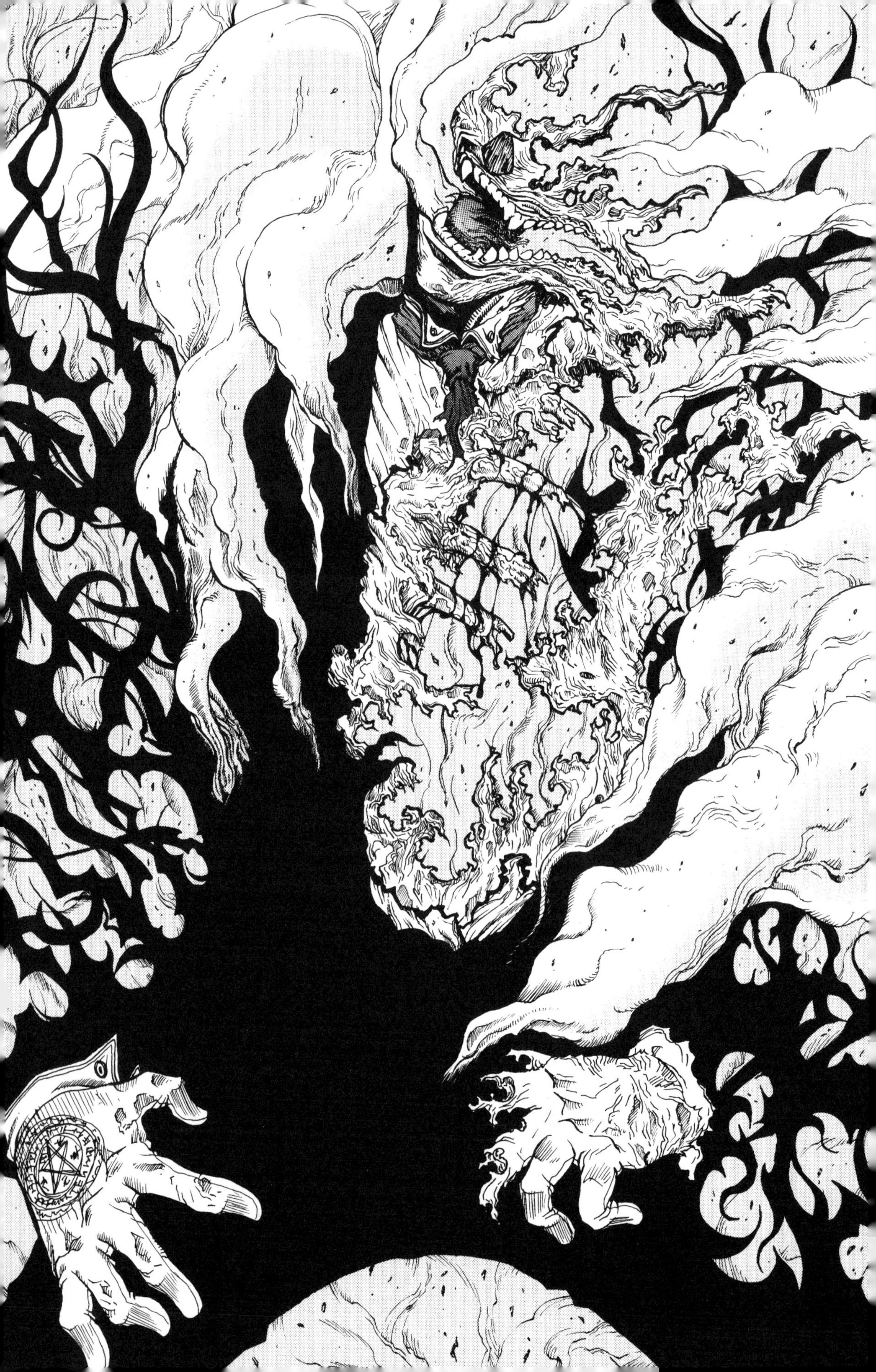

GREEEEEEEE
CHIK
CHIG
CHIK
CHIK
CHIK
CHIK
CHIK
CHIG
CHIK

ATTAAACK!
F...FIRE!
WHPP
BUDDA
BUDDA
BUDDA
BUDDA
BUDDA
DO
DO
DO
DO
DO
DO
DO
DO
DO
DO

HAND GRENADES!!
HAND GRENADES!!
GUNS ARE USELESS!!
ドドドドドドドドドドド
BUDDA
BUDDA
BUDDA
BUDDA
BUDDA
ガッ
GTUNK
ドッドッドドッドッ
DMP
DMP
DMP
DMP
DMP

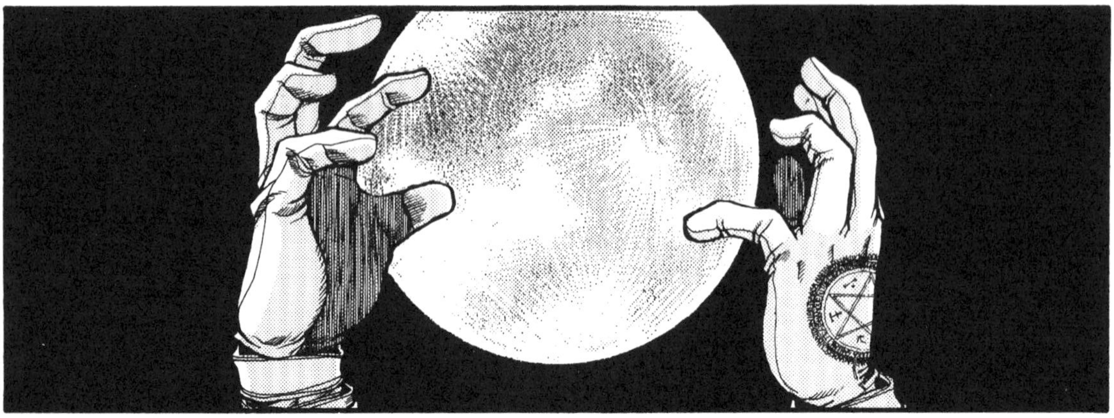

GOHH
GICH
GICH
GICH
GICH
GICH
GICH

GH
AA
AH
AH
AA
SHLUKK
OAAHAAAAA
BLAM
BLAM
BLAM
BLAM

VAT THE FUCK ARE YOU?!
BLCH

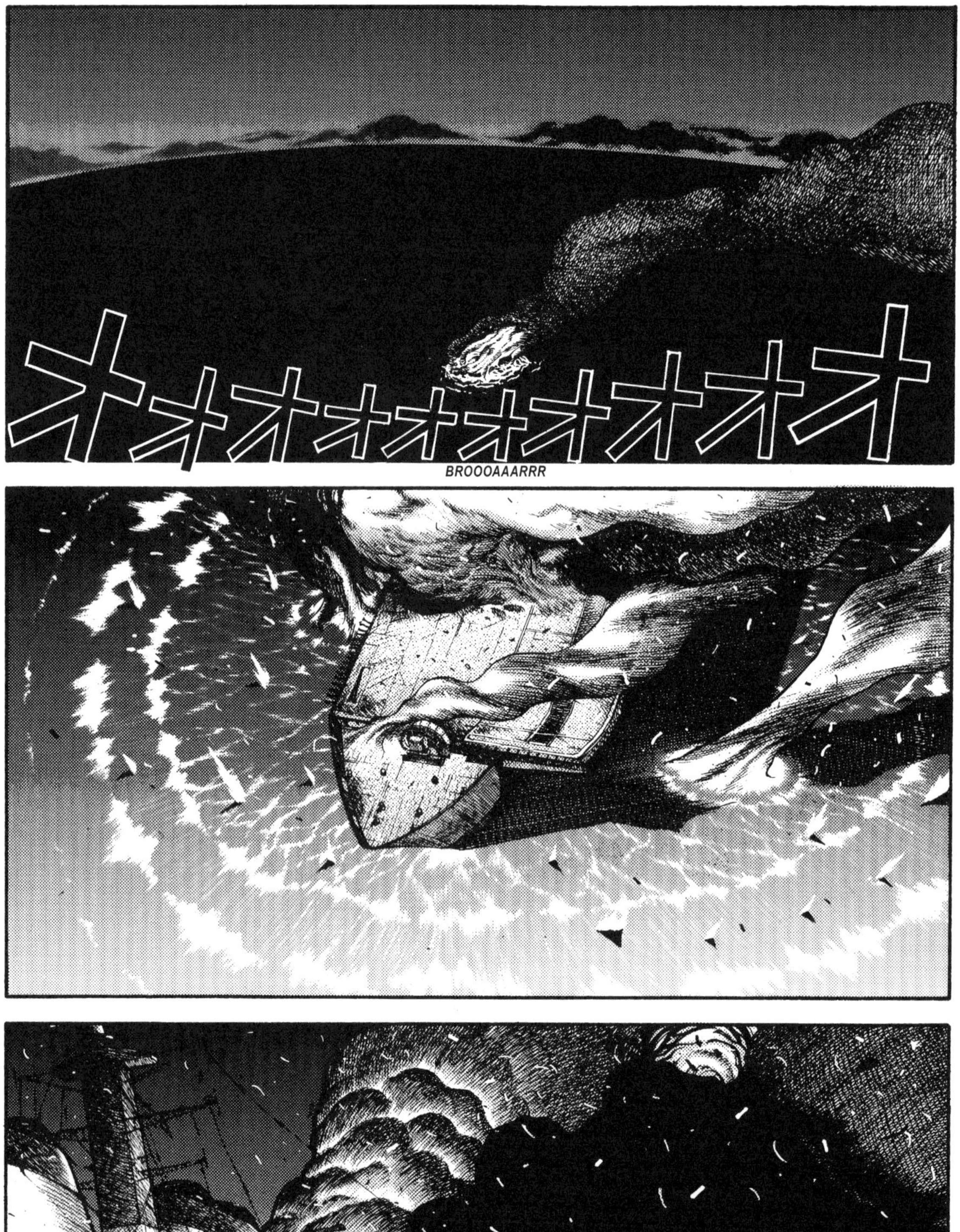
オオオオオオオオオオ
BROOOAAARRR
ゴゴゴゴゴゴゴ
ROARRRRR

ZAMEL...
ZAMEL...
ZAMEL... ZAMEL...
ZAMEL... ZAMEL...
ZAMEL... ZAMEL...
TWITCH
TWITCH TWITCH
TWITCH
ZAMEL...!!

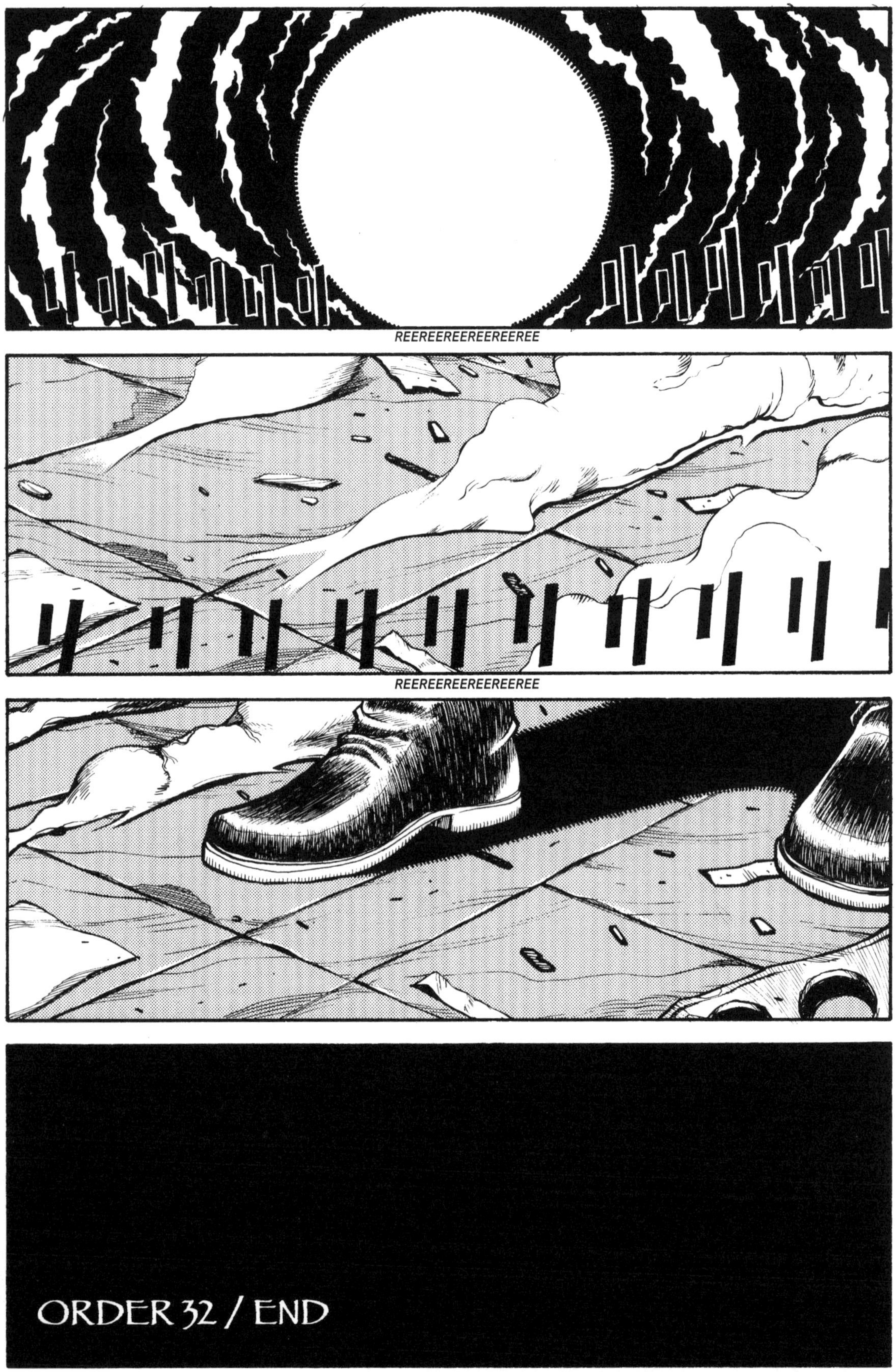
REEREEREEREEREEREE
REEREEREEREEREEREE
ORDER 32 / END

SHHH SHHHH
SHHH SHHHH
SHH SHHH
HASN'T THE RECON-NAISSANCE REPORT COME IN YET?!
WHAT'S HAPPENING?!
WE'RE HAVING TROUBLE MAKING ANYTHING OUT THROUGH THE SMOKE!!
THE EAGLE'S BECOME AN INFERNO!!
... ...THAT WOULD BE OUR WIN.
NATURALLY.
WHAT HAVE YOU DONE?! WHAT'S HAPPENING WITH THAT SHIP?!
SIR INTEGRA!!

ORDER 33 D⑧

ACTUALLY, I'VE BUT EMBARKED ON AN ORTHODOX SIEGE WAR.
ALTHOUGH THE BATTERING RAM'S TOTAL LENGTH WAS 30m AND SPEED MACH 3.2.
THUS WAS THE BATTERING RAM SWUNG AND THE CASTLE WALLS BROUGHT DOWN.
THE PALISADE DESTROYED, THE MOAT CROSSED.
MY SOLDIER ENTERS THE CASTLE TO ATTACK.
"WHAT IS HAPPENING?"
WHAT HAPPENS IN CASTLE TOWERS IN ALL TIMES AND PLACES JUST BEFORE SUR-RENDER?
ONE THING, AND ONE THING ONLY.
AN ABSOLUTELY ONE-SIDED...
...MASSACRE.

ジッリリリリリリリリリリ
BRIIIIIIIIING
ジッリリリリリリリリリリ
BRIIIIIIIIIING
ジッリリリリリリリリリリ
BRIIIIIIIIIING

HEE!!
HIGU...!
...!!
...HEE!!
TWITCH TWITCH TWITCH
...!!
...!!
...!!
KRUNCH
BRIIIIIIIIING
KRING
BRIIIING

!!
?!
バッ
TURN
コオォォォォオオ
BROARRRR

NOW!! WHAT WILL YOU DO?!
WHAT WILL YOU DO, RIP VAN WINKLE?!

HNN

MY VARHEAD VILL PUNISH...
...ALL VITHOUT DISTINCTION.
ZZZZZZZZ
ZZZZZ

GRIN
ニイイッ
BLAM

KPAK
WHMP
ZSSSSSH

ZEE
ZEE
ZEE
ZEE
ZEE
ZEE
ZEE
ZEE
ZEE
GWEEEE
KPOW

SWAYYY
BOMF
ZEE
ZEE
ZEE
ZEE
ZEE
ZEE
ZEE
ZEE
ZEE
ZEE
ZEE
ZEE
ZEE
ZEE
ZEE

THMPA
THMP
THMPA
ドガッ ドッ ドッ ガッ
FALL.
FALL.
FALL!!
FALL IN.
UND PERISH!!
キイイイイイイ イイ
KREEEEEEE

SHUDDER...
ぞく...
NA AH HAH YA.

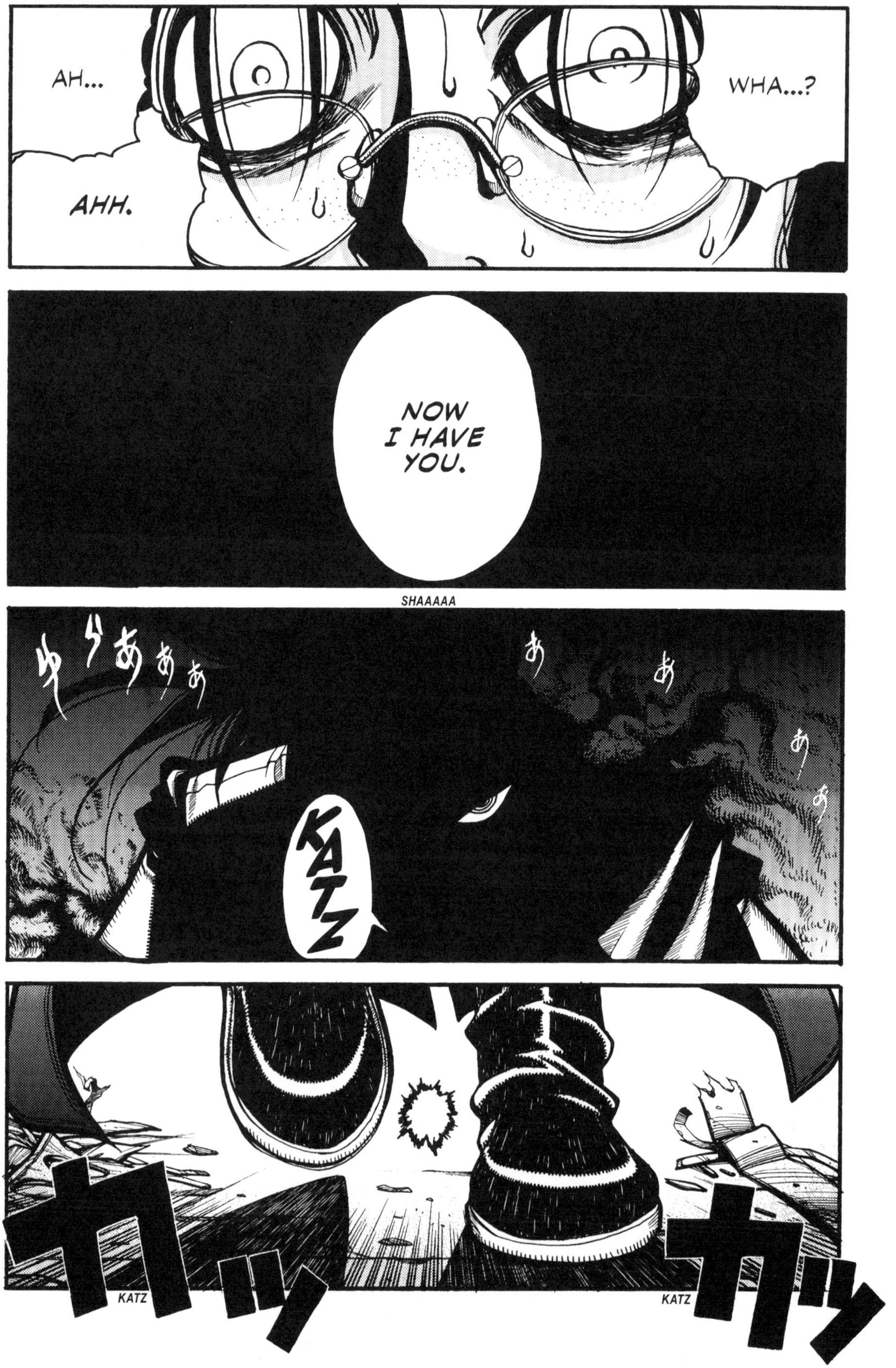

WHA...?
AH...
AHH.
NOW I HAVE YOU.
SHAAAAA
ゆらあああ
ああああ
KATZ
KATZ
KATZ

AH!
AH!
AH!
AGH!
AGHHHH! AGHHHH!
カッカッカッカッカッカッ
KATZ KATZ KATZ KATZ KATZ KATZ
カッカッ カッカッカッ
KATZ KATZ KATZ KATZ KATZ
カッカッ カッカッ
KATZ KATZ KATZ KATZ
カッカッカッカッ
KATZ KATZ KATZ KATZ

WHOM
BOKK
SLIDE
GUH...!
!!
GRAB

KAKK
!!
KEH
HA...
AGH
AGH...!
AGH
SQUEEZE
!!
SHOVE
SHFFF
AH
...
...!
AH
SHNNK

OH!
AH
AH
HEE!
ZSHH
KUAH!
AHH!
AHH!
ZSHH
SLSH
ZSHH
CRNCH

AH!
AH
AH...
WHOOOOOOOOO
WHOOO

Hindenburg II
WHOOOOOOO
ORDER 33/ END

ORDER 34

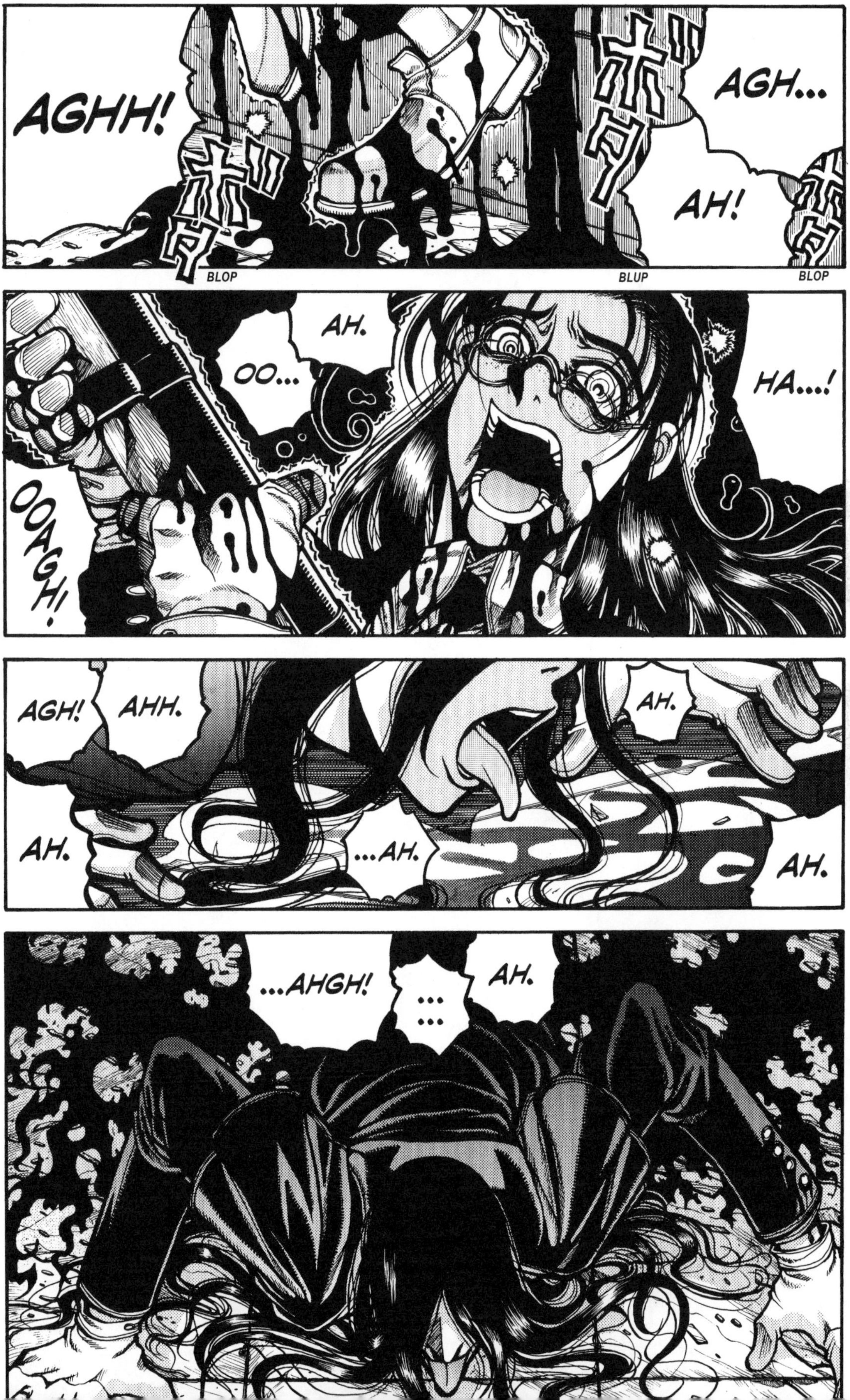

AGH...
AH!
BLOP
BLUP
AGHH!
BLOP
HA...!
AH.
OO...
OOAGH!
AH.
AH.
...AH.
AGH!
AHH.
AH.
AH.
...
...
...AHGH!

ORDER 34 D⑨

...!
!!
!!
HEE.
......
!
...!
....!!
わきわき
わきわき
わきわき
AGH!
KEE
KEE
KEE KEE
HEE.
AH.
AH.
AH.
AH.
AGH!

NN...
NG
GEE
GEE
GEE
GEE GEE
AHHHH
AHH
HA...
AH
GREEE

GAH...
AH
HEE...
AH
AH
TWITCH
...!
TWITCH
SHUDDER
HA!
OH
TWITCH
TWITCH
OH...
...AH
AH

GREEE
GREEE
GREEE
AH
AGH..
OH..
ギ!!
ギ!!
ギ!!
YOU'VE DONE VELL, LIEUTENANT.
THE OPERATION IST A SUCCESS. A TOTAL ONE.
オオオ
オオオオ
ROARRRRR

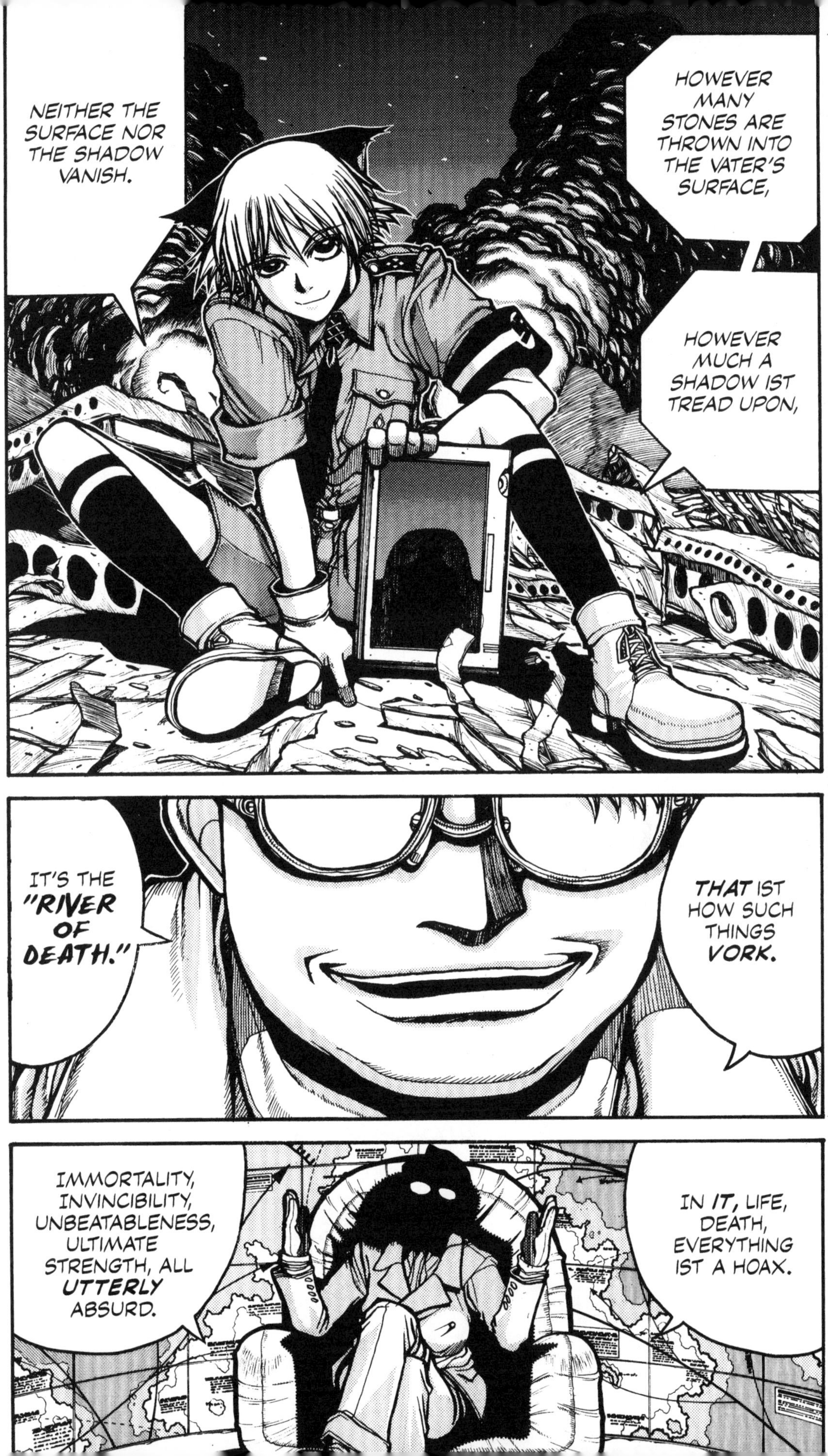
HOWEVER MANY STONES ARE THROWN INTO THE VATER'S SURFACE,
HOWEVER MUCH A SHADOW IST TREAD UPON,
NEITHER THE SURFACE NOR THE SHADOW VANISH.
THAT IST HOW SUCH THINGS VORK.
IT'S THE "RIVER OF DEATH."
IN IT, LIFE, DEATH, EVERYTHING IST A HOAX.
IMMORTALITY, INVINCIBILITY, UNBEATABLENESS, ULTIMATE STRENGTH, ALL UTTERLY ABSURD.

SHAKE SHAKE
...OGOHH...
OH...OH...
...OHH...
...OH...
SHIVER
SHIVER SHAKE
SHAKE SHAKE
BY THE SACRIFICE OF YOUR REPATRIATION, VE VILL OVERTHROW ALUCARD.
BUT VE VILL OVERTHROW HIM.

CLICK
CLICK
CLICK
SHHP
TO LEAVE THINGS LIKE THIS...
JAWOHL... B-BUT...
AH!!
STOP.
SHE HAST FULFILLED HER MISSION.
FULLY. PERFECTLY.
I VON'T PERMIT YOU TO FRY HER.
STAND
ACHTUNG!!
JA...
JA- JA--
JAWOHL.....

KRICH
KRICH
KRICH
KATZ
Ktak
Katz

AUF WIEDER-SEHEN, LIEUTENANT.
VE'LL MEET AGAIN IN **VALHALLA.**
AUF WIEDERSEHEN, AUF WIEDERSEHEN, LIEUTENANT.
AUF WIEDER-SEHEN, LIEU-TENANT.
AUF WIEDER-SEHEN.
AUF WIEDER-SEHEN.
AUF WIE-DERSEHEN, FRAU LIEU-TENANT.
AUF WIEDER-SEHEN.

CIAO.
RIP VAN.
SIEG HEIL.
SALUTE
LIFT

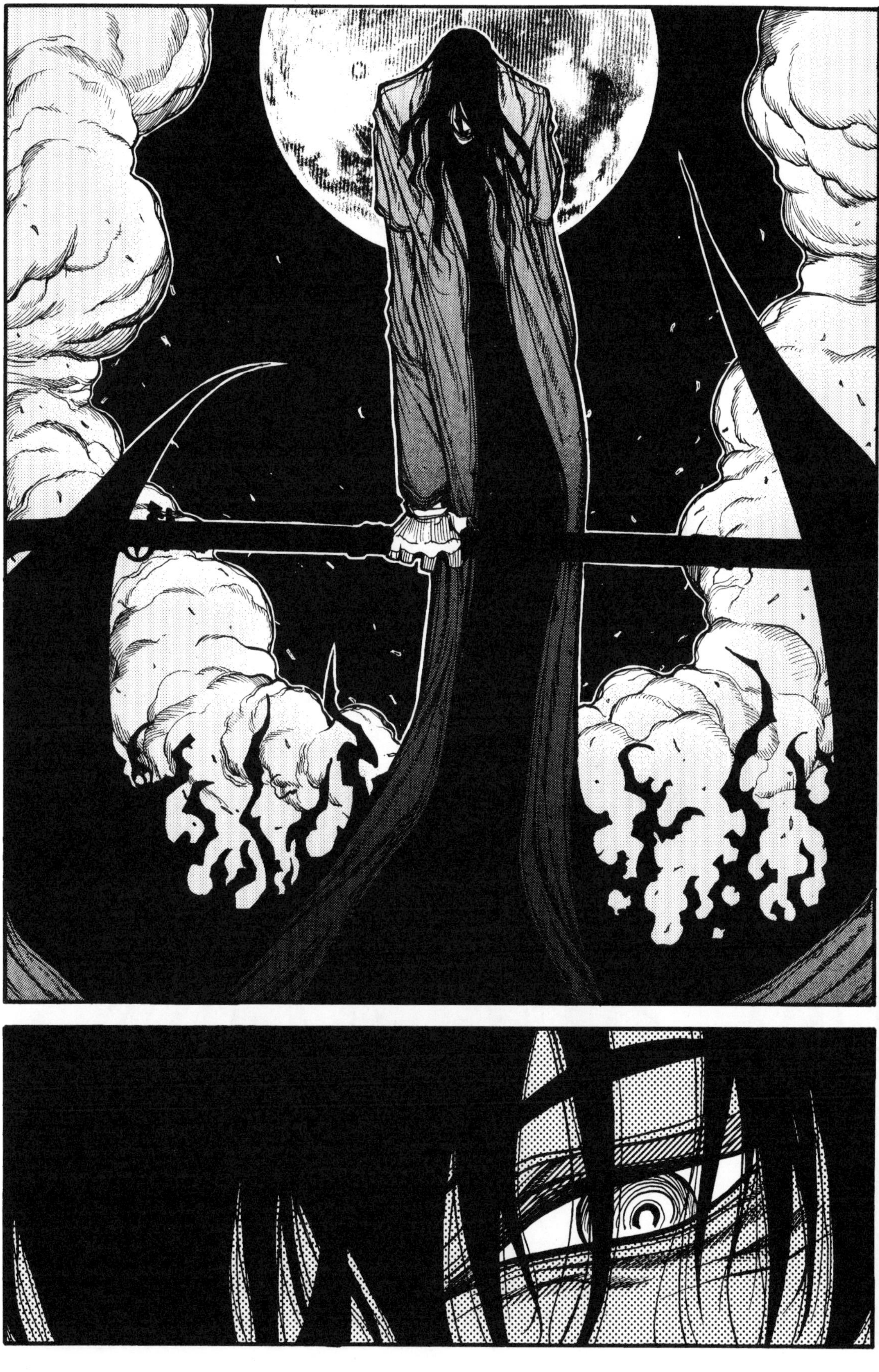

HA HA HA
ゴ
GO
ゴゴゴ
GO GO GO
ゴ
GO
HA HA HA
ゴ
GO
HA HA
HA HA HA
HA
HA HA HA
HA...
HA... HAHH
HA HA HA HA HA HA

IST IT FUN, ALUCARD?
VAR IS FUN!!
SING A VICTORY SONG, ALUCARD.
UND THEN VATCH FROM THERE.
I CAN SEE IT. EVEN THROUGH THESE NEARSIGHTED GLASSES I CAN SEE IT CLEARLY.
THE SPIRES OF THAT CITY!!
THE RADIANCE OF THAT CITY.
VWOOOOOO
LISTEN TO THE VICTORY SONG, ALUCARD.
UND JUST VATCH FROM THERE.

ORDER 34 / END

ORDER 35

IT'S EUROPE...
IT IST EUROPE...!
THOSE LIGHTS...?!
IST THAT IT?!
IST THAT LONDON?!
LONDON?
LOOK!! YOU CAN SEE IT NOW!! YOU CAN SEE IT!!
EUROPE...!!
THE LIGHTS OF EUROPE...
IT'S EUROPE!!
ォォオオォォオォオォ
VWOOOOOOO
THAT'S RIGHT. THOSE ARE AT LAST THE LIGHTS OF EUROPE VICH VE SO DESIRE.
AS PROMISED, GENTLEMEN, I HAF BROUGHT YOU HOME.
TO THAT LONGED-FOR BATTLEFIELD, THAT LONGED-FOR VAR.

HERR MAJOR!!
MEIN FÜHRER!!
MAJOR.
HERR MAJOR.
TRANSMIT THIS TO EACH MEMBER OF THE ***MILLENNIUM BATTALION!!*** UN ORDER FROM YOUR BATTALION LEADER!!
UND SEELÖWE HAST CROSSED THE OCEAN,
TO CLIMB ONTO THE SHORE.
COME, GENTLEMEN.
VE GO TO RAISE **HELL.**

ORDER 35

XANADO
ザナドゥ

*NOTE: GCHQ IS SHORT FOR GOVERNMENT COMMUNICATIONS HEADQUARTERS.

COMMUNICATIONS LOST WITH ATLANTIC FLEET COMMAND CENTER!!
NO CONTACT WITH THE MINISTRY OF DEFENCE'S INTELLIGENCE CONTROL DIVISION!!
CONTACT LOST WITH DESTROYER FORTE CREST ON THE THAMES RIVER!!
CONTACT LOST WITH ALL POLICE UNITS!!
IMPOSSIBLE... ...?!
YOU MEAN TO SAY SOME KIND OF WAR HAS BEGUN?!
A TELEGRAM FROM THE IRISH BRIGADE OF THE ROYAL GUARD!!
"WE'RE UNDER ATTACK!! WE'VE BEEN ENGAGED BY UNKNOWN ENEMIES!!
"THEY'RE MONSTERS. HELP US, THEY'RE MONSTERS!!"
IT'S BEGUN... YES, AT LONG LENGTH...
...THE WAR HAS STARTED.
BOOM

TRMP
TRMP
TRMP
TRMP
TRMP
!!
WHO?!
WHAT'S THE MEANING OF THIS?!
GRIN
CHAK
GCHAK
ZKAA
FROM HERE ON THIS FACILITY...
...IS UNDER THE CONTROL OF MILLEN-NIUM!!
I THINK THAT'S ABOUT ENOUGH OF YOUR QUESTIONABLE BEHAVIOR, SIR HELLSING.
CHIK

SSSSSS
SSS
COMMANDER!! Y-YOU ALL...
WHAT'S THE MEANING OF THIS?!
STUFF IT, YOU!!
THIS IS THE MEANING, ADMIRAL.
VAMPIRISM IS MAGNIFICENT!!
GRIN
HAHAHAHA
!!
HAH! HAHAHAHAH. TO THINK THAT I'D GET TO SNARE THE SIR HELLSING.
OH,
I DARE SAY THE FÜHRER WILL BE PLEASED!!
...nuhn.
...nuhn.
...nuhn.
nuhnuhn nuhn!
...

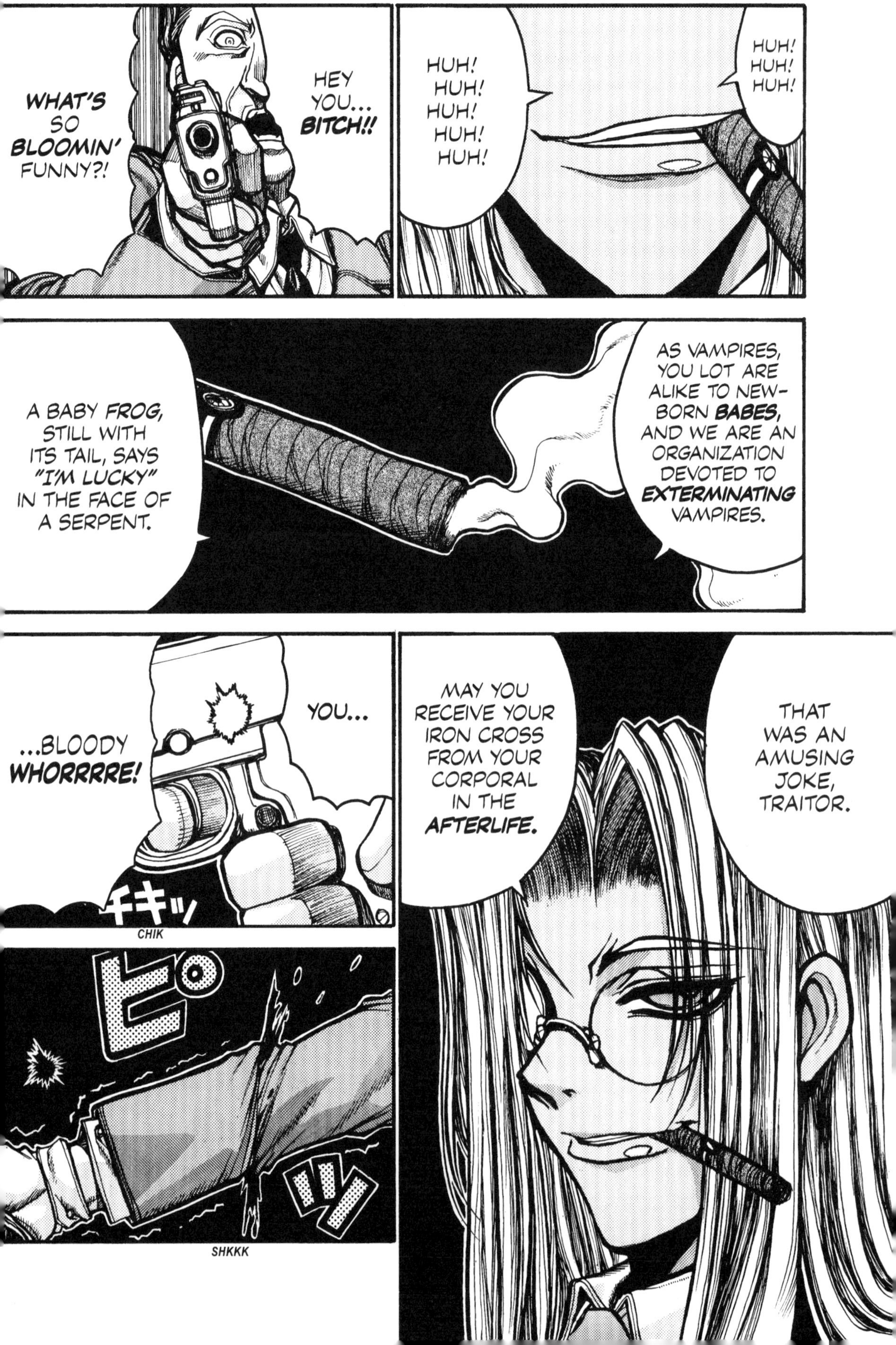
WHAT'S SO BLOOMIN' FUNNY?!
HEY YOU... BITCH!!
HUH! HUH! HUH! HUH! HUH!
HUH! HUH! HUH!
A BABY FROG, STILL WITH ITS TAIL, SAYS "I'M LUCKY" IN THE FACE OF A SERPENT.
AS VAMPIRES, YOU LOT ARE ALIKE TO NEW-BORN BABES, AND WE ARE AN ORGANIZATION DEVOTED TO EXTERMINATING VAMPIRES.
...BLOODY WHORRRRE!
YOU...
チキッ
CHIK
ピッ
SHKKK
MAY YOU RECEIVE YOUR IRON CROSS FROM YOUR CORPORAL IN THE AFTERLIFE.
THAT WAS AN AMUSING JOKE, TRAITOR.

BLAT
BUTLER.
DO YOUR WORK.
AYE.
MY LADY.

LITTLE BABES!!
COME, LET US SPAR TOGETHER!!
DASH
BRRRAP
BRRRAP BRRRAP BAP
!!
G-GOD-DAMNED
OLD SOD!
KEEEEEEEEEEE
GEENG

GEENG

SPASH
ビッシャ
PLIP
A THOUSAND PARDONS!!

ARE YOU **STILL** IN ONE PIECE, SIR PENWOOD?
I WAS JUST THINKING.
IT SEEMED **QUITE** POSSIBLE YOU HAD BETRAYED US.
WHILE I MIGHT BE ***INCOMPETENT...***
...I AM **NO SNEAK,** INTEGRA.
ADMIRAL!!
THIS IS ***DREADFUL,*** ADMIRAL!!
477 CIVILIAN AIRCRAFT HAVE REPORTED SEEING A NORTHBOUND FLEET OF AIRSHIPS SOUTH OF LONDON OVER NEWFIELDS...
SHMP
AIR-SHIPS...?!
YOU SAID ***AIRSHIPS?!***
ISN'T THAT SOME **KIND** OF MISTAKE?! ***AIRSHIPS?!***
THEY ***ARE*** AIRSHIPS.
WHAT'S MORE, THEY'RE **SO** GIGANTIC IT'S HARD TO BELIEVE.

VWOOOO
VWOOOOO
VWOOOOOO
MAXIMUM SPEED!! FLY!! FASTER!! FASTER UND FASTER!!
TURN THE ENGINES UNTIL THEY BURN OUT!! FASTER!! FASTER!! FASTER!!
VWOOOOO
VWOOOOOOOO
WHAT ABOUT RADAR?! WHAT WAS IT DOING?! HOW COULD NO ONE MANAGE TO NOTICE THEM GET THIS CLOSE?!
ALL SITES HAVE REMAINED SILENT!!
WHAT IS AIR DEFENSE HEADQUARTERS DOING?!
OUR COMMUNICATIONS WITH THEM ARE CURRENTLY DOWN!!
LONDON
THE STRAIGHT LINE DISTANCE FROM NEWFIELDS TO LONDON IS ABOUT 100 KILOMETERS!!
THE AIRSHIP FLEET WILL BE OVER LONDON IN A FEW DOZEN MINUTES!!

VWOOOOOOO
TURN TOWARDS THE SPIRES OF THAT DIMLY SEEN CITY UND DASH!!
DASH!! DASH!!
TURN TOWARDS THAT TUMULT UND SHOCK WE REMEMBER EVEN NOW UND DASH!!
DASH!! DASH!!
VWOOOOO

オオオオオオオ
VWOOOOO
All flesh is as grass, and all the glory of man as the flower of the grass. Because
The grass withers, and it's flower fall away
Amen!!
ORDER 35 / END

ORDER 36

WORLDWIDE LOVE AAAA
GIELGUD
...HOW YOU
SAY SOMETHING TO HER, MATE.
HEY, JANSEN!!
OH SHUT UP! YOU KNOW, I SHOULD...
WHY DON'T YOU GO PISS OFF?!
WHA ...?!
...THE MOON!
......!!
VWOOOOOOO

VWOOOOOOOOO
VWOOOOO

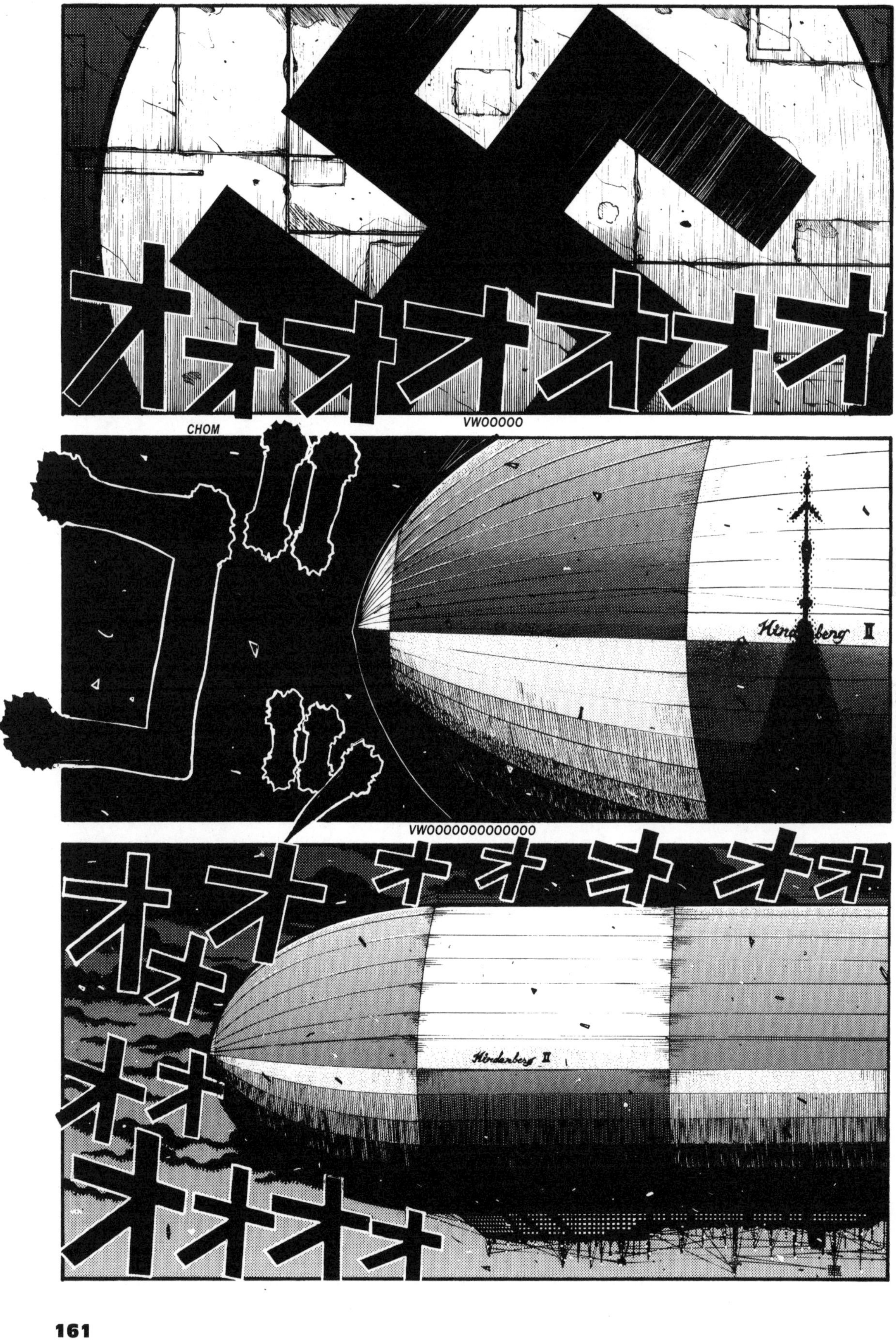
オォオオオオオ
CHOM
VWOOOOO
VWOOOOOOOOOOOOO
Hindenberg II

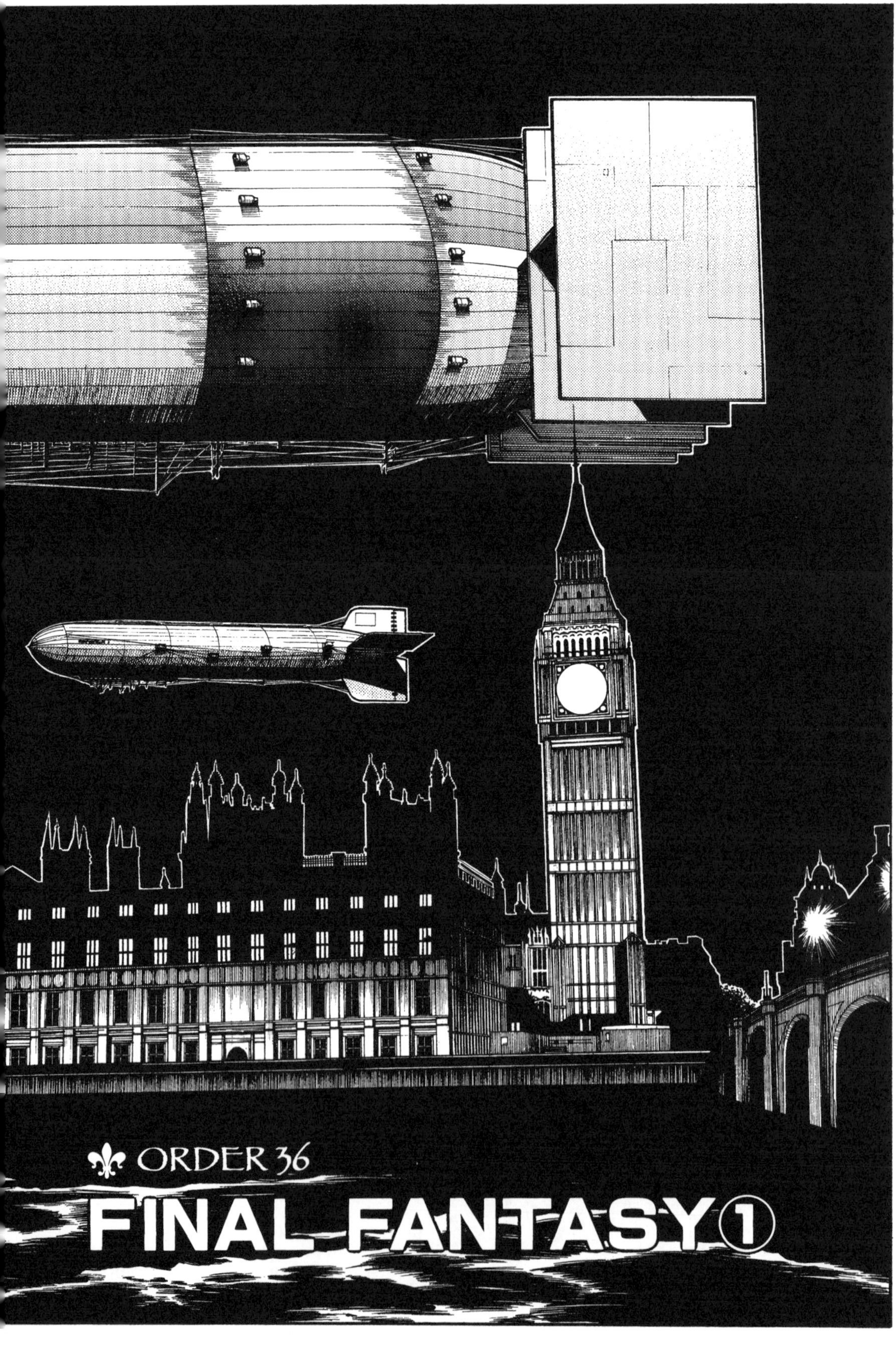
ORDER 36
FINAL FANTASY ①

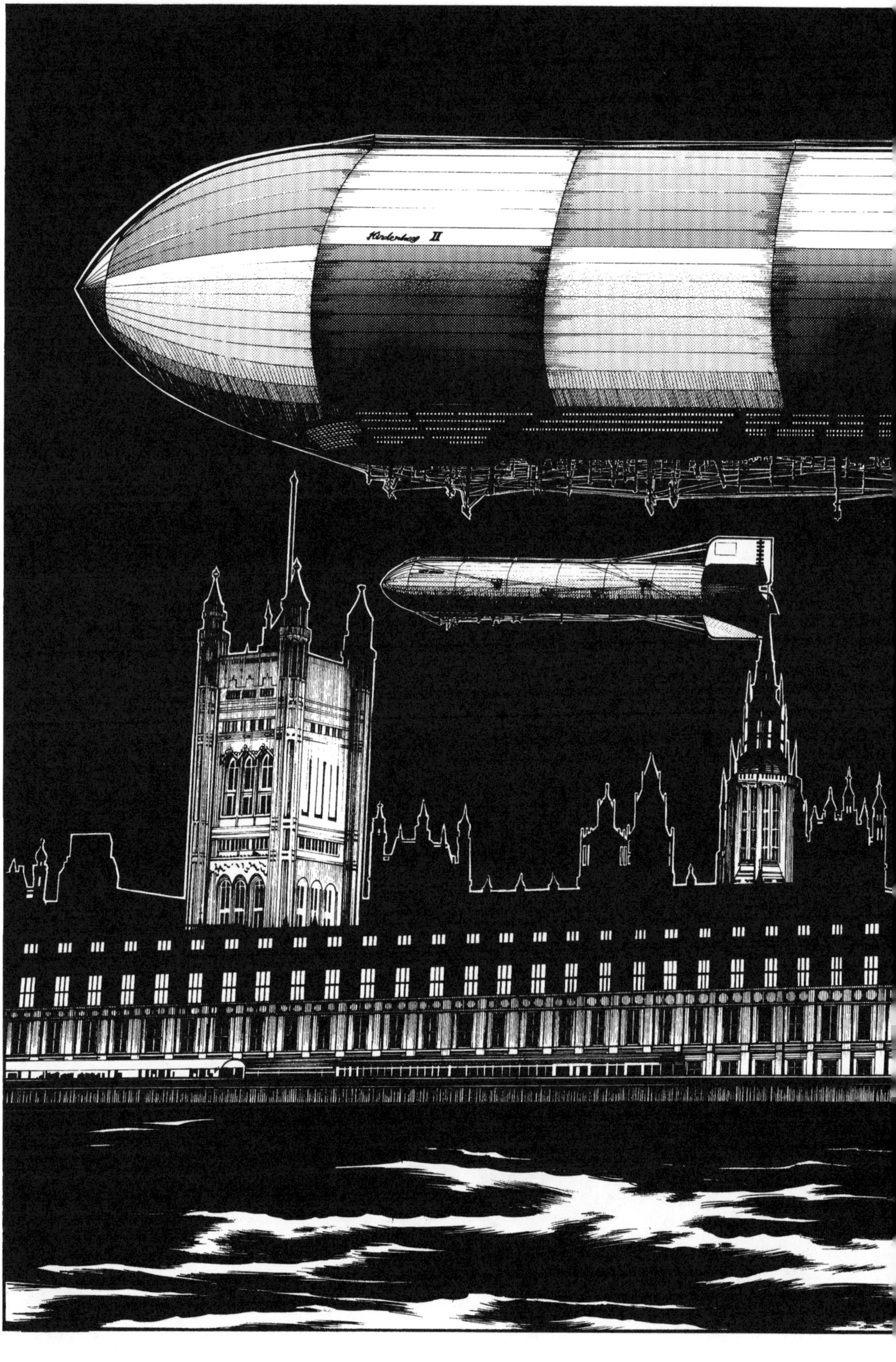

MAJOR!!
HERR MAJOR.
FÜHRER!!
カッ KATZ
カッ KATZ
カッ KATZ
カッ KATZ
カッ KATZ
カッ KATZ
カッ KATZ
MAJOR!!
HERR KOMMAN-DANT!!
MAJOR!!
カ KATZ
カッ KATZ
カッ KATZ
カッ KATZ
KATZ
KATZ
KATZ
KATZ
KATZ
KATZ
カ
FÜHRER!!
MEIN FÜHRER!!
カッ
カッ
カッ
カッ
MAJOR.
HERR MAJOR!!
カッ

ACHTUNG!!
ALL BATTALION MEMBERS!
SHKAA
ザガッ
GENTLEMEN.
NIGHT HAST COME.
MY UNBEATABLE TROOPS OF A BEATEN ARMY.
MY OLDEST VETERAN NEW RECRUITS.

THE NIGHT OF TEN THOUSAND FULFILLED VISHES HAST COME.

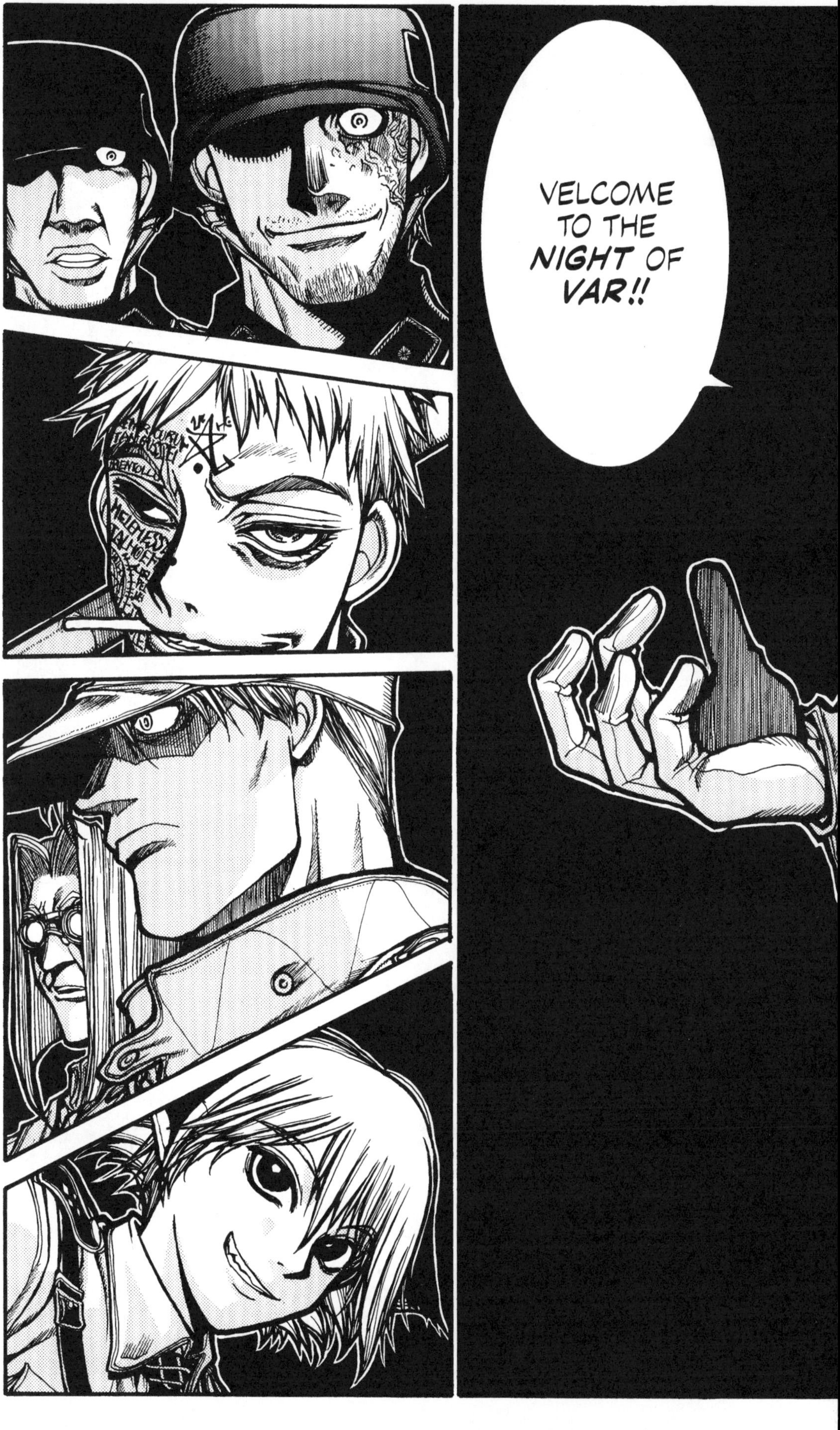
VELCOME TO THE NIGHT OF VAR!!

HURRA! HURRA!
Seelöwe 2
Landing operaion
kursbuch ①
ZPP
NOW IF EVERYVONE VOULD CONSULT THEIR HANDBOOK...
...THEIR ENGLISH INVASION LANDING OPERATION SEELÖWE 2 HANDBOOK...
PLEASE DIRECT YOUR ATTENTION TO PAGE 3, LONDON EXPLODES!! FEARSOME BATTLE VAMPIRES.

SHFF SHFF SHFF SHFF
ごそ ごそ ごそごそ
AH.
SHP SHP SHP SHP
バッ バッ
OHHH DEAR, VATEVER IS THE MATTER, SCHRÖ-DINGER?
UH... UMMM.
UH OHHH.
VAT ARE YOU DOING...?
SHIVER SHIVER SHIVER SHIVER SHIVER
プル
I'M SORRY.
I LOST MY HANDBOOK...
ANGH!! AH, FINE THEN. THERE'S NO FIXING IT NOW.
HAF THE CAPTAIN SHOW YOU HIS.
PEEK
そ～～～っ
WOWWW.

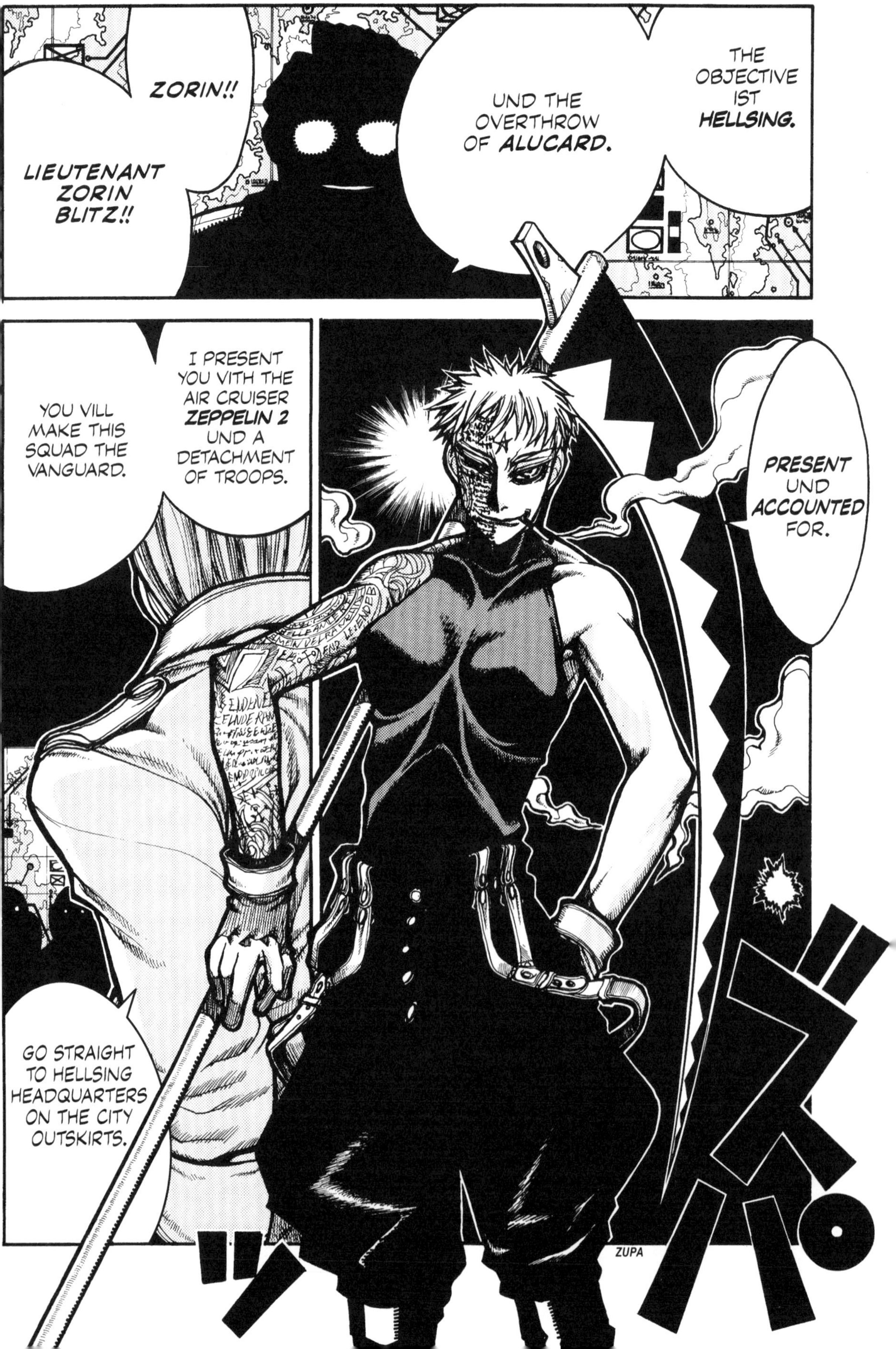
THE OBJECTIVE IST HELLSING.
UND THE OVERTHROW OF ALUCARD.
ZORIN!!
LIEUTENANT ZORIN BLITZ!!
PRESENT UND ACCOUNTED FOR.
I PRESENT YOU VITH THE AIR CRUISER ZEPPELIN 2 UND A DETACHMENT OF TROOPS.
YOU VILL MAKE THIS SQUAD THE VANGUARD.
GO STRAIGHT TO HELLSING HEADQUARTERS ON THE CITY OUTSKIRTS.
ZUPA

KATZ
カッ
ツン
HOWEVER, AVOID AGGRESSION.
YOU SHOULD VAIT FOR THE ARRIVAL OF MYSELF UND THE MAIN FORCE.
HAHAHA, IT IST NOTHING TO TROUBLE YOURSELF OVER.
A HELLSING VITHOUT ALUCARD...
...IST A BABE IN THE VOODS.
SHAKE SHAKE
フル
フル
SHAKE
フル
!!
THOSE GIRLS ARE THERE. DO NOT UNDERESTIMATE THEM.
?!
!!
DO NOT UNDERESTIMATE INTEGRA HELLSING UND SERAS VICTORIA!!

"SHE IST A DESCENDANT OF THE **HELLSINGS.** THE HEAD OF THE **MIGHTIEST** VAMPIRE HUNTING FAMILY IN HISTORY.
"***INTEGRAL FAIRBROOK WINGATES HELLSING.***
"ALUCARD RECOGNIZES **HER** AS HIS MASTER.
"THEN THERE IST THE 'POLICE GIRL VAMPIRE' ***SERAS VICTORIA.***
"SHE IST... ***HAHAHA.*** HER EXISTENCE IST SOMEVAT OF A MARVEL. YOU COULD EVEN SAY IT'S SOMEVAT OF A JOKE.
"PERHAPS SHE HERSELF HAST NOT EVEN NOTICED YET!!
THIS

THESE TWO ARE TERRIBLY INEXPERIENCED UND IMPERFECT, BUT ON THAT ACCOUNT...
...I DECIDE TO VALUE THEM AS ARCH ENEMIES, THE SAME AS ALUCARD.
AM I CLEAR, ZORIN? I SAY IT ONCE MORE.
DO NOT ATTACK. VAIT FOR MY ARRIVAL.
...JAWOHL.
JAWOHL, HERR KOMMANDANT.
GRIN
WERY GOOD.
WERY GOOD!! NOW, THEN...

CADILLY, SOHO, UTHVARK, RN IT ALL DOWN.
YOUR FIRST OBJECTIVE IST THE ANNIHILATION OF LONDON!!
THE HOUSES OF PARLIAMENT ON THE VEST BANK OF THE THAMES!! BIG BEN!! THE PRIME MINISTER'S OFFICIAL RESIDENCE!! THE HOME UND FOREIGN OFFICES! THE MINISTRY OF DEFENCE!! ALL THE GOVERNMENT BUILDINGS!!
BUCKINGHAM PALACE!! SAINT JAMES PALACE!! KENSINGTON PALACE!! WINDSOR CASTLE!! HAMPTON COURT!!
THE HORSE GUARDS!! SCOTLAND YARD'S MAIN OFFICE!! HER MAJESTY'S TREASURY!! VESTMINSTER CATHEDRAL!!
BURST THE DAM!!
BURST THE DAM ON THE MUDDY STREAM OF VAR!! GENTLEMEN!!

CENTRAL GOVERNMENT OFFICES!! LONDON CAVENDISH REGIMENTAL HEADQUARTERS!! SAINT PAUL'S CATHEDRAL!!
HERR MAJOR!! VAT ABOUT THE CABINET VAR ROOMS?
BLOW THEM UP!! NATURALLY, UND LET NOT ONE MOST ACCURSED FRAGMENT REMAIN.
HOW SHALL VE HANDLE TRAFALGAR SQUARE, HERR MAJOR?!
BURN IT. TOPPLE NELSON'S COLUMN.
THE TOWER OF LONDON, THE BRITISH MUSEUM, THE LONDON LIBRARY, DESTROY THEM ALL. THEY ARE UNPLEASANT.
UND THE TOWER BRIDGE?
BRING IT DOWN. LONDON BRIDGE, TOO. LIKE IN THE SONG.
VAT SHALL VE DO VITH THE IMPERIAL VAR MUSEUM?
BLOW IT UP.
AREAS

THIS EIGHT-MILLION-STRONG MORSEL OF UN IMPERIAL CAPITAL HAST TONIGHT BEEN REDUCED TO YOUR DINNER, GENTLEMEN.
EAT FREELY, DRINK FREELY.
VY SHOULD I CARE? DESTROY VATEVER CATCHES YOUR EYE ON ONE SIDE...
UND EAT WHOEVER CATCHES YOUR EYE ON THE OTHER.
NOW!! GENTLEMEN!! LET US KILL UND BE KILLED, DIE UND BRING DEATH.
I PROPOSE A TOAST.
THE FEAST HAST BEGUN TONIGHT, FROM THIS TIME FORWARD.
CHIK CHIK CHIK CHIK CHIK
GONG GONG GONG GONG

THE THING'S HUGE... GIGANTIC.
IT'S NAZIS, MATE!!
HEY!! WHAT IS THAT?! BLIMEY IT'S HUGE!! WHAT THE HELL!!
OI!! OVER HERE!! GET A PHOTO!! HURRY!!
IS THIS FOR A FILM OR SOMETHING?
HEY, TAKE A LOOK AT THAT!!
PROST!!
Please call Beth.....!!
PROST!!

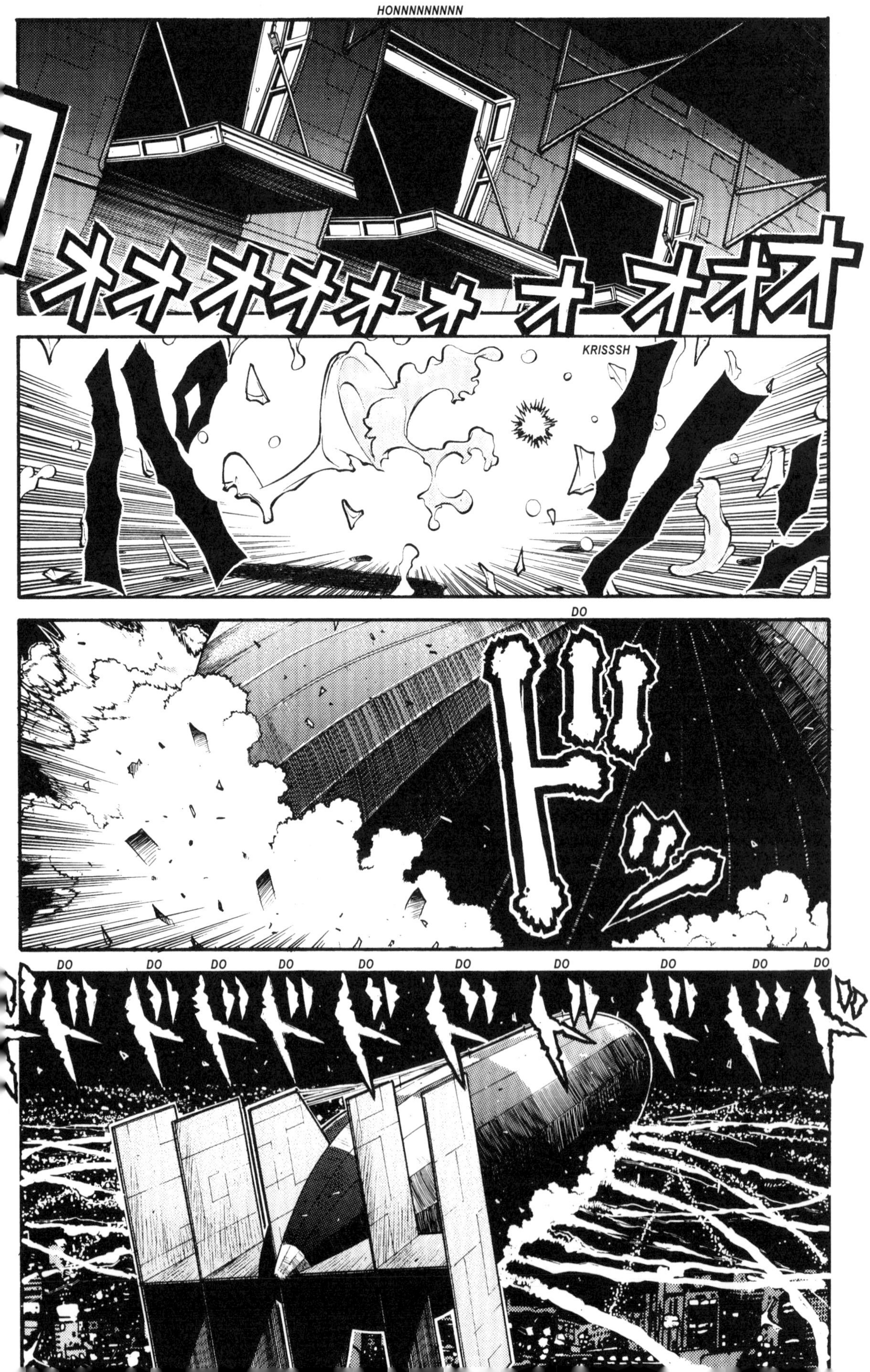
HONNNNNNNNN
KRISSSH
DO
DO DO DO DO DO DO DO DO DO DO

キィウァウァアァアアウウウアア
KEEEWAAAWAAAWAA
?!
?!
!!
?!
キイイイイイイイー
KEEEEEEEEEE
ゴユアア
GWAAA

BOMM
BDOOM
WHOOM

ボッ
BOMM
ドカッ
BDOOM
ドドッ
DADOM
AAA!!
UAA
GAAAAAAAA
AHAAAA
AIHAAA
AHAAAA
AHAHAHAA
AHAAAA
AHA
AHAHA

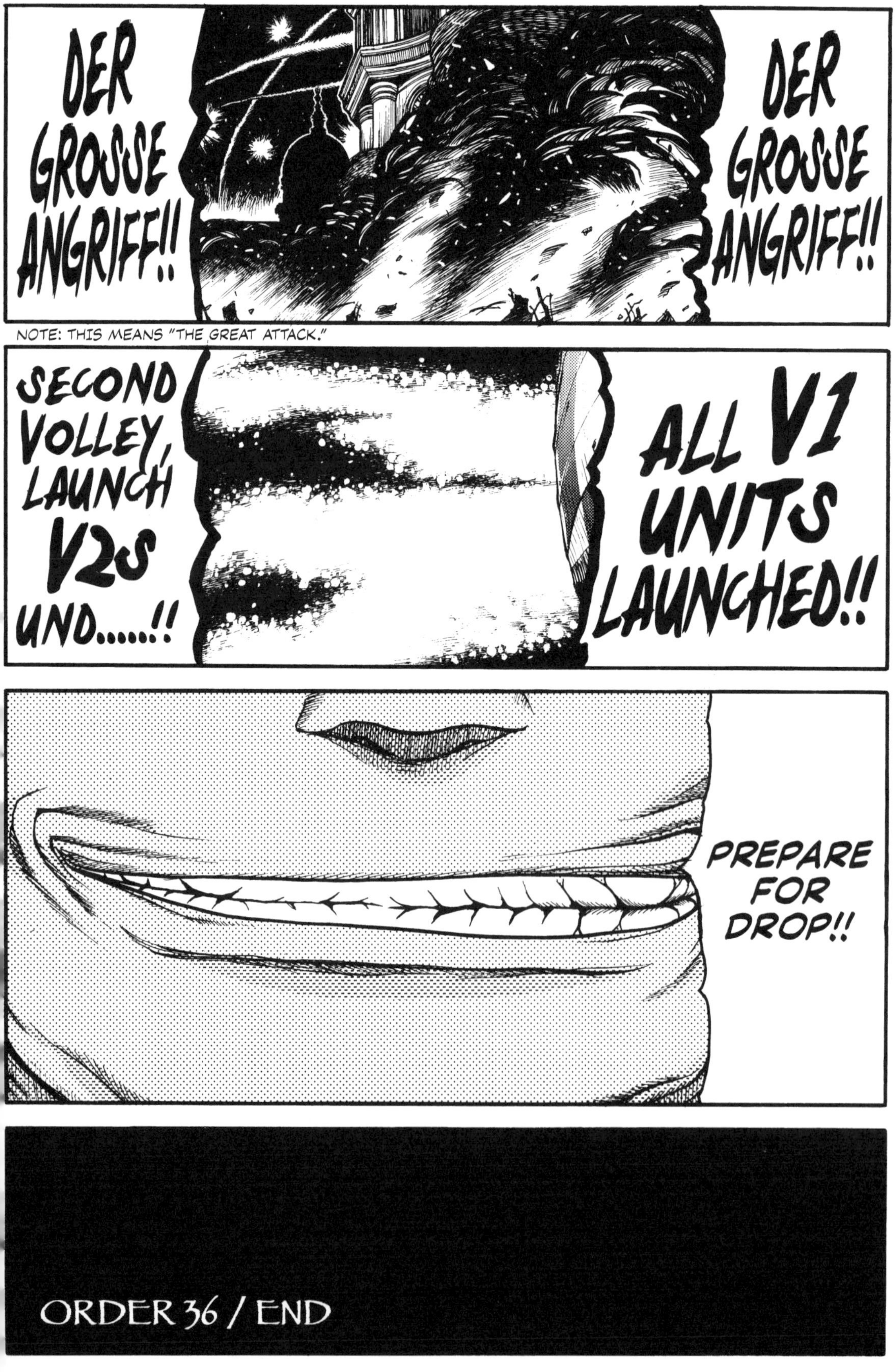
DER GROSSE ANGRIFF!!
DER GROSSE ANGRIFF!!
NOTE: THIS MEANS "THE GREAT ATTACK."
ALL V1 UNITS LAUNCHED!!
SECOND VOLLEY, LAUNCH V2S UND......!!
PREPARE FOR DROP!!
ORDER 36 / END

ORDER 37

DER GROSSE ANGRIFF.
ROOAARR
BROARR
BDOOM
BROARRRRR
DER GROSSE ANGRIFF!!
DER GROSSE ANGRIFF!!

MORE!!
MORE FRUITS OF BATTLE!!
MORE!!
MORE CONFLAGRA-TION!!

ORDER 37
FINAL FANTASY 2

ゴウウウウウウウウウ
GNNNNNNNNN
NNNNNNNNNNNNN
IT'S BEAUTI-FUL...!!
I CAN SEE HELL.
COMMENCE AIRBORNE GROUND VARFARE.
AIRBORNE CORP, SALLY FORTH.
LET'S GO, FRONT LINE SWINE.
IT'S TIME FOR FLIGHT.

SHMMMMMMMMM
5
Funf!
4
Vier!
3
drei!
CLICK
SHPP
2
Zwei!
ズッ
GEHEN
1
eins!
CHAK
SHOOM
0
Null!

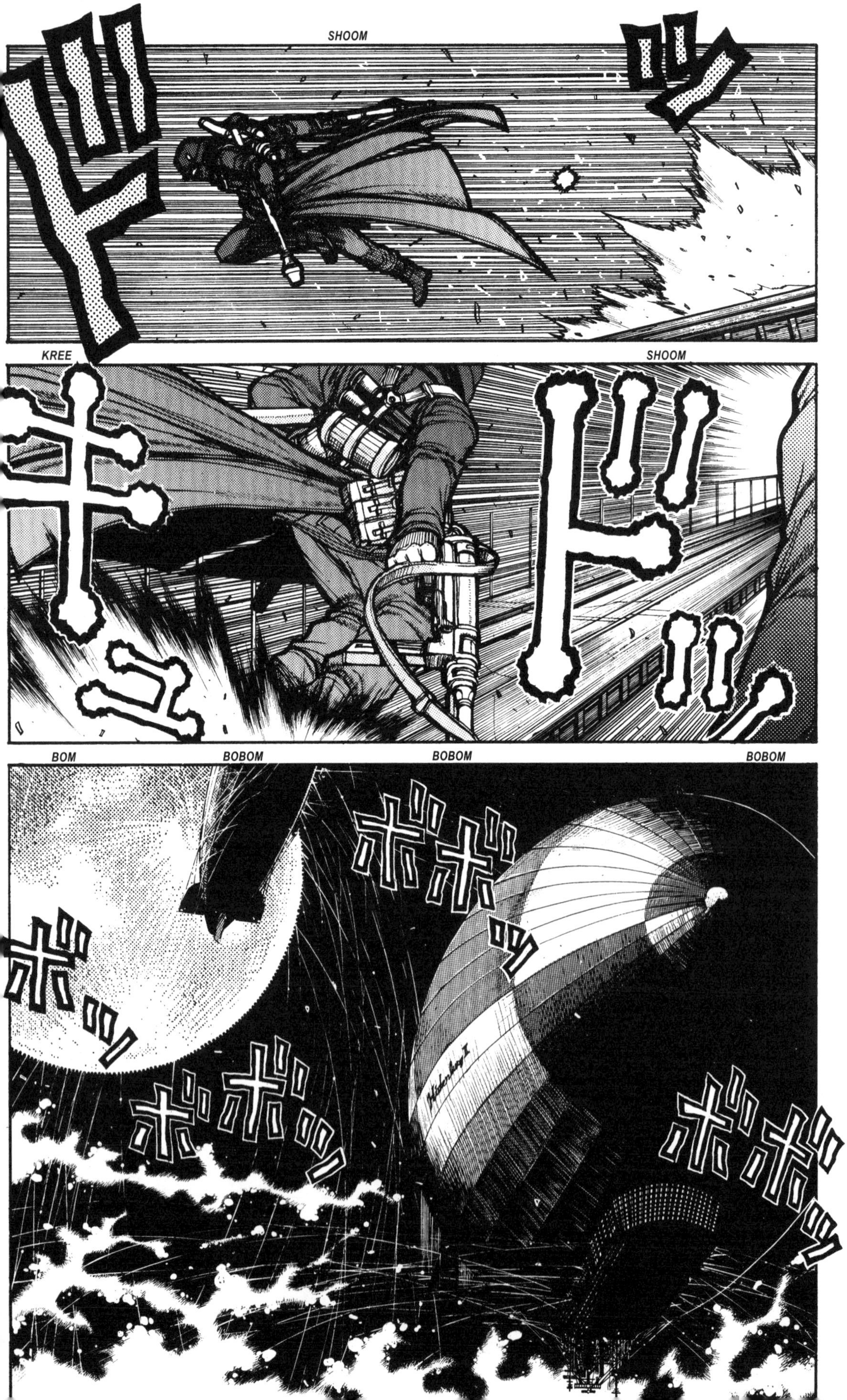
SHOOM
ドッ
SHOOM
ドッ
KREE
キュ
BOBOM
BOBOM
BOBOM
BOM

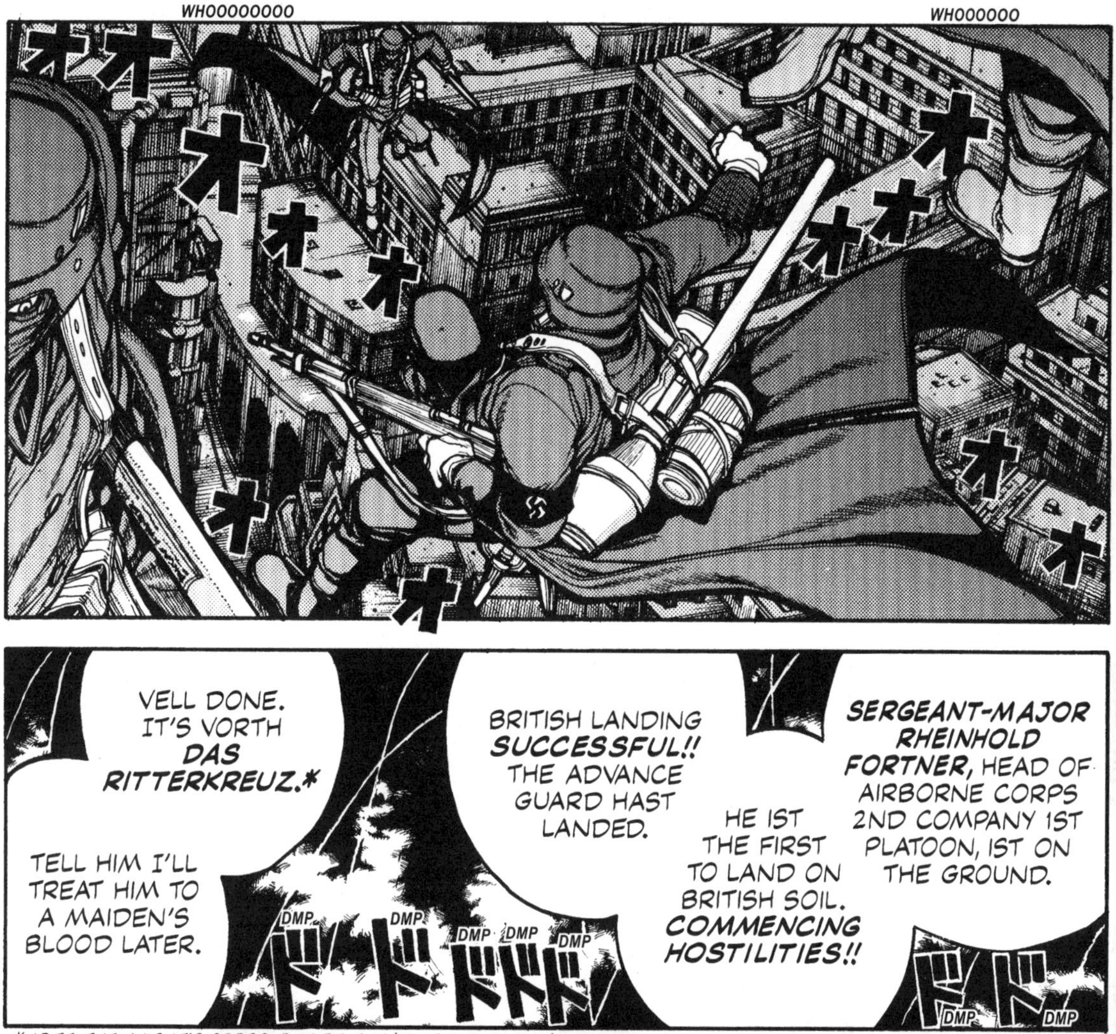

*NOTE: THE KNIGHT'S CROSS, ONE OF THE (IF NOT THE VERY) HIGHEST NAZI WAR DECORATIONS.

FLASH FLASH FLASH
FLASH FLASH FLASH
THE ENTIRE CITY IS UNDER ATTACK!
WOO WOO WOO WOO WOOON WOOON
A LARGE-SCALE CONFLAGRATION IS BREAKING OUT IN SOUTHWARK!!
IT'S A ROCKET ATTACK FROM THE AIRSHIP FLEET!!
EXPLOSIVE FIRES REPORTED IN OVER A HUNDRED FIFTY LOCATIONS AROUND LONDON!!
THE AIR FORCE... WHAT'S THE AIR FORCE DOING?!
COMMUNICATIONS LOST WITH RAF HEADQUARTERS AND EVERY BASE!!
WE CAN'T REACH THE PRIME MINISTER, GOVERNMENT, OR MILITARY HEADS.
OUR COMMUNICATION NETWORK AND COMMAND SYSTEM ARE TORN TO BITS.
THE APPROXIMATELY HUNDRED FIFTY PRINCIPLE MILITARY ESTABLISHMENTS, COMMUNICATIONS CENTERS, AND COMMAND CENTERS OF GREAT BRITAIN ARE EITHER EXPERIENCING...
...A MASS COMMUNICATIONS DISRUPTION, OR ARE LOCKED IN BATTLE WITH UNIDENTIFIED ENEMY FORCES.
!!
IT'S THE SAME AS THAT GROUP WHICH ATTACKED US EARLIER.
"ETERNAL LIFE." "VAMPIRISM."
IT MEANS THAT THERE WERE THAT MANY LURED AWAY BY SUCH SWEET FRUITS.
WHMP

THAT MANY TRAITORS.
THIS LOCATION MUST BE ONE OF THEIR OBJECTIVES.
YOU SHOULD ESCAPE IMMEDIATELY, SIR PENWOOD.
STAND
YOU, Y-YOU RETURN TO YOUR AGENCY STRAIGHT AWAY.
YOU HAVE RESPONSI-BILITIES THAT ONLY YOU CAN FULFILL...!!
I CANNOT ES-ESCAPE. I CAN'T RUN.
TH-THAT ALONE I CAN'T DO.
TROOPS ARE DEPLOYING FROM THE AIRSHIP FLEET HOLDING ABOVE THE CITY.
THIS! THIS IS PREPOS-TEROUS!
THEY... THEY'RE GERMAN TROOPS!
THEY'RE WAFFEN SS!!
WHA...
WHAT'D YOU SAY?!

ESCAPE, SIR PENWOOD!! ESCAPE!!
THE VAMPIRE SWARM WILL MAKE ITS WAY IN HERE IN HALF A MOMENT.
WOON
WOOON
WOON
AT THIS POINT, YOUR ABILITY TO COMMAND FROM HERE IS ALMOST NONEXISTENT.
DO YOU MEAN TO DIE?
WOOON
WOON
PERHAPS... PERHAPS COMMUNICATIONS WILL BE RESTORED AND ORDERS WILL COME IN.
SOME BASE SOMEWHERE MAY REPULSE THE ENEMY AND BE WAITING FOR INSTRUCTIONS FROM US.
I-I AM IN COMMAND HERE.
AS LONG AS THIS LOCATION IS INTACT, TH-THERE'S NO WAY I CAN LEAVE.
WOOON
WOOO
INTEGRA, I AM A USELESS MAN. INCOMPETENT. A COWARD.
I'M SO USELESS I DON'T EVEN KNOW MYSELF WHY I'M IN SUCH AN IMPORTANT POSITION.
IT'S AS IF MY LIFE HAS BEEN DETERMINED SOLELY BY PEDIGREE AND SOCIAL STANDING.
I DID NOT GET HERE BY ANY ASPIRATION OF MY OWN.
I'VE ALWAYS COME BY WAY OF STATUS AND DUTY GIVEN TO ME BY OTHERS.

...I FEEL I MUST FULFILL *THIS* DUTY...BUT...
SO, A-*AT* THE VERY LEAST...
YOU... HELLSING HAS A DUTY, WHICH ONLY *HELLSING* CAN FULFILL.
GO ON. *YOU* GO, INTEGRA.
GUNK
FLING
?
INSIDE THIS ARE ROUNDS TIPPED WITH *BLESSED GRANULATED SILVER*.
IT SHOULD PROVE *MORE* EFFECTIVE AGAINST THEM THAN AN ORDINARY GUN.

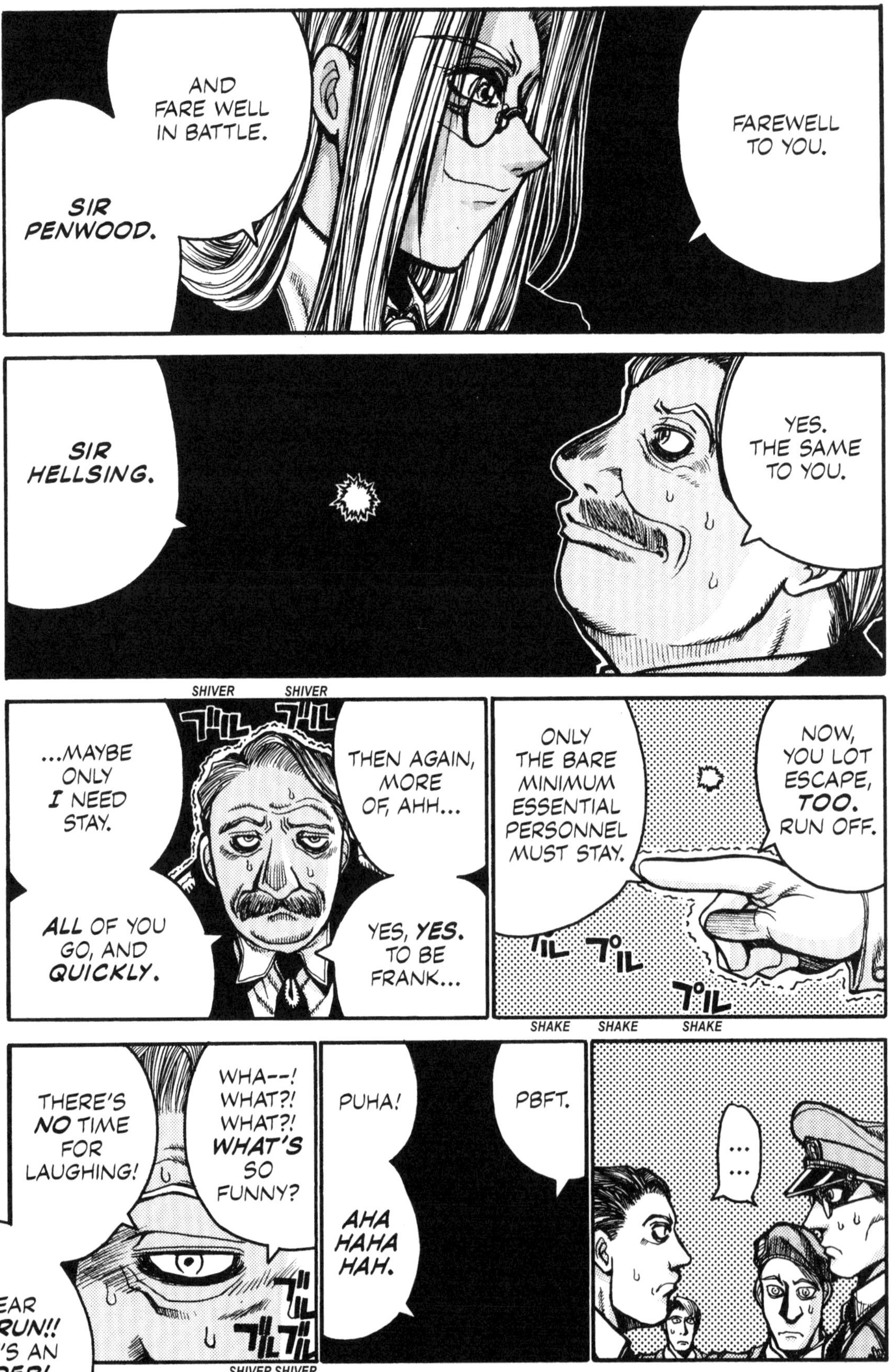
FAREWELL TO YOU.
AND FARE WELL IN BATTLE.
SIR PENWOOD.
YES. THE SAME TO YOU.
SIR HELLSING.
NOW, YOU LOT ESCAPE, TOO. RUN OFF.
ONLY THE BARE MINIMUM ESSENTIAL PERSONNEL MUST STAY.
SHAKE SHAKE SHAKE
SHIVER SHIVER
THEN AGAIN, MORE OF, AHH...
...MAYBE ONLY I NEED STAY.
YES, YES. TO BE FRANK...
ALL OF YOU GO, AND QUICKLY.
......
PBFT.
PUHA!
AHA HAHA HAH.
WHA--! WHAT?! WHAT?! WHAT'S SO FUNNY?
THERE'S NO TIME FOR LAUGHING!
SHIVER SHIVER
RUN!!

HURRY! HURRY AND ESCAPE!
WHAT ARE YOU DOING?!
ORGANIZE THE RANKS AND GO TO CONTACT THEM DIRECTLY!! ON FOOT IF YOU MUST!!
RE-ADJUST THE DAMAGE REPORT.
!!
WE MUST ATTEMPT TO CONTACT THE MINISTRY OF DEFENCE ONCE MORE.
WE MUST RESUME THE SEARCH FOR A FUNCTIONAL CIRCUIT.
BUILD BARRICADES AT THE ENTRANCES AND EXITS, QUICKLY!!
WHA...
WHAT?
HA!
SET UP A GARRISON! MOVE!!
ASSEMBLE THE REMAINING MEN, AMMUNITION, AND ARMS!!
WHAT ARE YOU DOING, YOU BARMY FOOLS?!
YOU CAN'T OPERATE A SINGLE CONSOLE, CAN YOU?
WHAT ARE YOU TALKING ABOUT, ADMIRAL?
YOU'RE INTERFERING WITH OUR WORK.
PLEASE TAKE YOUR SEAT.
THERE'S NO REASON FOR THIS!!

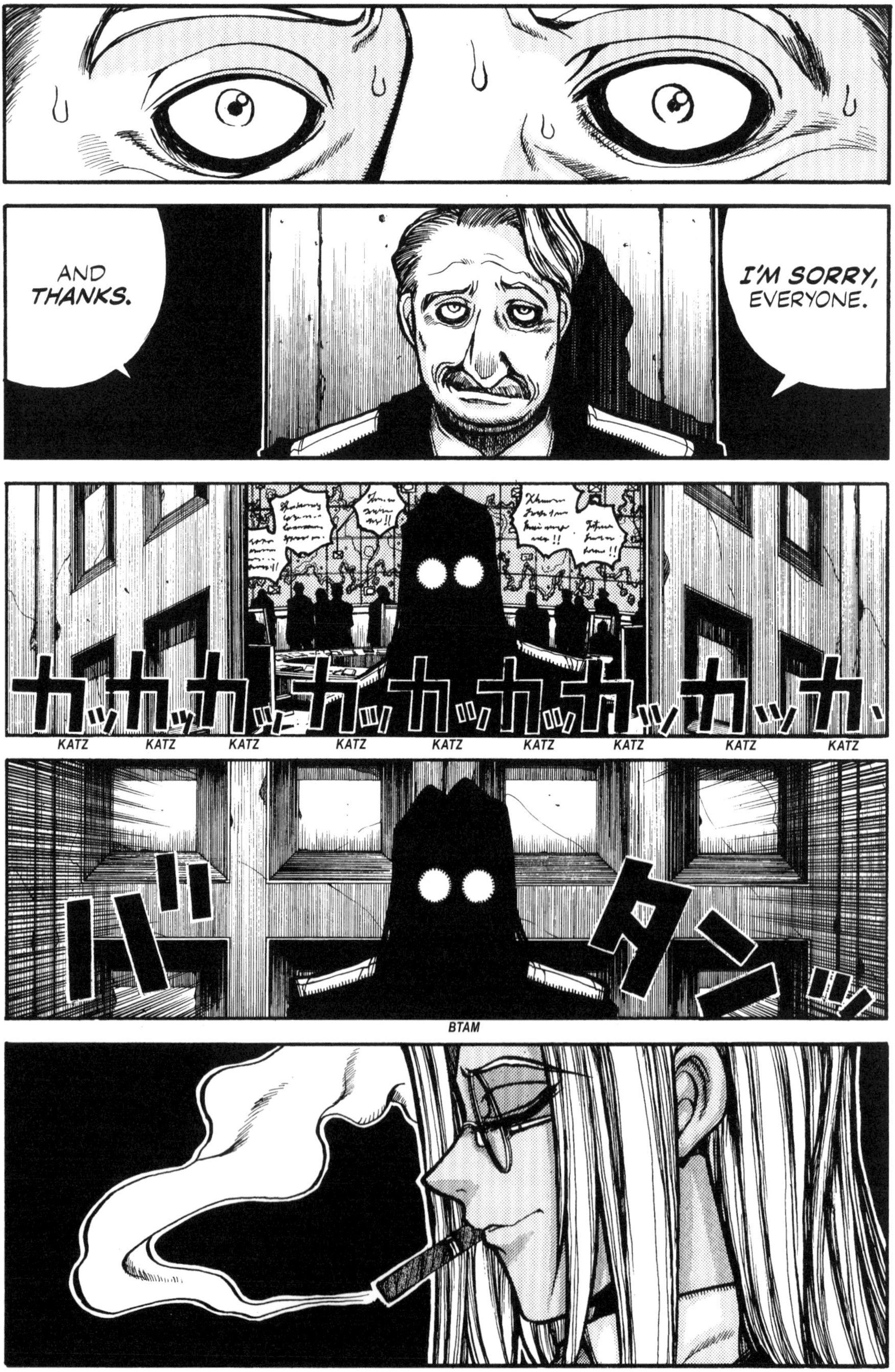
I'M SORRY, EVERYONE.
AND THANKS.
KATZ KATZ KATZ KATZ KATZ KATZ KATZ KATZ KATZ
BTAM

LET'S GO HOME, WALTER. WE'VE NOT A MOMENT TO LOSE.
YES M'LADY!
カッ KATZ
カッ KATZ
カッ KATZ
カッ KATZ
AS YOU WISH.
WE CAN CUT ACROSS THE CITY.
カッ KATZ
カッ KATZ
カッ KATZ
カッ KATZ
HELLSING WILL RESIST YOU TO ITS LAST BREATH.
I WILL DO MY OWN DUTY.
VAMPIRES!!
カッ KATZ
カッ KATZ
カッ KATZ
ボッ BOPH

HAHA
HAHA
HAHA
HAHA
HAHA
HAHA
ORDER 37 / END

ORDER 38

LYRICS BY TERUYUKI TAKAHASHI "DEVIL STOCKINGS"
JASRAC PERMIT #0314247-301

GYAHH!
BLAM
...AND MARCH DOWN THE ROAD...
KRAK KRAK KRAK
KRAK
KRAK KRAK
BRRRAP BRRRRRAP
...TO WAGE WAR UPON A DISTANT ENEMY.
BOOM

THEY KEEP MARCHING ON...
...JUST SO THEY CAN DIE...
...IN THIS TIME GONE MAD.

...!
...!!
...!!
WHO KNOWS WHY...
KSHH
KSHH
SPSHH
...THOUGH THE DEPTHS OF THEIR HEARTS...
ha!
ha!
ha!
hah!
...ARE SO TOTALLY DARK...
...NOTHING CAN BE SEEN.

THEY STAND IN A WIND-BLOWN FIELD...
...COUNTING THE NUMBER OF CORPSES.

IN THE PLAZA, THE SOLDIERS ARE DANCING IN A CIRCLE.
BUT THEY HAVE NO TIME FOR THAT.

TWITCH TWITCH
SHLLLP
TWITCH TWITCH
TO MAKE THEIR ESCAPE...
HUNNNNNH
...TO PROLONG...
...THE LENGTH OF THEIR LIVES...

...THEY WATCH HOW THE ROTTEN SHADOW...

...FROM THE CLOCKTOWER AT THE END OF THE WORLD...

...FALLS ACROSS THE RED FIELD.

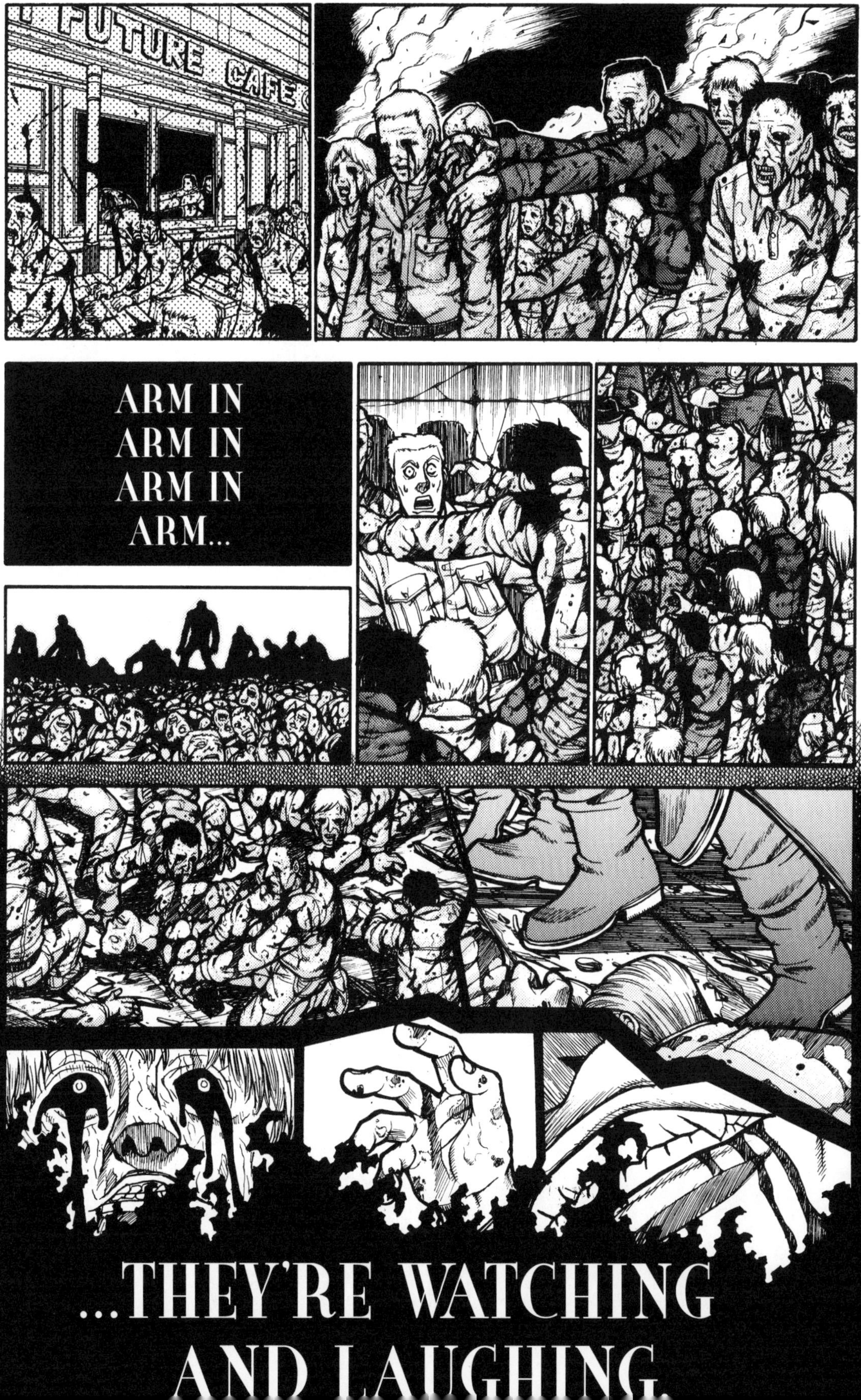
FUTURE CAFE
ARM IN ARM IN ARM IN ARM...
...THEY'RE WATCHING AND LAUGHING.

THE SOLDIERS LINE UP AND MARCH DOWN THE ROAD TO WAGE WAR UPON A DISTANT ENEMY.
THEY KEEP MARCHING ON JUST SO THEY CAN DIE IN THIS TIME GONE MAD.

THEY KEEP MARCHING ON. THEY KEEP MARCHING ON.
THEY KE MARCHI ON.

ORDER 38
FINAL FANTASY③

BLAM
BLAM
BLAM
KBLAM
FUCKIN' MONSTERS!!
BLAM
BLAM
KBLAM
C'MON YA BUGGERS!!
BLAM
BLAM BLAM
DAMN IT.
DAMN IT!!
DAMN IT.
BLAM
BLAM
BLAM
?!
Das ist aber nicht gut!
.....
Hölle auf Erden!

ZHAA
TAK
TAK
TAK
G... GODDAMN FREAK...!!
Y... YOU!
...! NGA... AHH...
BAM
BLAM
BAM
BAM
BLAM
HA HA!
HA!
HA! AA!

RATATATATATA
SMP
SMP
SMP
SMP
SMP
SMP
SMP
SMP
SMP
SMP
BLAM
BAM
BAM
BAM

THMP
THMP
THAP
THMP
!!
TICK
TICK
TICK
TICK
TICK
TICK
?!
?!
?!
BOMF
SKREEEEE

オーオオオ
オオオ
SHOOOO
SHOOOO
WELL DONE.
YOU HAVE ALL FULFILLED YOUR DUTY.
SLEEP NOW.

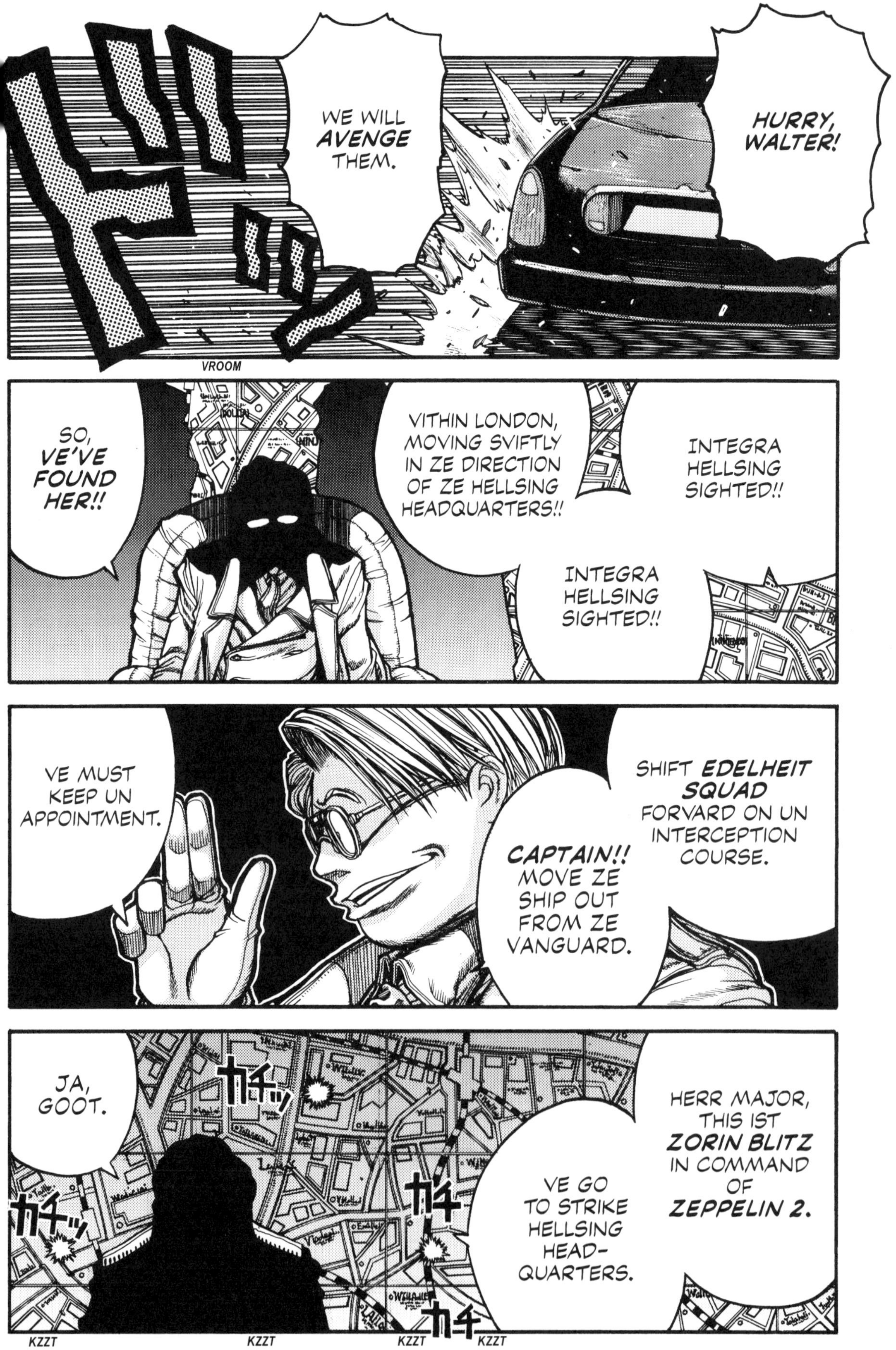
HURRY, WALTER!
WE WILL AVENGE THEM.
VROOM
INTEGRA HELLSING SIGHTED!!
VITHIN LONDON, MOVING SVIFTLY IN ZE DIRECTION OF ZE HELLSING HEADQUARTERS!!
INTEGRA HELLSING SIGHTED!!
SO, VE'VE FOUND HER!!
SHIFT EDELHEIT SQUAD FORVARD ON UN INTERCEPTION COURSE.
CAPTAIN!! MOVE ZE SHIP OUT FROM ZE VANGUARD.
VE MUST KEEP UN APPOINTMENT.
HERR MAJOR, THIS IST ZORIN BLITZ IN COMMAND OF ZEPPELIN 2.
VE GO TO STRIKE HELLSING HEAD-QUARTERS.
JA, GOOT.
KZZT
KZZT
KZZT
KZZT

SIEG HEIL.
SIEG HEIL.
HOW MANY V1S REMAIN?
NINE IN TOTAL.
LAUNCH ALL OF ZEM AT HELLSING HEAD-QUARTERS.
ZEY VILL BE ZORIN'S HERALD.
NOW HOW VILL YOU RESPOND, HELLSING?
THE BROWN INSANITY VILL BE YOUR OPPONENT.
SHOW ME YOUR CAPABILITIES.

ORDER 38 / END

ORDER 39

FINAL FANTASY④

... ...ENG ...LAND
... ...IS ...UN
... ...IS
... ...BY
LADY INTEGRA!!
I DON'T KNOW WHETHER **ANYONE** HEARS THIS TRANS-MISSION.
BUT I SEND IT IN THE BELIEF SOMEONE DOES.
...THIS IS... ADMI... PENWOOD... CURI... HEADQUAR-TERS.
KYEWIII!
KYEWII!
...I SEND MY **FINAL ORDERS.**
TO ANY **"HUMANS"** LISTENING AT THE HOME OFFICE...
THE MONSTERS ON THE OTHER SIDE OF THE DOOR,
WILL SOON COME HERE.
THIS LOCATION WILL SOON FALL.
NOT LONG FROM NOW.
RESIST...
...AND CARRY OUT YOUR DUTIES.

ADMIRAL...!! END OF THE ROAD, THEN!!
CAN'T SAY I'M MUCH FOR BECOMING A ZOMBIE.
CHEERS!!
BANG
WHOM
WHOM
WHOM
WHOM
KCHIK
THE NEW FAMILY HEAD?
YOU ARE...? OF HELLSING?!
WALTER!! A GIRL LIKE THIS?!

"A GIRL LIKE THIS."
SEEMS A RATHER EXTREME WAY OF PUTTING IT, SIR PENWOOD.
I AM THE FAMILY HEAD, INTEGRA HELLSING.
TO THAT END, I KILLED MY UNCLE AND INHERITED THIS POSITION.
I WOULD HAVE YOU STOP REFERRING TO ME AS "A GIRL LIKE THIS."
EH.
AH.
NO, I...
UH.
SHIVER
AH, NO, I...
Y-YES.
I-I SHOULDN'T HAVE.
S-SORRY.
WHILE HE WAS ALIVE, FATHER WOULD OFTEN TELL ME:
"WHENEVER YOU NEED A FAVOR, ASK SIR PENWOOD."
SHAKE SHAKE SHAKE
D-DID HE NOW? THAT RASCAL ARTHUR!!
SOMETHING WOULD COME UP AND HE'D MAKE SUCH UN-REASONABLE DEMANDS.
LIKE, "LET'S HAVE ONE OF THOSE NEW-ISSUE FIREARMS."
OR, "LET'S HAVE A HELICOPTER."
ALWAYS UP TO SOMETHING!
I DON'T THINK I WILL LOSE OUT TO MY FATHER WHEN IT COMES TO ASKING FOR THINGS.
HERE'S TO OUR FUTURE!!
EH.
EHHHHH?!

WHMP
KBAM
KATZ
CHF
CHF
CHF
CHF
CHF
YOU'VE BEEN MU TROUBL YOU GOOD-FOR-NOTHING
VAT'S SO FUNNY, HUMAN?
GRIN
Y-YOU LOT A-ARE...
Y-YOU'RE G-GOOD FOR EVEN L-LESS TH-THAN I AM.
LASMAND
BAGNAMIA

!!
!!
!!
G-GOD... GOD SPEED, I-INTEGRA.
I-IT'S BEEN FUN FOR ME, TOO.
GRIN
S--!
STOOOOOP!!
CHIK
NO!!
THAT'S ONE FAVOR I WON'T GRANT!!

ドッ
BOOM
ZHA!
BTTF-2
RUX:A/CF
RAT:D/GM
ZHA!
ZHAAAAA!
ZHAAAAA!
ZHAAAAA!
ZHAAAAA!
WALTER.

STEP ON IT!!
GRAHHHH
SKREEYEEYEE
VROOOOOOOO

KREEEEEEE
VROOOOOOO
REEECH
KREE

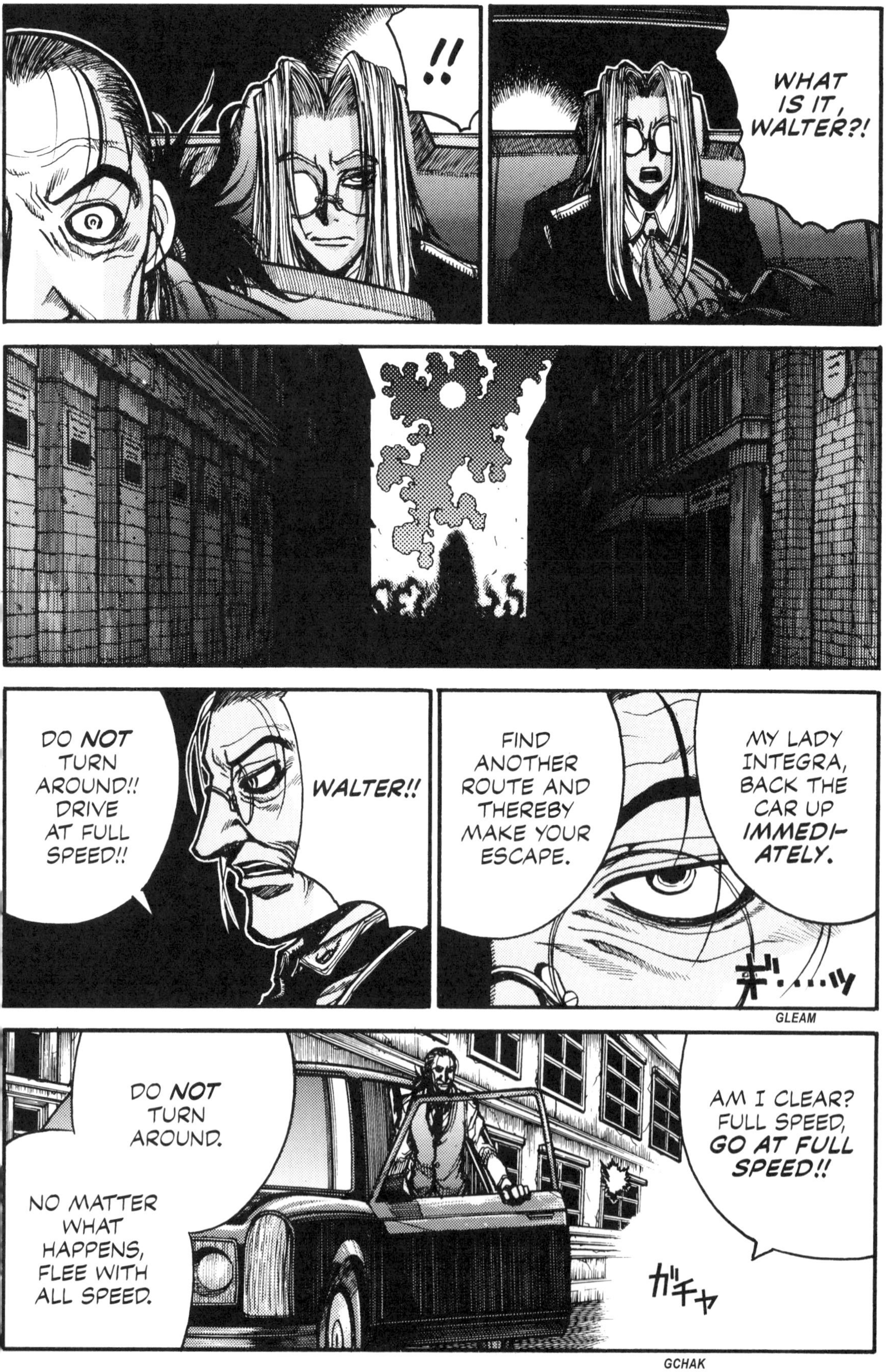
!!
WHAT IS IT, WALTER?!
MY LADY INTEGRA, BACK THE CAR UP IMMEDIATELY.
FIND ANOTHER ROUTE AND THEREBY MAKE YOUR ESCAPE.
ギ…ッ
GLEAM
WALTER!!
DO NOT TURN AROUND!! DRIVE AT FULL SPEED!!
AM I CLEAR? FULL SPEED, GO AT FULL SPEED!!
ガチャ
GCHAK
DO NOT TURN AROUND.
NO MATTER WHAT HAPPENS, FLEE WITH ALL SPEED.

WALTER!!
HURRY!!
IN MY PRESENT STATE I DO NOT KNOW JUST HOW LONG I CAN HOLD OUT AGAINST THAT CHAP OVER THERE.
GCHAK
ガチャッ
KATZ
BUTLER!!
YES, MA'AM!
KCHAK
THIS IS AN ORDER.
RETURN ALIVE AT ALL COSTS. SWEAR IT.
YES!
AS YOU COMMAND.

BTAM
KREEEEE
GROMMM
GROMM
OOON
OOOOON
KATZ
KATZ
KATZ

LICH RE
!!
AH
AHH
AH
FWSSSSS
OH
OH
SHAAA

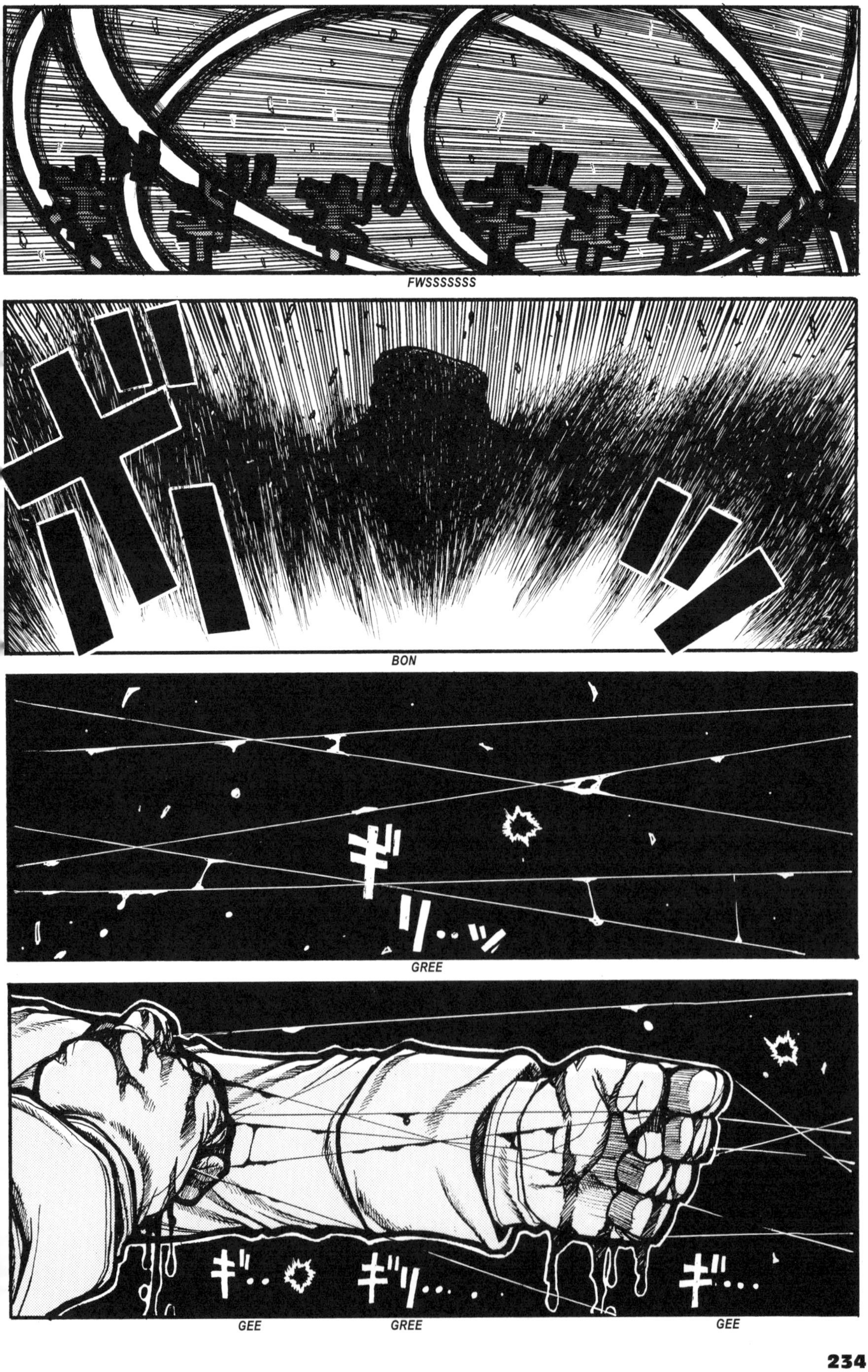
FWSSSSSSS
ボッ
BON
ギリ..ッ
GREE
ギ..
ギリ......
ギ...
GEE
GREE
GEE

SURE ENOUGH!
IT IS YOU!!

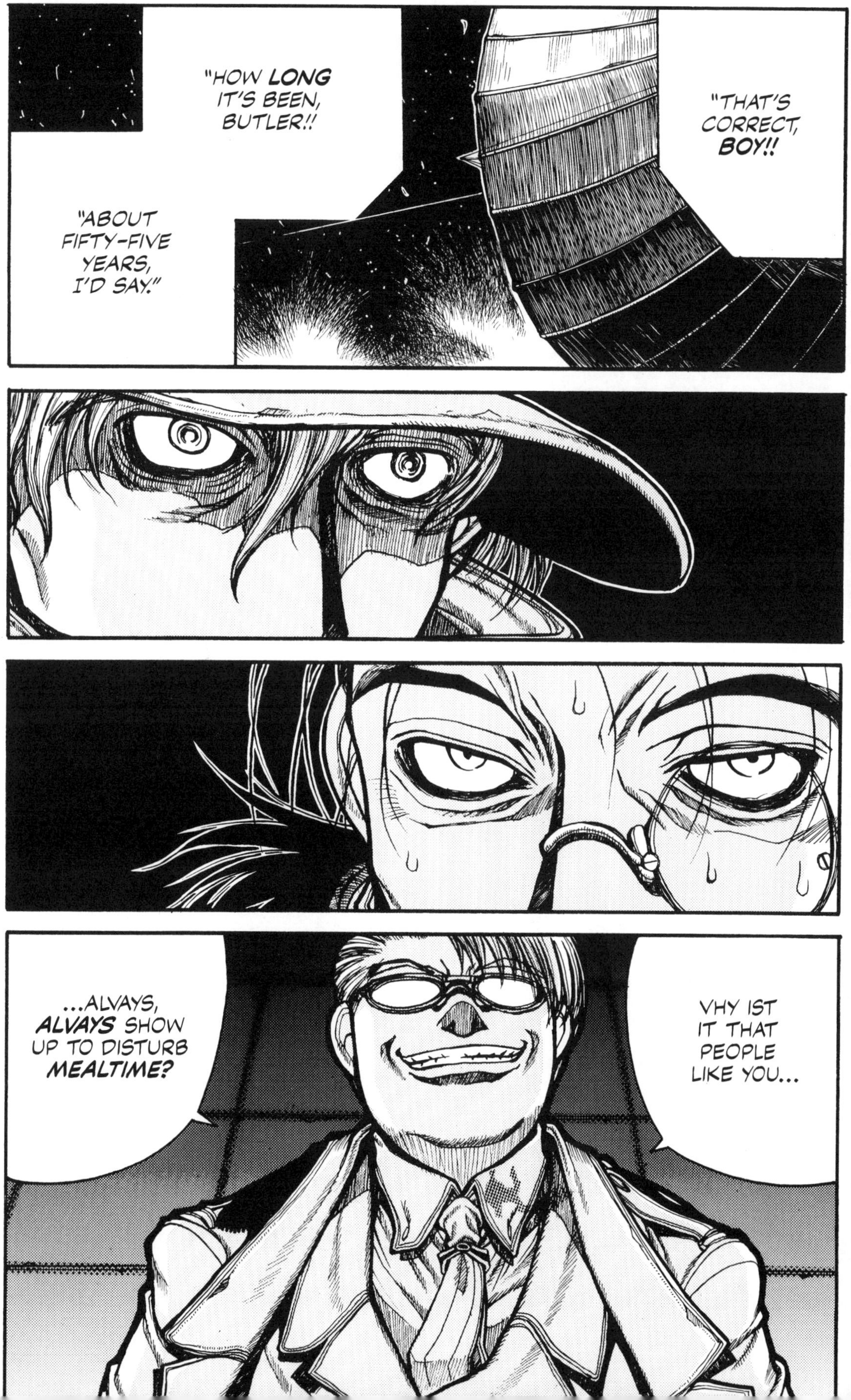
"HOW LONG IT'S BEEN, BUTLER!!
"ABOUT FIFTY-FIVE YEARS, I'D SAY."
"THAT'S CORRECT, BOY!!
VHY IST IT THAT PEOPLE LIKE YOU...
...ALVAYS, ALVAYS SHOW UP TO DISTURB MEALTIME?

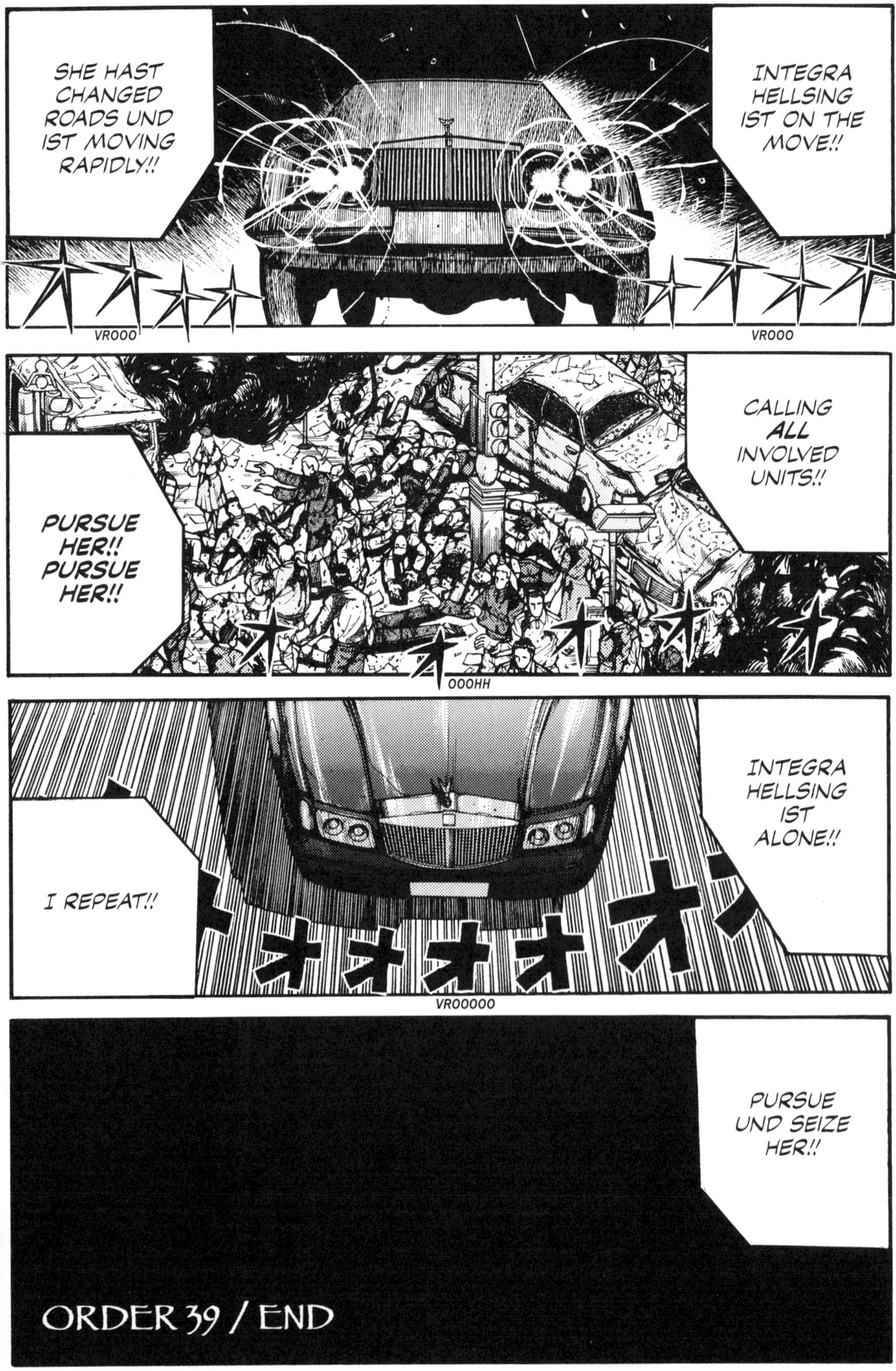
INTEGRA HELLSING IST ON THE MOVE!!
SHE HAST CHANGED ROADS UND IST MOVING RAPIDLY!!
VROOO
VROOO
CALLING ALL INVOLVED UNITS!!
PURSUE HER!! PURSUE HER!!
OOOHH
INTEGRA HELLSING IST ALONE!!
I REPEAT!!
VROOOOO
PURSUE UND SEIZE HER!!
ORDER 39 / END

⚜ ORDER 40

FINAL FANTASY⑤

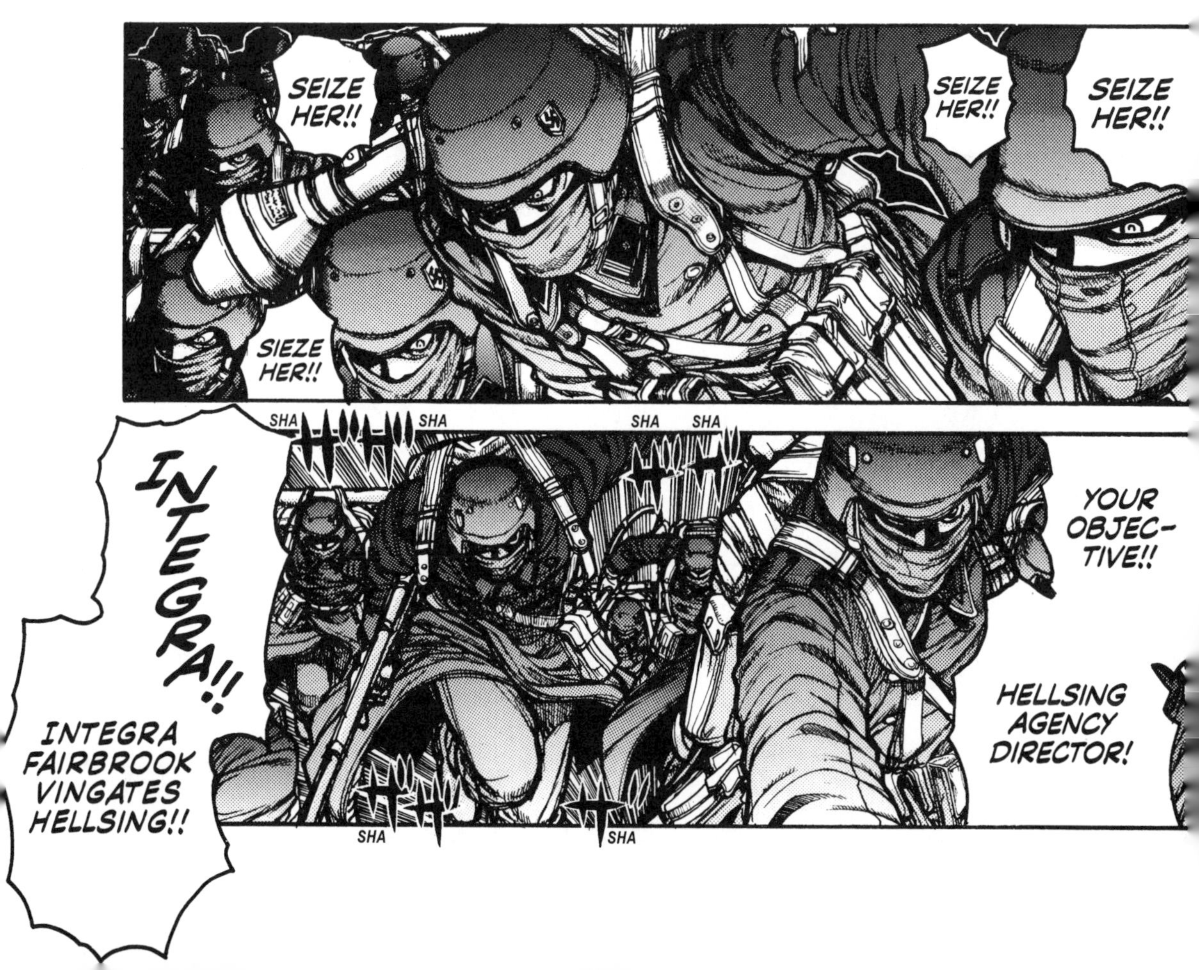

ドッ!!
WHOM
ドギャヤギャギャギャッ
SKREE
YEE
YEE
YEE

BOOM
DADOMM
BWOO
DERE SHE IZZZZT!
BROOOOOO

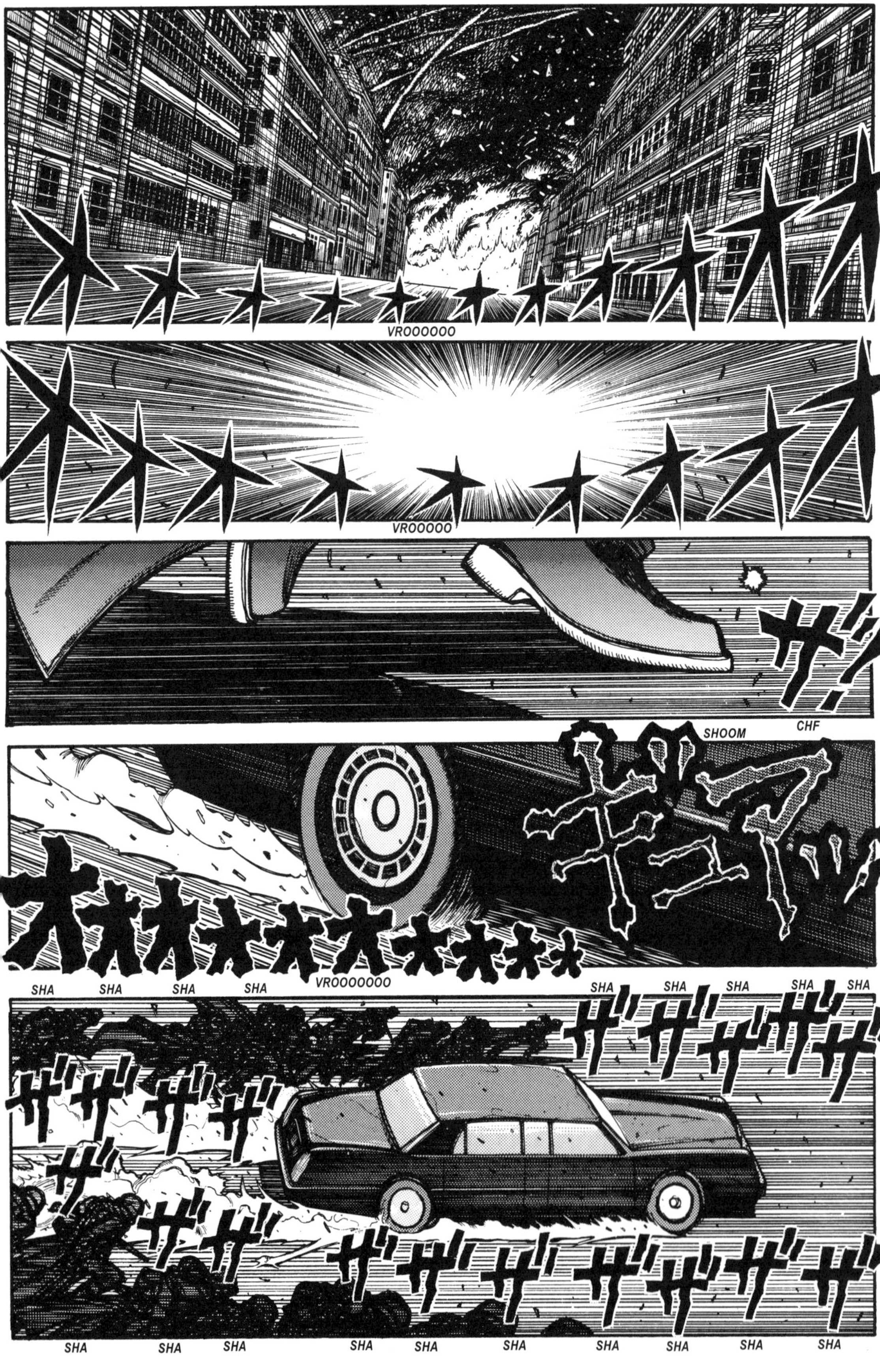
VROOOOOO
VROOOOO
CHF
SHOOM
VROOOOOOO
SHA SHA SHA SHA SHA SHA SHA SHA SHA
SHA SHA SHA SHA SHA SHA SHA SHA SHA SHA SHA

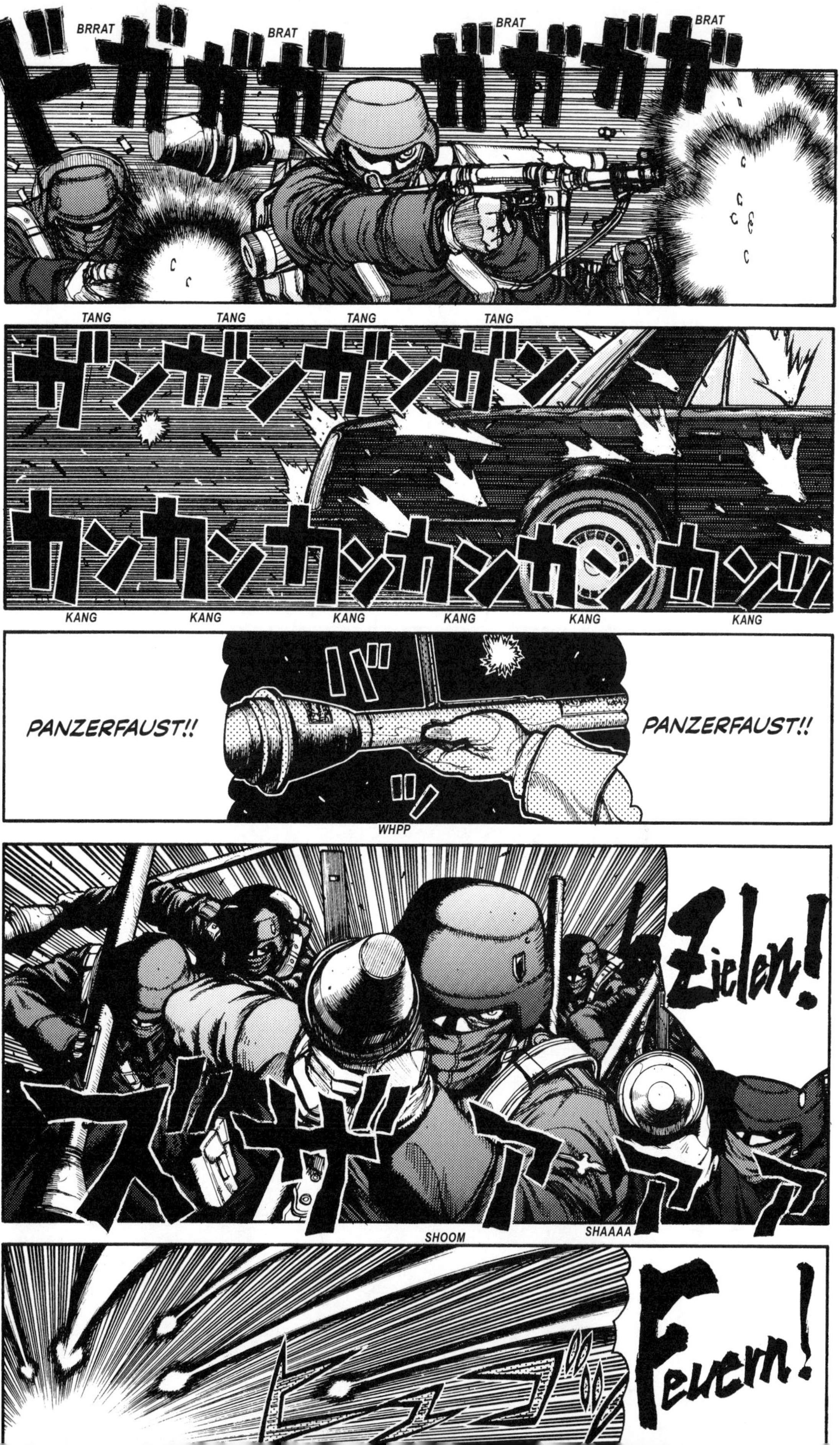

BRRAT
BRAT
BRAT
BRAT
TANG
TANG
TANG
TANG
KANG
KANG
KANG
KANG
KANG
KANG
PANZERFAUST!!
PANZERFAUST!!
WHPP
Zielen!
SHOOM
SHAAAA
Feuern!

ドォッ!
DOOM
ギュ…ォォォォォォ
BYOOOOM
ギャギャギャギャ
SKREEEEEE
ドガッ!!
KRASH

INTEGRA HELLSING!!
オオオオオオオ
TMP
BROARRRR
LEAP
ダンッ
SWSSS
BY ORDER OF MEIN BATTALION KOMMANDANT!!
PREPARE YOURSELF!!
ズアッ
ZWIP
ズッ!!

SHKK
HAHH
HAHH
HAHH
HAHH
HAHH
HAHH
THE FRÄULEIN IST A BAD LOSER.
HOWEVER MUCH YOU STRUGGLE, HOWEVER MUCH YOU RUN....
IT'S USELESS.
SHA
SHA
SHA
SHA
SHA
SHA
SHA
SHA

GIVE UP.
GIVE UP, HUMAN!!
YOUR KIND NO LONGER HAST ANYVHERE TO RUN...
...OR HIDE FROM THE MIDIANS IN LONDON.

STICK
"GIVE UP"?
"GIVE UP," YOU SAID.
OF COURSE, SUCH FITTING WORDS FOR YOUR KIND.
YOU WHO COULD NOT STAND BEING HUMAN?
DON'T UNDERESTIMATE HUMANITY, FREAKS.
COME, I WILL FIGHT WITH YOU.

STRAIIIN
VERY VELL THEN, BITCH!!
HUH! HU-HUH!
.......!!
...!
SUITS ME!!
LUNGE
SHMM
SHMM
SHMM

VHA...
...VHA
......
VHAT
...
......AH
VH...AT
NGAH
ZA
OGH
VHAT
IST
DIS?!
MY BODY
IST
CRUMB...
THESE
ARE...!
BA!
...BA!
BA...!
TH...
シュオオオオオオン
SHWOHHHH
BA!
BAY!
BAYONETS!!

BOSH
!!
SHLLL
IT'S YOU......!
THE VATICAN!
SECTION XIII ISCARIOT...!!
HIT MAN.
KILLING JUDGE.
REGEN-ERATOR.
ANGEL DUST.
BAYONET.
SSSSSSSS
SSSSS!
FATHER

ALEXANDER ANDERSON!!

HAHAHAHA! VHAT'S COME OVER YOU, FATHER ANDERSON?
I THOUGHT OUR STANDING ORDERS FROM FATHER MAXWELL VERE JUST TO OBSERVE.
!!
WHAT'S MORE, YOU RESCUED THE HELLSING.
ISN'T THAT AN ACT OF GROSS MISCON-DUCT?

HA HA HA HA HA HA
HA HA HA HA HA HA
DID YE HEAR, HEINKEL?!
DID YE HEAR, YUMIE?!
WITH AE BLEEDING NOSE AND AE VERITABLE SWARM O' THE FREAK FORCE AFORE HER!
COME AND GET ME?
AH WILL FIGHT YE?
GYEHA HA HA HA HA HA!
NAE MISTAKING IT.
SHE, THIS WOMAN, AND A' WITH HER...
...ARE OOR SWORN ENEMIES!

WE WILL DEFEAT THEM.
NAE ONE CAN HAVE THAT RIGHT.
WE ARE THE ONLY ONES WHA MAY.
NAE ONE CAN INTERFERE.
NAE ONE! NAE ONE!!
YOU'RE FROM ISCARIOT!!
DO YOU MEAN TO HINDER US?!
GLARE
SHUT YER MOUTHS!!
NAE TALKING FOR THE DEID!!

AFORE MY VERY EYES...
...THE DEID WALK.
THE UNDEID FORM AN ARMY...
...LINE UP, AND MARCH FORTH.
FOR THOSE WHA WOULD ATTEMPT TAE EMBRACE THAT ULTIMATE PRINCIPLE O' BACKWARDS HERESY...
...WOULD THE VATICAN...
...WOULD SECTION XIII...
...WOULD AH FORGIVE THEM?
AFORE YE EVEN HAVE AE CHANCE TAE TREMBLE...
...YE'LL PERISH LIKE STRAW.

ORDER 40 / END

⚜ ORDER 41

THE SCREAMER

KATZ
KATZ
KATZ
KATZ
WHIT ART THOU?!
WE ASK O' THEE.
KATZ
KATZ
KATZ
KATZ
KATZ
KATZ

WE ART ISCARIOT.
THE ZEALOT JUDAS!!
(looking up)
!!
ZAM
OOOOOOO

SHA
SHA
SHA
SHA
SHA
SHA
IN THAT CASE, ISCARIOT. WE ASK O' THEE...
...WHIT DOST THOU HOLD IN THY RIGHT HAND?!
DAGGERS!!
AND POISONS!!
ZAM

UOHHH!
ZHA
IN THAT CASE, ISCARIOT. WE ASK O' THEE...
...WHIT DOST THOU HOLD IN THY LEFT HAND?!
THIRTY SILVER PIECES!!
AND A ROPE!!
IN THAT CASE!!
WHMM

SHNNK
AH
WHIT ART THOU?!
IN THAT CASE, ISCARIOT.
BLORP

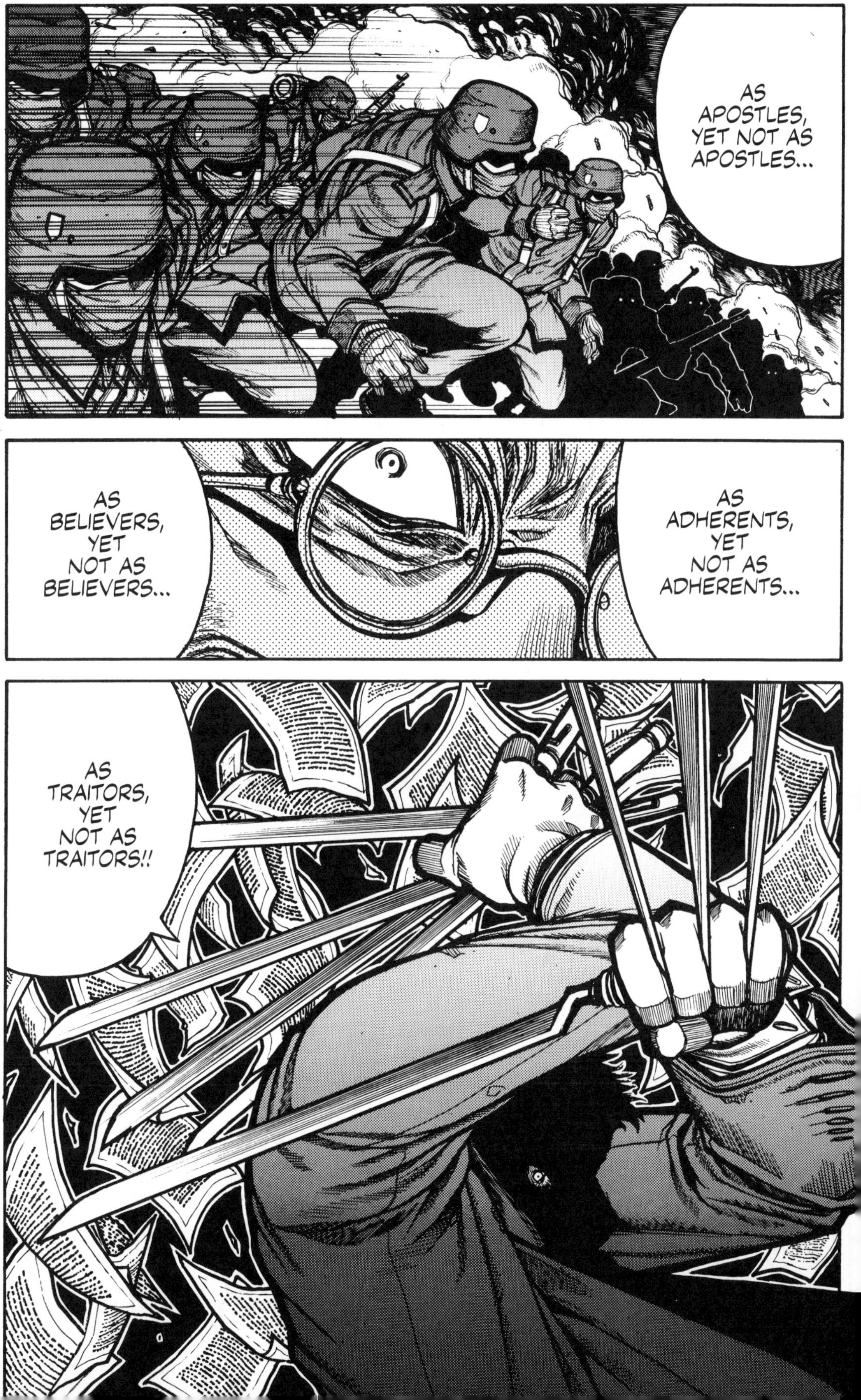
AS APOSTLES, YET NOT AS APOSTLES...
AS ADHERENTS, YET NOT AS ADHERENTS...
AS BELIEVERS, YET NOT AS BELIEVERS...
AS TRAITORS, YET NOT AS TRAITORS!!

WE ART DISCIPLES OF DEATH.
THE DEATH DISCIPLE GROUP.
ONLY BOWING AND PRAYING FORGIVENESS OF THE LORD.

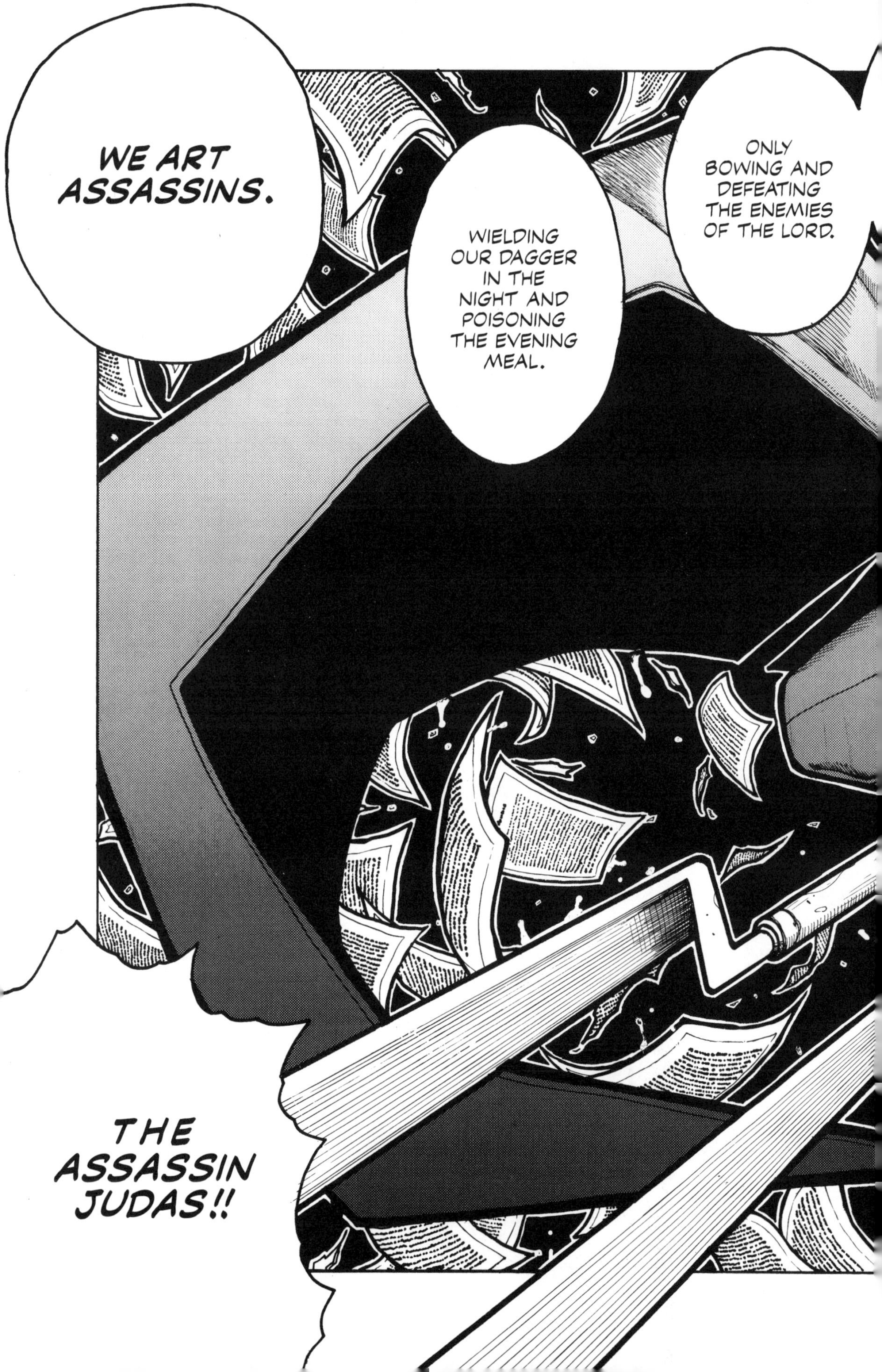
ONLY BOWING AND DEFEATING THE ENEMIES OF THE LORD.
WIELDING OUR DAGGER IN THE NIGHT AND POISONING THE EVENING MEAL.
WE ART ASSASSINS.
THE ASSASSIN JUDAS!!

SHNK
SHNK
SHNK
WHEN THE TIME COMES WE SHALT CAST OUR THIRTY SILVER PIECES AT THE ALTAR...
...AND HANG THY HEAD FROM OUR *ROPE*.

THEREBY WE SHALT FALL TO HELL IN CABAL.
LINED UP IN SQUARE FORMATION...
CHIK
CHIK
CHIK
...WE SEEK TO DO BATTLE WITH THE SEVEN MILLION, FOUR HUNDRED FIVE THOUSAND, NINE HUNDRED TWENTY-SIX DEMONS OF HELL.
SHPOP
SHRUKK

APOCALYPSE NOW!!
ORDER 41 / END

THMP THMP THMP THMP THMP THMP THMP THMP
SHNK
BRRRRAP
BRRRRRRAP
SAAAAAAA!

ORDER 42
AUBIRD FORCE

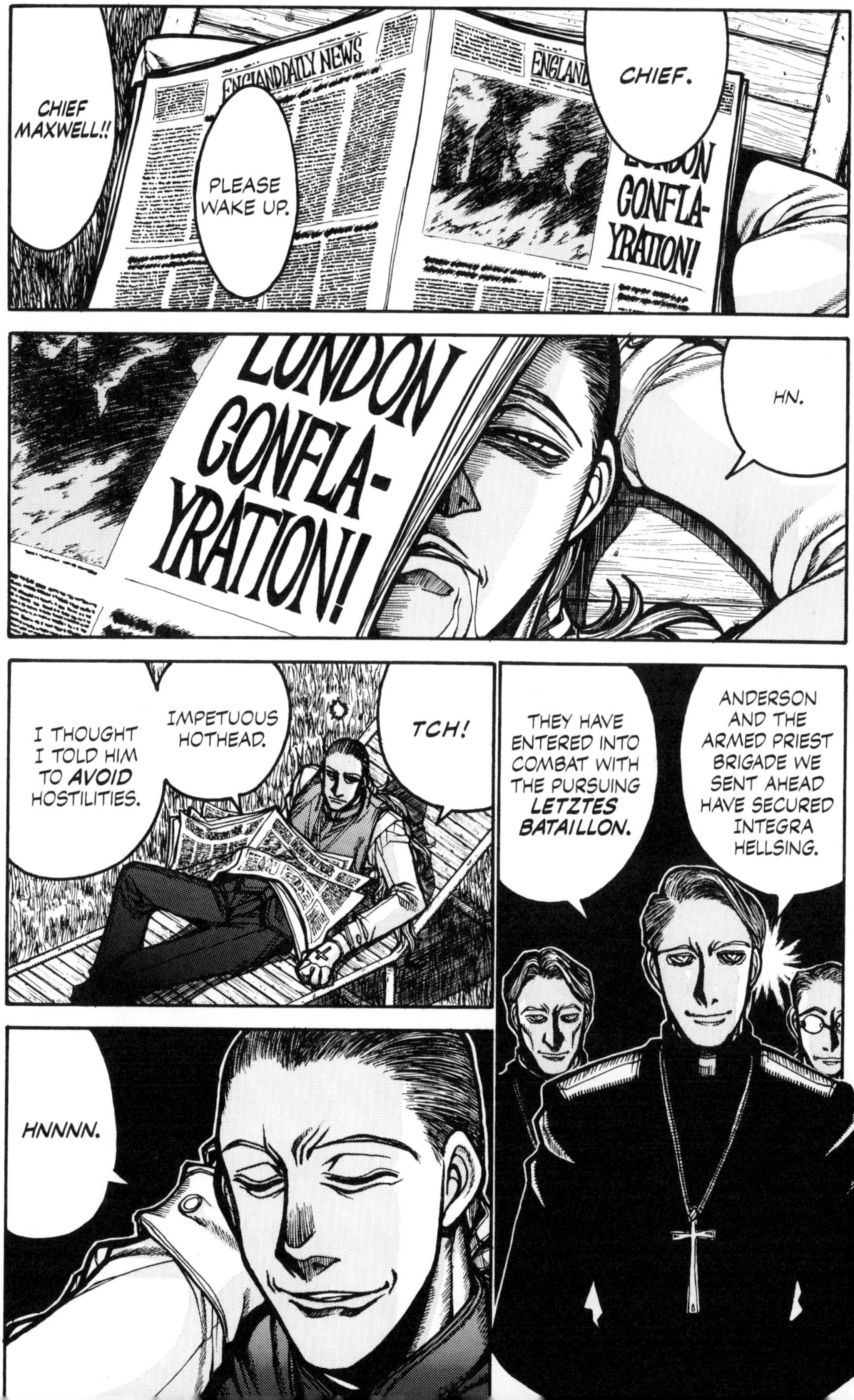
CHIEF.
PLEASE WAKE UP.
CHIEF MAXWELL!!
ENGLAND DAILY NEWS
LONDON CONFLA-YRATION!
LONDON CONFLA-YRATION!
HN.
ANDERSON AND THE ARMED PRIEST BRIGADE WE SENT AHEAD HAVE SECURED INTEGRA HELLSING.
THEY HAVE ENTERED INTO COMBAT WITH THE PURSUING *LETZTES BATAILLON*.
TCH!
IMPETUOUS HOTHEAD.
I THOUGHT I TOLD HIM TO ***AVOID*** HOSTILITIES.
HNNNN.

RMMMMMMM
RMMMMMMMM
HOOO.
THAT IS QUITE A FIRE.
THE IMPERIAL CAPITAL LONDON IS IN A STATE OF DEVASTATION.
SINCE THE GREAT LONDON AIR RAID, A LARGE CONFLA-GRATION HAS CONTINUED TO SPREAD.
JUST LIKE PURGATORY.
RMMBL
WE ARE UNABLE TO ESTIMATE THE NUMBER OF DEAD...
...NOR HOW MANY HAVE BECOME UNDEAD.
IT'S DIVINE PUNISHMENT.

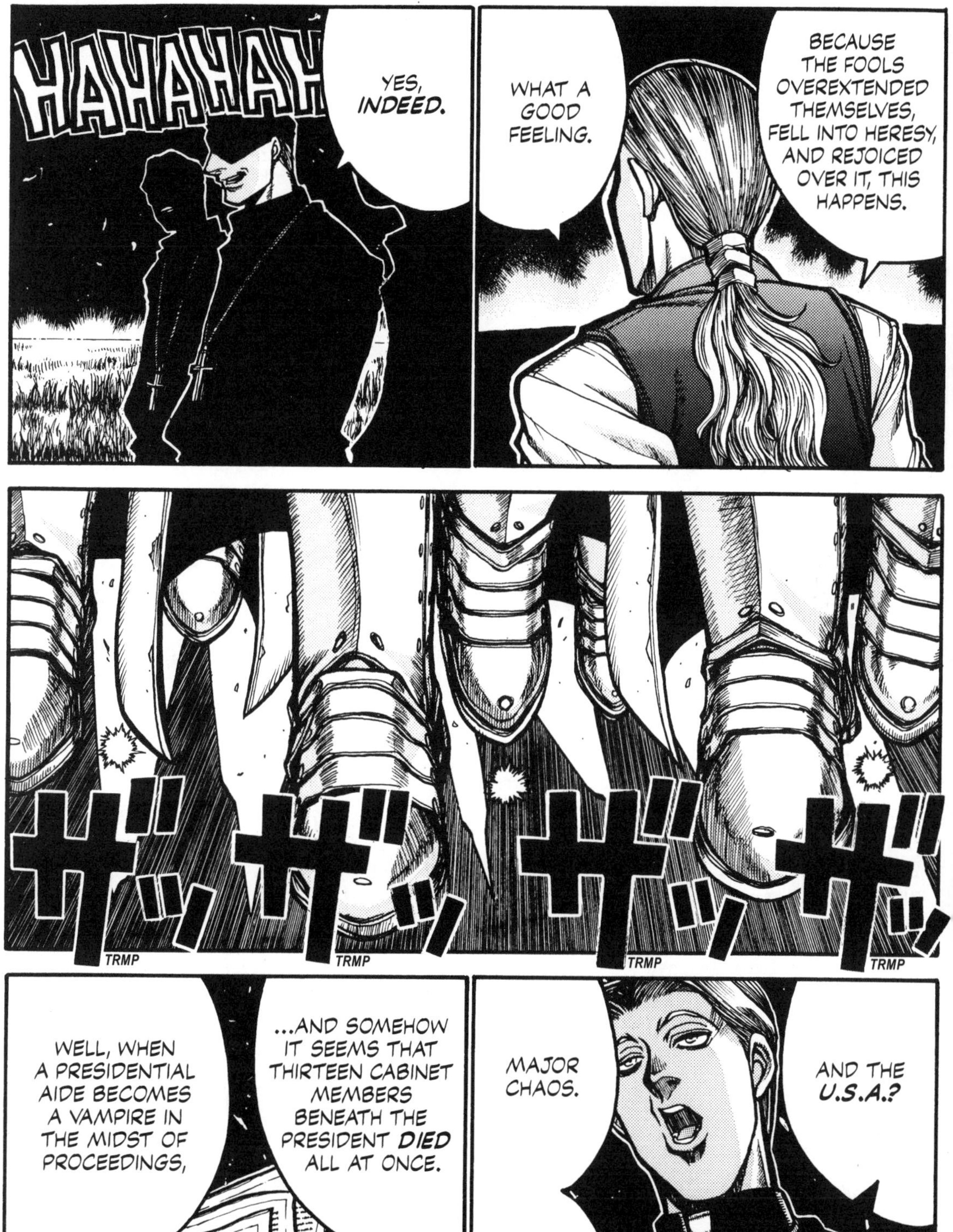
WHAT A GOOD FEELING.
BECAUSE THE FOOLS OVEREXTENDED THEMSELVES, FELL INTO HERESY, AND REJOICED OVER IT, THIS HAPPENS.
YES, INDEED.
HAHAHAH
TRMP
TRMP
TRMP
TRMP
AND THE U.S.A.?
MAJOR CHAOS.
AS OF NOW THE WHITE HOUSE IS IN FLAMES...
...AND SOMEHOW IT SEEMS THAT THIRTEEN CABINET MEMBERS BENEATH THE PRESIDENT DIED ALL AT ONCE.
WELL, WHEN A PRESIDENTIAL AIDE BECOMES A VAMPIRE IN THE MIDST OF PROCEEDINGS,
I SUPPOSE THAT WOULD HAPPEN.

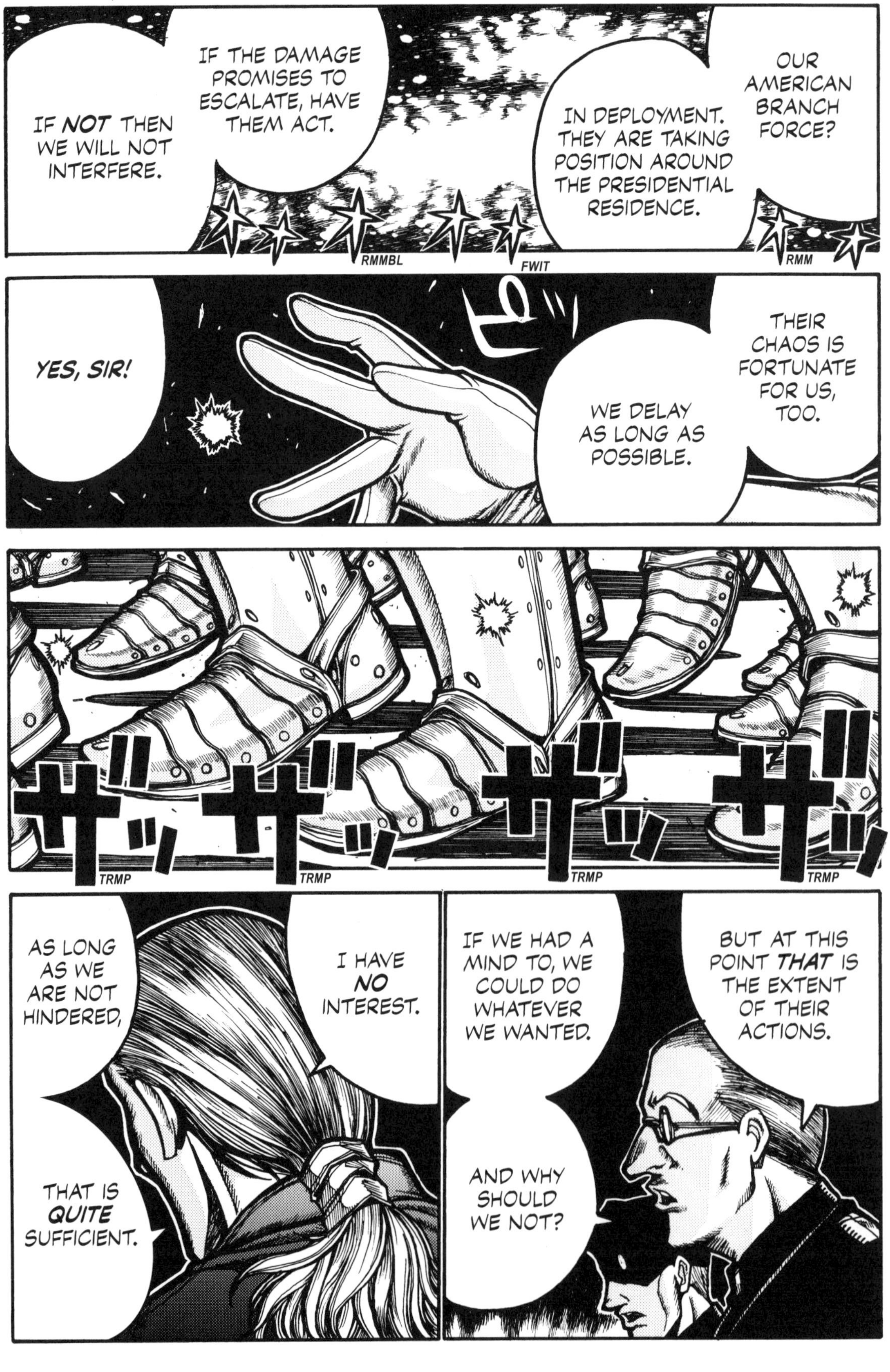
OUR AMERICAN BRANCH FORCE?
RMM
IN DEPLOYMENT. THEY ARE TAKING POSITION AROUND THE PRESIDENTIAL RESIDENCE.
FWIT
IF THE DAMAGE PROMISES TO ESCALATE, HAVE THEM ACT.
RMMBL
IF **NOT** THEN WE WILL NOT INTERFERE.
THEIR CHAOS IS FORTUNATE FOR US, TOO.
WE DELAY AS LONG AS POSSIBLE.
YES, SIR!
TRMP
TRMP
TRMP
TRMP
BUT AT THIS POINT ***THAT*** IS THE EXTENT OF THEIR ACTIONS.
IF WE HAD A MIND TO, WE COULD DO WHATEVER WE WANTED.
AND WHY SHOULD WE NOT?
I HAVE **NO** INTEREST.
AS LONG AS WE ARE NOT HINDERED,
THAT IS ***QUITE*** SUFFICIENT.

WITH THE EXCEPTION OF GREAT BRITAIN, HELLSING, AND ALUCARD, I DON'T CARE.
THAT FAT MAJOR...
...LIES OUTSIDE EVEN **OUR** SACRED INTERESTS.
TiTRMP TiTRMP TiTRMP TiTRMP TiTRMP
ザッ ザッ ザッ ザッ ザッ
ザッ ザッ ザッ ザッ ザッ
TRMP TRMP TRMP TRMP TRMP
SO, **WHY NOT?**
"WE WILL HIT THEM FROM THE FLANK WITH EVERYTHING WE HAVE."
BUT OF COURSE.
WE SHALL RECAPTURE BRITAIN FOR EUROPE FROM THE **HERETICS** AND **FREAKS.**

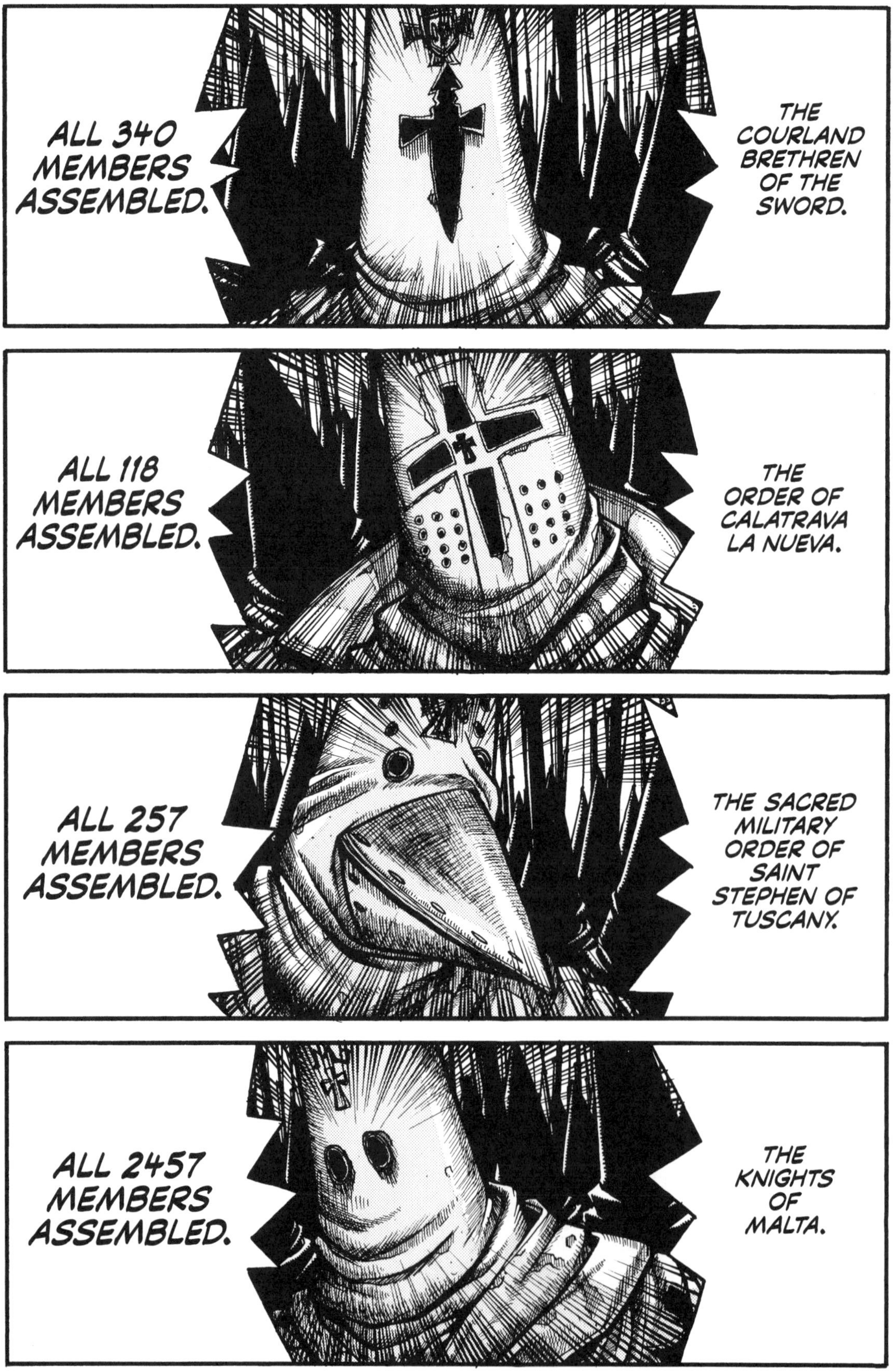
THE COURLAND BRETHREN OF THE SWORD.
ALL 340 MEMBERS ASSEMBLED.
THE ORDER OF CALATRAVA LA NUEVA.
ALL 118 MEMBERS ASSEMBLED.
THE SACRED MILITARY ORDER OF SAINT STEPHEN OF TUSCANY.
ALL 257 MEMBERS ASSEMBLED.
THE KNIGHTS OF MALTA.
ALL 2457 MEMBERS ASSEMBLED.

THE SHORE OPPOSITE DOVER.
AMIENS, FRANCE.
SHNGG

AT THE REQUEST OF HIS HOLINESS, WE HAVE GATHERED TOGETHER HERE.
ALONG WITH OUR ASSEMBLAGE COMES YOUR PROMOTION, BISHOP MAXWELL.
YOU ARE NOW ARCHIE-PISCOPUS* MAXWELL.
*LATIN FOR ARCHBISHOP.
SHOO
OUR ARMIES FORM THE 9TH CRUSADE.
WE ENTRUST ULTIMATE COMMAND AUTHORITY TO YOUR GRACE, ARCHBISHOP MAXWELL.
GRAB
SHOO
AMEN.
I FULLY ACCEPT, BODY AND SOUL.

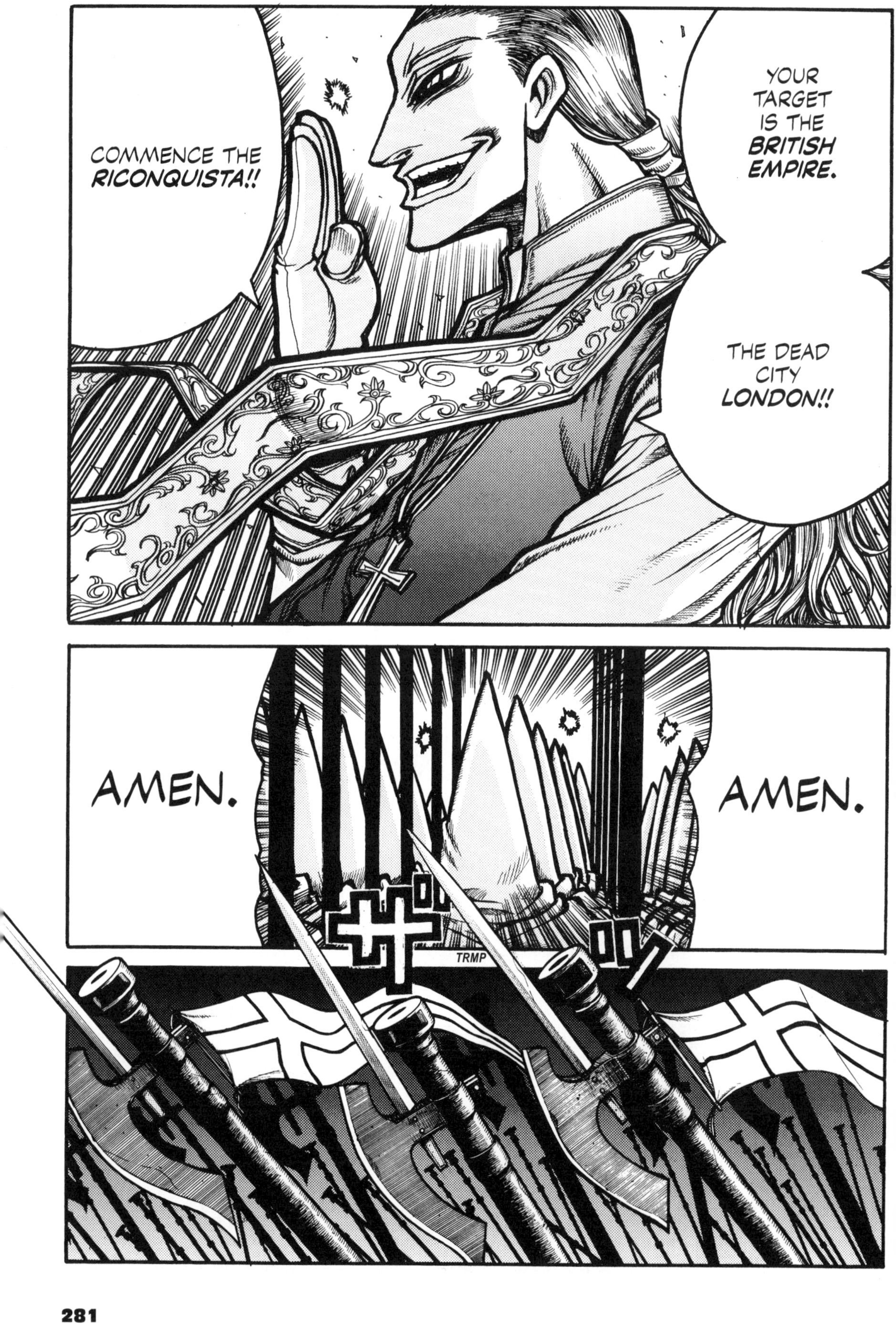
YOUR TARGET IS THE BRITISH EMPIRE.
COMMENCE THE RICONQUISTA!!
THE DEAD CITY LONDON!!
AMEN.
AMEN.
TRMP

TRMP TRMP TRMP TRMP TRMP TRMP TRMP
HEH!
HEHEHEH! HEHEHEH!
HEHEH!
TWITCH TWITCH TWITCH TWITCH
HEHEHE HEHEH! HEHEHE HEHEH!
HEHEHE HEHEHE HEHE HEHEHEH!
I...! I OF SECTION XIII...!
THE ONE WHO WAS LOATHED, CALLED DEVIL CHILD AND A FAILURE...
...AN ARCHBISHOP!! LEADER OF AN ARMY!!
HEHE HEHE HEHE HEHE HEHE HEHEH.
CHIEF!!
WHAT IS IT?

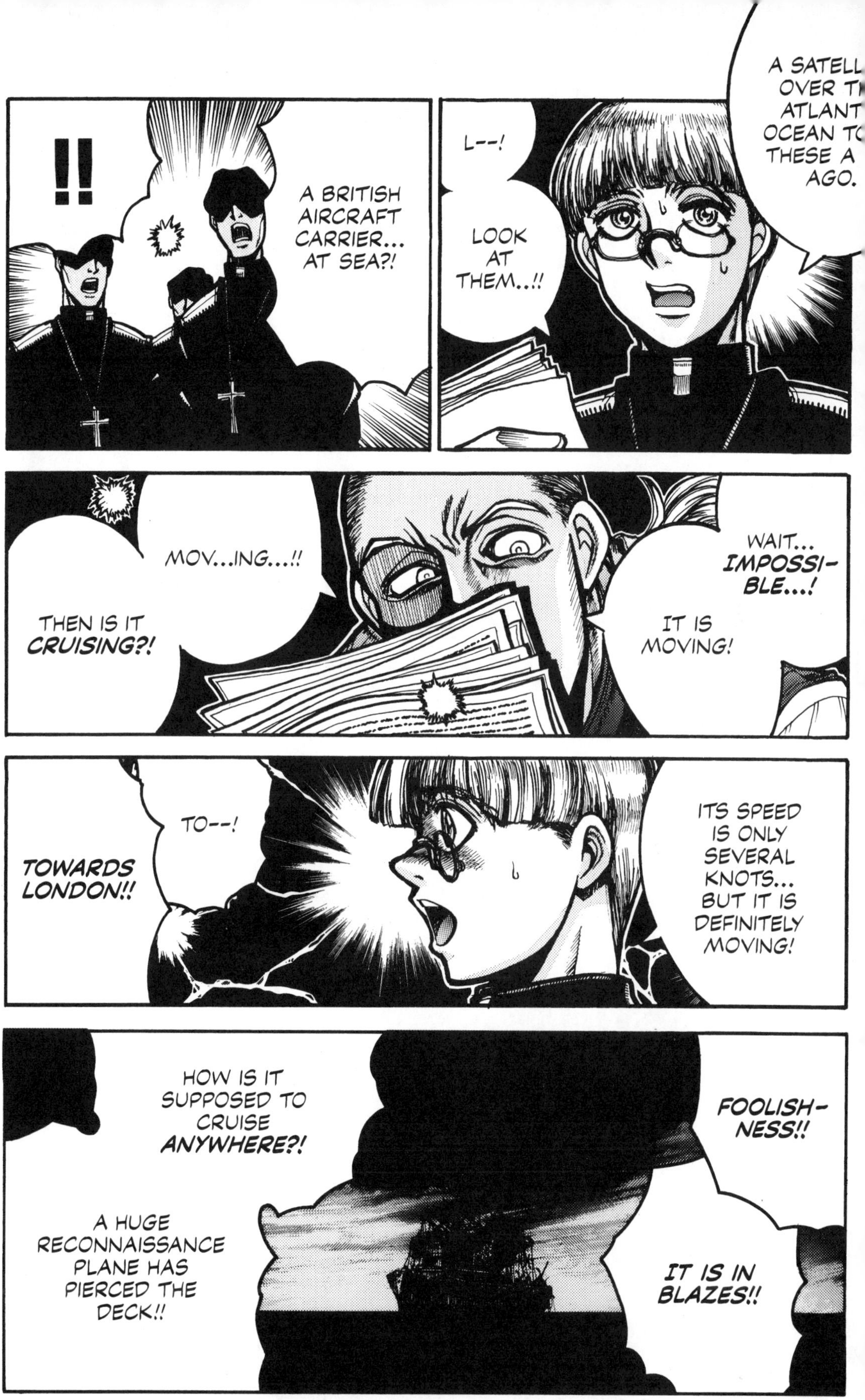
A SATELL
OVER T
ATLANT
OCEAN T
THESE A
AGO.
L--!
LOOK AT THEM..!!
!!
A BRITISH AIRCRAFT CARRIER... AT SEA?!
WAIT... IMPOSSIBLE...!
IT IS MOVING!
MOV...ING...!!
THEN IS IT CRUISING?!
ITS SPEED IS ONLY SEVERAL KNOTS... BUT IT IS DEFINITELY MOVING!
TO--!
TOWARDS LONDON!!
FOOLISH-NESS!!
IT IS IN BLAZES!!
HOW IS IT SUPPOSED TO CRUISE ANYWHERE?!
A HUGE RECONNAISSANCE PLANE HAS PIERCED THE DECK!!

GOHH

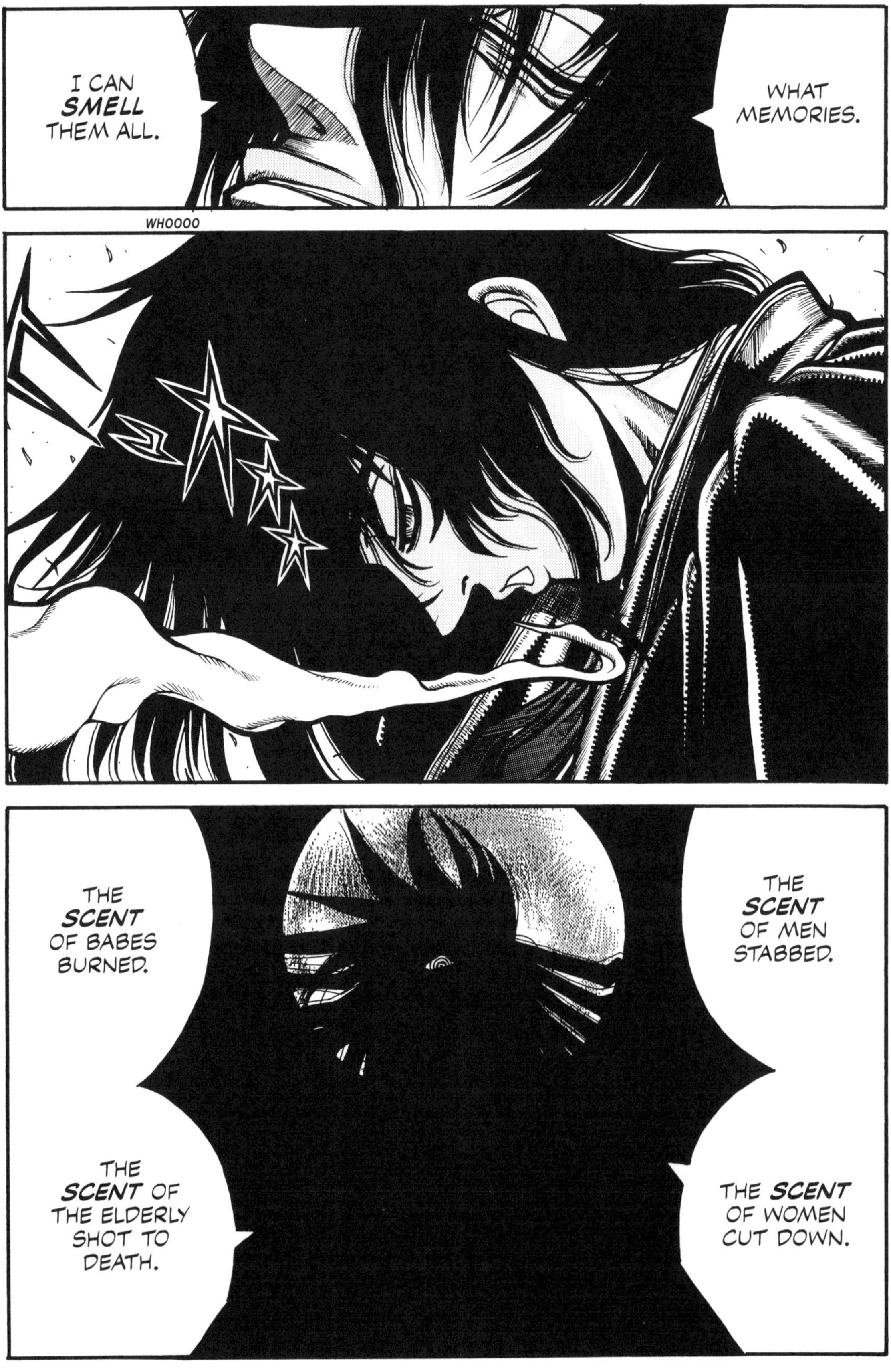
WHAT MEMORIES.
I CAN SMELL THEM ALL.
WHOOOO
THE SCENT OF MEN STABBED.
THE SCENT OF BABES BURNED.
THE SCENT OF WOMEN CUT DOWN.
THE SCENT OF THE ELDERLY SHOT TO DEATH.

THE SCENT OF DEATH.
THE SCENT OF WAR.

ALUCARD...
...WILL COME.
I CARE NOT!
STOMP
HIS MASTER INTEGRA IS IN OUR HANDS.
WHAT DOES ONE SERVANT MATTER?
SHAA
HELLSING, MILLENNIUM, AND ALUCARD...
...WILL ALL CEASE TO BE!!

RECRUITING AN ASSISTANT. PLEASE HELP ME. HELP ME. HELP...ME.... I'M SEEKING HELP FROM SOMEONE IN THE ADACHI, TOKYO AREA ABOUT 5-7 DAYS A MONTH. CONTACT THE EDITORIAL OFFICE FOR DETAILS. NO PREFERENCE GIVEN TO EXPERIENCE, GENDER, OR AGE. PLEASE CONSIDER IT. PLEASE. PLEA...

GNN GNN GNN GNN GNN GNN
BADDA BADDA BADDA
BADDA BADDA

RROOOO
RROOOOO
THEY ARE ALL SO FILLED WITH GLEE...
...AS THEY TURN TOWARDS HELL AND LAUNCH THEIR ASSAULT.
BADDA
BADDA
BADDA
BADDA
WHO IN THE WORLD AMONG THAT KILLING FIELD...
...WILL BE LEFT ALIVE IN THE END?
NO DOUBT.
EVERY ONE OF THEM WILL HAPPILY DIE...
...IN THE GATHERING TWILIGHT.

RESTART ENGINES!!
CHUN
CHUN
CHUN
CHUN
CHUN
CHUN
ZORIN BLITZ TASK FORCE...
...MOVE OUT!!
YOUR TARGET... HELLSING HEAD-QUARTERS!!
BWOOOOOOOO
ORDER 42 / END

ORDER 43

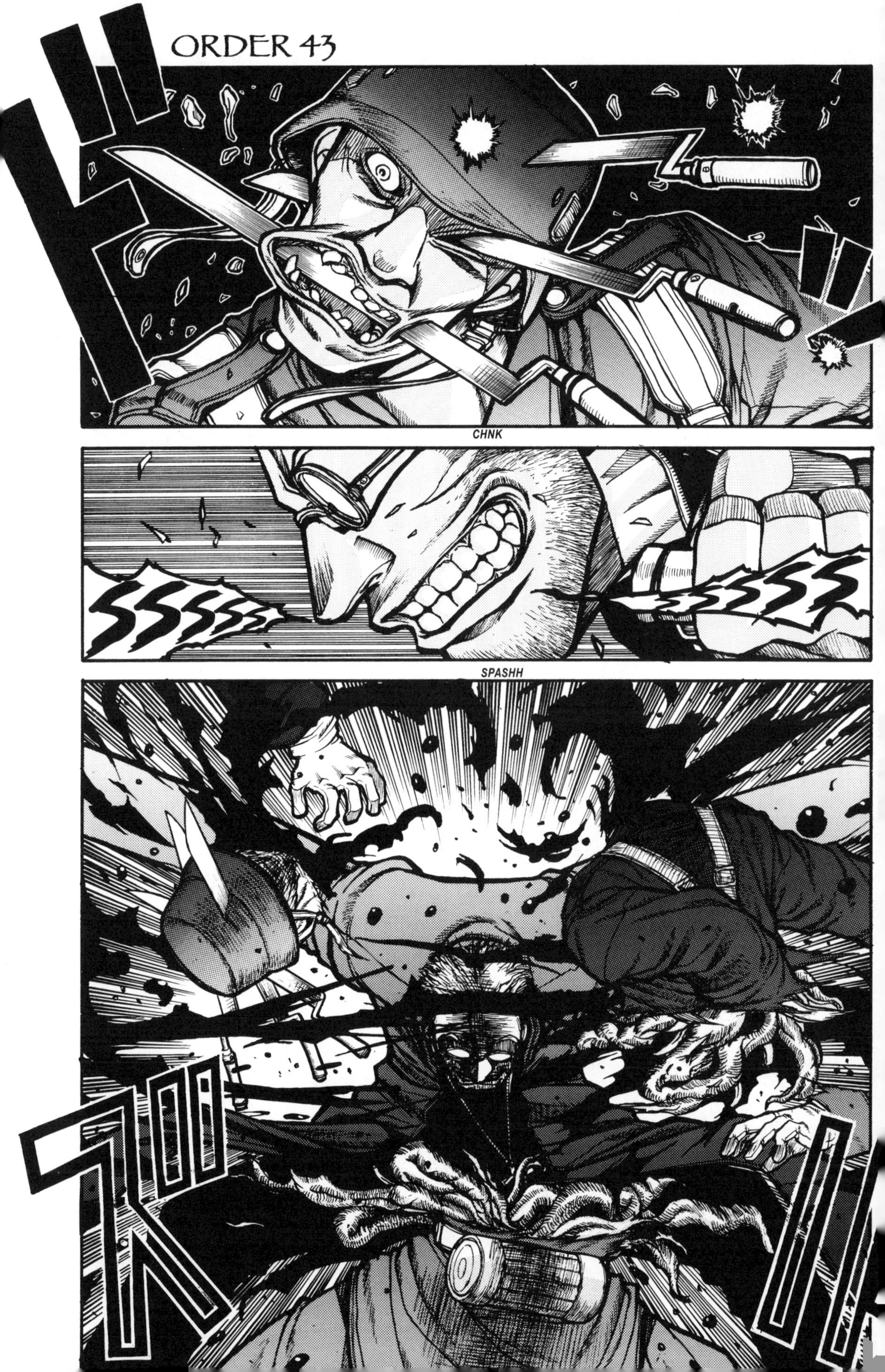

ORDER 43

GUN BULLET

SHNK
HOW MANY O' US ARE LEFT?!
HALF VERE TAKEN.
THEY'RE BETTER THAN VE THOUGHT.
GCHAK
THER-MITE!!*
INCINERATE THE BODIES OF THE NAZIS. LEAVE NO REMAINS.
*INCINERATION POWDER.
CHOMP

!!
I'M GOING HOME.
VHERE ARE YOU GOING?!
TO MY MANSION.
I MUST RETURN.
CHAK
KCHAK
ジャカッジャカカッ
VE VON'T LET YOU!!
KATZ
KATZ
KATZ
KATZ
KATZ
KATZ
KATZ

I MUST RETURN HOME.
THEY ARE AWAITING ME THERE.
I AM IN COMMAND OF AN AGENCY. I MUST ISSUE ORDERS.
I DON'T THINK SO.
THE ORDER VE RECEIVED VAS TO SECURE YOU.
VE VILL NOW BE TAKING YOU INTO CUSTODY.
MIGHT I GET A LIGHT FOR MY CIGAR?
SO THOUGHTLESS OF YOU.
ドオオン
ドンッ
BOOOM BOOM
A LIGHT.
ゴゴゴオオオ
BROARRRRR
?!

FIRE.
HUHHHHH?
...
...HUH.
FIRE.
...YOU DO REALIZE THE POSITION YOU'RE...
NEIN, JUST...
A LIGHT.
FWFF
FWFF
CHA
FWIT FWIT
FWIT
FOOOOO

THE THREAT OF GUNS DOES NOT AFFECT ME. I'M GOING HOME.
IF YOU MEAN TO ATTACK ME, THEN DO IT.
HMPH
ムカ
INCH INCH
INCH
ジリ…
ジリ ジリ
STAND DOWN, YUMIE.
VHAT SHOULD VE DO? I'M NOT SO GOOD VITH THIS TYPE.
SHOULD VE ATTACK?
W-WE COULD ALL TIE HER UP...
...A-A-AND JUST TAKE OFF WITH HER.
I CAN HEAR ALL OF THAT!
IS THAT ACCEPTABLE, SECTION XIII?
IS IT ACCEPTABLE, ANDERSON?
TYING ME UP AND TAKING ME AWAY?
O' COURSE NO.

SHOCK

BWOMMMM

TURN

SHFF
SILENCE
SHFF
SHFF
SHFF
SHFF
もく もく もく もく もく もく
ZHFF
ZHFF
ZHFF
ZHFF
ZHFF
ZHFF
VHAT... VHAT IN HIMMEL...
THIS HAST REALLY GOTTEN COMPLICATED......
WH-WH-WHAT DO WE DO?
THE CH-CHIEF'LL GET MAD AGAIN.
FRET FRET
VELL, EVEN THIS IST STILL "SECURING" HER IN A SENSE!
HE VON'T GET MAD!
TH-TH-THAT'S A SOPHISM!
SHUT UP!
FRET FRET FRET FRET FRET
IS THIS ALRIGHT, FATHER ANDERSON?
IT WILL BE SEEN AS A BREACH OF AUTHORITY.
AH DINNAE CARE.
MAXWELL'S WAY O' DOING THINGS IS TOO CLEVER.
THIS WAY IS BEST.
HEINKEL, FIND US AE RIDE.
WE'RE DUCKS IN AE BARREL LIKE THIS.
JAA.

VOOOOO
VE VILL SOON BE ABOVE HELLSING HEADQUARTERS.
GOOD.
ALL HANDS, PREPARE FOR COMBAT.
ゴゴゴゴゴ
RMMMMMM
BA
SUPPORT ATTACK INCOMING FROM THE FLAGSHIP!!
THEY ARE V1S.
HERALDS FROM THE DEUS EX MACHINA.
LET HELLSING FILL ITS BELLY VITH THEM!!
SHOOOOM
SHOOOOM

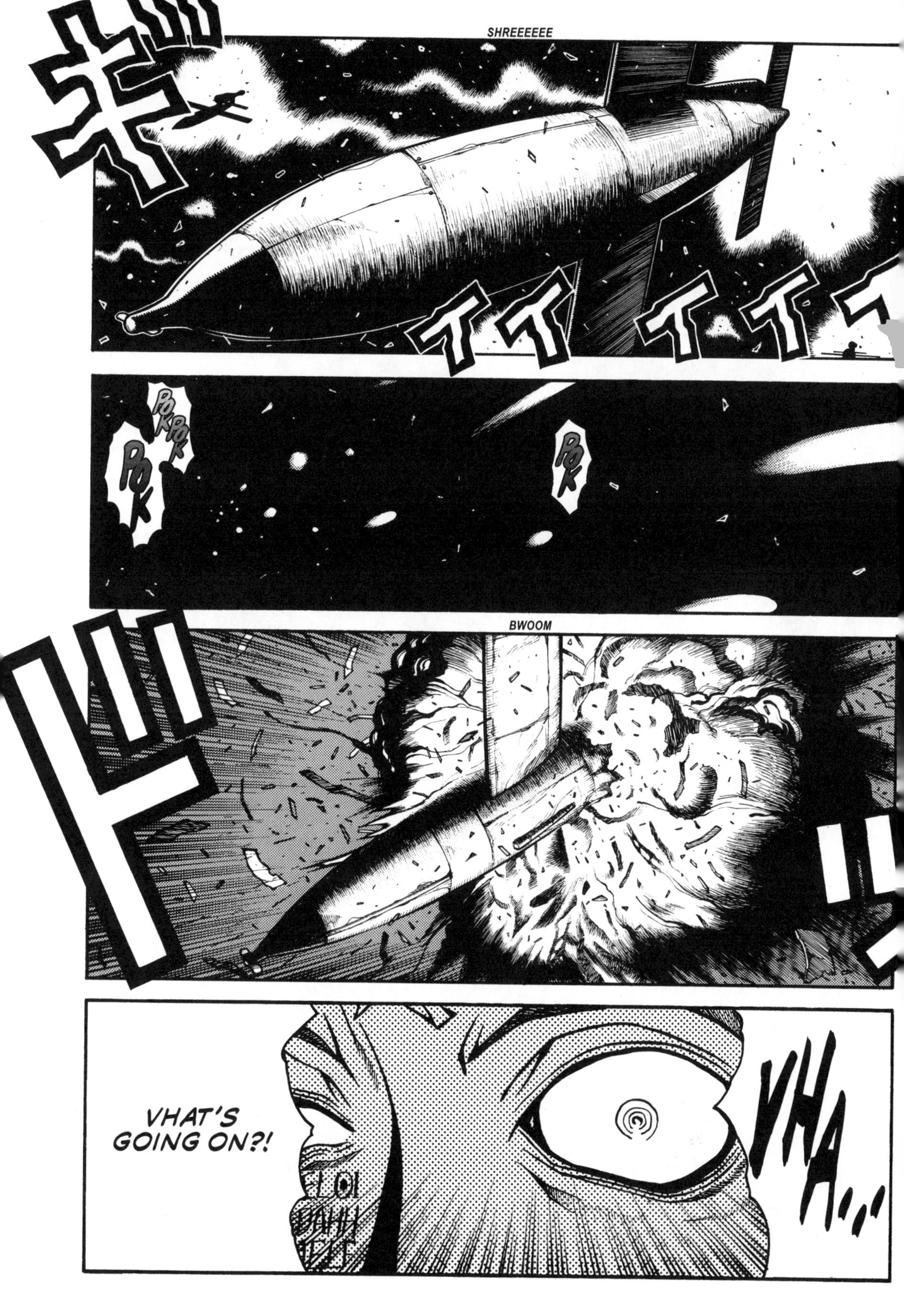
SHREEEEEE
POK POK
POK
POK
BWOOM
VHA...
VHAT'S GOING ON?!

BRANNK
KABOOM
VHAT!?
VHAT'S HAPPENING TO THEM?!
BOM BOM
BOM
BOM
BOM BOM
BOM
BOM
BOM

KANG
KANG
KANG
KANG
ガン ガン ガン ガン
DOOM
DOOM
DOOM
DOOM
DOOM
ドドドドド
HA!
バッ
THEY ARE BEING SNIPED!!
WE ARE BEING FIRED UPON BY HELLSING HEADQUARTERS!!
WHBOOM
VHAT DID YOU SAY?!

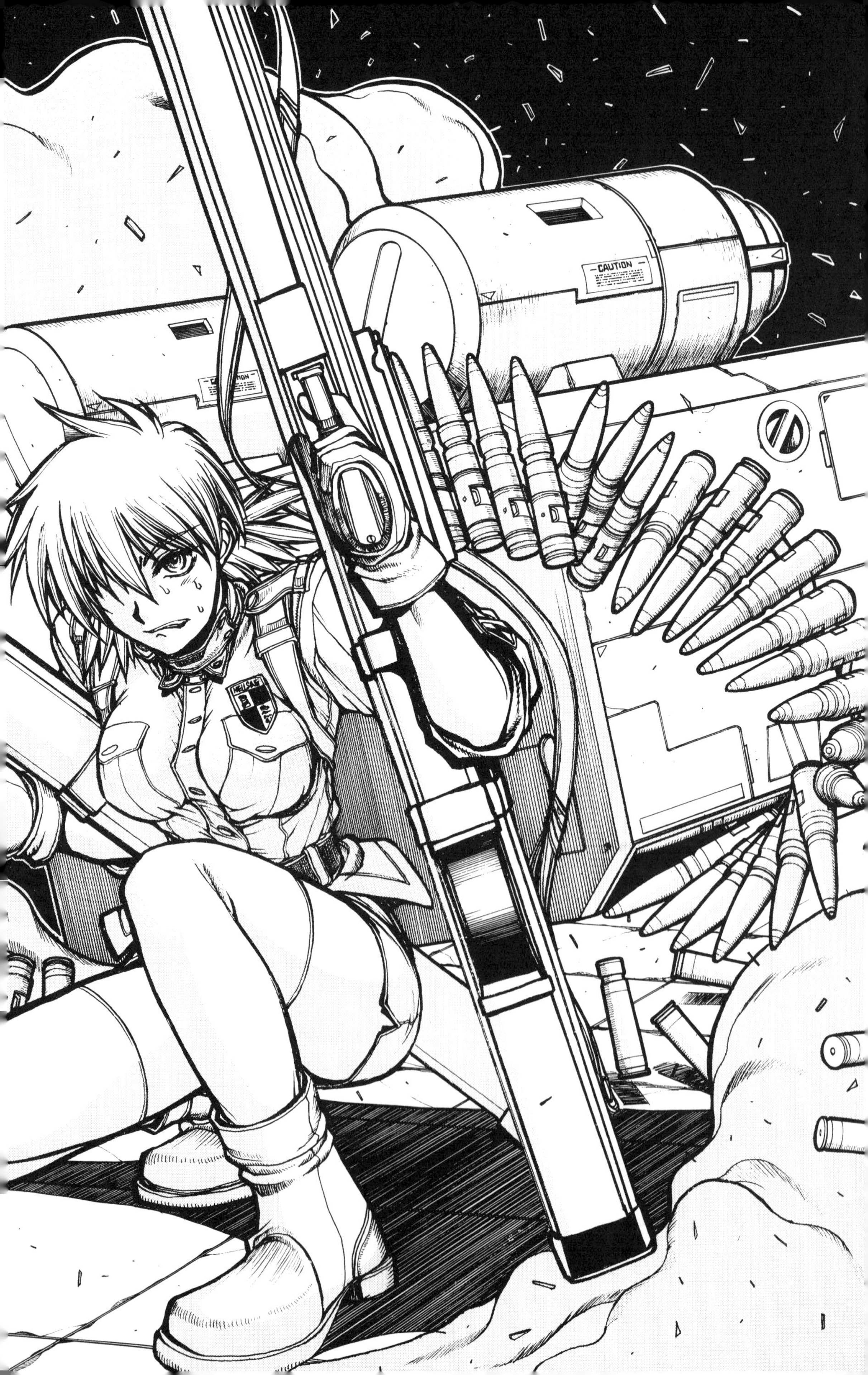
CAUTION

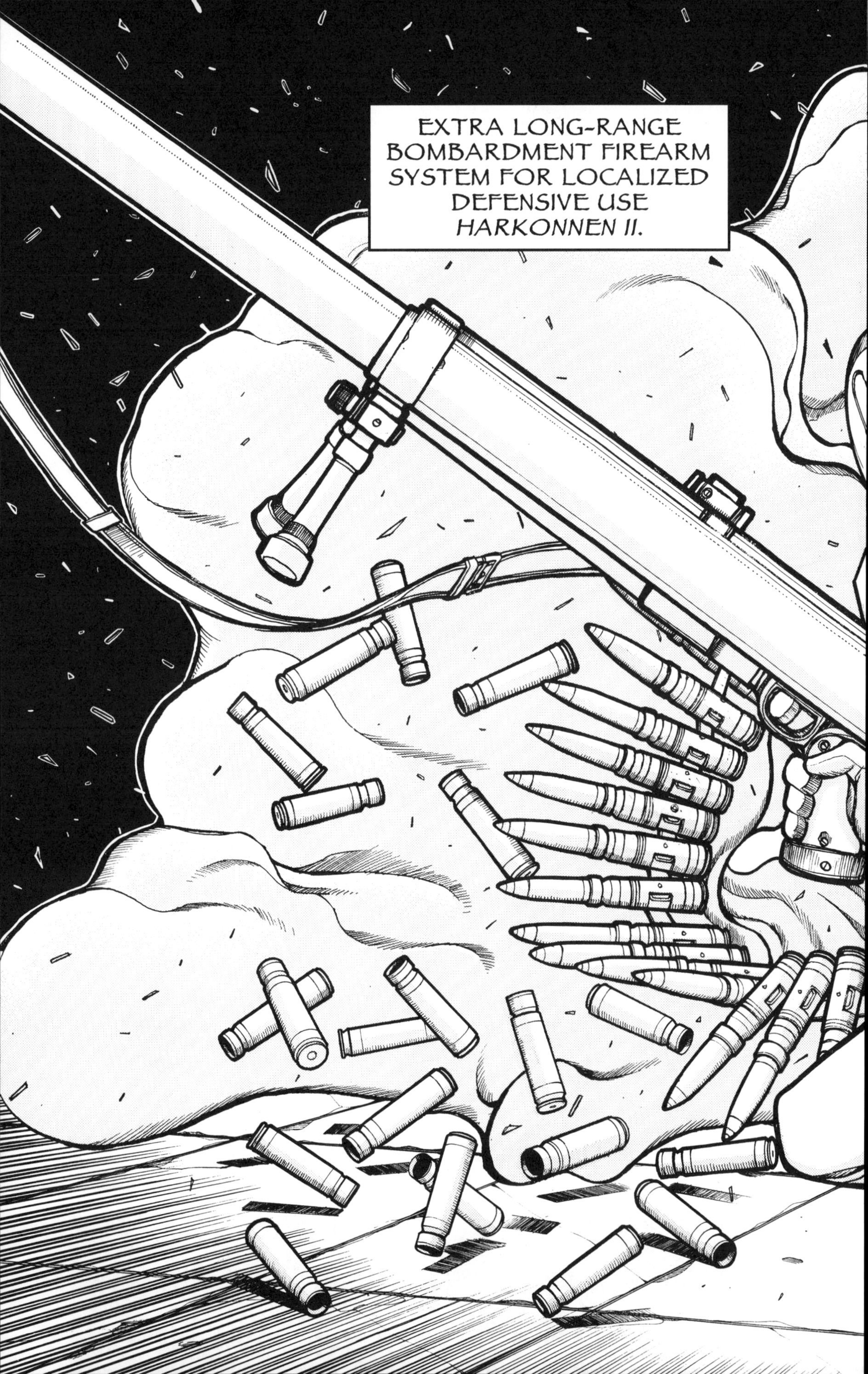
EXTRA LONG-RANGE BOMBARDMENT FIREARM SYSTEM FOR LOCALIZED DEFENSIVE USE *HARKONNEN II*.

ALL BOGEYS SHOT DOWN, GIRL.
ZE NEW GEAR'S ZE DOG'S BOLLOCKS, ISN'T IT GIRL?
'ARKONNEN II.
A 30mm SEMI-AUTO "CANNON."
MAXIMUM RANGE 4000m!! GROSS WEIGHT 345kg.
IT'S LIKE SOME BLOOMIN' JOKE TO MOBILIZE ZAT ZING, GIRL.
MR. VERNEDEAD! DO YOU THINK YOU COULD STOP CALLING ME "GIRL?!"
I HAVE A NAME, "SERAS"...
HA! HA! HA! SORRY 'BOUT ZAT!! "GIRL!!"
LET'S GET REVENGE FOR LONDON.
LIGHT ZEM UP, SERAS!!
ORDER 43 / END

ORDER 44

BOM
BOM
BOM
BOM
BOMF
BOM
ALL TWENTY-FOUR OF THEM VERE ATTACKED AT VONCE!
YOU CAN'T BE SERIOUS!!
THEY'RE ALL SHOT DOWN!!
THE V1S!
IT'S HER.
SEARCH-LIGHTS!!
SEARCH-LIGHTS!! SHINE THEM ON HELLSING HEAD-QUARTERS!!
PLEASE, DON'T!!
VE VILL BE FIRED UPON!!
I DON'T CARE!!
SHE CAN ALREADY SEE US!!

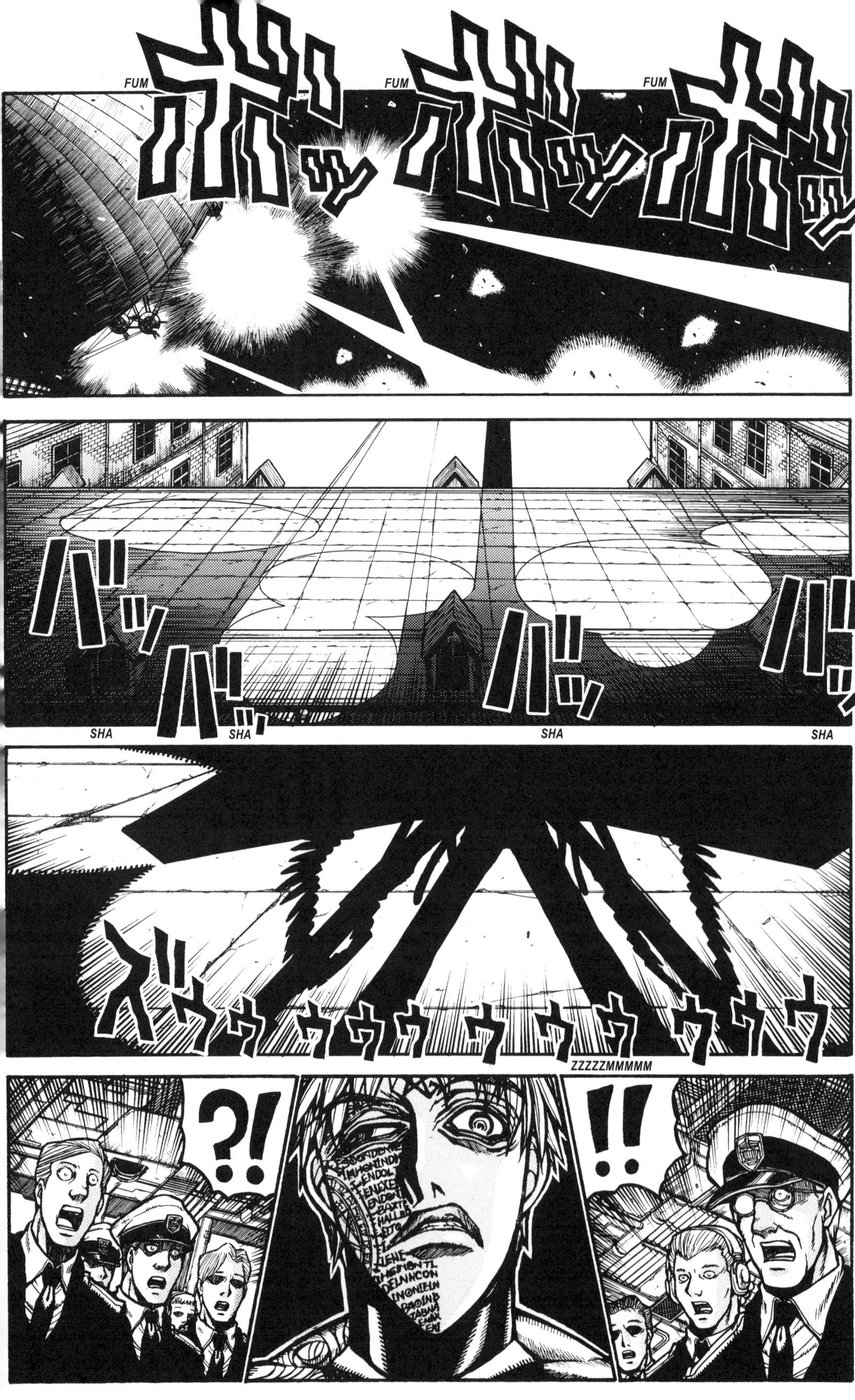
FUM
FUM
FUM
SHA
SHA
SHA
SHA
ZZZZZMMMMM
?!
!!

オォォォォオオオオ
WHOOOO
DOM

ORDER 44
BALLOON FIGHT
A 01
HARKONNEN
VLadimir HARKON

VWOOOOOOO
VWOOOOO
CAN YOU SEE LONDON, GIRL?
I CAN SEE IT!!
PICCADILLY, SOHO, AND COVENT GARDEN ARE ALL IN ASHES.
TODAY'S LONDON...
...IS SYNONYMOUS WITH HELL.
ME, I 'ATE LONDON.
I FOUND IT TOO OLD-FASHIONED.
I DIDN'T ZINK IT SUITED ME ONE BIT.
BUT YOU KNOW, AT ZE CABARET WE'D GO TO ON WEEKENDS ZE BEER WAS COOL AND RIGHT TASTY.
LOTS OF ZE 'ORES IN ZE BROZELS ARE STINGY AND UGLY.
ZE BLOKE TENDING BAR IS ZIS DUMB PRAT 'OO LOVES TASTELESS DIRTY JOKES.
BUT STILL, EVERYONE'S KIND ENOUGH. NONE OF ZEM DESERVE WHAT'S 'APPENING.

ZERE'S ZIS OLD LADY AT A CAFÉ ON VERBIE ROAD.
IT DON'T MATTER ZAT I DON'T ASK FOR IT, SHE ALWAYS BLOODY COOKS ME FISH AND CHIPS.
EVERY TIME SHE SAYS IT'S BECAUSE I'M A FOREIGNER, BECAUSE IT'S ZEIR SPECIALTY.
EVEN ZOUGH IT'S SO GREASY I CAN'T STAND IT...
...I DON'T WANT TO 'URT 'ER FEELINGS, SO I FORCE MYSELF TO EAT IT EVERY TIME.
SO ME, I 'ATE LONDON.
BUT YOU KNOW, ZE BARTENDER, ZE 'ORES, ZE OLD LADY.
ZIS FIGHT 'AS NOT A ZING TO DO WIZ ZEM.
WAR, NAZIS, VAMPIRES.
ZE MAJOR, SECTION XIII, ZE LETZTES BATAILLON, ***EVEN WE*** AT 'ELLSING.
ZEY'VE NEVER EVEN ***'EARD*** OF ANY OF IT.
NOT A DAMN ZING.

BUT RIGHT NOW ZEY'RE TURNING INTO CORPSES 'OO EAT OZER CORPSES.
AND AS FOR ME...
...I CAN'T FORGIVE ZAT.
GRIND
SERAS, LET'S GET REVENGE.
LET'S BEAT ZEM.
BEAT ZE SHIT OUT OF ZEM.
...YEAH.
I HEAR YOU.
I HEAR YOU, CAPTAIN.
ZASSH
I HEAR YOU!!

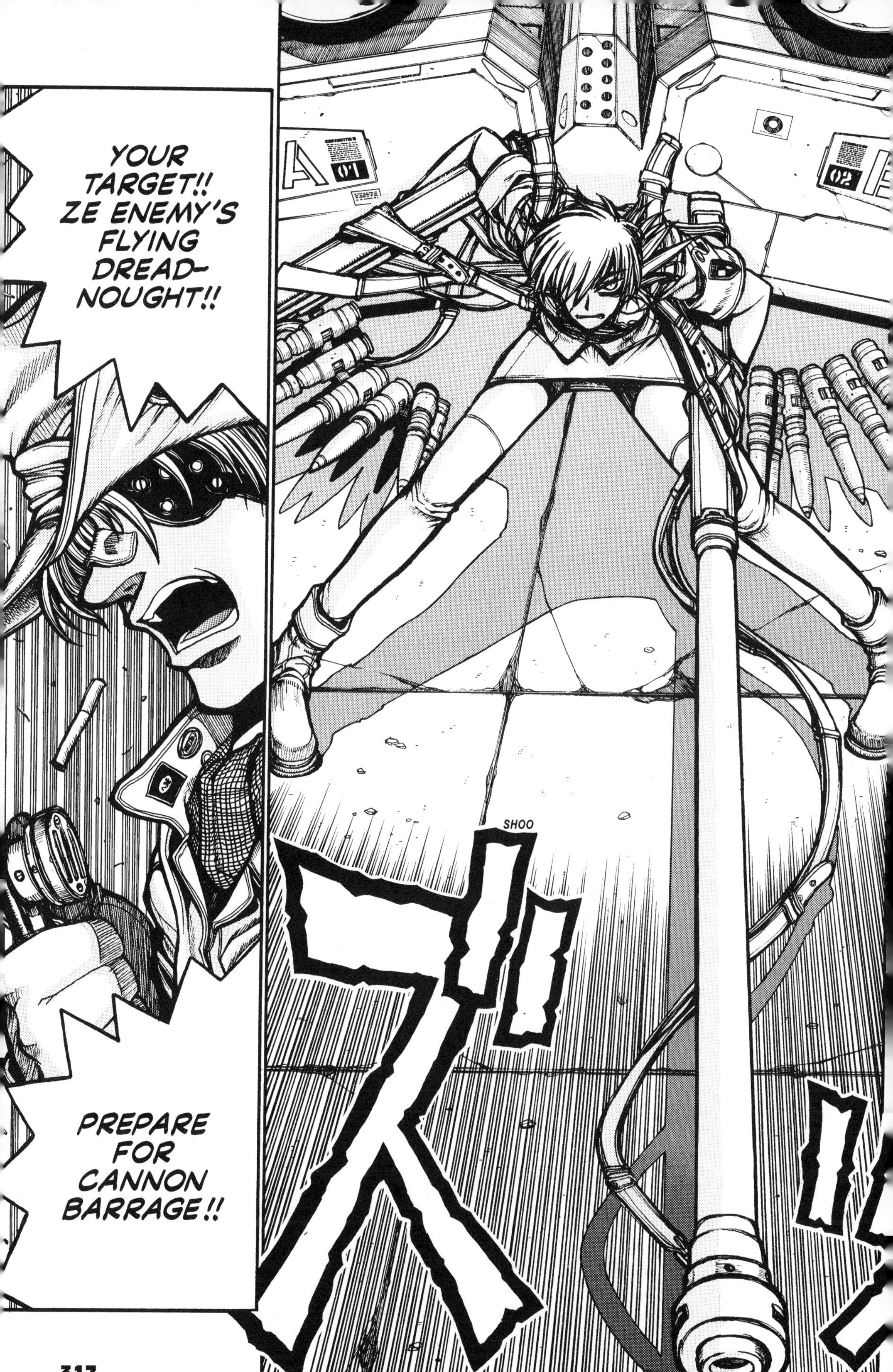
YOUR TARGET!! ZE ENEMY'S FLYING DREAD-NOUGHT!!
PREPARE FOR CANNON BARRAGE!!
SHOO

BOOM
BOOM
FIRE!!
BOOM
GON
GON
GON
GON
GON

BDOOM BDOOM BDOOM BDOOM BDOOM
CLATA CLATA CLATA CLATA CLATA
BOOM BA BA BA BA
BOOM BA BA BA BA

BAM
BAM
BAM
BAM
ガンガンガン
WHOM
WHOM
ゴン
ゴン
ゴン
ゴン
ゴン
ゴン
BOM
BOM
BOM
BOM
BOM
BOM
GRAF ZEPP
ドカッ
ドカッ
BOOM
BTOOM
BTOOM

ドドドドドドド
BOOM BOOM BOOM BOOM BOOM BOOM BOOM
BLOCK 7 TAKING FIRE!! BLOCK 3 TAKING FIRE!!
UN EXPLOSION IN TROOP READY ROOM 2!!
FIRE BREAKING OUT IN BLOCK 4!!
STERN ENGINES FOUR UND FIVE HAF COLLAPSED!!
ボボボボボボボ
BOM BOM BOM BOM BOM BOM BOM
FLIGHT CAPABILITY DOWN BY 32%!!
ドドドドドドド
BOOM BOOM BOOM BOOM BOOM BOOM BOOM

BOM
BOM
BOM
L... LIEUTENANT!!
IF VE...! IF VE DON'T VITHDRAW THE SHIP...!
TOO LATE FOR THAT!!
BOOM
BOOM
BOOM
IN THE FACE OF THAT CANNON, THIS SHIP'S LIGHT ARMOR MIGHT AS VELL BE PAPER.
VE CAN'T RUN IN SOMETHING THIS BIG.
DIVE!!
MAKE US LAND!!
A FORCED LANDING!!
INTO HELLSING HEAD-QUARTERS... NO!!

CRASH INTO HER!!
GN
GN
GN
FWMM
VWOOOO

MON DIEU!!
SERAS!! LEG IT!!

KSHAK
CAUTION
JUT
ガッ
THMP
SHHHNK

VLadimir HAL
VLadimir HALCONNEN
THWOK
"VLADIMIR."
RAAH!!
EXPLOSIVE INCENDIARY GRENADE LAUNCHER FOR WIDE-AREA FIELD DOMINANCE.
AAAHHHHH
RAAAAAA

BWOOM
VOOOOSH

BOOM
CONTROL LOST!! CONTROL LOST!!
VE ARE ASHING!!
VE...
RMMMBBBLL

ゴォォ……
WHROOM
ボッ
BWOOOSH

BROARRRRRR
SHE DID IT!!
OHH!
ALRIGHT!
NO, NOT YET!!
TALLY HO!
TALLY HO!
DON'T BLINK, 'ERE ZEY COME!!
ZAT'S RIGHT. NOT YET, LADIES.

SHA
SHA
SHA
SHA
SHA
SHA
SHA
SHA
SHA
ZEY ESCAPED JUST BEFORE IMPACT.
THAT'S IMPOSSIBLE!! WITH NO SUSPENSION?!
ZAT'S RIGHT. ZEY AREN'T 'UMAN.
SHOCK
ZEY'RE MONSTERS!!
'ERE ZEY COME, GEESE!! WE'RE ON ZE JOB!! ROCK'N ROLL!!

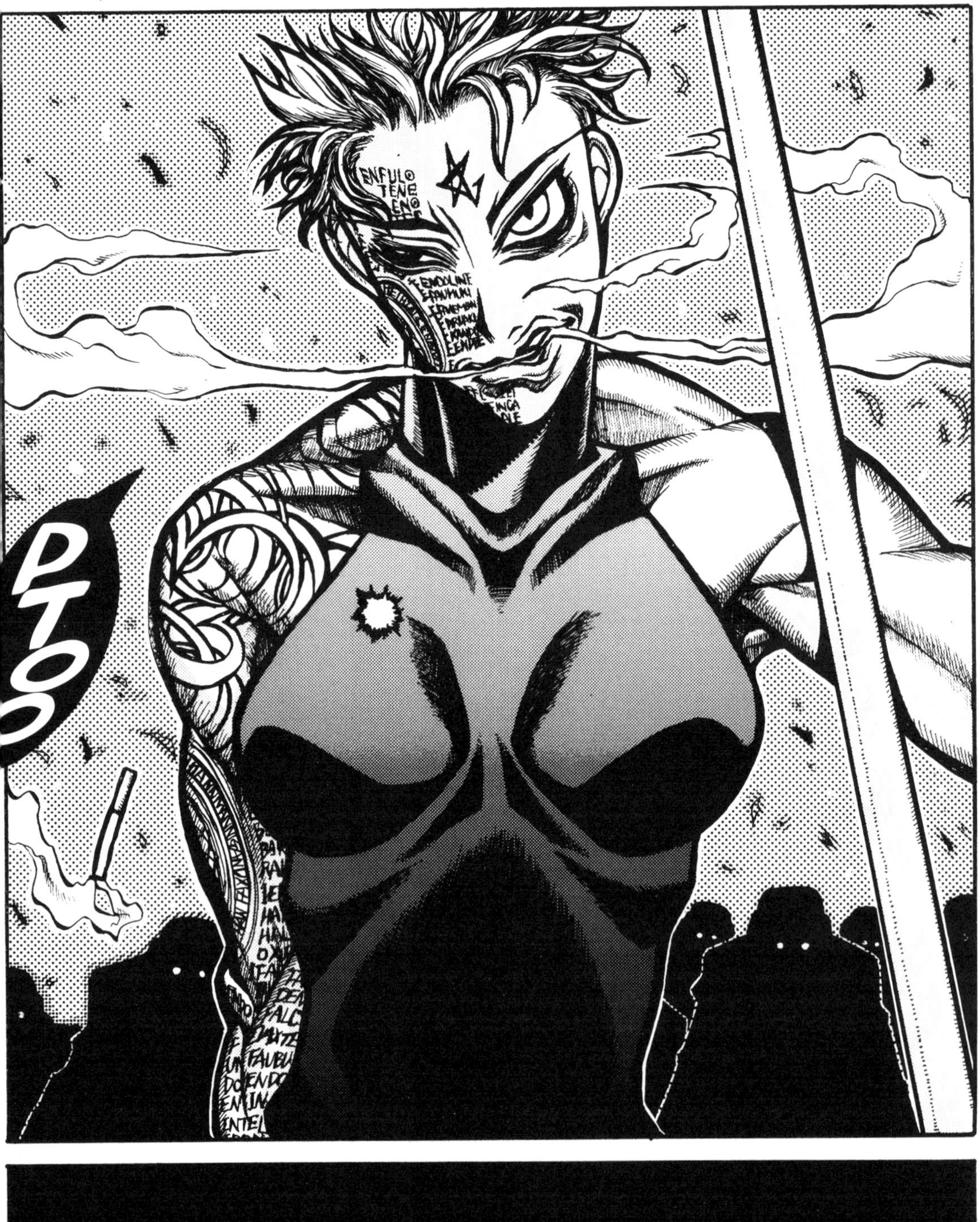

ORDER 44 / END

ORDER 45

OO......
OO...
UWEH!
HENGH!
HENGH!
-HIC!-
-HIC!-
-HIC!-
WHAT'S ZE MATTER?
WHY'RE YOU CRYIN'?
E-EVERY-ONE AT SCHOOL!
ZEY SAY I'M A CHILD OF MURDER-ERS...!
ZAT OUR FAMILY IS PAID TO GO OFF AND KILL IN WARS!
ZAT'S RIGHT.
IT'S ZE TRUTH.

WE'VE BEEN A MERCENARY FAMILY FOR AS FAR BACK AS EIGHT GENERATIONS.
SINCE YOUR GRANDPA'S GRANDPA'S GRANDPA'S GRANDPA.
EVEN YOUR OWN **PAPA** WAS KILLED IN COLOMBIA.
'E GOT IN OVER 'IS 'EAD TRYING TO RAISE MONEY FOR YOUR DELIVERY.
WHAT, YOU MEAN YOU STILL DIDN'T **KNOW**?
G-G-GRANDPA,
'AVE YOU **KILLED** PEOPLE **TOO?!**
OH, SURE I 'AVE.
A **'OLLLE LOT** OF ZEM.

WH--!
WHY?!
WHY WOULD YOU KILL SOMEONE?!
WHY DO MERCENARIES DO ANYTHING?
FOR MONEY.
ZE GOALS OF ZOSE WE FOUGHT WERE SUCH ZINGS AS...
...PRINCIPLES AND ASSERTIONS, OVERZROWING ZE ESTABLISHMENT AND MAINTAINING ZE ESTABLISHMENT.
FOR AGGRESSION, FOR DEFENSE, FOR 'OMELAND.
FOR FAMILY, FOR WOMEN, FOR NARCOTICS, FOR FOOD, FOR LOTS OF ZINGS.
BUT WE DON'T UNDERSTAND ALL ZAT.
WE KNOW ZAT SUCH ZINGS ARE IMPORTANT. BUT YOU KNOW...
...I RECKON ZEY WORK ZEMSELVES OUT EVEN WIZOUT FOLKS TAKING UP ARMS.
ZAT IS, WHEN YOU PICK UP A GUN...
...DOES IT 'AVE TO 'OLD A MEANING LIKE ZAT?
I FIGURE, AIN'T IT ENOUGH TO EARN A BIT OF DIRT-CHEAP PAY?
SSSSS

ON ZE OZER 'AND...
...A DIRT CHEAP PIECE OF SHIT REWARD IS ENOUGH FOR US TO STAKE OUR LIVES ON.
FOR DIRT-CHEAP PAY WE RUN 'ERE AND ZERE TO BATTLEFIELDS ALL OVER ZE WORLD.
FOR DIRT-CHEAP WE KILL AND ARE KILLED.
AND IT'S NOT LIKE ANYONE TOLD US TO DO IT, WE CHOSE TO.
ON ZE BATTLE-FIELD, DIRT-CHEAP IS MORE IMPORTANT ZAN YOUR OWN LIFE OR SOMEONE ELSE'S.
YOU COULD SAY OUR FAMILY LINEAGE IS ZE REAL SCUM OF ZE EARTH.
I'M SORRY, BUT MAYBE GETTING PICKED ON AT SCHOOL CAN'T BE 'ELPED.
NO, ZEN AGAIN PER'APS ZE TIME WILL COME WHEN YOU UNDERSTAND.
'EY, AFTER ALL,
YOU'RE OUR GRANDKID.

ORDER 45
SOLDIER OF FORTUNE①

BROAARRRRRR
CAPTAIN!!
YOU GET DOWN 'ERE AND RE-EQUIP, GIRL.
CHANGE YOUR GEAR!! 'URRY!!
SHF
SHF
SHF
ZE'RE COMING.
FOREPLAY'S OVER.
NOW IT'S OUR TURN.
WATCH CLOSELY, GIRL.
WE'LL SHOW YOU 'OW GEESE FIGHT.

GO GO GO GO GO
ゴゴゴゴゴ
ROARR
オォ
ROARRRR
オォオ
VE HAVE FORTY-TWO REMAINING TROOPS!!
THOSE ROUNDS VERE **NOT** REGULAR ISSUE.
VE LOST MORE THAN HALF OUR NUMBER UND ALL OF OUR HEAVY VEAPONRY.
BUT OUR MORALE IST HIGH!!
GIVE US ORDERS!! **LIEUTENANT ZORIN BLITZ!!**
GOOD ENOUGH.
IT'S GOOD ENOUGH THAT VE KILL THEM ALL!!

KILL THEM.

KILL ALL OF THEM.

THRUST
ZHA
ZHA
ZHA
ZHA
ZHA

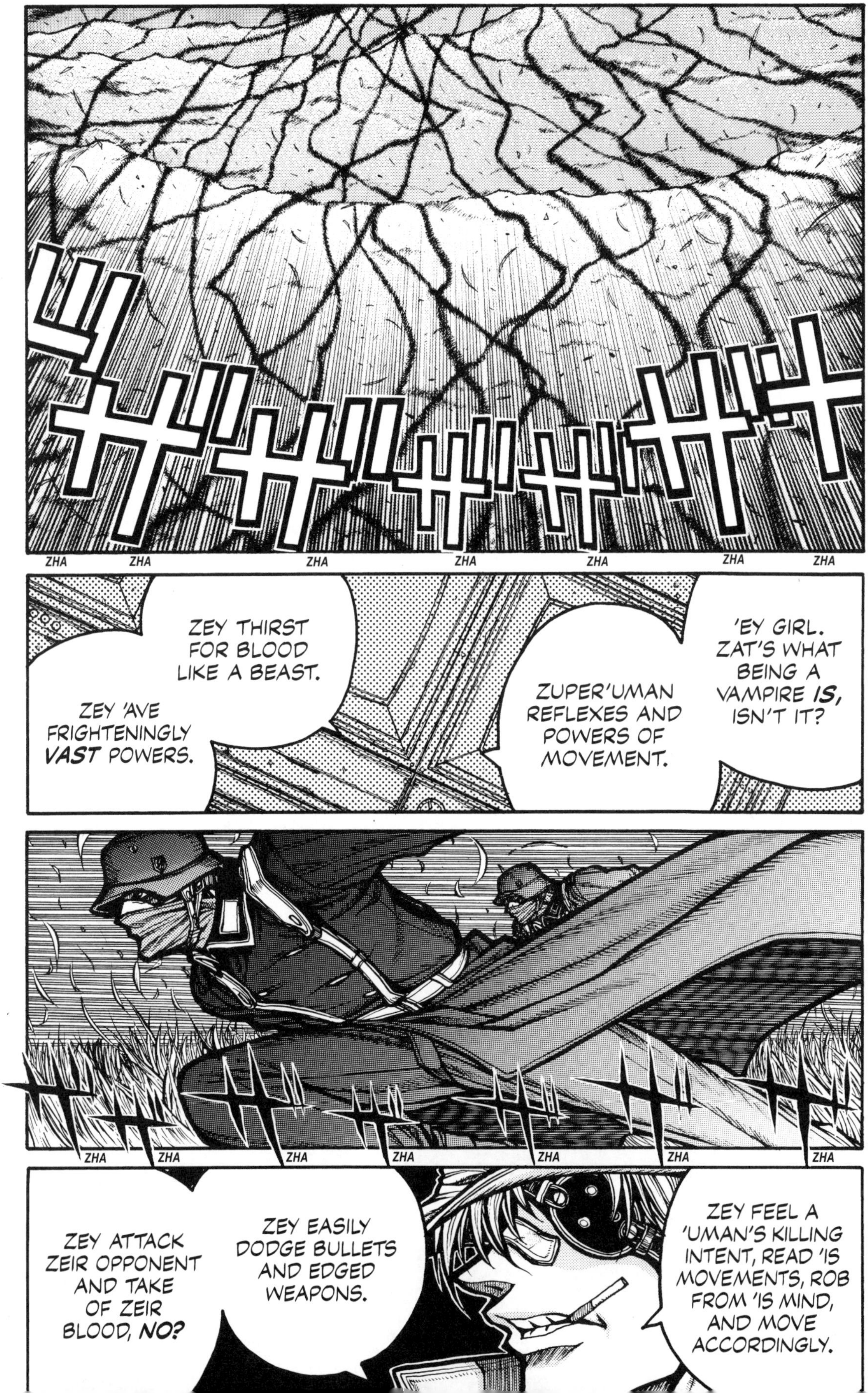
ZHA ZHA ZHA ZHA ZHA ZHA ZHA
'EY GIRL. ZAT'S WHAT BEING A VAMPIRE IS, ISN'T IT?
ZUPER'UMAN REFLEXES AND POWERS OF MOVEMENT.
ZEY THIRST FOR BLOOD LIKE A BEAST.
ZEY 'AVE FRIGHTENINGLY VAST POWERS.
ZHA ZHA ZHA ZHA ZHA ZHA ZHA
ZEY FEEL A 'UMAN'S KILLING INTENT, READ 'IS MOVEMENTS, ROB FROM 'IS MIND, AND MOVE ACCORDINGLY.
ZEY EASILY DODGE BULLETS AND EDGED WEAPONS.
ZEY ATTACK ZEIR OPPONENT AND TAKE OF ZEIR BLOOD, NO?

WELL ZEN.
'OW WILL ZEY LIKE ZIS?
CHIK
BDOOM
BOMM
YA
.....?!

(sudden stop)
IT'S A MINEFIELD!!
MINEFIELD!!
ZE'VE STOPPED.
DO EET.
KLIK KLIK
KLIK
KLIK
DOOM

BOOM
DOOM
DOOM
DOOM
DOOM
DOOM
DOOM
DOOM

WHMP
WHMP
WHMP
WHMP
AHAAAA
AAA
GAAAA
ROARRRRRR
......
......!!

BINGO!!
ZAT'S WHAT YOU GET FOR SCREWIN' WITH MR. 'UMAN!
LEER
Y...YOU!
YOU PLANNED THIS TRICK!!
TRICK?
ZEY'RE ZE BLOODY IDIOTS FOR RUSHIN' IN 'EADLONG.
EQUIPMENT WITH NO KILLING INTENT, MIND, OR MOVEMENT.
A DIRECT, UNAVOIDABLE GENERAL AREA ATTACK.
A WELCOME MAT OF SIXTY BALL-BEARING CLAYMORE MINES, ALL DETONATING AT ONCE!
IF ZEY CAN DODGE ZAT, I'D FANCY A LOOK-SEE!
'CAUSE WE'RE WEAK IN A FIGHT.
SO, AGAINST ZEM, WE'RE NOT ABOUT TO FIGHT FAIR AND SQUARE!!

ORDER 45 / END

ORDER 46

ドドドドドド
DOOM
DOOM
DOOM
DOOM
DOOM
DOOM
DON'T GIVE ZEM ANY ROOM TO BREATHE!!
KEEP A WIDE FIELD OF FIRE GOING!!
ZIRD FLOOR!! GRENADE VOLLEY!!
RIFLE SQUAD, CONCENTRATE ALL YOUR FIREPOWER IN BARRAGES OVER LIMITED INDIVIDUAL PERIMETER RANGES!!
FORWARD!! ZOROUGHLY ATTACK ZE FORWARD AREA.
BOM
BOM
BOM
BOM
BOM
ボン
ボン
ボン
ボン
ボン
CAUTION

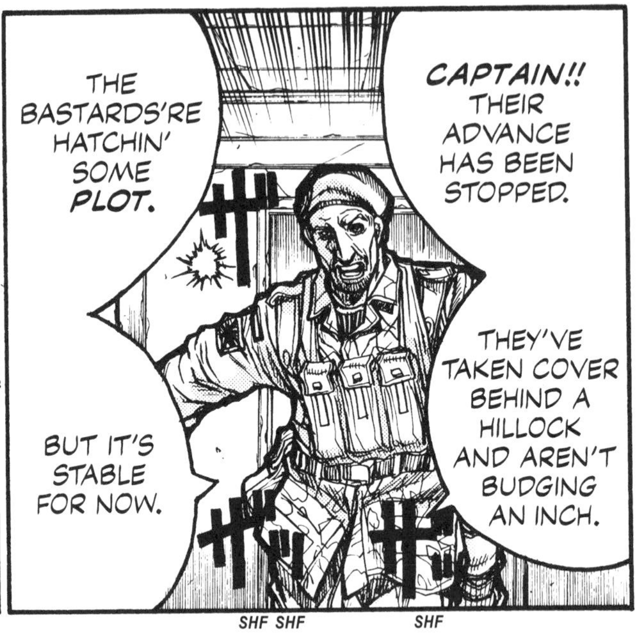

❧ ORDER 46

SOLDIER OF FORTUNE②

BABABAM
BABABAM
DOOM
DOOM
DOOM
DOOM
DOOM
DOOM
I WONDER IF THEY'LL WITHDRAW?
IF ZEY WERE NORMAL, IF ZEY WERE 'UMAN.
'UMANS WOULD WIZDRAW.
WOULD 'AVE ALREADY, NO DOUBT.
BUT...
...ZEY AIN'T 'UMAN.
ZEY'RE FREAKS.

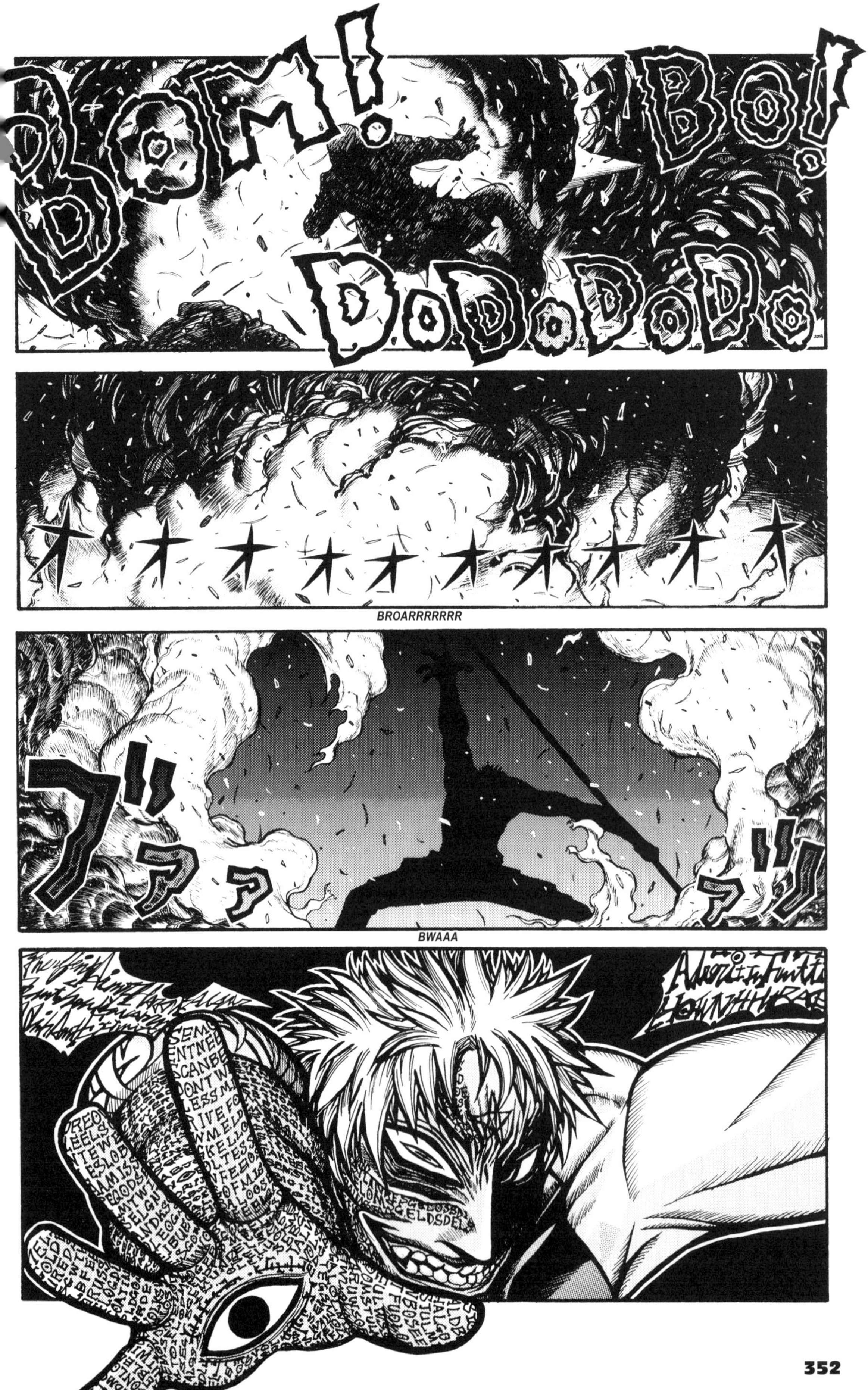
BOOM!
BO!
DODODODO
ォォォォォォォォォォ
BROARRRRRRR
ブァァァァッ
BWAAA

BAM
ZU ZU ZU ZU ZU ZU
ZHWAA

ZU ZU ZU ZU ZU ZU ZU ZU ZU ZU ZU
?!!
ZU ZU ZU ZU ZU ZU ZU ZU ZU ZU
?!
WHAT'S THAT?!

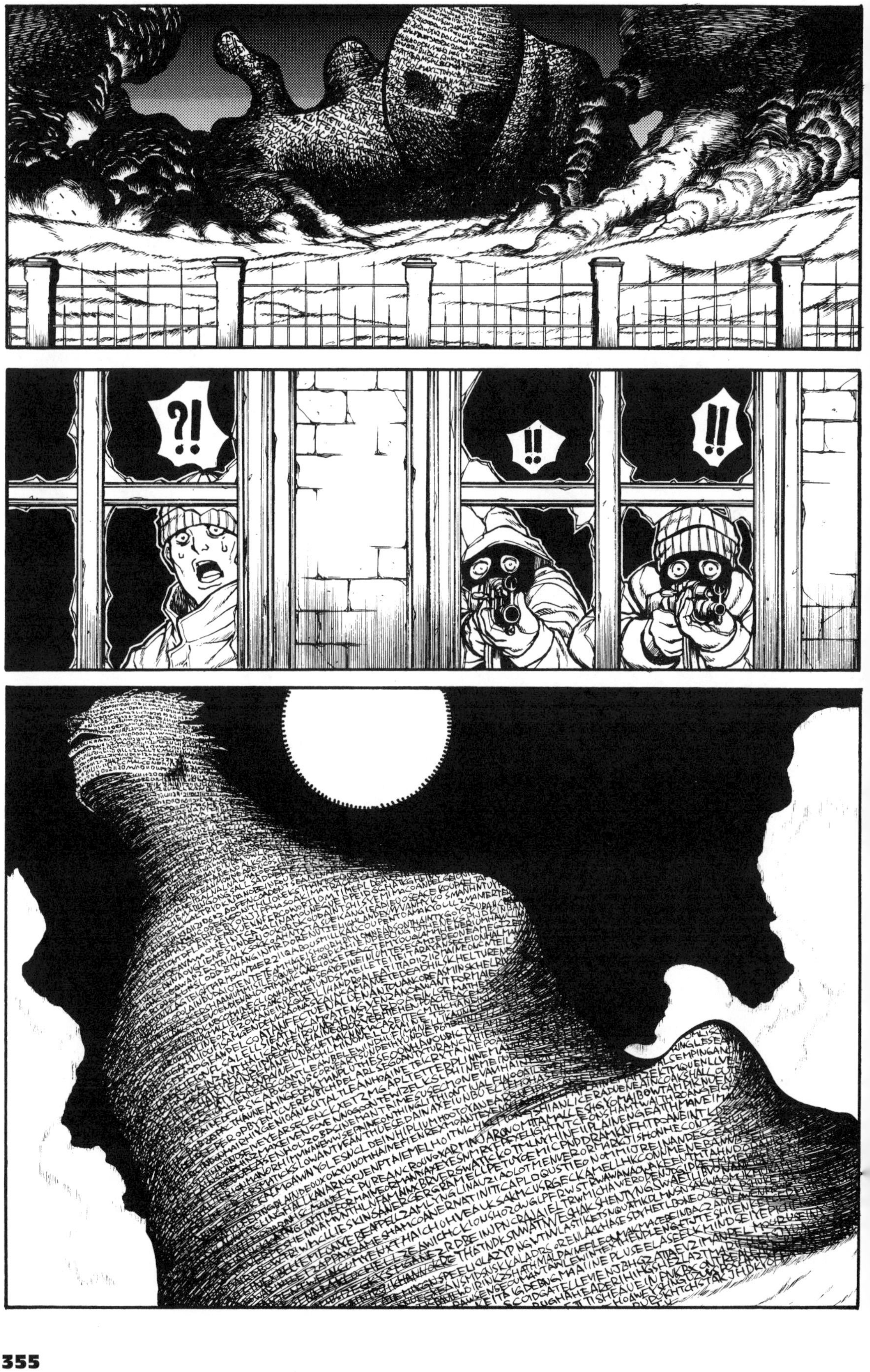

WOHHHHHH
UWAHHHHHH!
WH-WHAT THE HELL IS THAT?!
WHAT THE--?!
WHAT'S GOING ON?!
ZU ZU ZU ZU ZU ZU
ZU ZU ZU

!!
OY...
C'EST UNE BLAGUE ...?
OY!!
WHAT 'APPENED?!

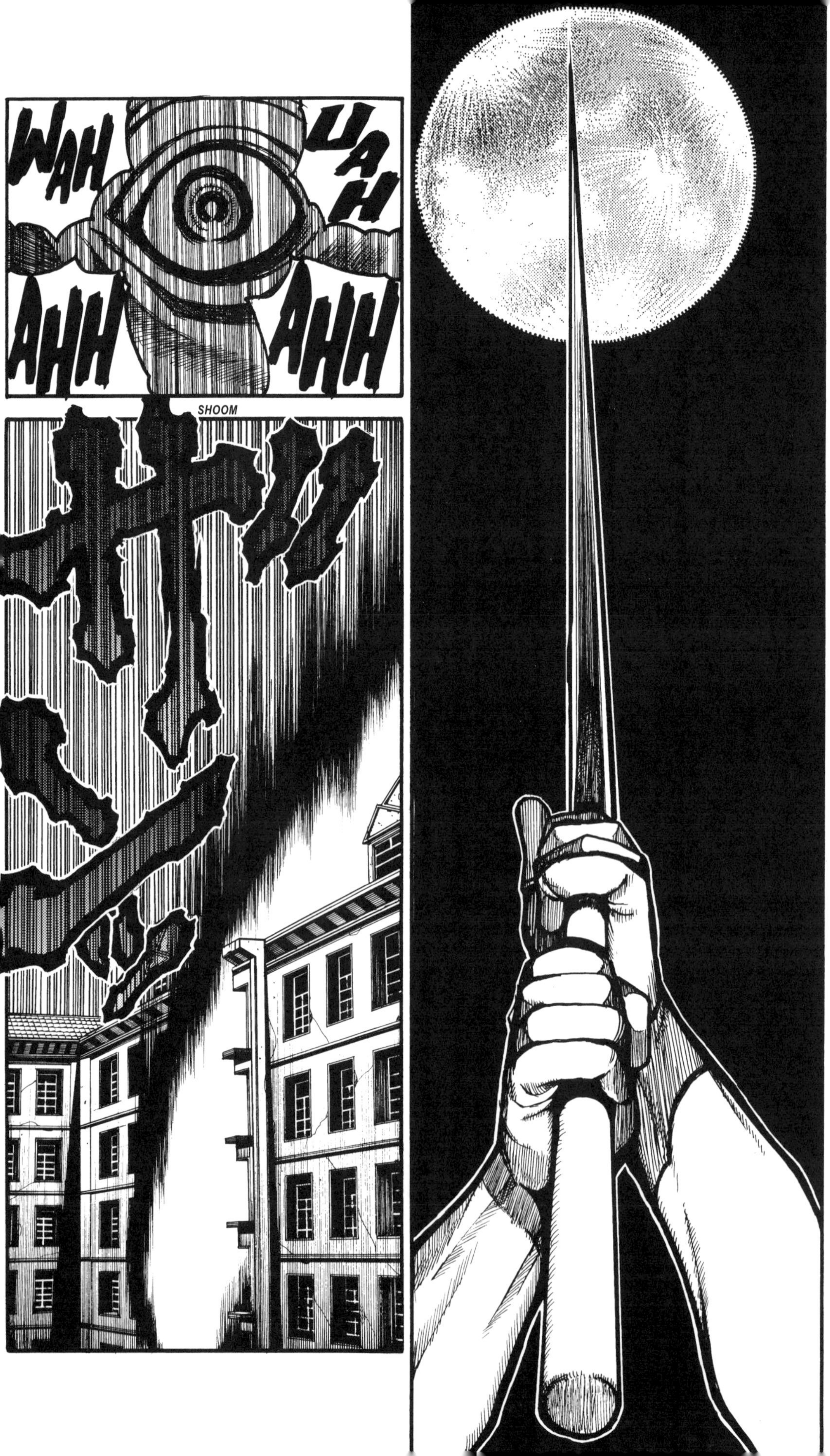
WAH UAH
AHH AHH
SHOOM

BTOOM
AH
OH
OH
OH
AH
AH
RMMMMMMBLLLL
UWOHHHHH!!
KKRRMMBBLLL
Z-ZIS, ZIS!
ZIS CAN'T POSSIBLY BE 'APPENING!!

RUMMMBLLL
ドドドドド
WHA...AH!
AGHH!
IT'S A LIE.
THIS IS A LIE!!
I DON'T KNOW WHY! BUT...
...SOMETHING INSIDE ME IS TELLING ME THAT.
"THE OTHER EYE IN YOUR FOREHEAD."
DIDN'T I TEACH YOU?

YOUR THIRD EYE.
CAST ASIDE YOUR HUMAN EYES.
THIS WOULD BE A PROBLEM FOR A HUMAN.
BUT YOU ARE NOT HUMAN ANYMORE.
THIS WOULD BE A PROBLEM FOR A HUMAN.
BUT YOU ARE NOT HUMAN ANYMORE.
(seeing through illusion)
ヒュボッ

AN ILLUSION?!!
IT'S A HALLUCI-NATION!!
UWA HHHH!
HELP.. HELP MEEE!
IT.. IT'S A MONSTERRR!
MY LEG! MY LEG'S BEEN...!!
HELP MEEE I CAN'T MOVE!!
S-STEADY ON! PULL YOUR-SELVES TOGETHER!
IT'S AN ILLUSION!
YOU WERE HALLUCI-NATING!
MY ARM!
MY ARM!
WHA...!

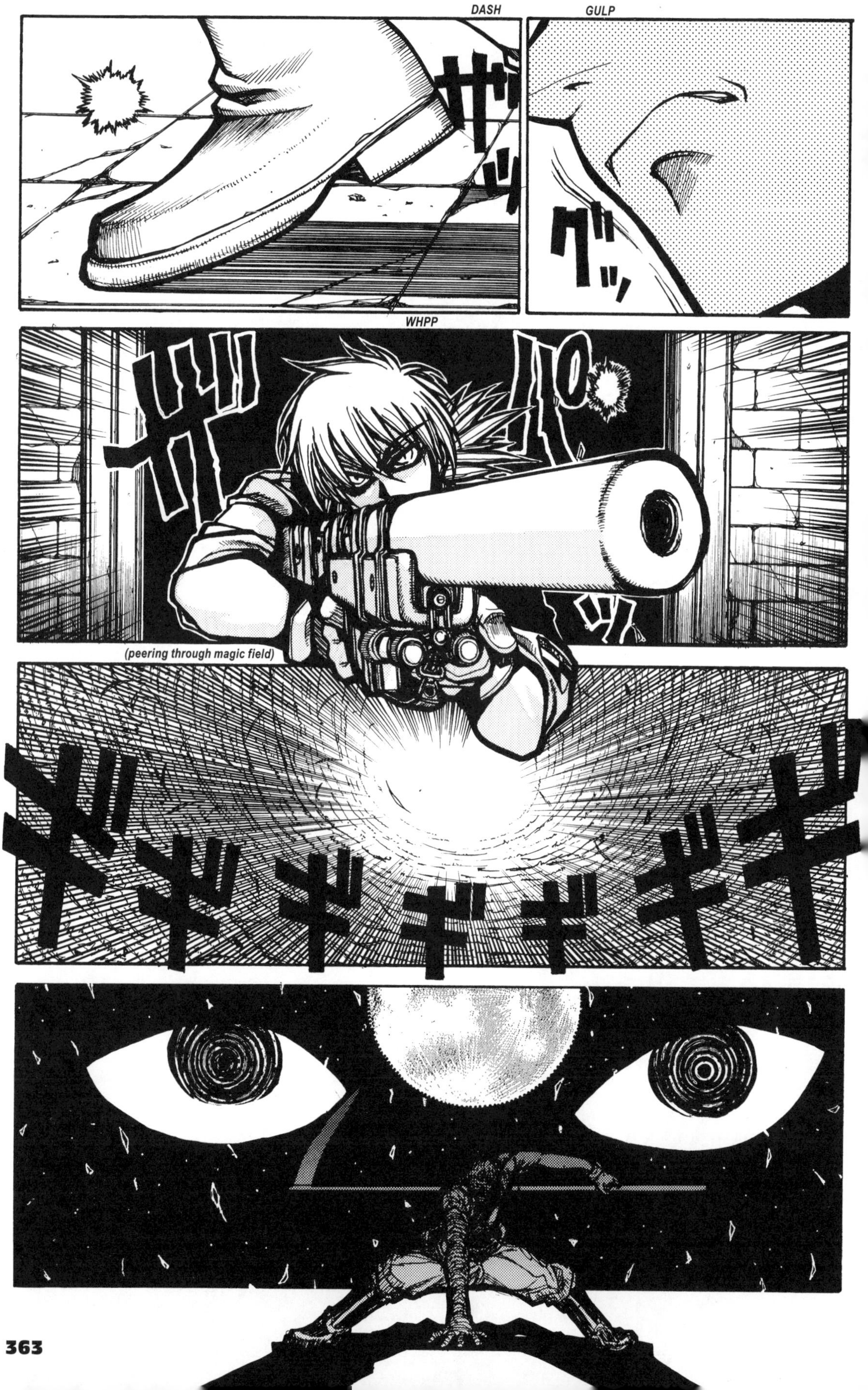
GULP
DASH
WHPP
(peering through magic field)

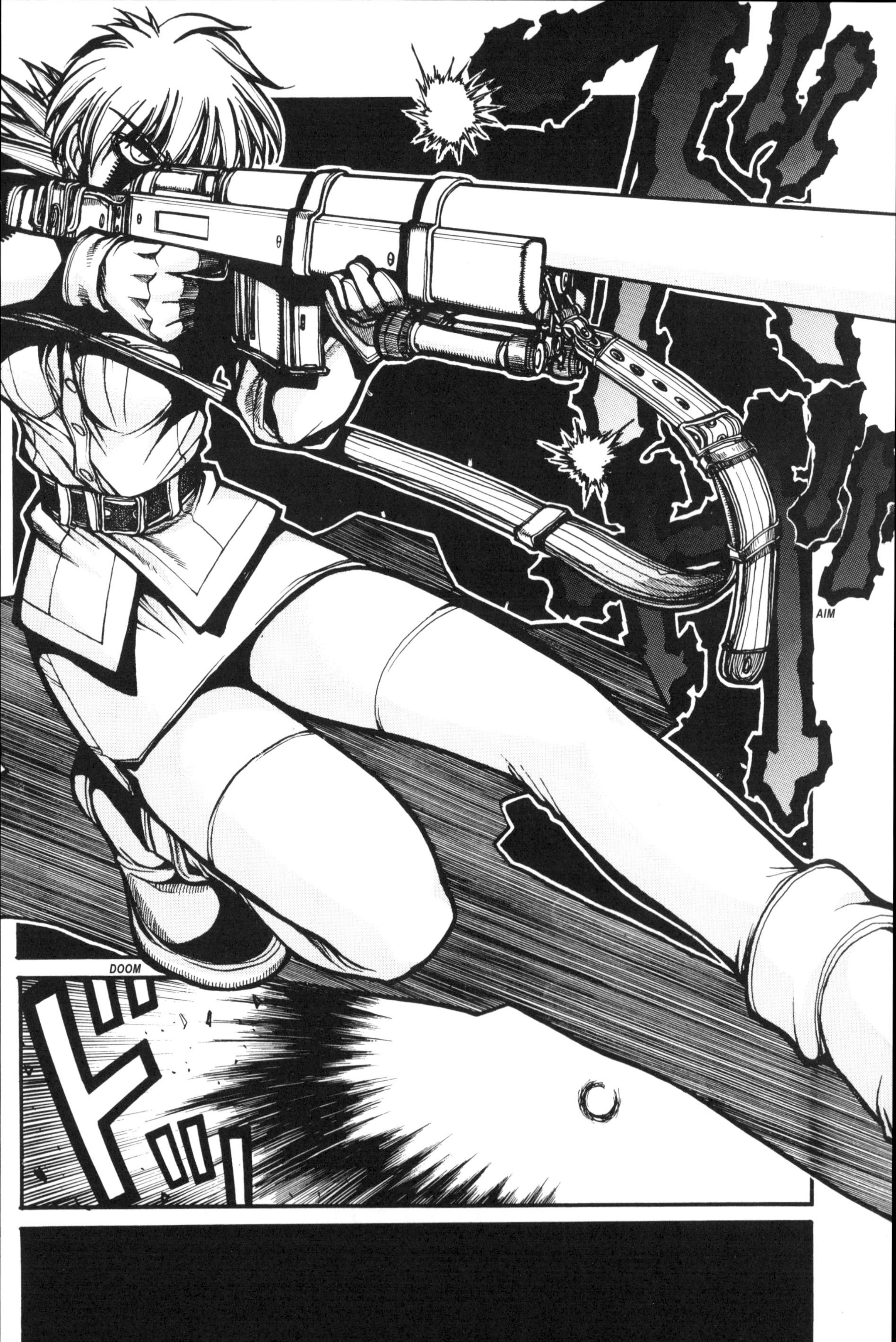

ORDER 46 / END

AH!
AH!
WAHH!
AHH!
RMMBBBLLL
ORDER 47
SOLDIER OF FORTUNE ③

バズッ
BSHOOM
バズッ
BSHOOM
バズッ
BSHOOM
バズッ
BSHOOM
FWEE
FWEE
FWEE
FWEE
FWEE
ZWAAAAA
SHPP

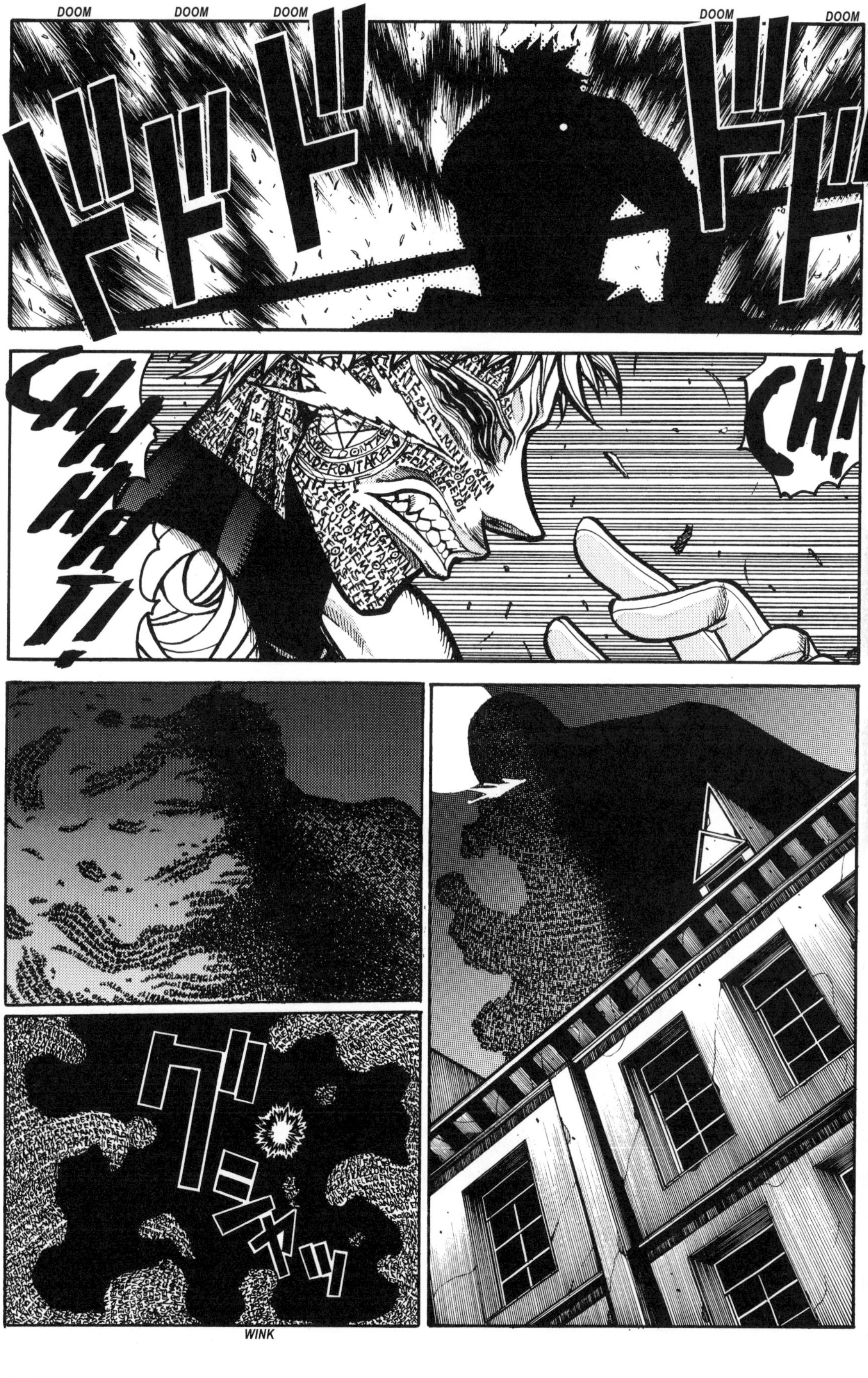
DOOM
DOOM
DOOM
DOOM
DOOM
ドドドドドドド
CHHHHAT!!
CH!!
グシャッ
WINK

ZAZAAAAA
!!
WHAT WAS THAT?!
WHAT THE?
WHA...
WHA...?!
!!
?!
BA
SORCERY?!
ZAT WAS AN ILLUSION?!
PLEASE, GET YOURSELVES SORTED!!
IT'S AN ILLUSION! SORCERY OR SOMETHIN'!!
BUT YOU'RE TOO LATE!!
BUT...
THAT'S RIGHT, UN ILLUSION!!
YOU DID VELL TO SEE THROUGH IT, SERAS VICTORIA!!

CRASH
SHSKK
RASSK
WHA!
WHA!
AH!
GEHA!
GEH!
ZSHHH
CHNKK

GRAHH!
WHNK

AH
RAH
AH
AH
AH
AH
AH
BOOM

SHPAM
HAH!
HAH!
HAH!
HAH!
HAH!
HAH!
ZNNNNN
ZNNNNNN
?!
WE'RE IN SOME DEEP MERDE.
OUR FRONTAL DEFENSE IS TOAST.
THIS IS THE ENTRANCEWAY POST.
ENEMY SOLDIERS ARE STORMING THE DOORS!!
WE'RE BEING INVADED!!

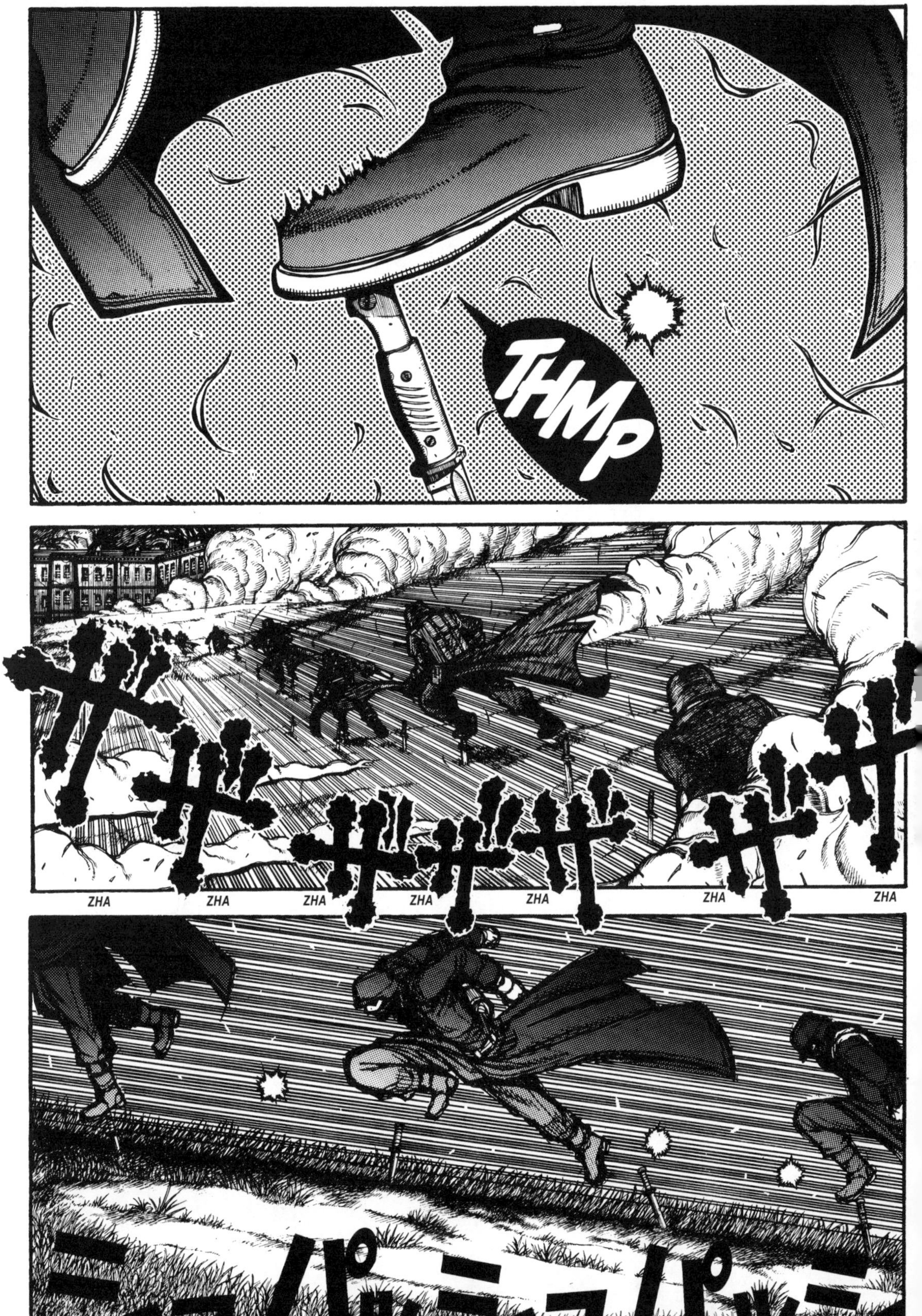
THMP
ザザザザザザザ
ZHA
ZHA
ZHA
ZHA
ZHA
ZHA
ZHA
シュパッシュパッ
SHHHP
SHHHP

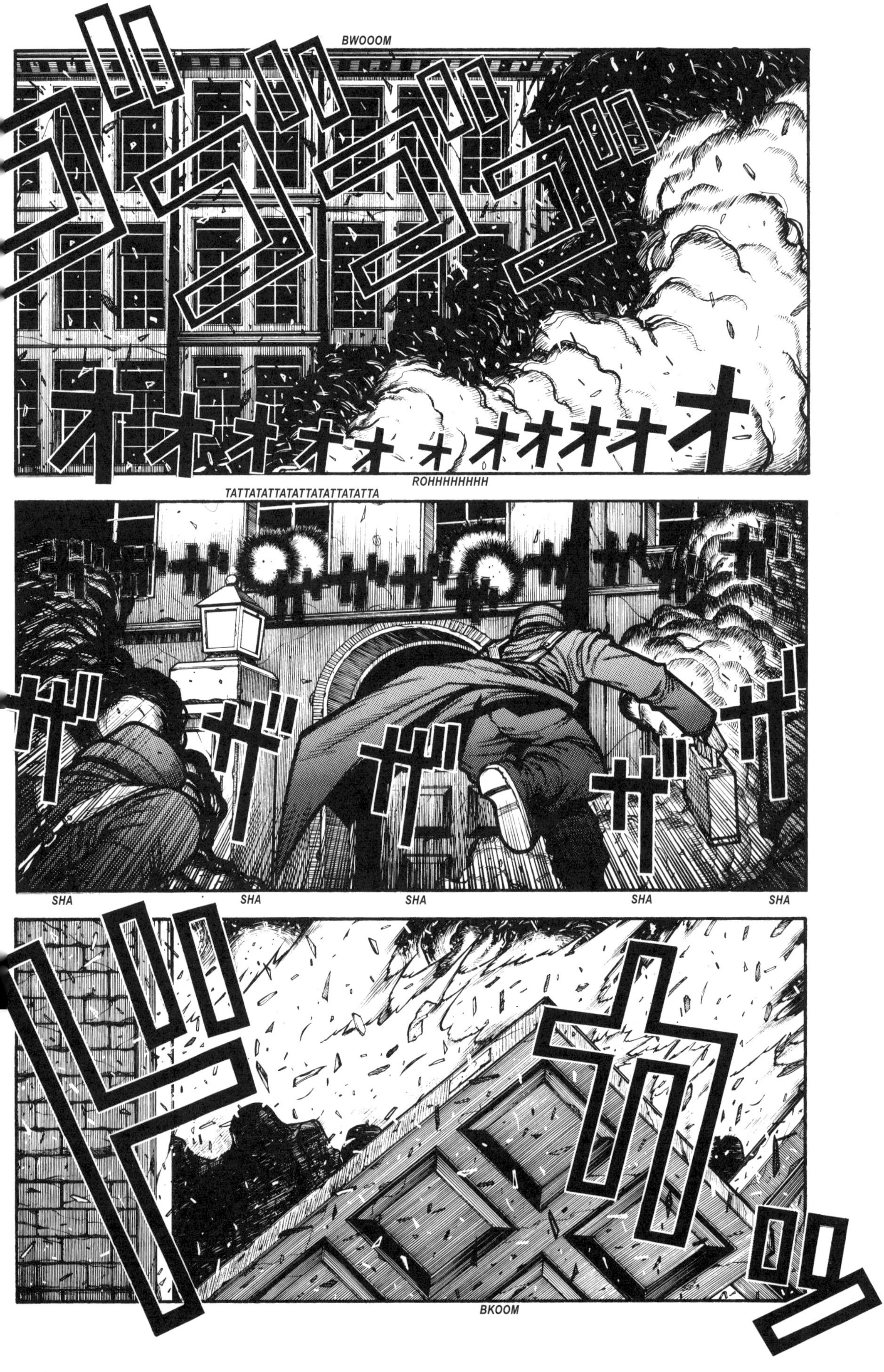
BWOOOM
ゴゴゴゴ
オオオオオォォオオオオオ
ROHHHHHHHHH
TATTATATTATATTATATTATATTA
ザザザザザ
SHA
SHA
SHA
SHA
SHA
ドカッ
BKOOM

NOWWW VE VON'T SPARE YOU!!
KHA! KHA! KHA!
NOWWW NO ONE VILL SURVIVE!!
ビギビ ビギビギ
HZZZZZZZ
Stürm!
Stürm!!
Leven!!
Stürm!
Stürm!!
ザザザザザ
ZHA
ZHA
ZHA
ZHA
ZHA
NOWWWW!!
KILL THEM ALL SVIFTLY!!

CHAK
SHA
CHAK
ASSEMBLE ZE UNIT.
'AVE ALL DEPLOYED TROOPS CENTER PEEL.
REASSEMBLE ALL REMAINING FORCES 'ERE!!
EQUIP ALL AVAILABLE AMMO AND 'AND GRENADES.
GIRL!!
Y--! YES SIR!
WE'LL 'OLE UP IN ZIS PART OF ZE BUILDING.
WHILE WE PROTECT ZIS AREA...
WE'LL BE ZE DEFENSE AND YOU BE ZE OFFENSE.
...YOU GO TAKE ZEM OUT, GIRL!!
Y--!
YAHHH!
YOU'RE OUR TRUMP CARD.
...DO IT BEFORE ZEY COME MAKE MINCEMEAT OUT OF US.
GET ZEM!! BUT...

SWAT
HYAH!
WE'RE COUNTIN' ON YA.
HEHEH.
!!
R---!
RIGHT, THEN!
AH, I FORGOT ONE IMPORTANT ZING.
?
?
ぼそり
MUMBLE
SERAAAAS!!
!!
GAAA!
CLOSE YOUR EYES!
!!

FWOOF
GIIYAH HHHH!
GYAHHHH!
ドムッ
WHAT'RE YOU DOING?!
WHAT'RE YOU DOING?! WHA! WHA!
FEH!

WHA! WHA!
WHAT'RE! WHA! WHA
WHAT WAS THAT ALL ABOUT?!
AHH! NO FAIR!
HOW COULD YOU, CAPTAIN?!
RIGHT YOU LOT, GO ON ZEN.
CHOP CHOP!!
FLARE
ME TOO.
AND ME.
AND ME.
AND ME.
AND ME.
I--!
IGNORANT CLOTS!
HEHEHEH...
SERAS, GIRL.
DON'T TURN YOUR TOES UP.
DON'T DIE.

YOU TOO, CAPTAIN!!
AND ALL OF YOU!!
DASH
ダッ
RIGHT!! OFF YOU GO!!
OFF I GO!!

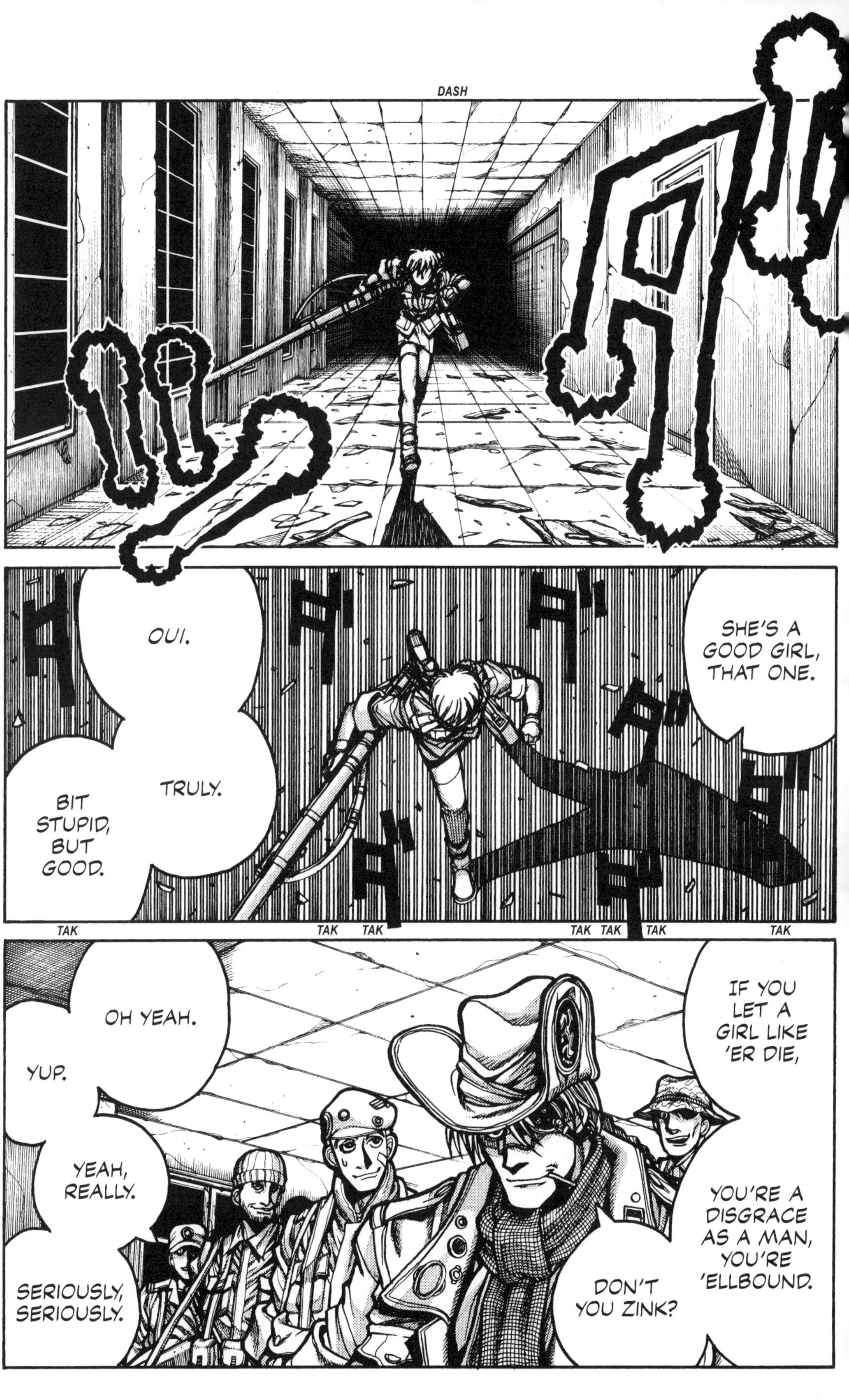
DASH
SHE'S A GOOD GIRL, THAT ONE.
OUI.
BIT STUPID, BUT GOOD.
TRULY.
TAK
TAK TAK
TAK TAK TAK
TAK
IF YOU LET A GIRL LIKE 'ER DIE,
YOU'RE A DISGRACE AS A MAN, YOU'RE 'ELLBOUND.
DON'T YOU ZINK?
OH YEAH.
YUP.
YEAH, REALLY.
SERIOUSLY, SERIOUSLY.

I'M SORRY, BUT ZIS IS WHAT I ASK.
ZIS IS ZE PLACE YOU GUYS LAY DOWN YOUR *LIVES.*
ZINK OF IT AS YOUR GRAVEYARD.
YOU KNOW, CAPTAIN...
USUALLY RIGHT NOW IT'D BE THE OTHER WAY. "ANYONE WHO WANTS TO RUN, RUN!!"
YOU'D LET YOUR MEN ESCAPE AND STAY BEHIND ALONE OR SOMETHING.
WHAT THE 'ELL'S *ZAT* ABOUT?
YOU LOT'RE ALL BAD *SONS 'OO* BECAME FIGHTERS
FOR SMALL CHANGE AND ZE FUN OF IT.
GSHAK
NOW, ZEN. LET'S GO AND DIE, *DOGS.*
LET'S DIE WHILE YELLING *"FUCK, FUCK."*
AS WE TAKE GUT-SHOTS. AS WE WRIZE IN AGONY.
HEHEHEH.
ZAT'S RIGHT.
MAKE *NO* MISTAKE.
NO MISTAKE ABOUT IT.
ORDER 47 / END

ORDER 48

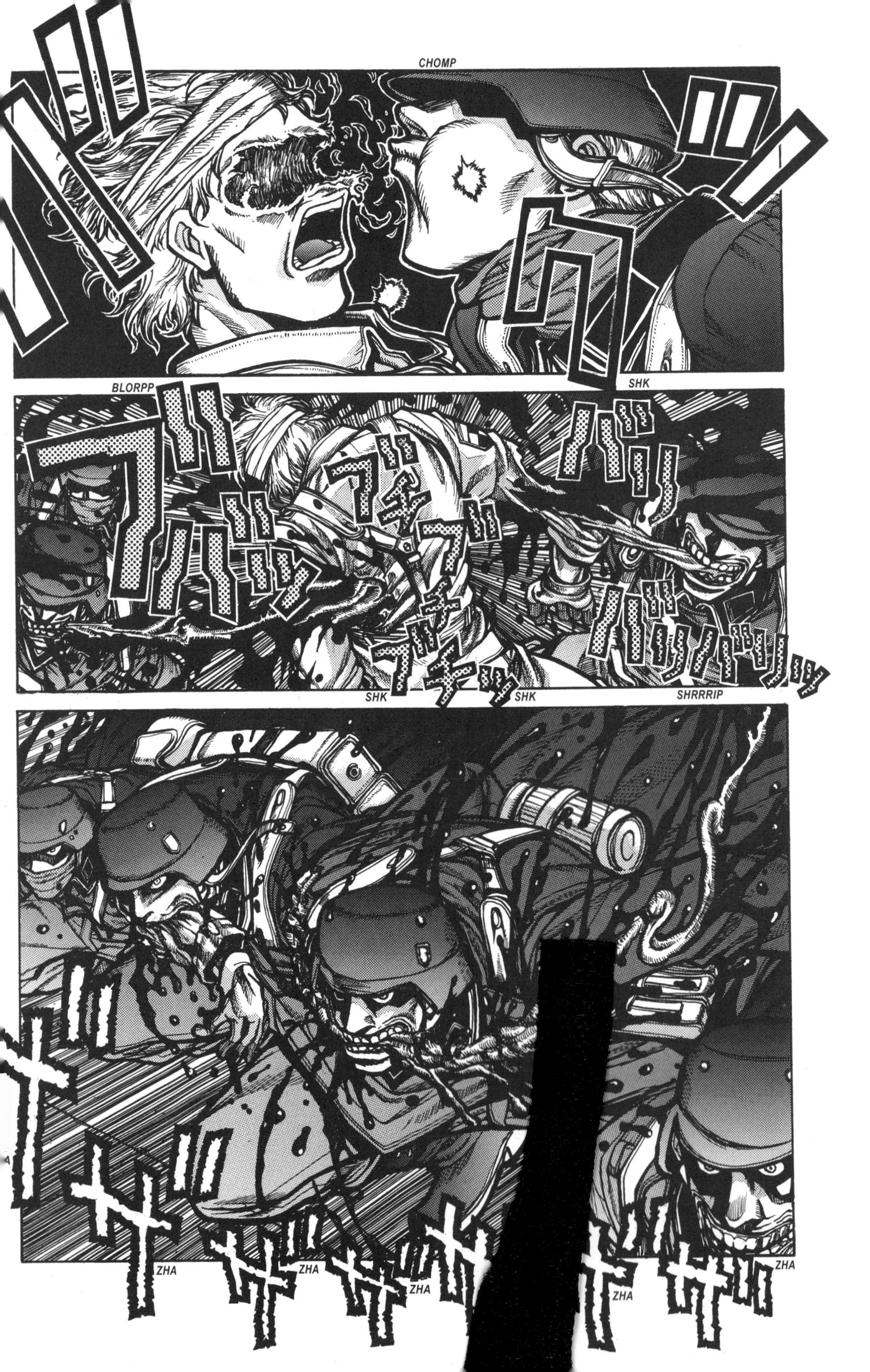
CHOMP
SHK
SHRRRIP
SHK
SHK
BLORPP
ZHA
ZHA
ZHA
ZHA
ZHA

AGGHHHH!
HELP ME!! HELP ME!! HELP ME!!
DOOM DOOM DOOM DOOM DOOM DOOM DOOM
DAMMIT, THEY'RE GETTING THROUGH!
THE SHOTS!! THEY'RE NOT HITTING THEM!!
SHOOT!! SHOOT!! SHOOT!!
TAT TAT TAT TAT TAT TAT TAT TAT
TAT TAT TAT TAT TAT
SON OF A BITCH, WE'RE CUT OFF! FUCK!!
WITHDRAW!! RETREAT!!
FUCK!! FUCK!! FUCK!!
MEDIC!! MEDIC!!
Es wurde ihnen

HELLSING ARMS. INDUSTRY
HELLSING
ORDER 48
SOLDIER OF FORTUNE④

THIS IS B BLOCK!! CAPTAIN!! OUR RETREAT'S BEEN CUT OFF!
IT'S IMPOSSIBLE TO LINK UP WITH YOU THERE!!
GET OUT OF ZERE, FOOLS!!
GET 'ERE IF YOU 'AVE TO CRAWL!!
BLAM BLAM BLAM BLAM
WE'RE DIGGING IN 'ERE AT ZE ROUND TABLE OFFICE.
ZIS SPOT IS ZE FIRMEST. WE CAN 'OLD OUT 'ERE FOR A WHILE.
YOU'LL SIMPLY DIE ZERE. DON'T GIVE UP.
WE'LL OPEN ZE BARRICADE FOR YOU!! FIND A WAY TO GET 'ERE!!
NO, CAPTAIN IT'S USELESS
WE'RE HEAP CASUAL MYSE INCLUD
WE'LL DO ALL THAT WE CAN HERE.
TATTATAT TATTATAT
THIS BLIGHTER'S DEAD ALREADY.
GET RID OF HIM QUICK OR HE'LL TURN GHOUL.
WATER.
...GIVE ME WATER.
CLOSE THAT BARRICADE, PLEASE!! GOOD FORTUNE!!
CHEERS.
YOU DAFT ASS'-OLE!!

WELL, BLOODY FUCKING 'ELL.
ALRIGHT, DIE ZEN.
IT'S BEEN FUN, YOU KNOW.
FOR ME TOO, CAPTAIN.
SEE YOU IN HELL!!
OVER!!
SHMP
SEAL ZE BARRICADE!!
TURN ZIS 'UGE ROUND TABLE OVER AND USE IT, TOO.
PILE UP ANYZING, I DON'T CARE.
CAPTAIN, WHAT ABOUT B-BLOCK...?
ZEY'RE DONE FOR.
I SEE.
THAT'S TOO BAD.

IT'S NO USE. WE'RE FINISHED!
SHUT UP, YOU THICK BASTARD!!
NO MORE FIGHTING MONSTERS FOR ME!! I'VE HAD ENOUGH!!
INTEGRA AND ALUCARD HAVE GONE AND CAST US OFF!!
WHAT'RE YOU ON ABOUT?
YOU CAN'T GO ANYWHERE, NOT ZAT I'D LET YOU!
I'M LEAVING!! FORGET THIS!!
WHERE DO YOU PLAN TO GO? YOUR GRAVE'S RIGHT 'ERE.
YOUR TOMBSTONE'S ZIS RUDDY 'UGE MANSION.
YOUR GRAVE KEEPER'S ZAT TERRIFYING GIRL, INTEGRA.
YOUR EPITAPH GOES LIKE ZIS.
"'ERE ZE MERCENARIES 'AD AT ZE EVIL NAZIS IN 'IGH STYLE AND 'ERE ZEY SLEEP IN 'IGH STYLE."
BUT BECAUSE OF YOUR BAWLING, IT'S YOUR FAULT IT GETS CHANGED.
"WASTED AND GUTLESS, ZEY DIE LIKE BUGS WHILE WEEPING LIKE WOMEN."

I DON'T ZINK SO! YOU'RE GOING TO DIE IN STYLE IF I 'AVE TO FORCE YOU TO!!
YOU GET PAID TO GO TO WAR BECAUSE YOU LIKE IT!! RIGHT, SOLDIER?!
ZEN FIGHT AND DIE BECAUSE YOU LIKE IT!!
SHIT...!
SHIIIT!
FUCK!
FUCK!!
WHUMP
BESIDES, IT'S NO GIVEN YET ZAT WE'RE GOING TO DIE.
COME ON!! PUT ZAT BARRICADE TOGEZER PRONTO!!
WE'RE ZE DEFENSE.
ZE OFFENSE WILL TURN ZE TABLES.

ボッ
BOOM
ボオッ
BOOOM
ボオオオッ
BOOOOM
GYAHH!
ドッ
DOOM
BOOM
DM
DM
DM
DM
DM
DM
ドドドドドド

COME AND GET SOME, FREAKS!!
COME ON, FREAKS!!
BUGGER-ALL, CONNECT!!
SHIT! SHIT!
DM
DM
DM
DM
DM
DM
DM
SHPP
KRAKK
AGGHH!

CLOMP
CLOMP
CLOMP
CLOMP
DON'T RUN, FIGHT!!
IT'S THEM! WE'RE DEAD!
KEEP AT IT!
TAT
TAT
TAT
TAT
TAT
TAT
AHAA!!
AH!!
BUDDA BUDDA BUDDA BUDDA BUDDA
TATATATATAT
BUDDA
BUDDA

BURN, BURN!!
ILL ZEM
LL, KILL
EM ALL!!
THIS IST THE POWER OF HELLSING?!
THIS IST THE ORDER OF ROYAL PROTESTANT KNIGHTS?!
DON'T MAKE ME LAUGH!!
BLAM
hahh
hahh
hahh
hahh
hahh
hahh

SHMP
DM DM DM DM DM DM DM DM

(eerie effect of hand extending)
I'M SICK...
...UND TIRED OF THESE PIP-SQUEAKS!!

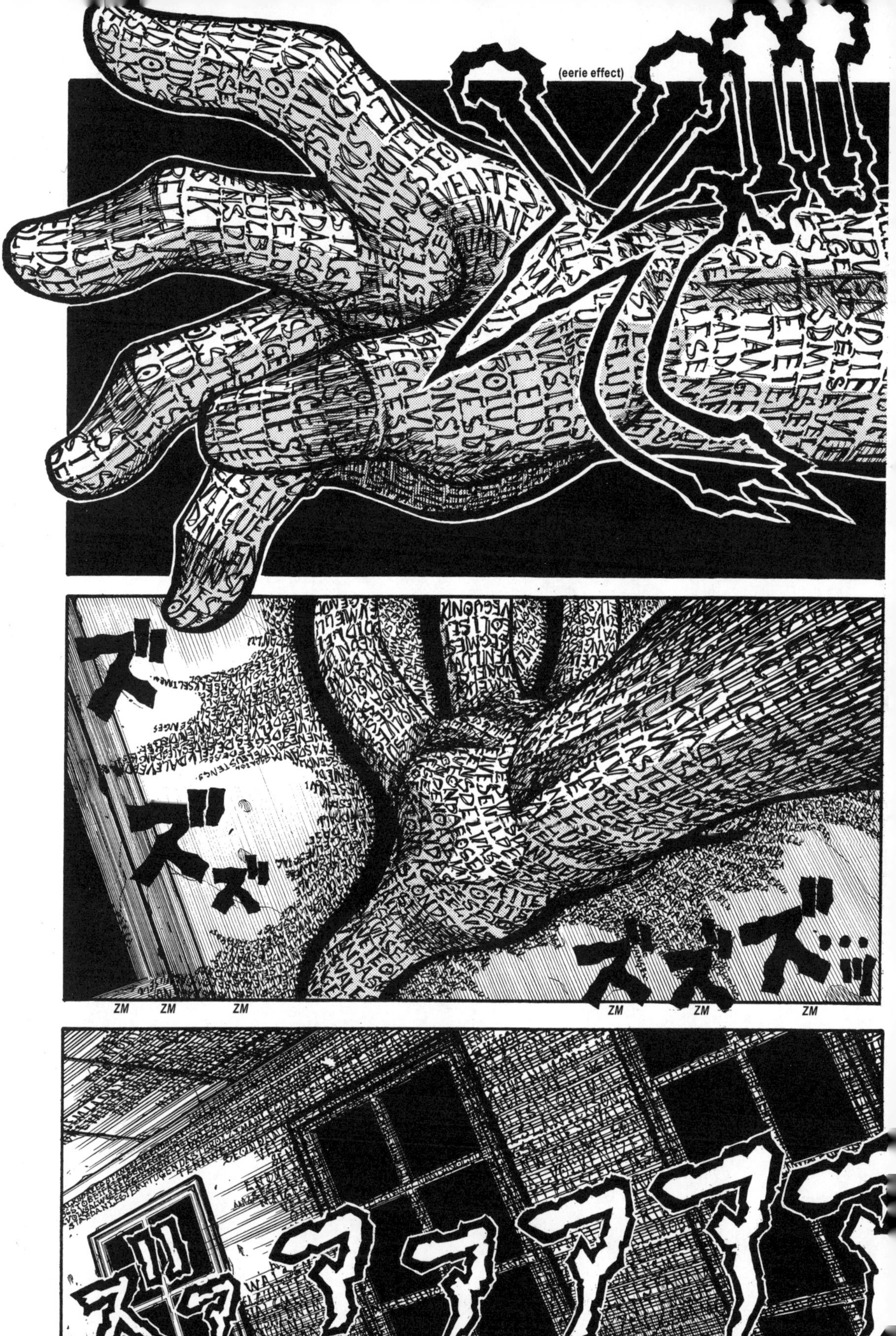
(eerie effect)
ZM ZM ZM
ZM ZM ZM
ZWAAAAA

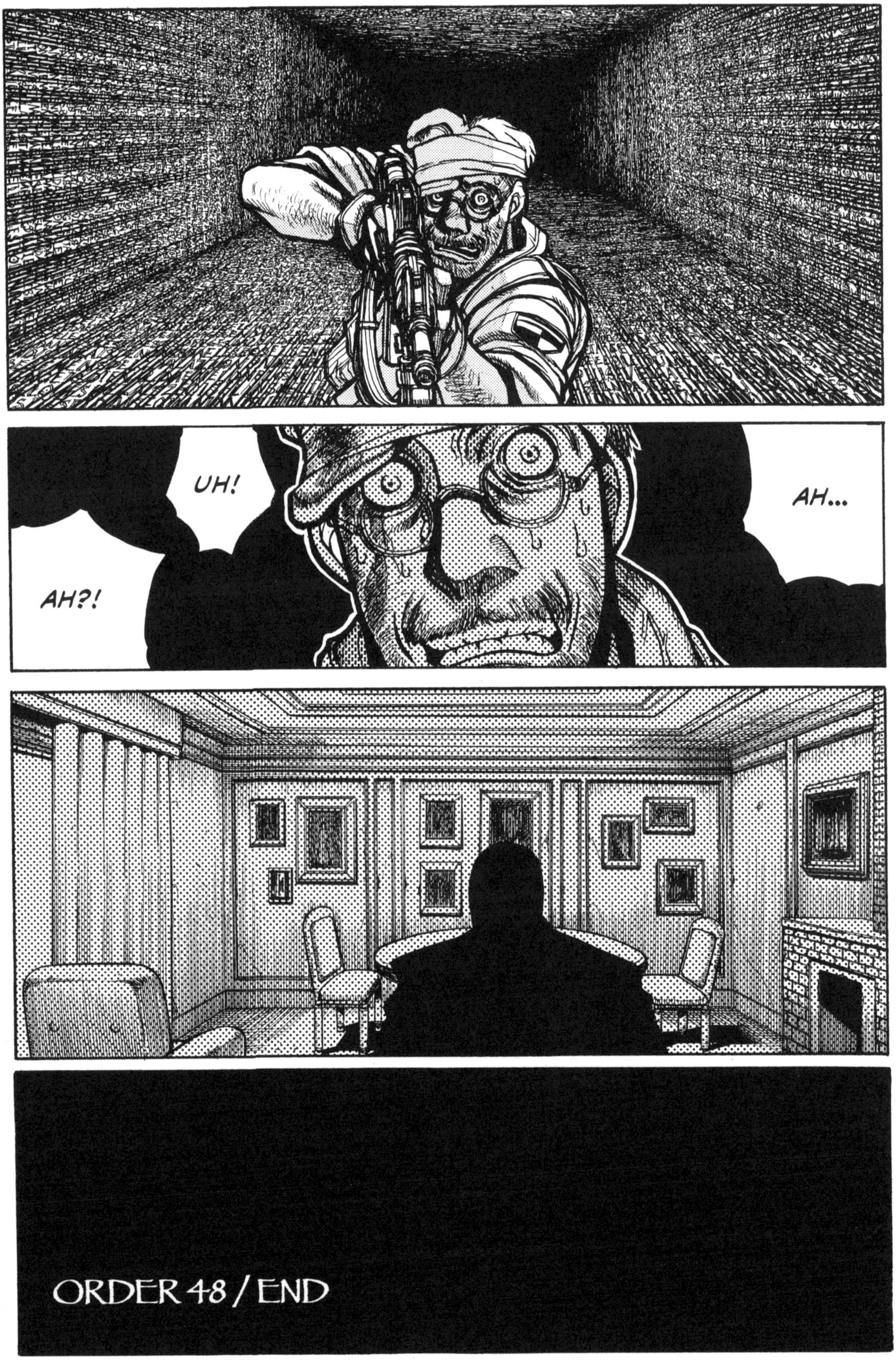
UH!
AH...
AH?!
ORDER 48 / END

⚜ORDER 49

SOLDIER OF FORTUNE⑤

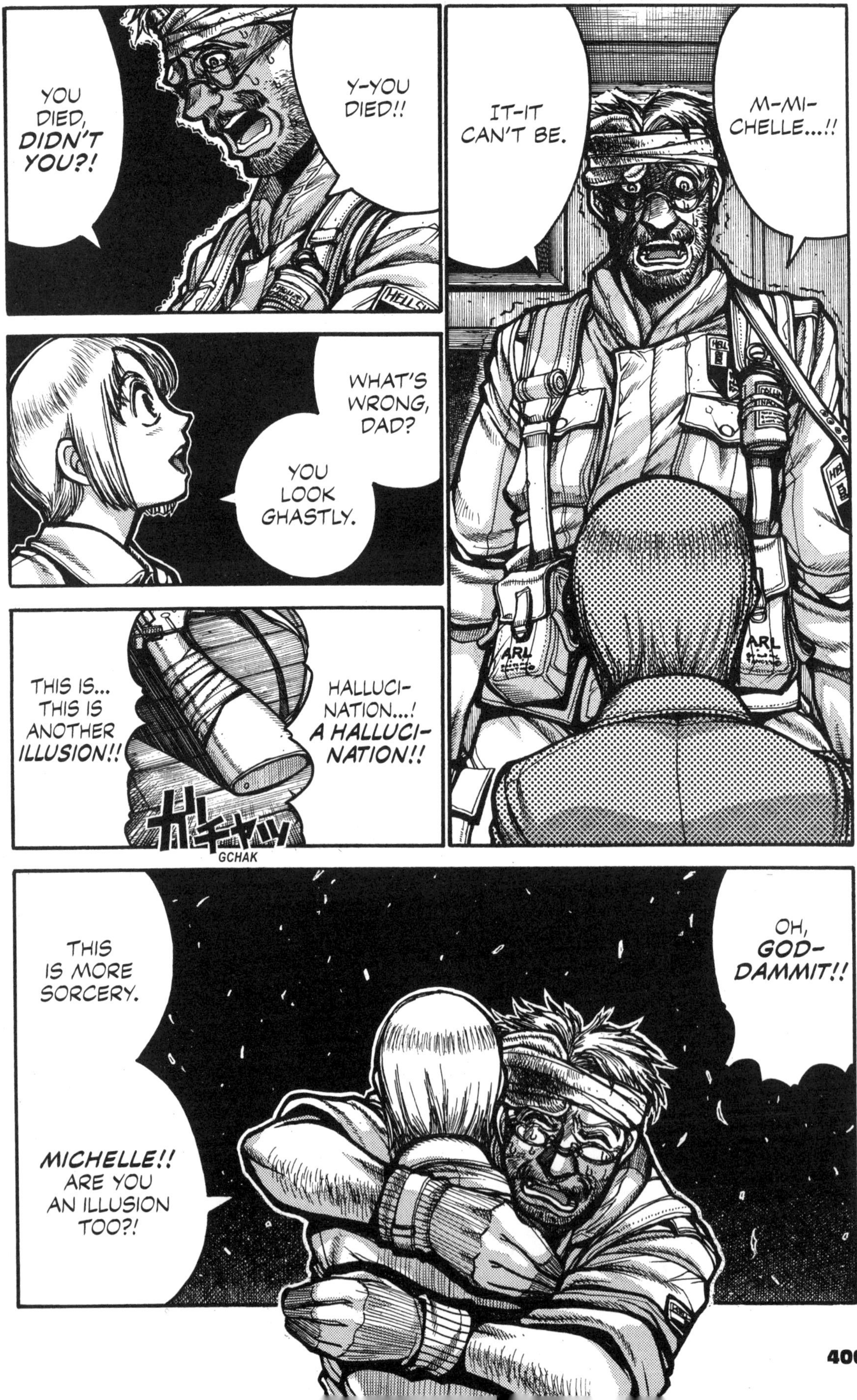
M-MI-CHELLE...!!
IT-IT CAN'T BE.
Y-YOU DIED!!
YOU DIED, DIDN'T YOU?!
WHAT'S WRONG, DAD?
YOU LOOK GHASTLY.
HALLUCI-NATION...! A HALLUCI-NATION!!
THIS IS... THIS IS ANOTHER ILLUSION!!
ガチャッ
GCHAK
OH, GOD-DAMMIT!!
THIS IS MORE SORCERY.
MICHELLE!! ARE YOU AN ILLUSION TOO?!

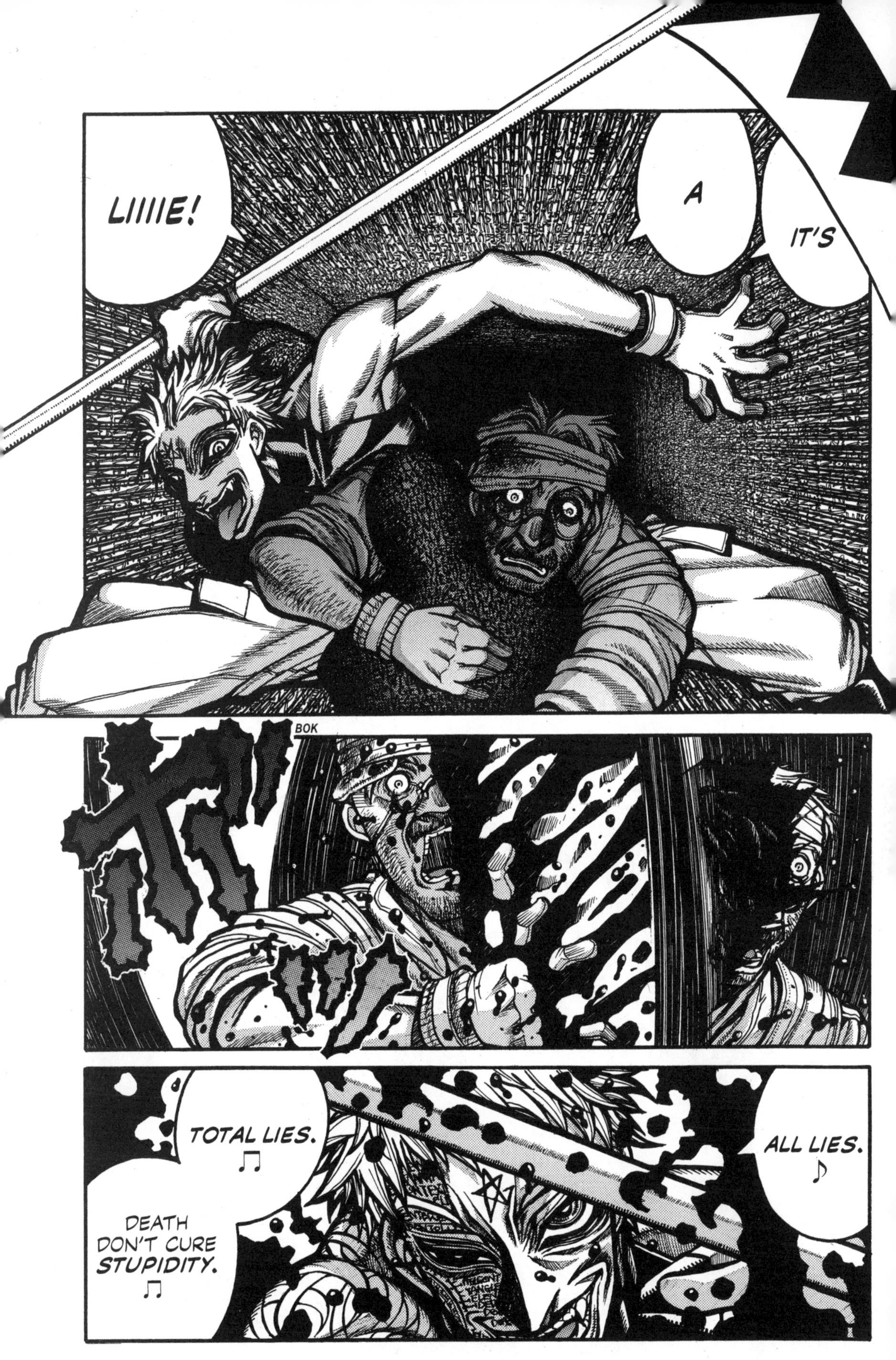
IT'S
A
LIIIIE!
BOK
ALL LIES. ♪
TOTAL LIES. ♫
DEATH DON'T CURE STUPIDITY. ♫

HOW 'BOUT THAT ONE, SERGEANT-MAJOR?
MMM, JUST A MOMENT.
THIS SOURNESS... JA
HMM.
SLSH SLSH SLSH
TYPE A, RH NEGATIVE!!
VELL, DID I GET IT THIS TIME?
MUMBLE MUMBLE
OHO!! AMAZING.
ABSOLUTELY CORRECT!!
YOU'RE SKILLED AT THIS.
THE THICKNESS UND SMOOTHNESS ARE DIFFERENT.
SEE?
ARE THEY? IMPRES-SIVE.

IT GOES DOWN DIF-FERENTLY.
UND BESIDES,
TYPE A IST, HOW SHOULD I SAY...
HYNN
BOMF
WHOM WHOM
WHOM
WHOM
WHOM

DOOM
Ladimir HALLCONNEN
Ladimir HALLCONNEN
WHOM
ORRRRR

I-I'LL BEAT THEM!
I WILL!
ALL-ALL OF THEM.
YES, I'LL BEAT THEM!!
GYNN
GYNN
GYNN
GYNN

OH
ザ
ZHA
ザ
ZHA
ザ
ZHA
ザ
ZHA
ザ
ZHA
ザ
ZHA
OH
OH

OH
WHOM
WHOM
WHOM
WHOM
WHOM
WHOM

BWOOM
AH!
WHMP
GYAHH! AGHH!
MY EYES! MY EYYYES!
SHIT! ZE BARRI-CADE!
BUDDA BUDDA BUDDA BUDDA BUDDA
MEDIC!! OVER 'ERE!!
BRING ZOSE CHAIRS, QUICK!
MOVE YOUR ASS!
ZE BARRI-CADE! 'URRY!!

TU ES FOU?!
STAY BE'IND COVER!
FUCK YOU!!
FUCK YOU!
DASH
AH!!
AAA
AAAAA
AH
AAH
BLAM BLAM BLAM BLAM BLAM BLAM BLAM BLAM
BLAM
IT-IT'S HOPELESS.
OH, SHUT IT, YOU SON OF A BITCH!!
BLAM
BLAM
BLAM
MERDE!
OHH!
BLAM
BLAM
BLAM

THIS IS THE LAST OF IT.
WE'RE FRESH OUT OF BLESSED SILVER BULLETS.
hah hah
hah hah
hah hah
hah hah
hah hah
REDISTRIBUTE ZE REMAINING AMMO.
I DON'T WANT TO DIE!
ENOUGH, CAPTAIN!
I'M DONE FOR! I CAN'T SEE!
KILL ME!
KILL ME!
IT'S NOT LIKE I REALLY WANNA DIE EIZER!
PUT A ZOCK IN IT!

ORDER 49 / END

GIMME AMMO!! 'AND IT OVER!!
AMMO! GIMME AMMO!!
STAY DOWN!! OR YOU'LL DRAW FIRE!!
HE'S ALREADY DEAD.
DON'T MOVE! YOU'LL DIE IF I DON'T STOP THE BLEEDING!
CAPTAIN!! TAKE THESE!!
THEY MARK THE END OF THE ROAD.
WE'RE FINISHED.
SHUT UP!
EVEN IF WE SURRENDER, WE'LL ALL BE RIPPED APART!!
THOSE THINGS'RE MONSTERS!! WE'RE GONNA BE *EATEN!!*
IT FEELS JUST LIKE THAT TIME.
UGANDA, JAUNGAIDE!!
OUR DETACHMENT AT THE AIRFIELD!!
TAT TAT TAT TAT TAT TAT TAT
REINFORCEMENTS MADE IT THERE.
THIS TIME... SHIT, NOT *THIS* TIME.
ZAT'S BOLLOCKS, LIEUTENANT!!
THUP THUP BUDDA BUDDA BUDDA BUDDA BUDDA BUDDA BUDDA

ORDER 50 **SOLDIER OF FORTUNE⑥**

GOD-DAMN! A ROCKET!
MERDE! ZEY STILL HAD SOME-ZING LIKE--
STAB
GHH!
GLCH
GRIND
EVERYONE REPORT IN!!
LIEUTENANT!! DAMAGE REPORT...
LIEUTEN-ANT!!
!!
LIEU--!

LIEUTEN-ANT!!
'EY!! LIEUTEN-ANT!!
I FEEL SO TIRED.
CAN I REST NOW, SIR?
YEAH.
AT EASE, MAN.
ADIEU.

ZZZSSSHHHH

GROHHHH
DIRECT HIT.
SHALL VE ADVANCE?
NO, NOT YET.
FIRE ANOTHER SHELL.
VE ONLY HAVE ONE PANZERFAUST ROUND LEFT. VOULD IT BE A VASTE?
I DON'T CARE. DO IT.
BLOW THEM AVAY.
BLOW THIS PITIFUL BUNCH TO SMITHER-EENS!!
JAWOHL.
チャカッ
CHAK
shit

KILL THEM!!
CHIK
SHPP
SHROP
GEBOBOBOBOBO
GEBOBOBO BOBOBOBO
BOOM
VHA--?!

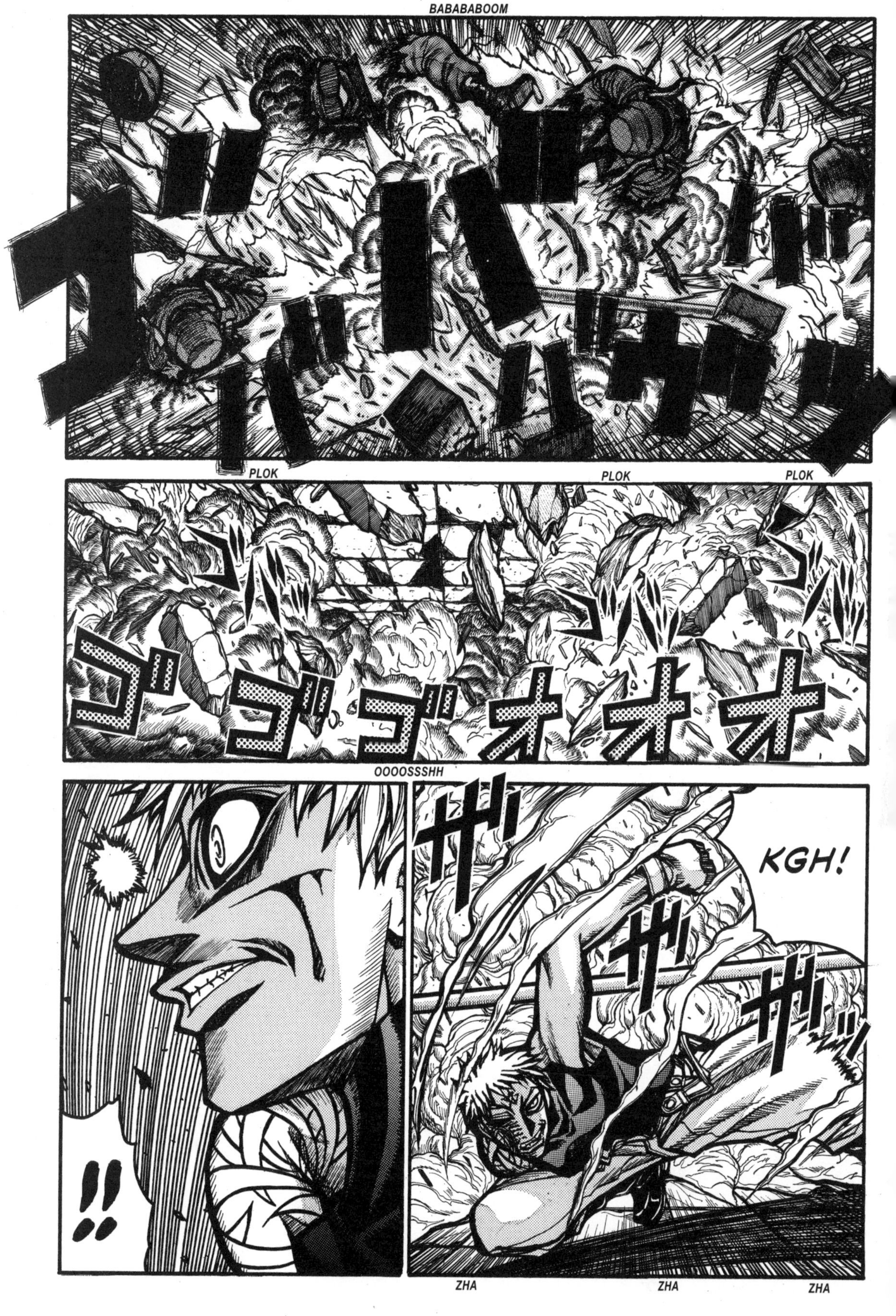
BABABABOOM
PLOK
PLOK
PLOK
ゴゴゴオオオ
OOOOSSSHH
KGH!
ZHA
ZHA
ZHA
!!

OOOSSSSHHH
SHPP
KLANK
KLANK
KLANK
KLANK
DIRECT CANNON SUPPORT...!!
IT'S YOU!!

CAPTAIN...!
YEAH.
SHE'S 'ERE.
JUST AS SHE PROMISED.
ボタッ ボタボタ
PLIP PLIP PLIP
ZE GIRL REALLY CAME.
TO KILL ALL ZE *FREAKS* BY 'ERSELF.
HEH, FUCK, SHIT!
SHE'S *REALLY* A GOOD GIRL.
ボタボタボタ
PLIP PLIP PLIP
SON-OF-A-BITCH, HEH!
I WISH I'D KISSED 'ER, EVEN IF I'D 'AD TO FORCE IT.
HEH HEH HEH!

KLANG
CLICK
CLICK
CLICK
SERAS.
SERAS VICTORIA!!
THE ONLY ONE LEFT...
...IS YOU!!

DO
YOU
HINK
ARE?!
I

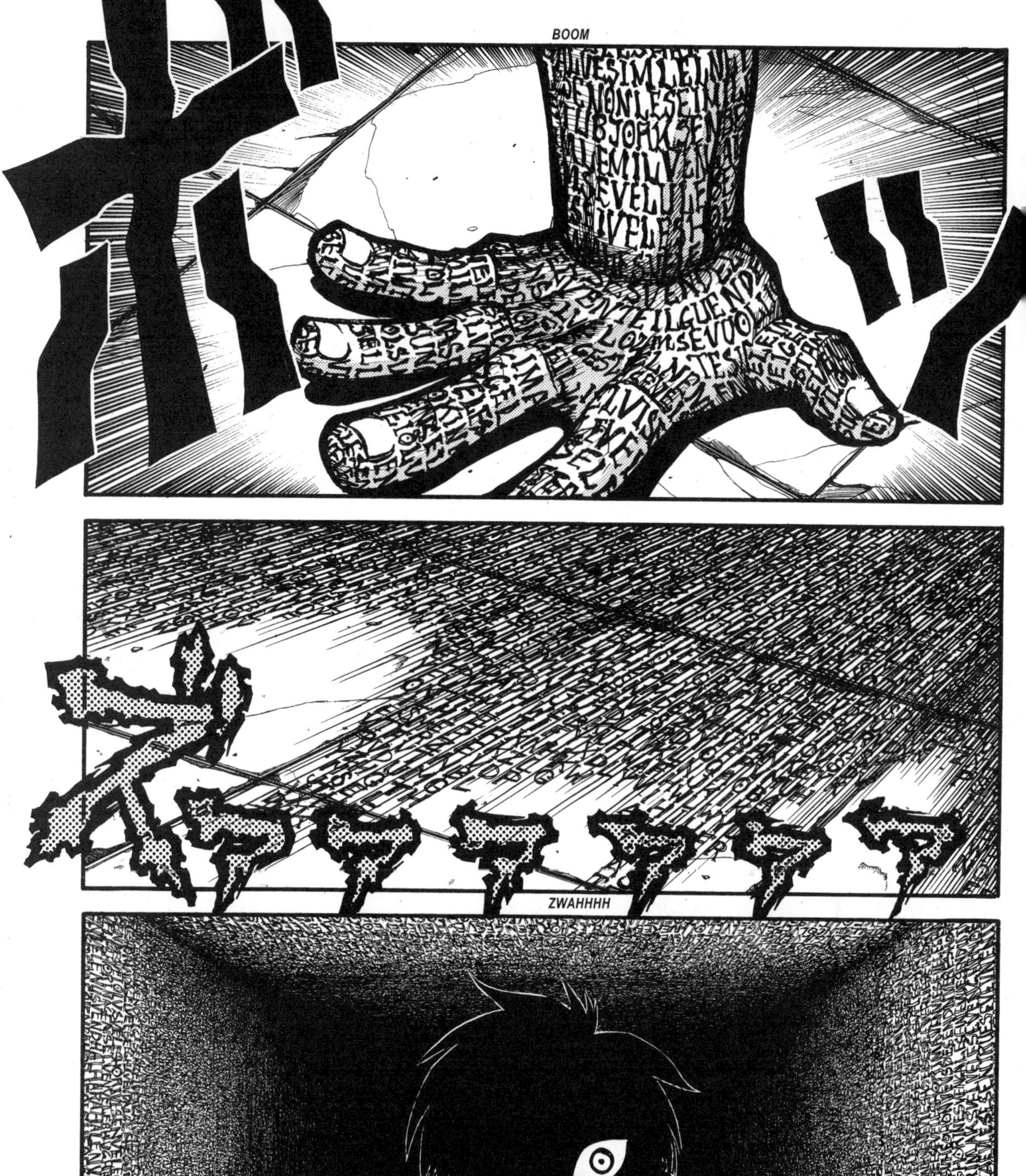
BOOM
ZWAHHHH

AAAAAAAAAAAA
OHMMMM
IT'S A HALLUCINATION!
IT'S A HALLUCINATION!
IT'S A HALLUCINATION!
IT'S A HALLUCINATION!
HALLUCINATION, IT'S A HALLUCINATION!
IT'S A HALLUCINATION, A LIE!
IT'S AN ILLUSION!!
DON'T BE DECEIVED!
FURTHER IN!!
FURTHER!
DEEPER!!

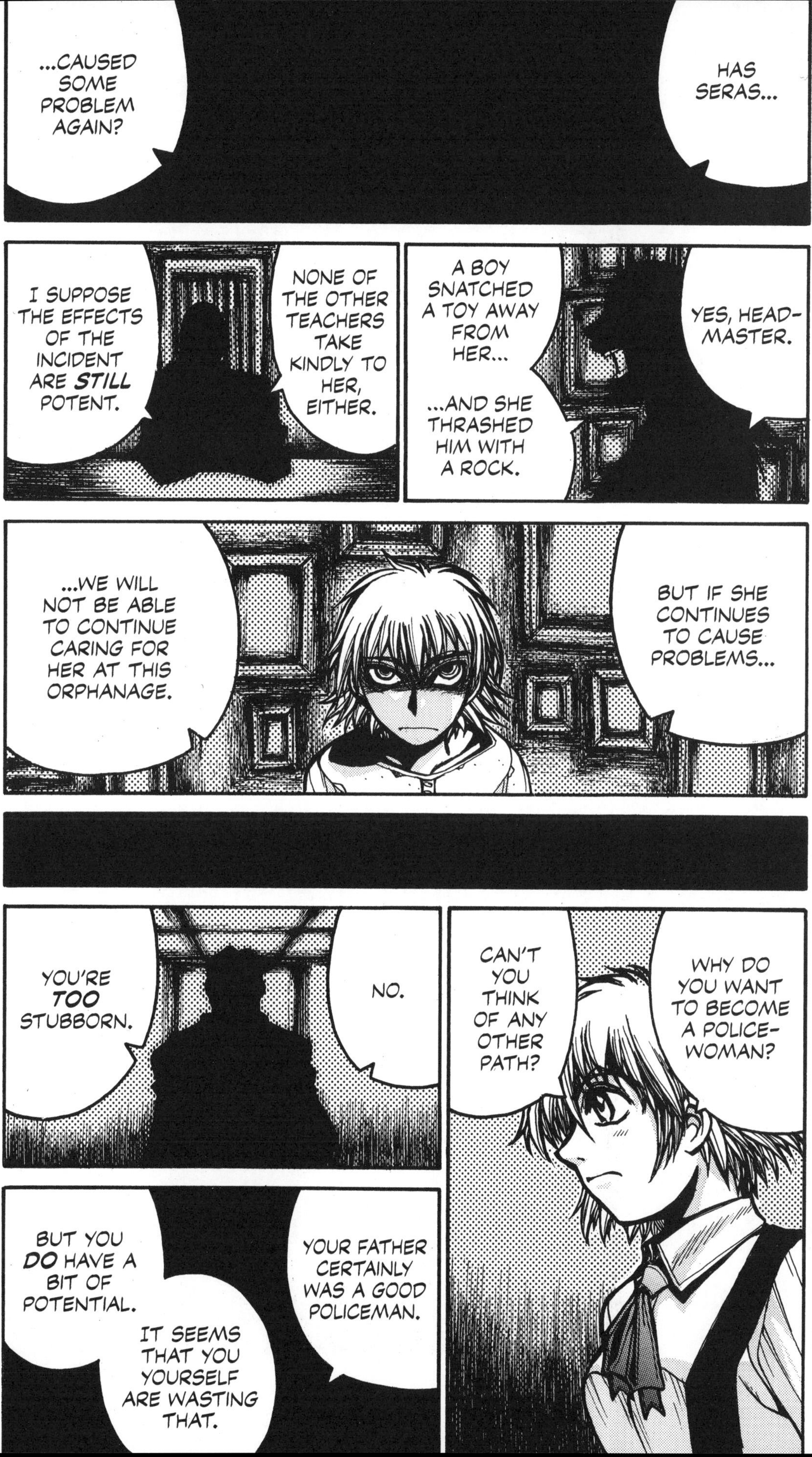
HAS SERAS...
...CAUSED SOME PROBLEM AGAIN?
YES, HEAD-MASTER.
A BOY SNATCHED A TOY AWAY FROM HER...
...AND SHE THRASHED HIM WITH A ROCK.
NONE OF THE OTHER TEACHERS TAKE KINDLY TO HER, EITHER.
I SUPPOSE THE EFFECTS OF THE INCIDENT ARE **STILL** POTENT.
BUT IF SHE CONTINUES TO CAUSE PROBLEMS...
...WE WILL NOT BE ABLE TO CONTINUE CARING FOR HER AT THIS ORPHANAGE.
WHY DO YOU WANT TO BECOME A POLICE-WOMAN?
CAN'T YOU THINK OF ANY OTHER PATH?
NO.
YOU'RE **TOO** STUBBORN.
YOUR FATHER CERTAINLY WAS A GOOD POLICEMAN.
BUT YOU **DO** HAVE A BIT OF POTENTIAL.
IT SEEMS THAT YOU YOURSELF ARE WASTING THAT.

ORDER 50 / END

EHEE HEE, HEY, **HEY!**
YOU DEAD, **COPPER?**
YOU DEAD? YOU DEAD?
YEAH.
HE'S **PLENTY** DEAD ALRIGHT.
IS HE DEAD? IS HE DEAD?
THIS IS WHAT HAPPENS TO A PUNK COP...
...WHO GETS IN TOO DEEP. GOT THAT?
FUCKIN' PIG. YOU REGRET IT NOW, FUCKIN' PIG?

ORDER 51

LAST MISSION

LISTEN VERY CAREFULLY TO ME, SERAS!!
NO MATTER WHAT, STAY IN HERE.
MUM!
MU...!
MUM!
MU...!
BANG
BABANG
BANG
......!
......!
......!
......!
......!

AHH
AH
AH
AH
DASH
AH
AH
AH
AH
!!
GRAB
VOOM

SHUNK
GYAHHHH!
!!
GOD-
FORSAKEN...
...LITTLE
BRAT!!
WHPP
BLAM

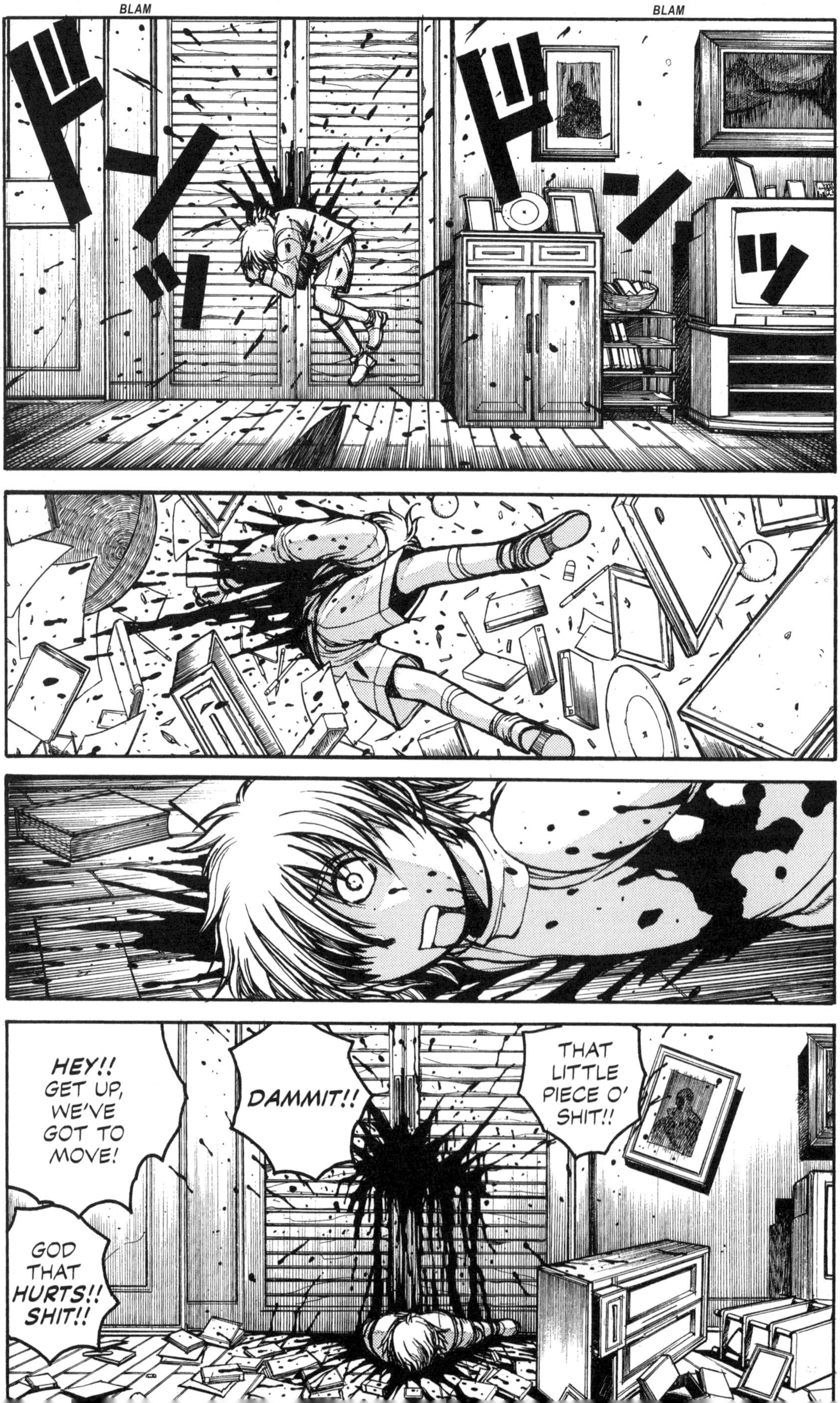
BLAM
BLAM
ドーン
ドーンッ
THAT LITTLE PIECE O' SHIT!!
DAMMIT!!
HEY!! GET UP, WE'VE GOT TO MOVE!
GOD THAT HURTS!! SHIT!!

BLOODY 'ELL! THIS DIDN'T EVEN SEEM WORTH IT.
I'M GONNA RAPE THE OLD BAG!
SHE'S DEAD, YOU ASS.
NO PROBLEM, SHE'S STILL WARM.
RRIP
RIP
KREEK KREEK
KREEK
KREEK
KREEK
KREEK

HELLSING
AH
AH
AH
AH
AH
AH
AH
GOOD MORNING, LITTLE SERAS!!
DID YOU HAVE SVEET DREAMS?!

SHOKK

AH
AH
AH
AHHHAH
WHRRRL
VONE MORE!
VONE MOOORE!!
ZASH

AH HAHH HAHA! ♡
VHAT A TOUGH VENCH YOU ARE!!
WHUMP
YANK
SHPP

KSSSH
SLASH
AH
AH
AH
AHH
AH

FILTH SCU
SLOPPY SLUT,
AH
AH
AH
AH
AHH
AH

NOW, THENNN.
MAYBE, JUST MAYBE...
...I FINISH YOU OFF NOW.
ボタ
PLIP
ボタ
PLIP
SHOVE OFF, 'AG.
ボタ
PLIP

ORDER 51 / END

ORDER 52
GET AWAY
Pip Vern
Live up to
BRITANICA COWBOYS

AGH
GH
AH
AHH
H
AGH
AGH
AH
ZHA
ZHA
ZHA
JUST LOOK AT YOU.
THIS ISN'T VHAT I VAS EXPECTING AT ALL.

WHOK
VMM
HAHAHA! VHAT ARE YOU?! A BUG?! A FROG?!
HNAHH
KAHA
GUH...
GAHA!
SHLLK
NOW I THINK I'FE HAD ENOUGH FUN!!
TIME TO STOP DAWDLING UND TAKE THAT HEAD OF YOURS!!

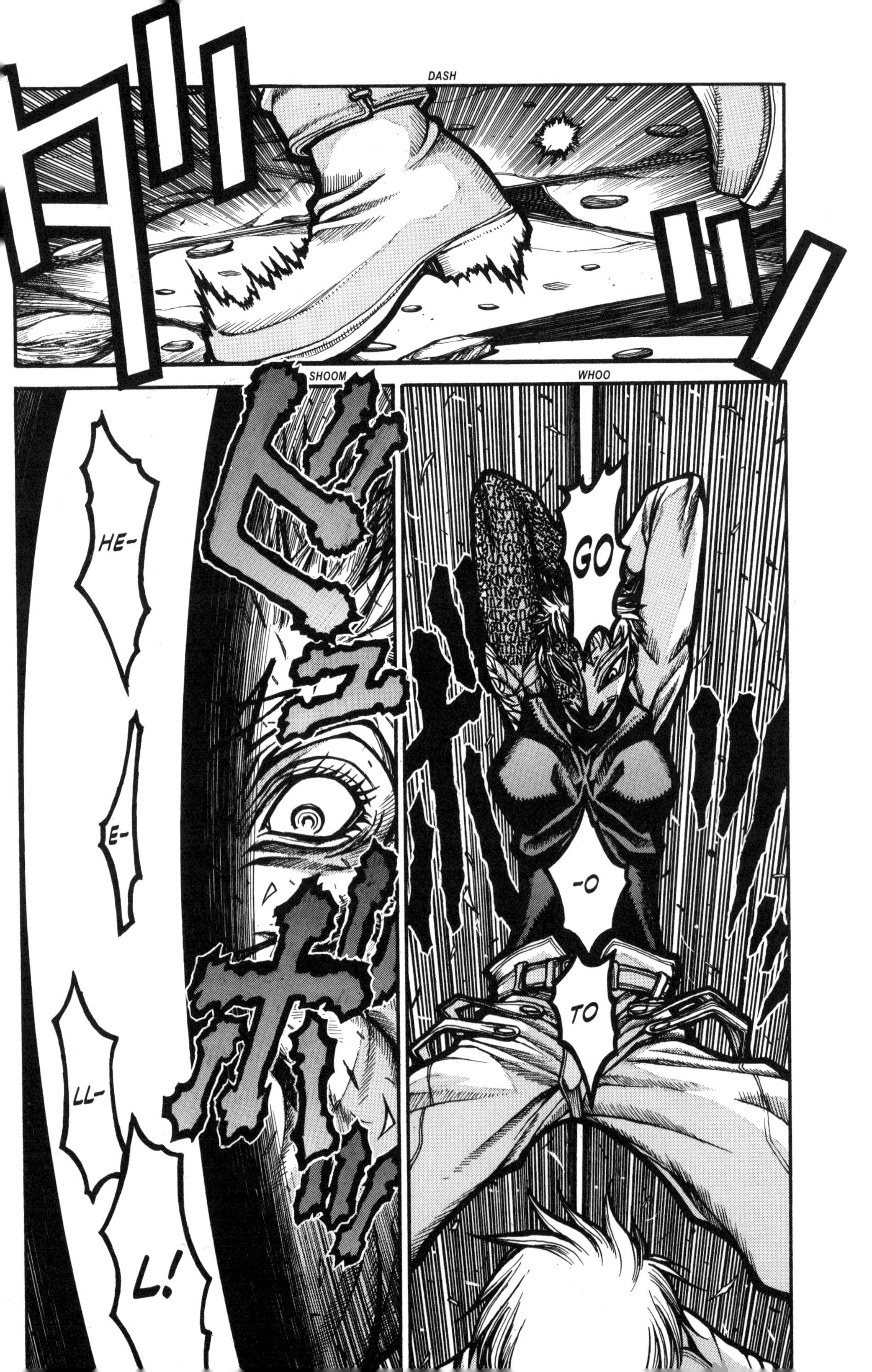
DASH
WHOO
GO
-O
TO
SHOOM
HE-
E-
LL-
L!

SHOVE OFF, 'AG.
VHA...
?!
BAM
WHOO

WHOK
VH...
T
A
CHAK
'ERE'S A BONUS!!
KLIK

BLAM
BLAM
BLAM
ZHAAAAA
YOU TALK TOO MUCH!!
BLOODY 'AG!!

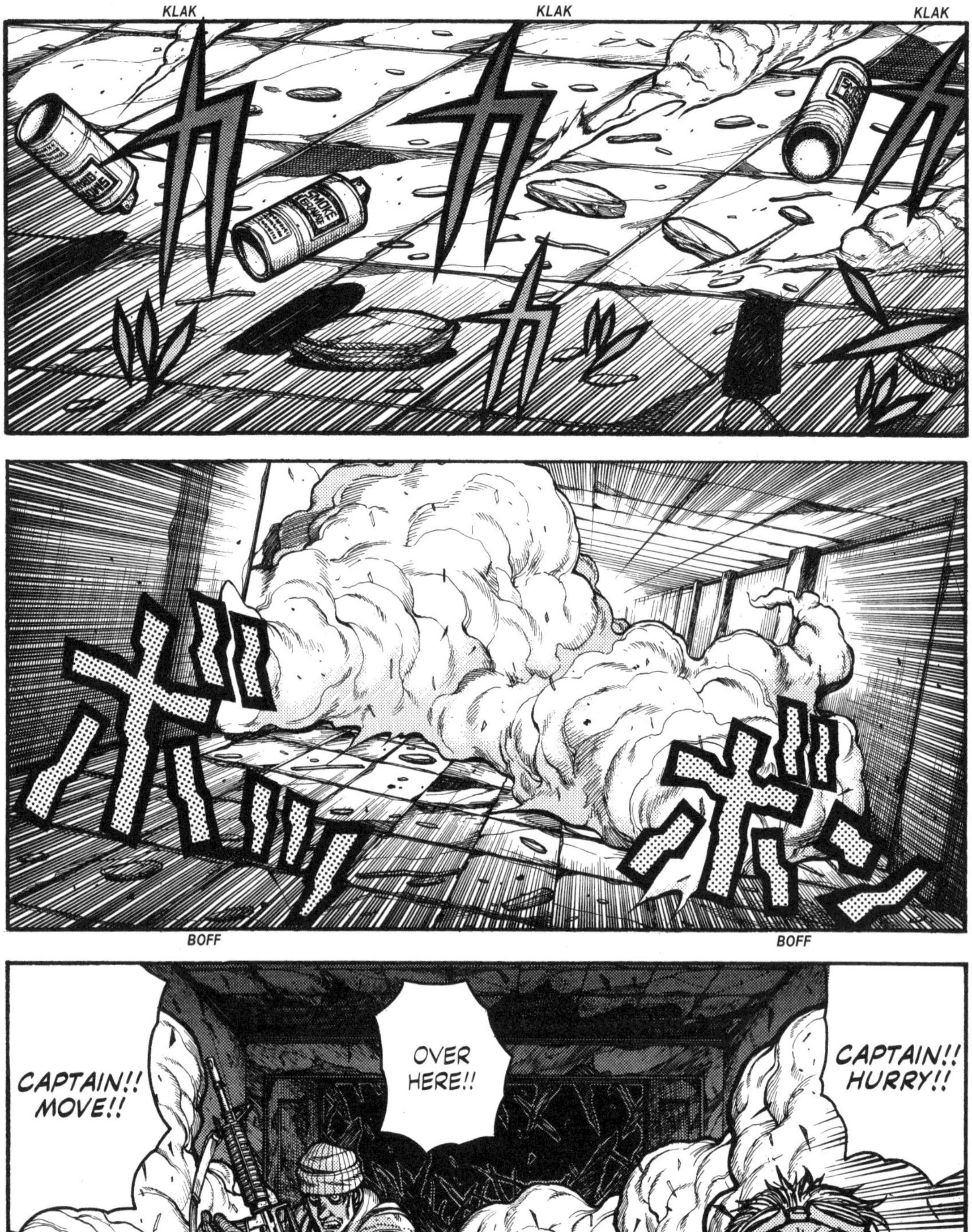
KLAK
KLAK
KLAK
BOFF
BOFF
CAPTAIN!! HURRY!!
OVER HERE!!
CAPTAIN!! MOVE!!
BSSSSSHHHH

GRAB
TALLY 'O!
CAP...TA--
VER...NE--
KEEP QUIET!!

ダッ
TMP
ダッ
TMP
ダッ
TMP
ダッ
TMP
hahhh
hahhh
hahhh
hahhh
hahhh
hahhh
hahhh
hahhh
ボタッ
PLIP
ボタッ
PLIP
ビキッ
KNCH
ミシッ
GRIND
hahhh
hahhh
hahhh
hahhh
hahhh
hahhh
ボタッ
PLIP
ボタッ
PLIP
ボタタッ
PLAP
hahhh
hahhh
hahhh
hahhh
hahhh
hahhh
hahhh

SHFF
CHAK
CHAK
CHAK
CHAK
CHAK
CHAK CHAK
BLA
BLAM
BLAM

STAGGER
!!
GH...!
BAM
GRRN
MERR-
GRRN
GRRN
DEEE!
HRRN

MR. VERNEDEAD!
MR. VERNEDEAD!
D-DON'T BOTHER WITH ME!
R-RUN FOR IT!
I TOLD YOU...
TO...
...SHUT UP!!
TATTA
TATTA
TATTA
TATTA
FUCK YOU!!
BASTARD!!
BSHH
BSHH
DM
DM
DM
DM

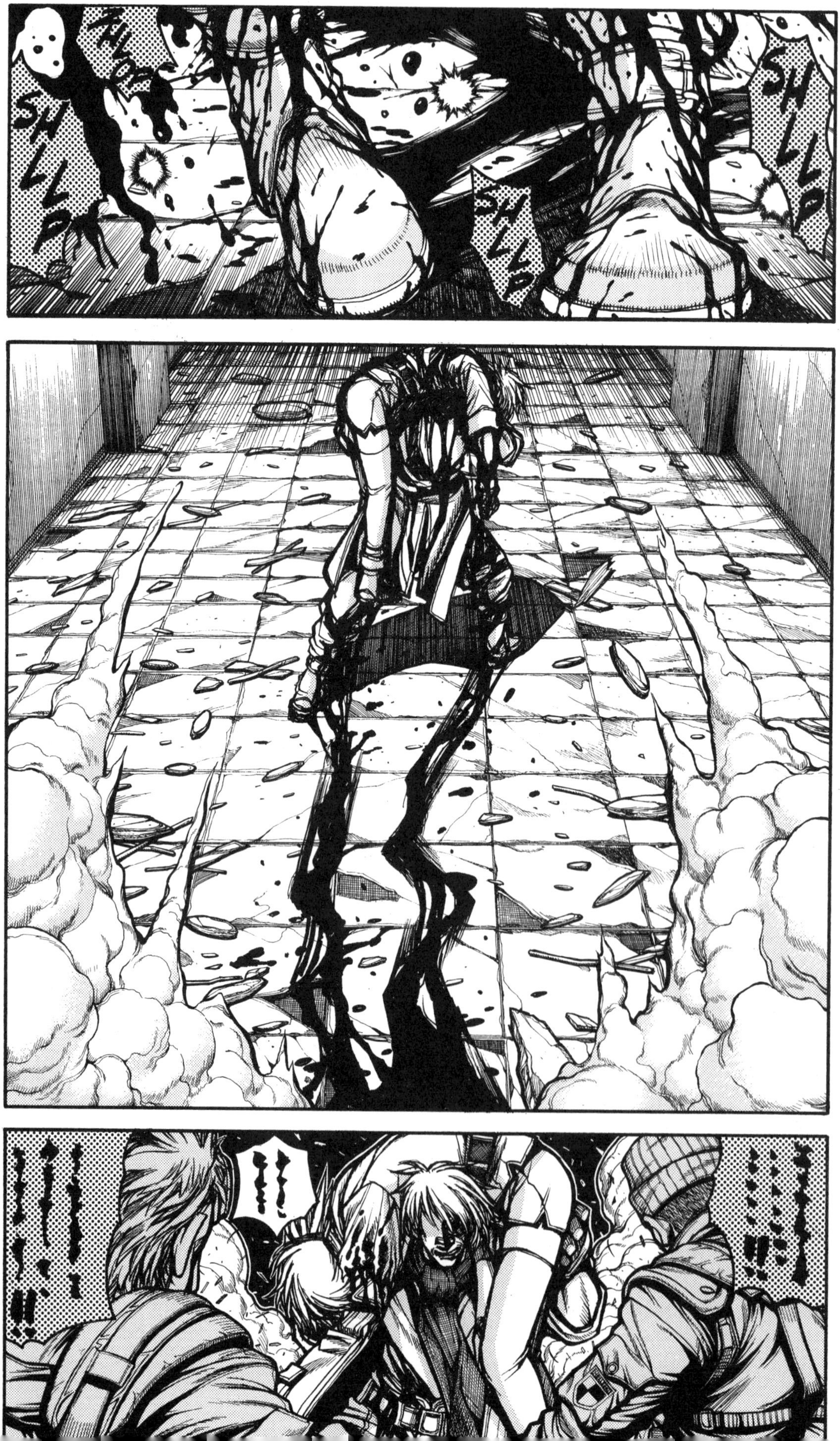
SHLLP
SHLLP
SHLLP

CHONK
KUH
OH
OO
KAH

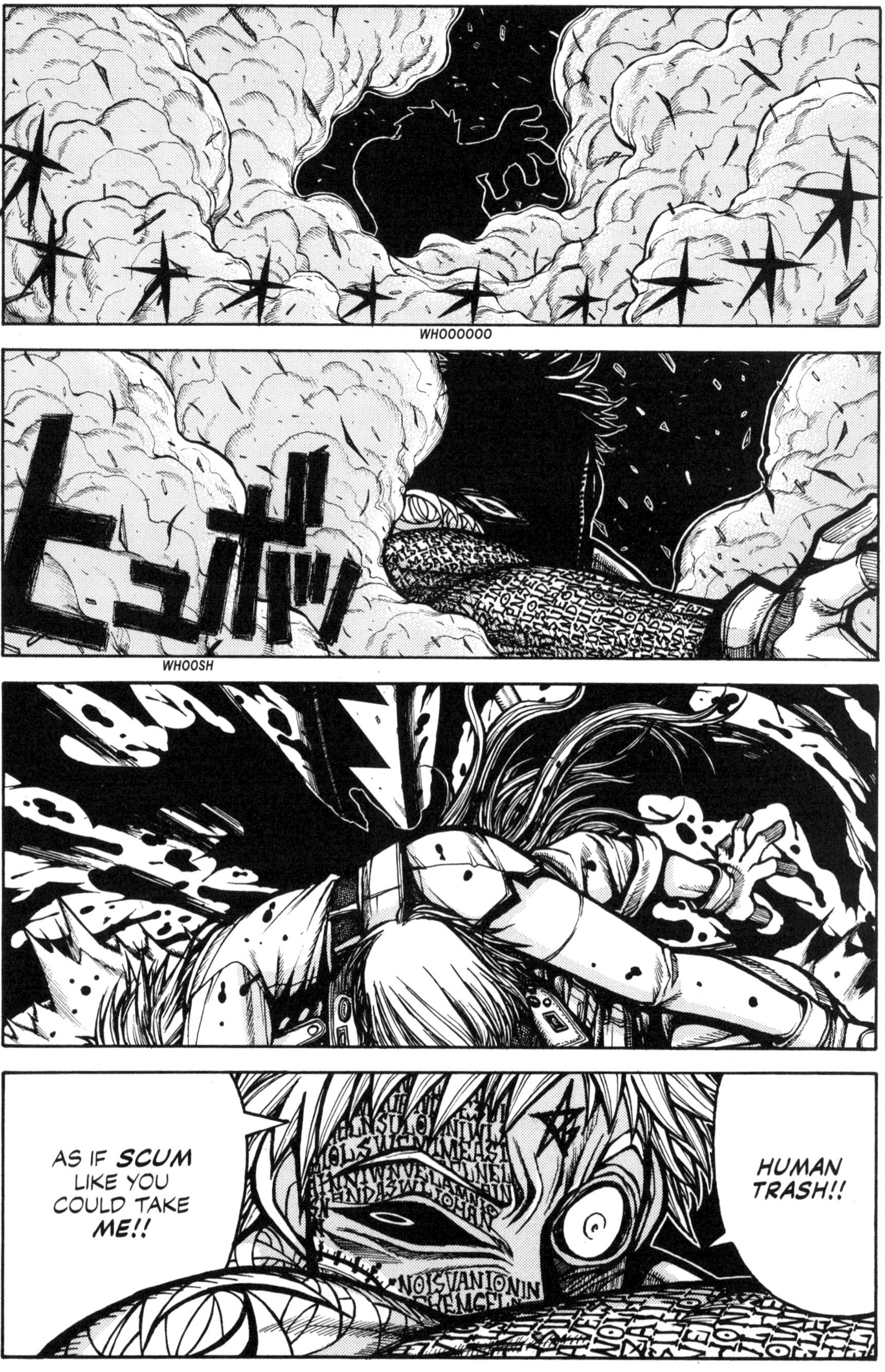
WHOOOOOO
ヒュボッ
WHOOSH
HUMAN TRASH!!
AS IF SCUM LIKE YOU COULD TAKE ME!!

MR. VERNEDEAD!
MR. VERNEDEAD!
S...SILLY GIRL.
HEH HEHEH... YOU CAME TO SAVE ME...!
AND I WENT AND SAVED YOU. 'O...'OPELESS.

PTEP...!
VERNEDEAD!
MR. VERNEDEAD!
V...!

...KEH! HAHA!
GAHA! GOHO!
ZAT WAS FOR MAKING IT EASY.
KEHEHEH!
I *FINALLY* STOLE A KISS...!
DON'T CRY NOW, SERAS.
YOU'RE ONE TOUGH WOMAN.
FEED ON ME.
ズル...
SHLFF
FEED ON ME...
...AND LET'S BEAT ZEM TOGEZER, SERAS.

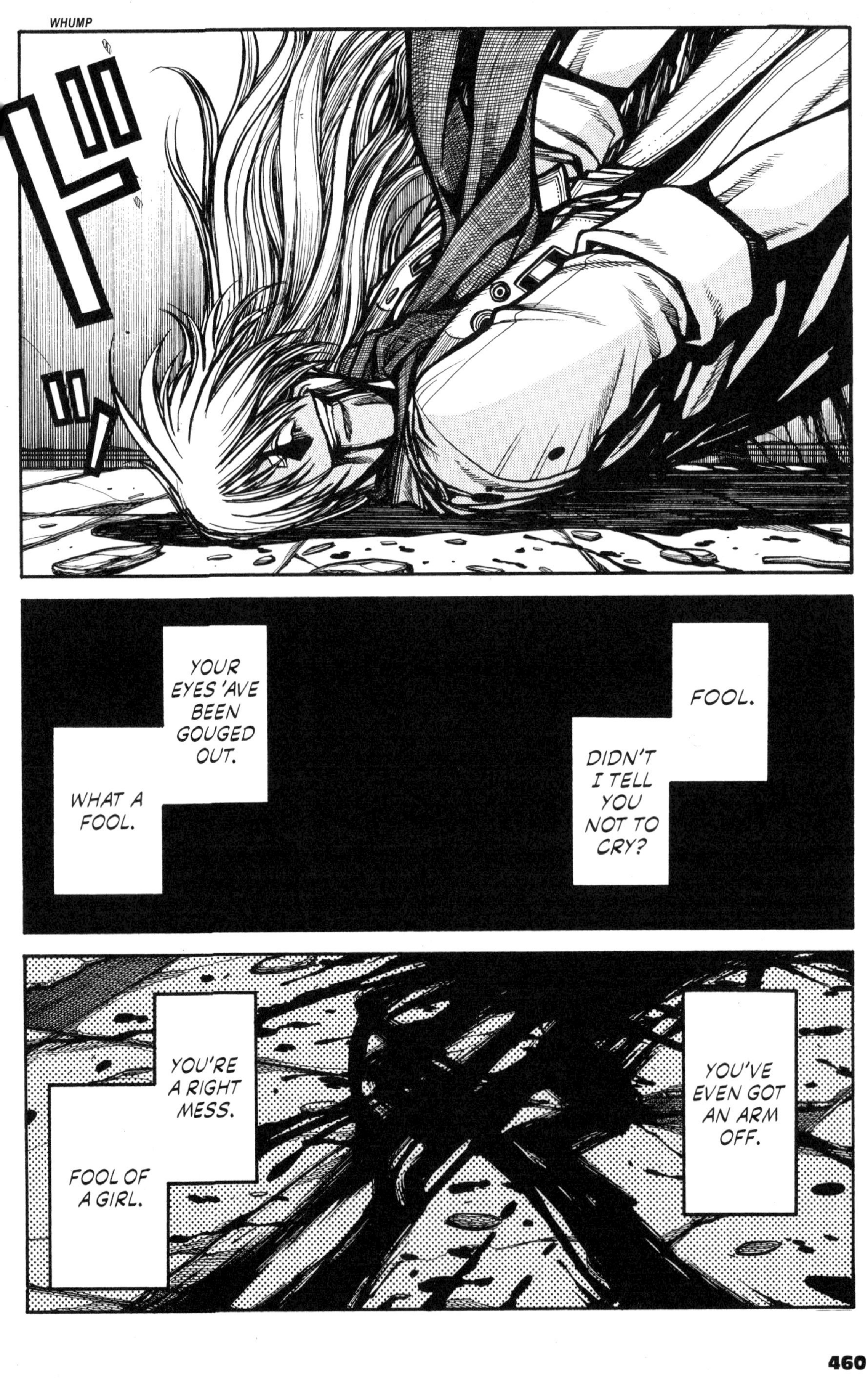
WHUMP
FOOL.
DIDN'T I TELL YOU NOT TO CRY?
YOUR EYES 'AVE BEEN GOUGED OUT.
WHAT A FOOL.
YOU'VE EVEN GOT AN ARM OFF.
YOU'RE A RIGHT MESS.
FOOL OF A GIRL.

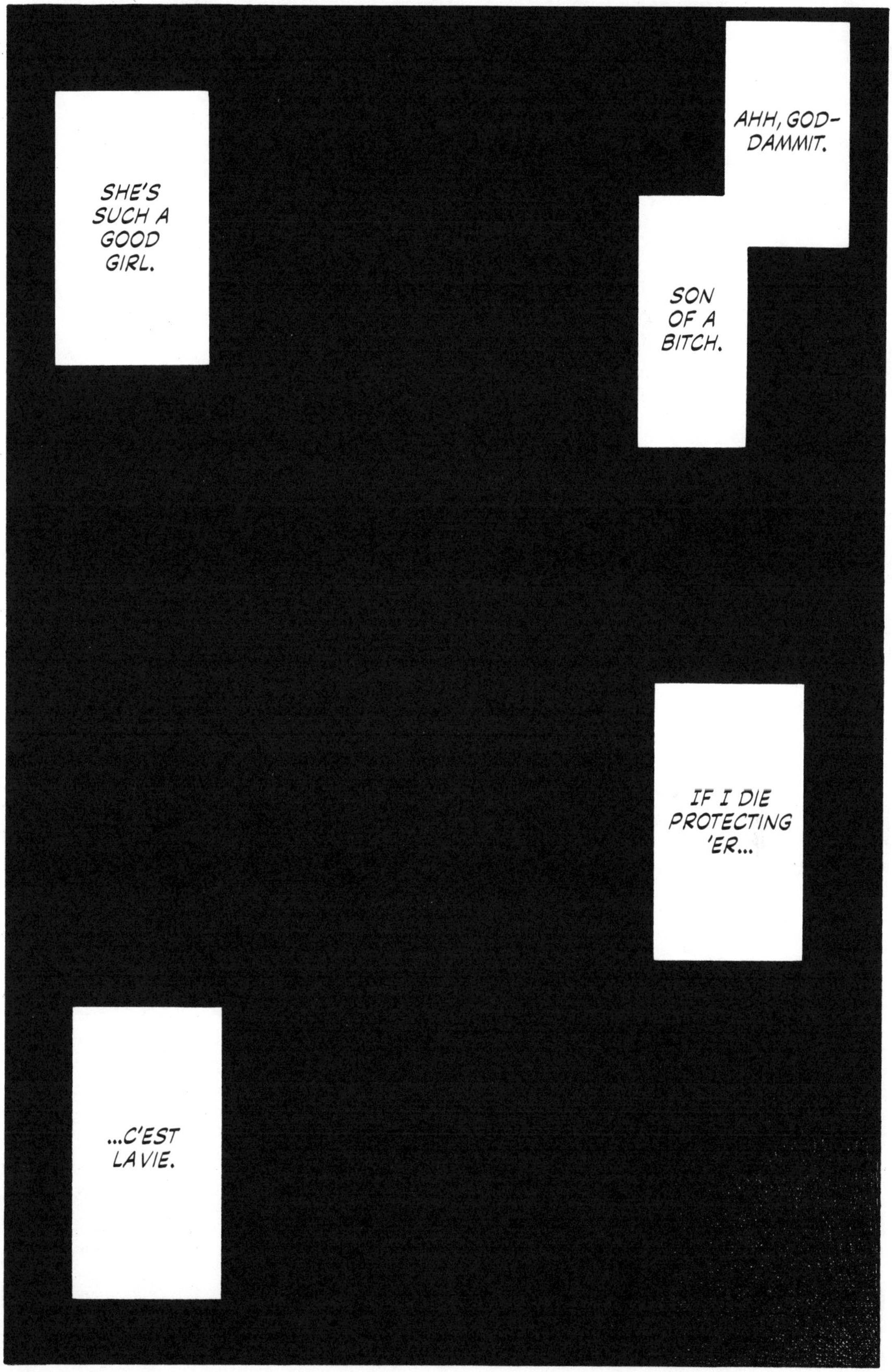
AHH, GOD-DAMMIT.
SON OF A BITCH.
SHE'S SUCH A GOOD GIRL.
IF I DIE PROTECTING 'ER...
...C'EST LA VIE.

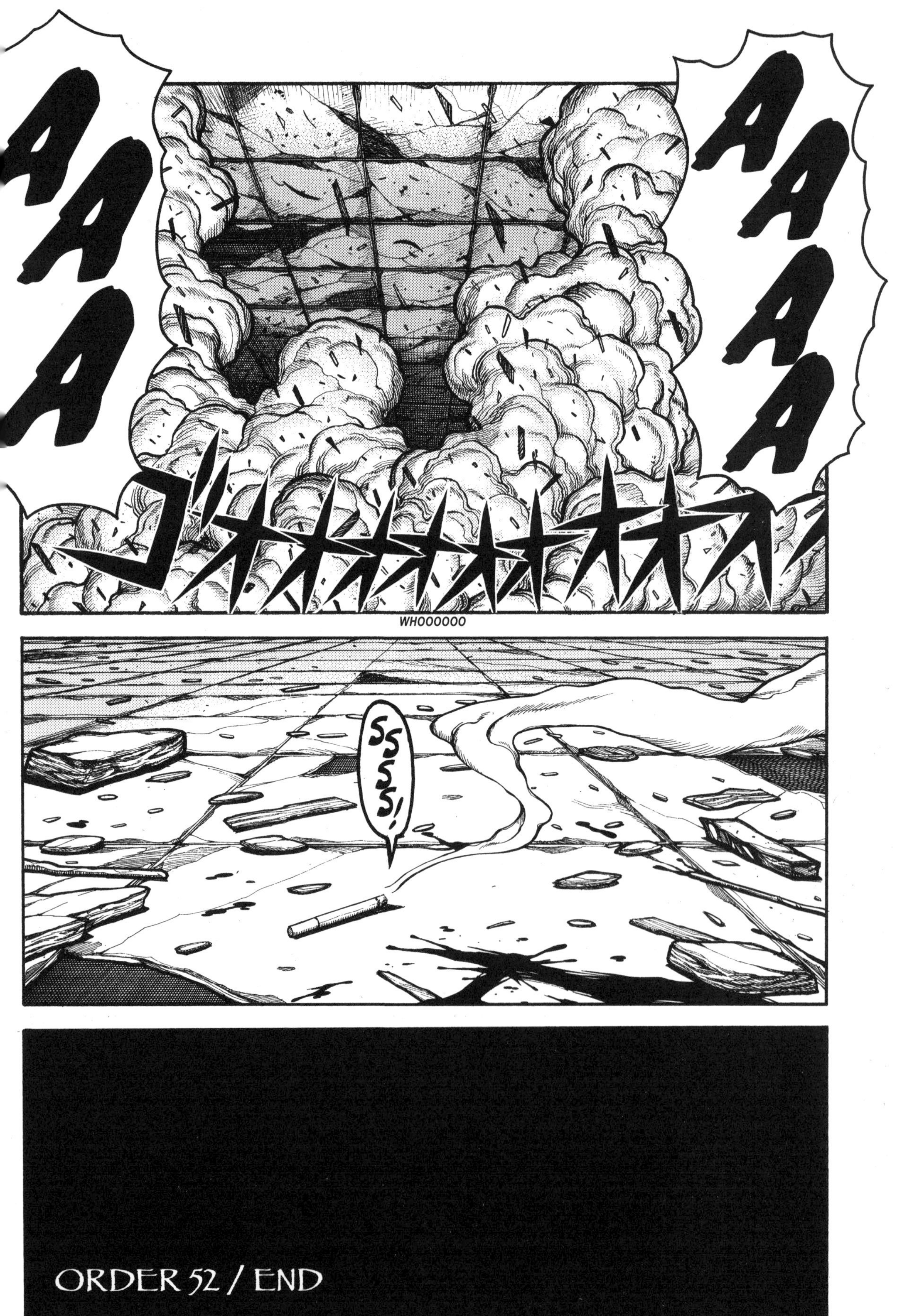
AAAA
AAAAA
WHOOOOOO
SSSS!
ORDER 52 / END

ORDER 53

UWAHH
AH
AHH
AGHAAAGH
AH
AHH
AH
AH
SHIT! SHIT!
NO...
...CAP-TAIN!
AHH
AH
AH
オオオオオオオオ
WHOOOO

UWAH
AHH
AHH
AH
HH
AH
AH
HH
AH
ORDER 53 YAKSA
ヤシャ
KATZ
カッ
IT MAKES YOU CRY, EHH?!

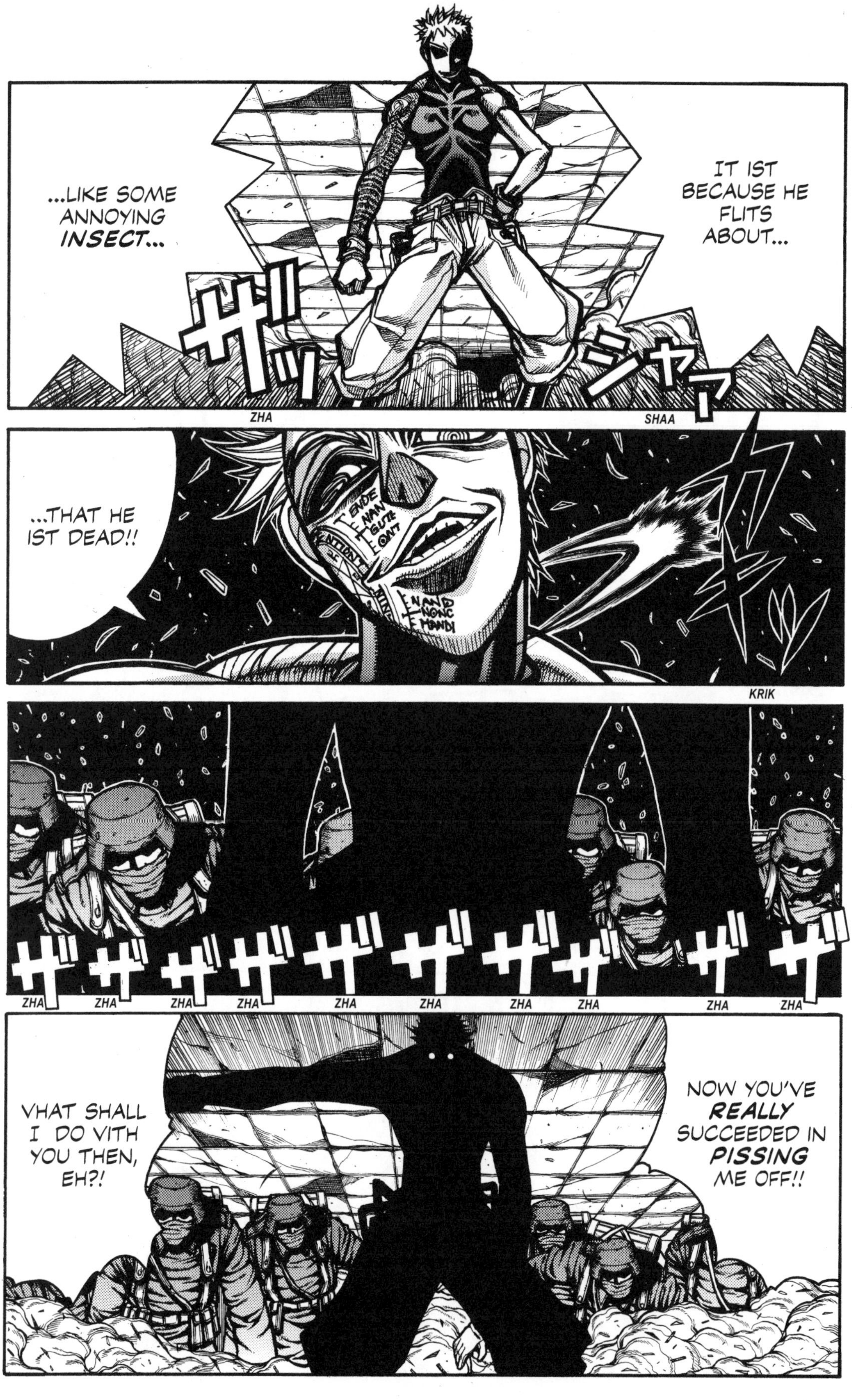
IT IST BECAUSE HE FLITS ABOUT...
...LIKE SOME ANNOYING *INSECT*...
ZHA
SHAA
...THAT HE IST DEAD!!
ENDE NAN GUTE OANT
NAND NONC HANDI
KRIK
ZHA
ZHA
ZHA
ZHA
ZHA
ZHA
ZHA
ZHA
ZHA
ZHA
NOW YOU'VE *REALLY* SUCCEEDED IN *PISSING* ME OFF!!
VHAT SHALL I DO VITH YOU THEN, EH?!

I'LL SVAT THE LITTLE BUZZING BUGS...
...VITH THE PALM OF MY HAND.
(hand opening)
UAH!
SH...!
SHIT-- SHIIIT!
THAT IST HOW A BUG'S LIFE...
...EEEE ENDS!
WHOM

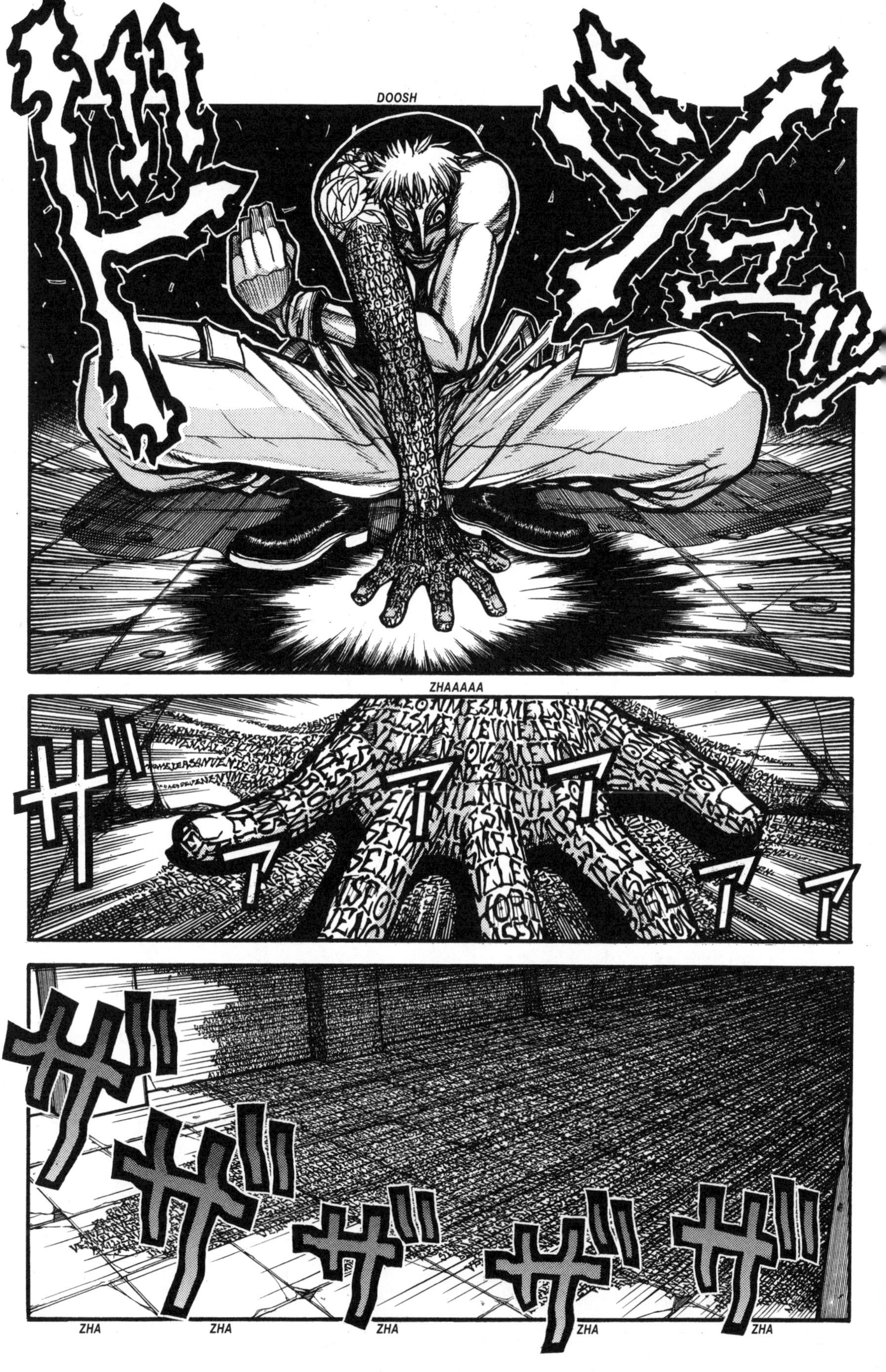
DOOSH
ZHAAAAA
ZHA
ZHA
ZHA
ZHA
ZHA

BOMM
OO
AHH!
AH!
AGAIN?!
AGAIN, DAMMIT?!
ZHA
ZHA
ZHA
ZHA
ZHA
ZHA

BUG, YOU SAID?!
YOU CALLED...
...THIS MAN AN INSECT?!
!!
I WON'T HAVE IT.
I WON'T HAVE IT!!
I WON'T HAVE IT!!

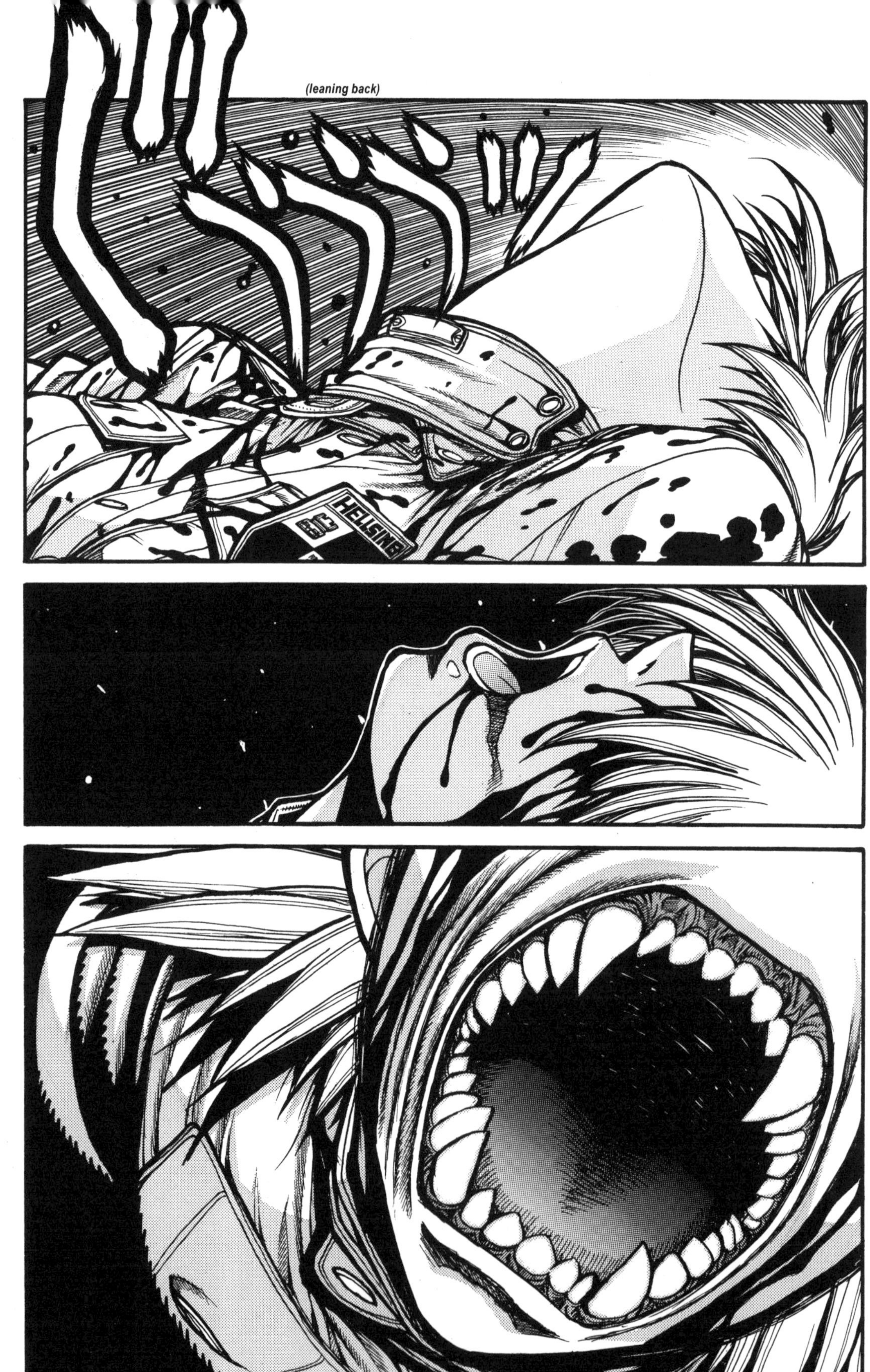
(leaning back)
HELLSING

CHNK

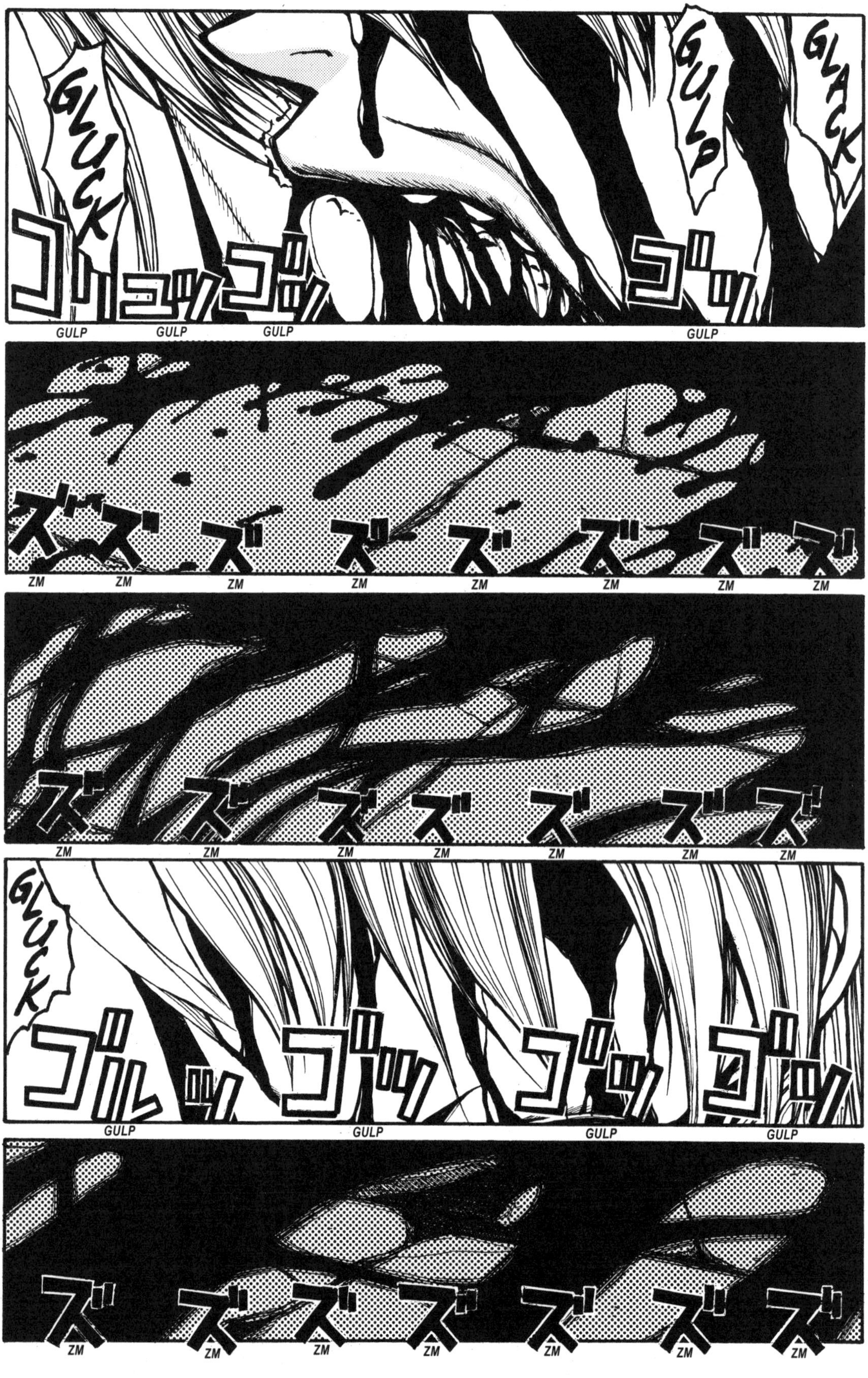
GLACK
GULP
ゴッ
GULP
ゴッ
GULP
ゴリュッ
GULP
GULP
GLUCK
ズズズズズズズズ
ZM ZM ZM ZM ZM ZM ZM ZM
ズズズズズズズ
ZM ZM ZM ZM ZM ZM ZM
ゴッ
GULP
ゴッ
GULP
ゴッ
GULP
ゴルッ
GULP
GLUCK
ズズズズズズズ
ZM ZM ZM ZM ZM ZM ZM

SHOOSH
ボタボタボタボタボタボ
PLIP
PLIP
PLIP
PLIP
PLIP
PLIP

ぼだッ
ぼだッ
ぼだ
BLUP
BLUP
BLUP

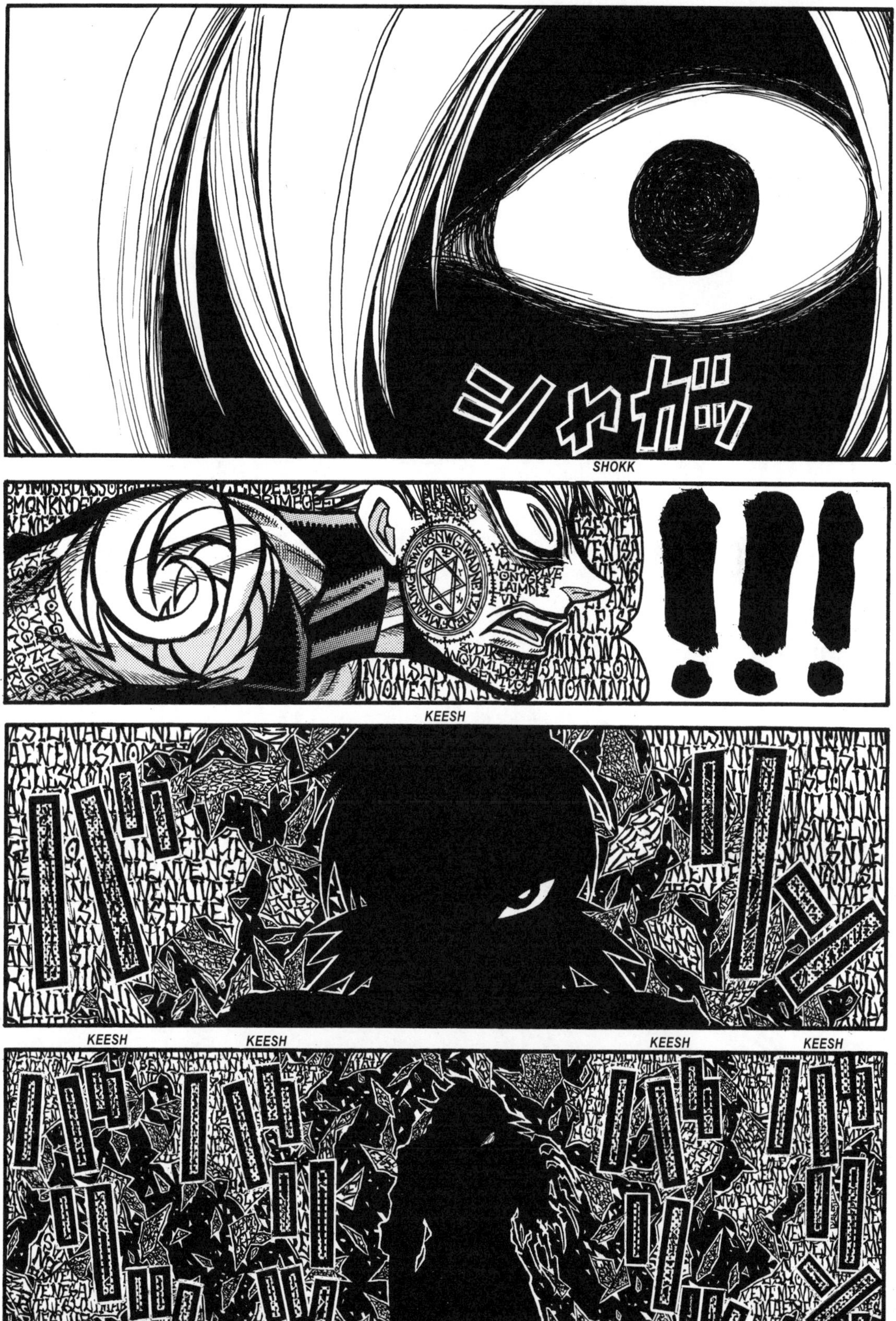
シャガッ
SHOKK
!!!
KEESH
KEESH
KEESH
KEESH
KEESH

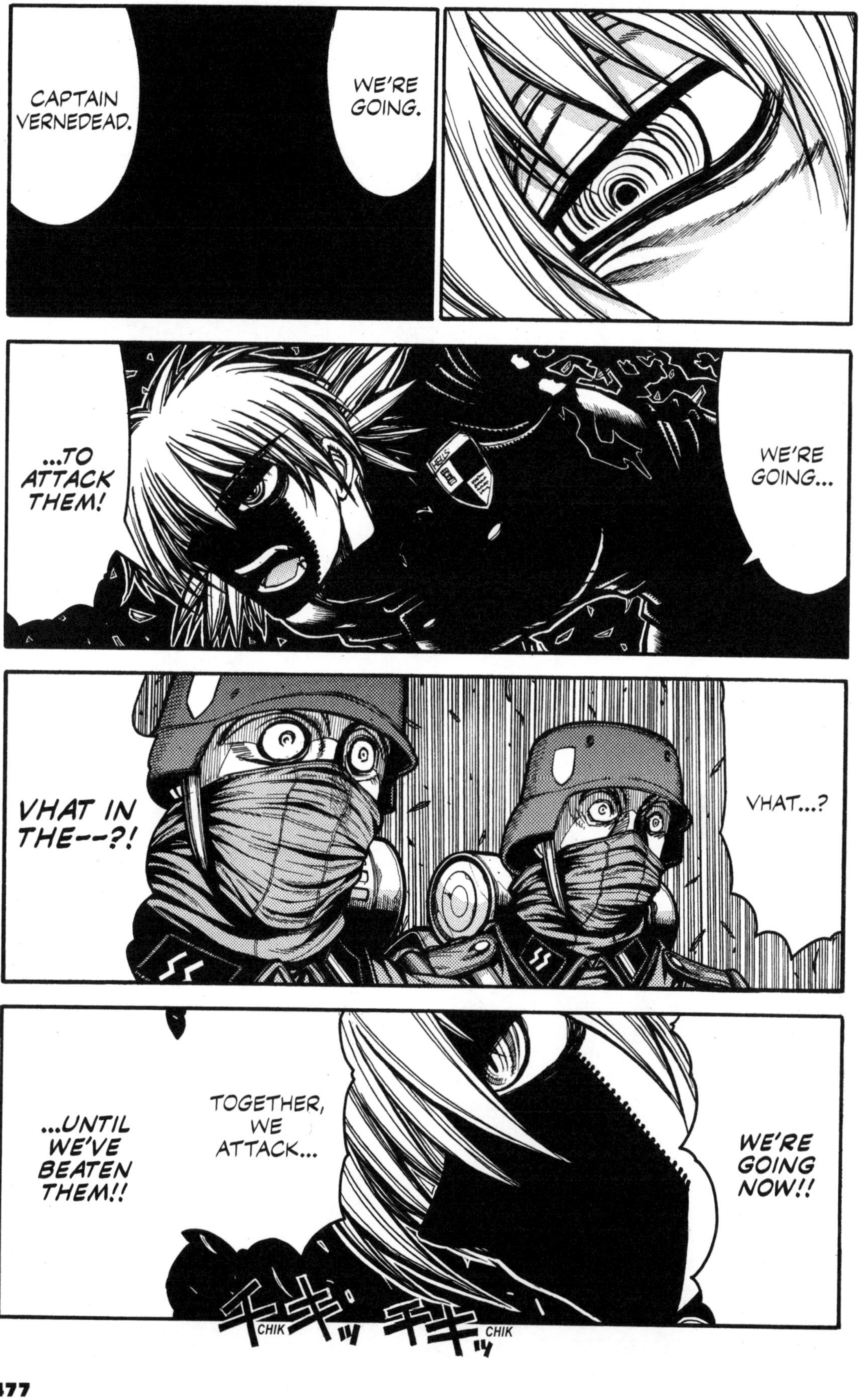
WE'RE GOING.
CAPTAIN VERNEDEAD.
WE'RE GOING...
...TO ATTACK THEM!
VHAT...?
VHAT IN THE--?!
WE'RE GOING NOW!!
TOGETHER, WE ATTACK...
...UNTIL WE'VE BEATEN THEM!!
CHIK
CHIK

LUNGE
FIRE!! FIRE!!
F-FIRE!!
GEBOBOBOBOBOBOBO
BOBOBO BOBO

OO!
ZHWAA
OOH

ORDER 53 / END

ORDER 54

VHAT?!
VHAT IST THIS?
THE SOLDIERS ARE TERRIFIED.
VAMPIRES, TERRIFIED!
VETERAN WAFFEN SS, WHO DOMINATED THE BATTLE-FIELD...
...UND DASHED RIGHT THROUGH ARTILLERY FIRE.
THEY'RE TERRIFIED OF ONE GIRL BEFORE THEIR EYES.
...OF A SINGLE GIRL COVERED HEAD TO FOOT IN VOUNDS!!
GREEEEEEEE
VHAT THE...
...HELL IST SHE?!

ORDER 54
THE MAN I LOVE

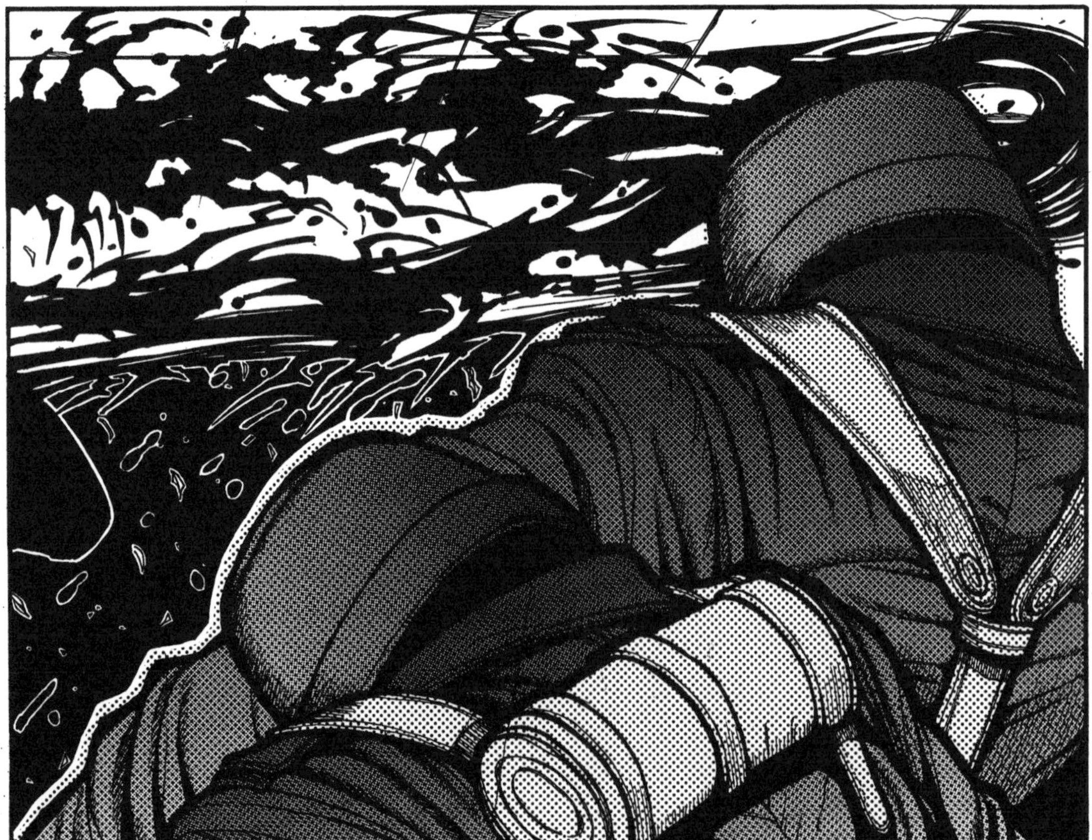

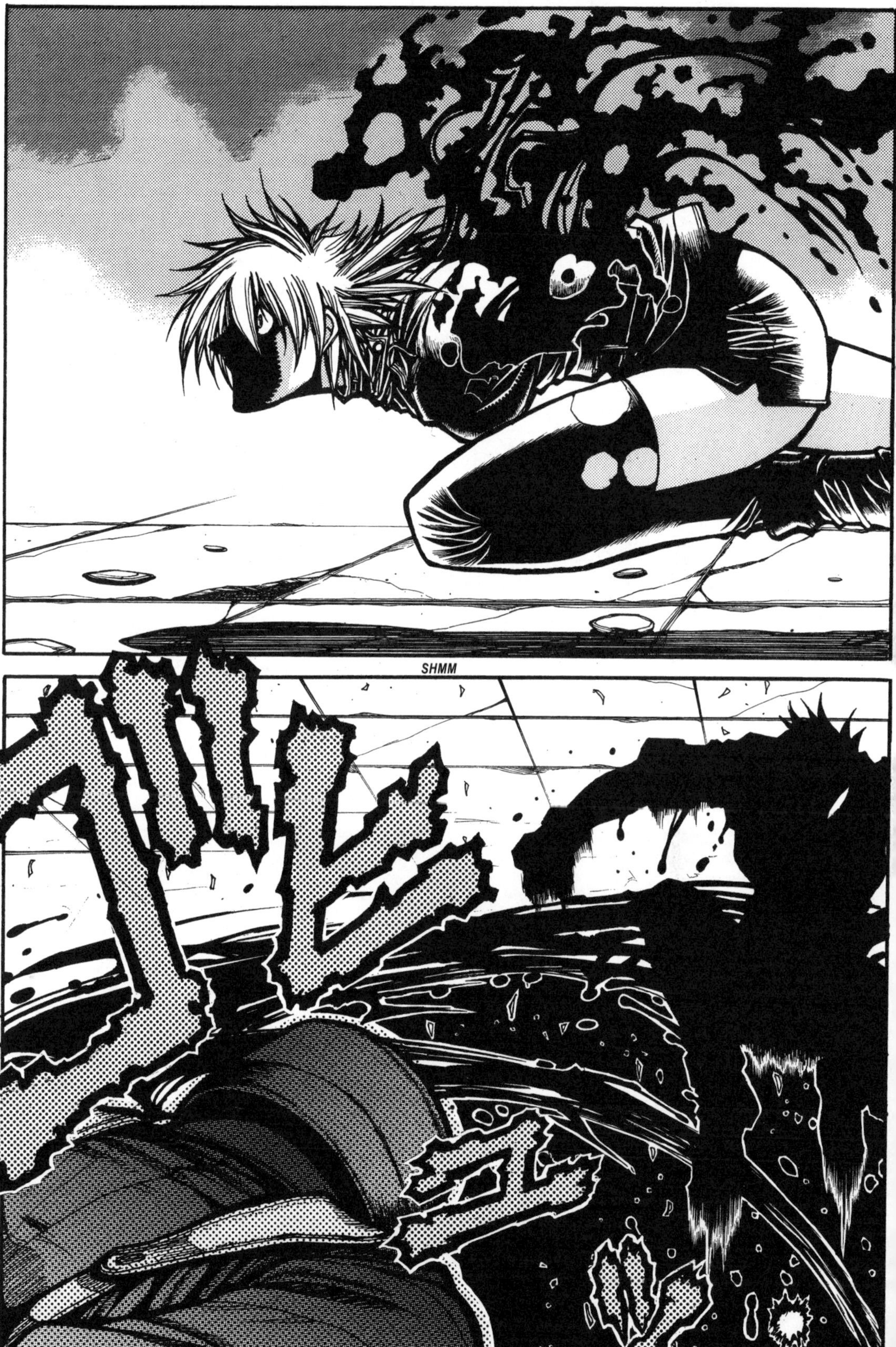
SHMM

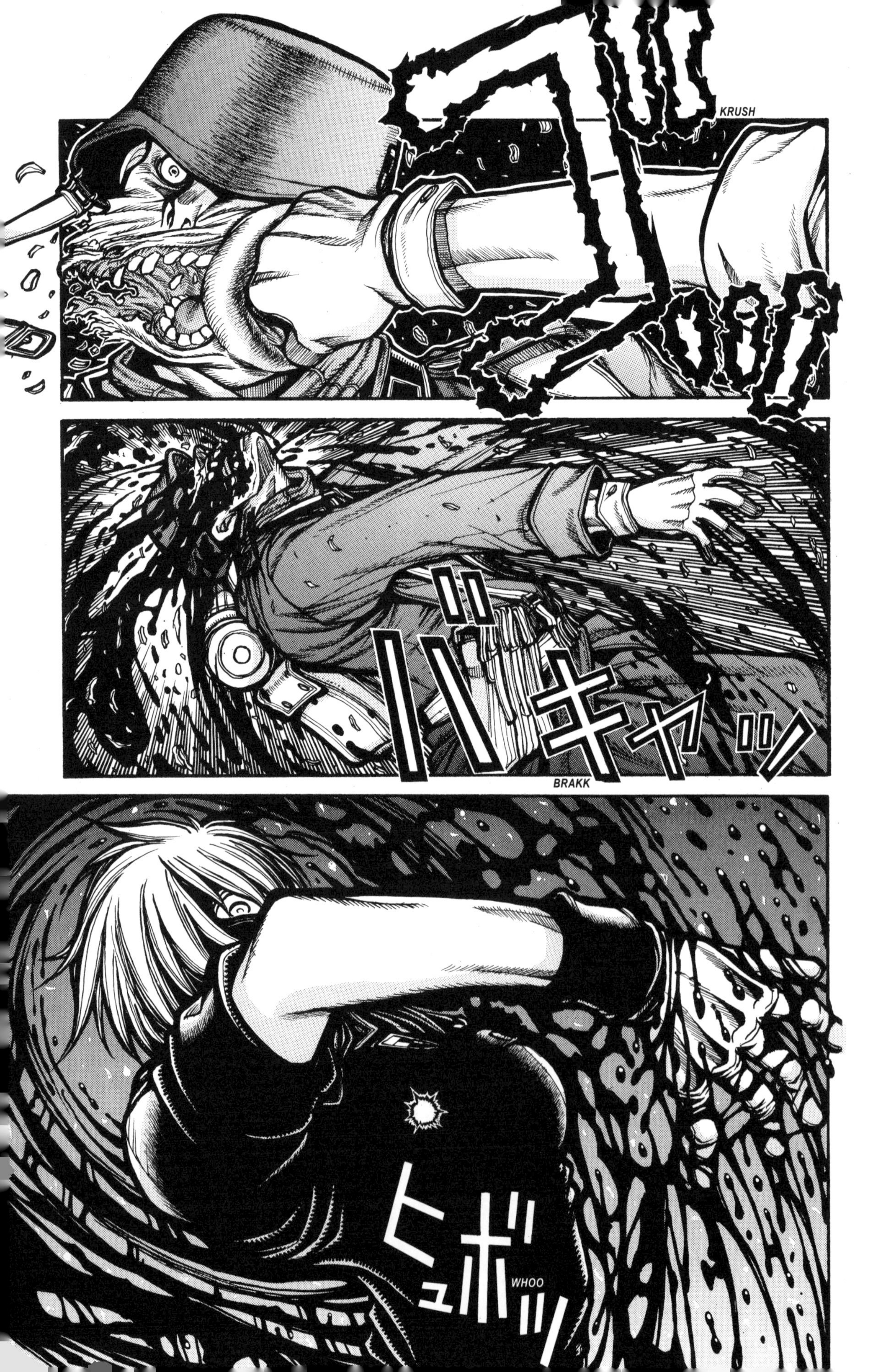
グシャッ
KRUSH
バキャッ
BRAKK
ヒュボッ
WHOO

WHOKK

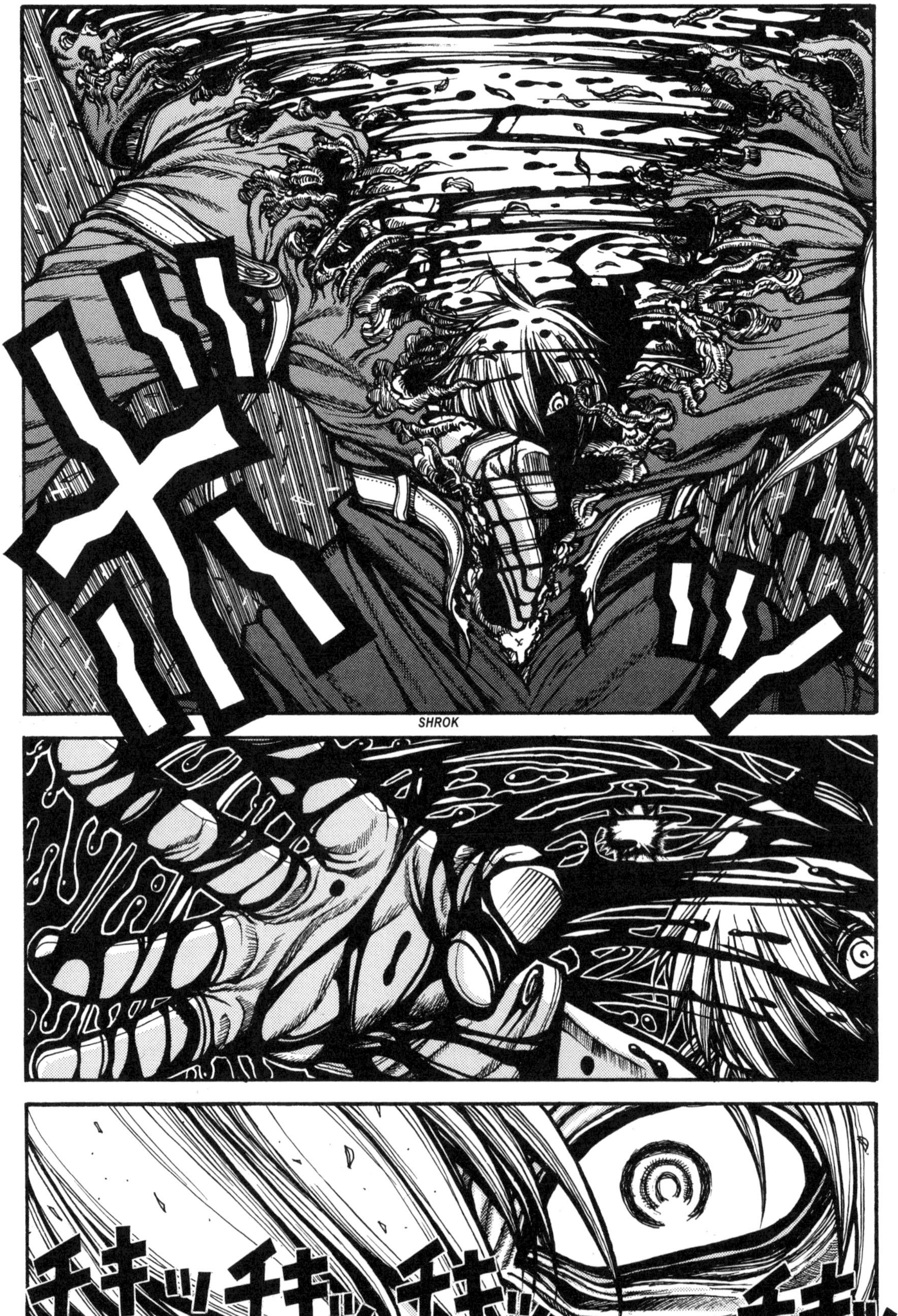
ズド
ッ
SHROK
チキッ
CHIK
チキッ
CHIK
チギッ
CHIK
チギッ
CHIK

WOKK
ORDER 54 / END

ORDER 55

SCHEISSE!!
SCHEISSE.
...THIS IST...
GRRN!
HRRRAAAAH
I DON'T REALLY UNDER-STAND, BUT...
...DEEP SH--

GRIND
GRIND
ギリギチギリ
OG...
MGH...!!
GRIND
ギリ
GOGHHH!!

ギリ…ッ
GRIND
BUOH...!
OGH... BOH!
BOHH
BOGH!
BH!
ギ…
GRRN

⚜ ORDER 55

OGRE BATTLE

(leaning back)
CHOMP
GHEE!
EEEEE!
PUH

I'M NOT ABOUT TO DRINK...
...ONE DROP, ONE BIT, ONE MICROLITER OF YOUR BLOOD!
ZHA ZHA ZHA
ZHA ZHA ZHA
I WON'T!!
I WON'T!!
AGH...
OGH...
OGH
OGHHGGH-AGHH
WHAM

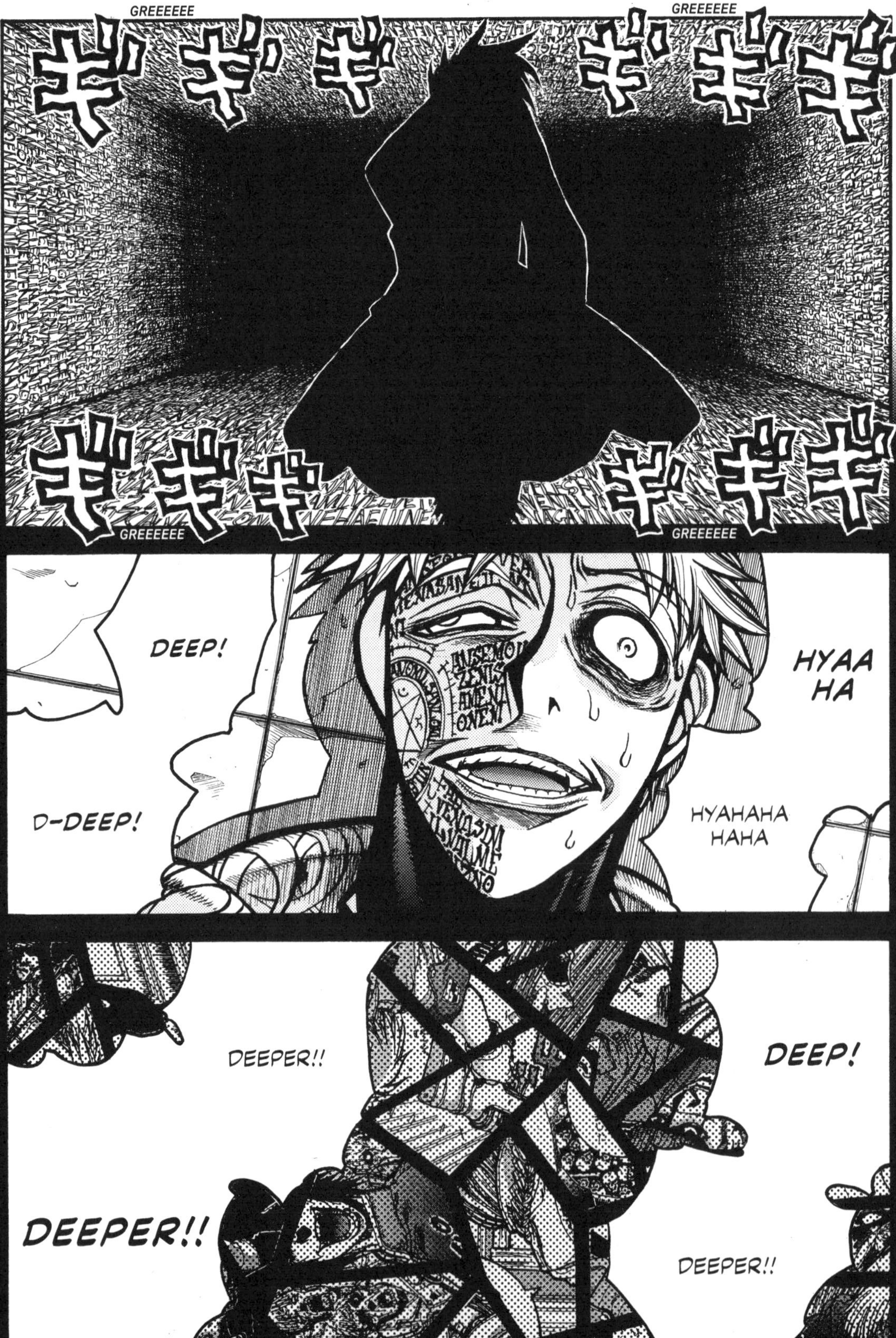
GREEEEEE
ギギギ
GREEEEEE
ギギギ
GREEEEEE
ギギギ
GREEEEEE
ギギギ
HYAA HA
HYAHAHA HAHA
DEEP!
D-DEEP!
DEEP!
DEEPER!!
DEEPER!!
DEEPER!!

ZOOSH
VH--
WHO IST THIS?!
VHAT?!
VHAT IST THIS?!
CHIK CHIK CHIK CHIK
NO!! THIS IST NOT HER!
THEY'RE BLENDING TOGETHER!
THE "MEMORIES"...! THE "SPIRIT"...!
VAHT!? WHO!? WHOSE SPIRIT IST THIS!?
CHIK CHIK CHIK CHIK

THE MAN I CALLED UN INSECT!!
IT'S HIM!!
THIS IST VHAT THEY MEAN.
THE SUCKING OF BLOOD, THE GIVING OF BLOOD,
BLOOD IST THE CURRENCY OF THE SOUL, THE DAGUERREO-TYPE OF VILL.
HOW ARE YOU? STILL ALIVE?
SCHRÖDINGER!!
I'M EVERYVHERE, UND NOVHERE.
DON'T BE SO SURPRISED.
ZORIN, I HAF A MESSAGE FOR YOU FROM THE MAJORRRR.

"...UND LOST PRECIOUS SOLDIERS IST IN TURN THE COMMANDER'S ESSENCE," HE SAID.
"...PASSING JUDGMENT ON INCOMPETENT SUBORDI-NATES...
"...WHO DISOBEYED ORDERS...
"JA, OF COURSE.
"IN THAT CASE...
"CHARGING FORVARD TO STRIKE FIRST IST THE SOLDIER'S ESSENCE.
...BUT THE MAJOR UND DOK HAF THEIR HANDS ON A MOST INTERESTING TOY...
...UND THEY SAY THEY HAF NO TIME TO PAY ANY MIND TO YOU UND YOUR ENGROSSED SELF OVER THERE.
IF THAT'S TRUE, YOU VOULD HAF BEEN BURNT TO CINDERS LONG AGO...
THIS VAMPIRE VILL SEE TO THE MATTER OF YOUR PUNISHMENT!!
THIS MONSTER...
...IST NO LONGER THE SERAS VICTORIA SHE VONCE VAS.
CIAO. ♡

KEESH
!!

WRANK
ZHA ZHA ZHA
GREEEEE

SKRANKK
GOH
IGH!
OGH...
GEHH
OH!
HRRRRRRRRASK
SOD OFF, BITCH!!
OUT OF MY SIGHT!!
OUT OF MY MIND!!

HRRRRRRASK
GHREEEE
SHRASK
SHRASK
SHRASK
BOGOOOOB
GO GAO... GEH
OGOO
OGH BOHH
SHRUSK
GHREEEE

THAT'S... THAT'S...!
THAT SAME GIRL...?!
ボタ ボタ ボタ ボタ
BLUP
BLUP
BLUP
BLUP
GSHH
GSHH
GSHH

FLING
WHUMP

ゴゴオッ
BROARR
ボッ
BOPH

KATZ
I'M OFF.
!!
YOU'RE... OFF...?!
WH-WH-WHERE TO?!

I MADE A PROMISE, TO YOUR COMMANDER...
...THAT I'D BEAT THEM.
SO, I'M OFF.
I'M OFF TO GO AND BEAT THEM.
AH...
OHH.
I GET IT.
CAPTAIN.
THIS IS WHERE YOU DIED.
RIGHT HERE.
BUT YOU,
YOU'RE ALSO THERE.
HALF A MOMENT!!

SHMP
KLAK
SHF
SHF
Yes, Sir!
Sir.

NOD
ダダダダダダダダダダ
TMP
TMP
TMP
TMP
TMP
TMP
TMP
TMP
TMP
TMP

SPRING
BRASH

THE NIGHT HAS STARTED LIGHTEN-ING.
THE DAY WILL DAWN.
WITHOUT REGARD EVEN FOR THE LIGHT OF THE SUN...
...LIKE AN ARROW FROM A FULLY DRAWN BOW...
BABOM BOM BOM
...I FLY.
...TOWARDS THE DEAD CITY.
WHMM
A DAWN DISPATCH!

オォオォ
オオオオ
BROHHHHH

THIS IST IT!!
VHAT I VANTED TO SEE!!
AHH.
SO GOOD.
ZORIN DIED, MAJOR.
KATZ
LIKE A BUG.
HAHAHA, I KNEW IT.
THE FOOLISH FRÄULEIN.

OUR RUIN HAST BEGUN.
MY HEART DANCES.
YOU'RE ONE CRUEL PERSON.
YOU MEAN TO LEAD EVERYONE AROUND...
...UND MAKE EVERY LAST VONE OF THEM CHARGE OFF TO HELL.
THAT IST VAR.
HELL IST *HERE*.
WHOOO

FOR THAT REASON, I HAF COME THROUGH DAY OF TREACHERY UND NIGHT OF RESIGNATION TO STAND HERE NOW.
I VILL TAKE UND BE TAKEN FROM VITHOUT LIMIT.
I VILL DESTROY UND BE DESTROYED VITHOUT LIMIT.
BROHHHHHH
LOOK.
BADDA BADDA BADDA BADDA BADDA
HERE COMES DEFEAT.
AND VITH IT, VICTORY.

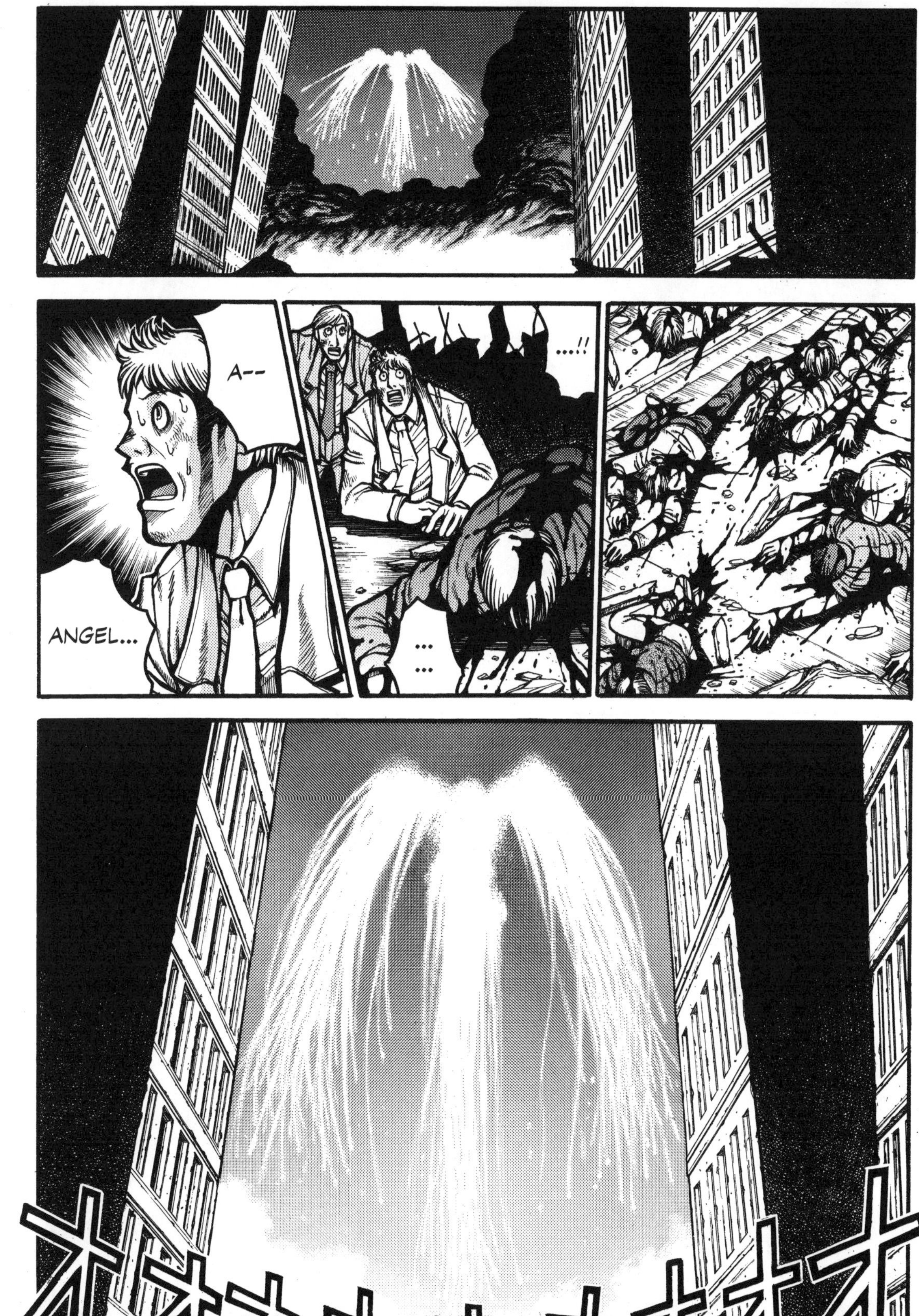

...!!
...
...
A--
ANGEL...
オオオオォ オオオオ
OMMMMM

CHRISTUS REGNABIT...
CHRIST WILL RULE...
CHRISTUS VINCET...
CHRIST WILL WIN...
CHRISTUS...
CHRIST...
CHRISTUS IMPERAT.
CHRIST REIGNS SUPREME.

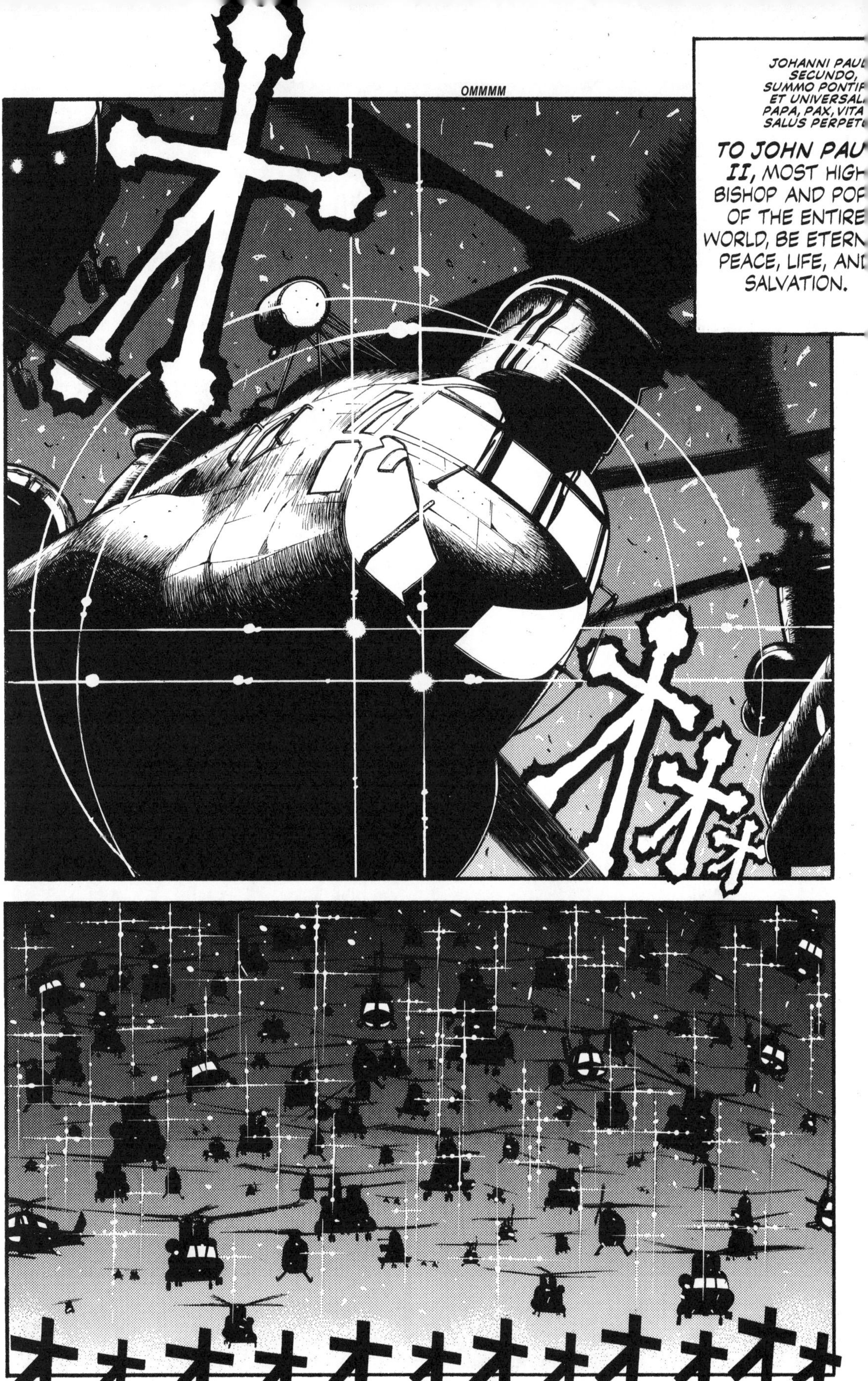
JOHANNI PAUL
SECUNDO,
SUMMO PONTIF
ET UNIVERSAL
PAPA, PAX, VITA
SALUS PERPET
TO JOHN PAU II, MOST HIGH BISHOP AND POP OF THE ENTIRE WORLD, BE ETERN PEACE, LIFE, AN SALVATION.
OMMMM
OMMMMMMMM

ET OMNI CLERO EI COMMISSO PAX...
AND TO ALL OF THOSE CLERGY DEVOTED TO HIM...
VITA ET SALUS PERPETUA.
BE ETERNAL PEACE, LIFE, AND SALVATION.

ORDER 55 / END

ORDER 56

BOM
BOM
BOM
BOM
BOM
IT'S ANGELS!!
IT'S ANGELS.
ANGELS...!!
HOW RIG
YOU ARE!
ARE AGE
OF THE A
OF DEAT
THE INQUISITION WILL NOW RENDER ITS JUDGMENT!!

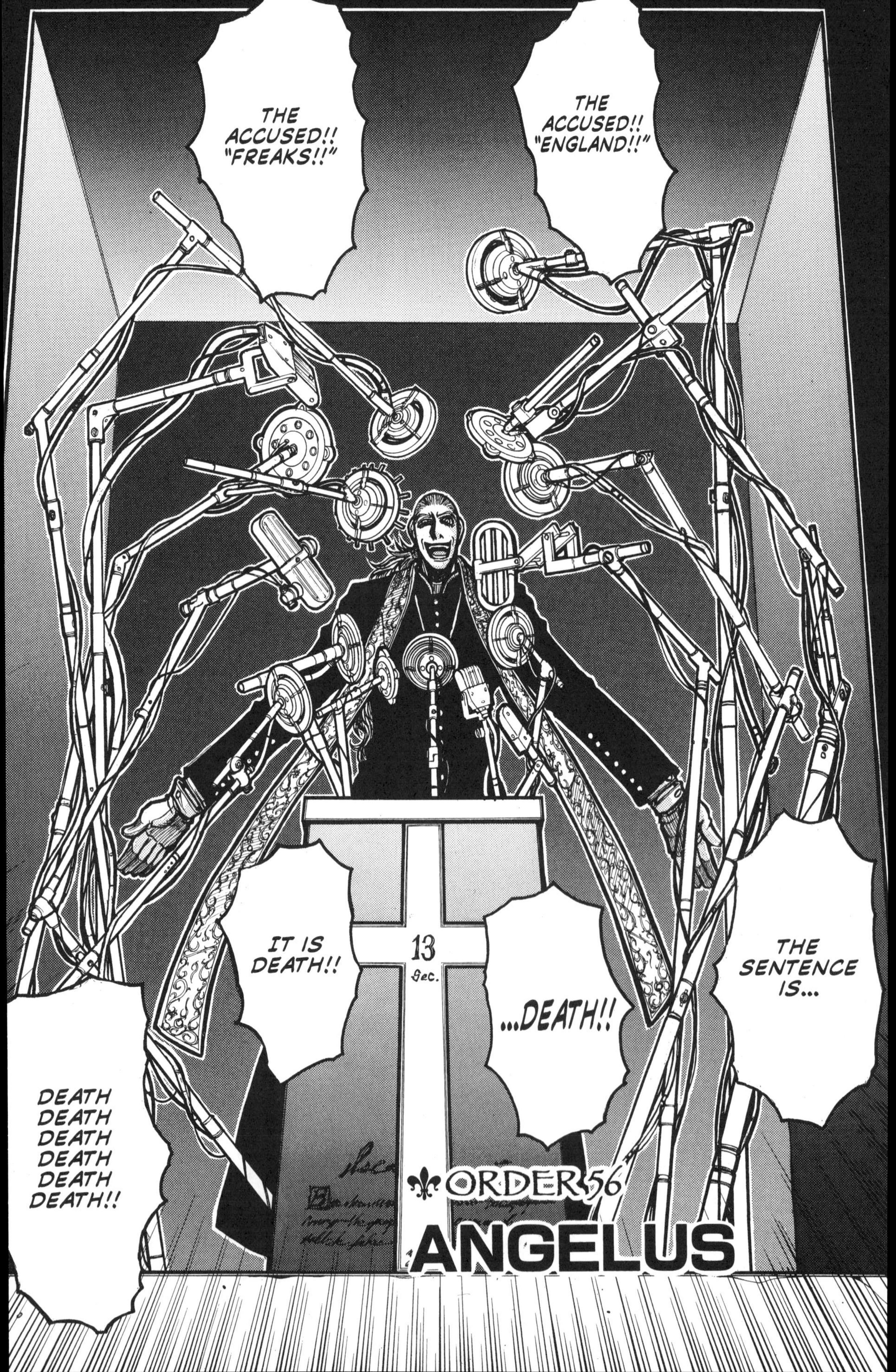
THE ACCUSED!! "ENGLAND!!"
THE ACCUSED!! "FREAKS!!"
THE SENTENCE IS...
...DEATH!!
IT IS DEATH!!
DEATH DEATH DEATH DEATH DEATH DEATH DEATH!!
13 Sec.
ORDER 56
ANGELUS

BADDA
BADDA
BADDA
BADDABADDABADDABA

YOU ALL ARE PITIFUL.
BUT I WILL NOT FORGIVE YOU!!
FLOAT LIKE A BUTTER-FLY...
..DIE IKE A BEE!!
DIE IN AIN LIKE RUITLESS, BURNING LOWERS!
OMMMMMMMMM
WIRE 04

VELL!!
HE IST NOT BAD VHEN HE PUTS HIS MIND TO IT.
THAT BOY.

BADDA
BADDA
BADDA
BADDA
BADDA
BADDA

BADDA
BADDA
BADDA
BADDA
BADDA
BADDA
BADDA
BADDA
BADDA

ALL BATTALION FORCES, ACHTUNG!!
COUNTER-UV RAY EQUIPMENT!!
ASSEMBLE!!
スパッ
WHPP
ZHA
ZHA
ZHA
ASSEMBLE!!

MASKS!
BATTALION!
ASSEMBLE!!
GPOP
BATTALION!
ASSEMBLE!!
ZHA
ZHA
ZHA
ZHA
ZHA
ZHA
ZHA
HA!
HAHH
HAHH
のた
のた
U-UP HERE OF ALL PLACES!
THIS IST HAZARDOUS. PLEASE COME INSIDE!!
!
のた のたのた
HAHH
TEETER
TEETER
TEETER
DOK.
CAN VE USE IT YET?

(anger)

(Dok becoming annoyed)

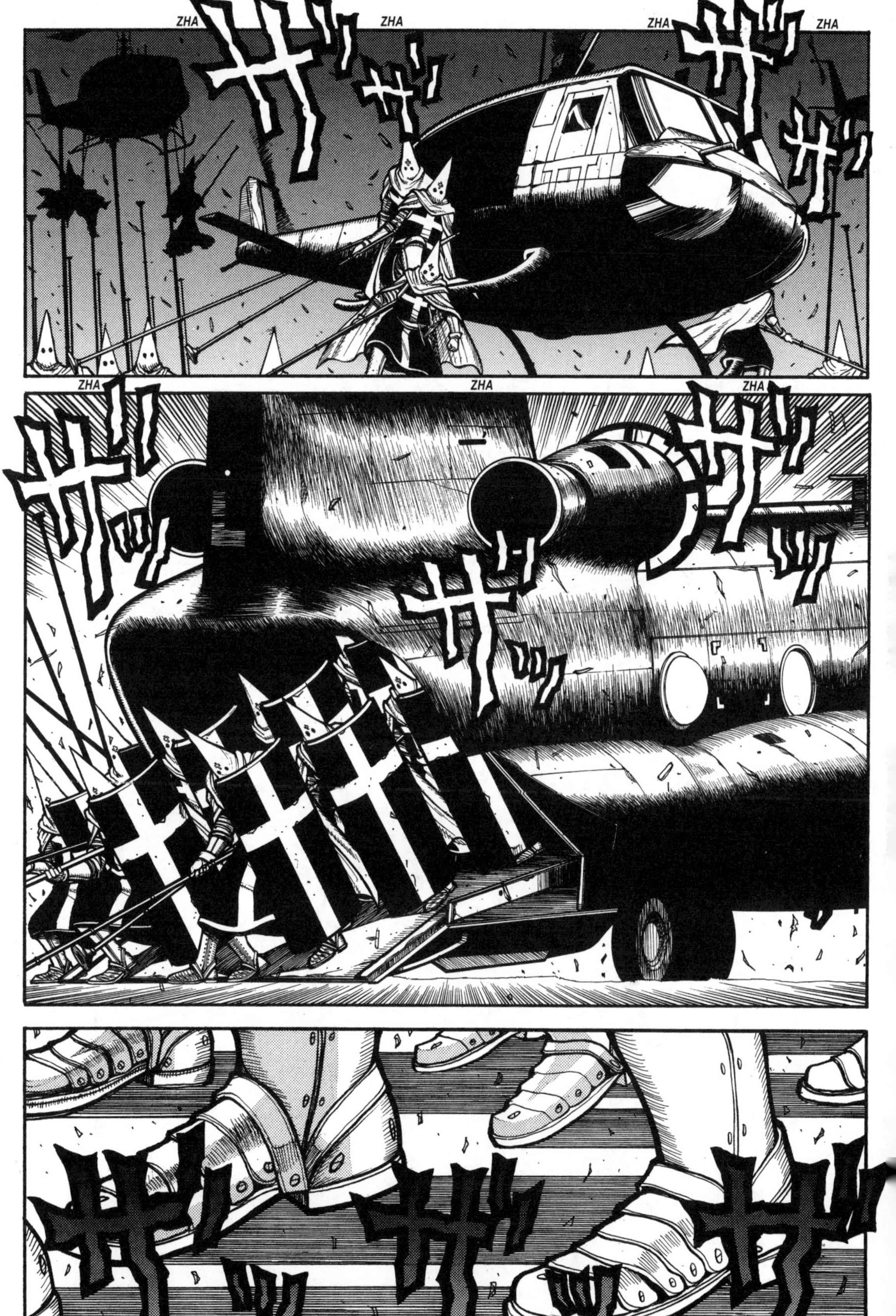
ZHA
ZHA
ZHA
ZHA
ZHA
ZHA
ZHA
ZHA
ZHA
ZHA

LOOK OVER THIS WAY!!
LOOK OVER THAT WAY!!
SEE TO THE...
...ERADICATION OF OUR ENEMIES!!
BCHING
YOUR OBJECTIVE LIES BEFORE YOU!!
EXECUTION!

ボ ボ ボ ボ ボ ボ ボ ボ ボ
SHMM SHMM SHMM SHMM SHMM SHMM SHMM SHMM SHMM
キュワッ
キュワッ
キュワッ
SHREE
SHREE SHREE

SHMM
ボッ
SHMM
ボッ
SHMM
ボッ
ボッ
SHMM
ドドドド
DOOM
DOOM
DOOM
DOOM
WAH
ドドドドッ
ドドッ
UWAH!
HYAHHHHHH
DOOM
DOOM
DOOM
DOOM

INSIDE, YOU MUST GET INSIDE!
EVEN VITH THIS SHIP'S SPECIAL LIGHT METAL ARMOR, IT VON'T HOLD...
IF VE DO NOT MOVE THE SHIP...!
...FOR LONG IN THIS ATTACK!!
ズゥ ズ ズ ズ ズ ズ ズ ズ
ZMM ZM ZM ZM ZM ZM ZM
MAJOR!!
MA...
...!!

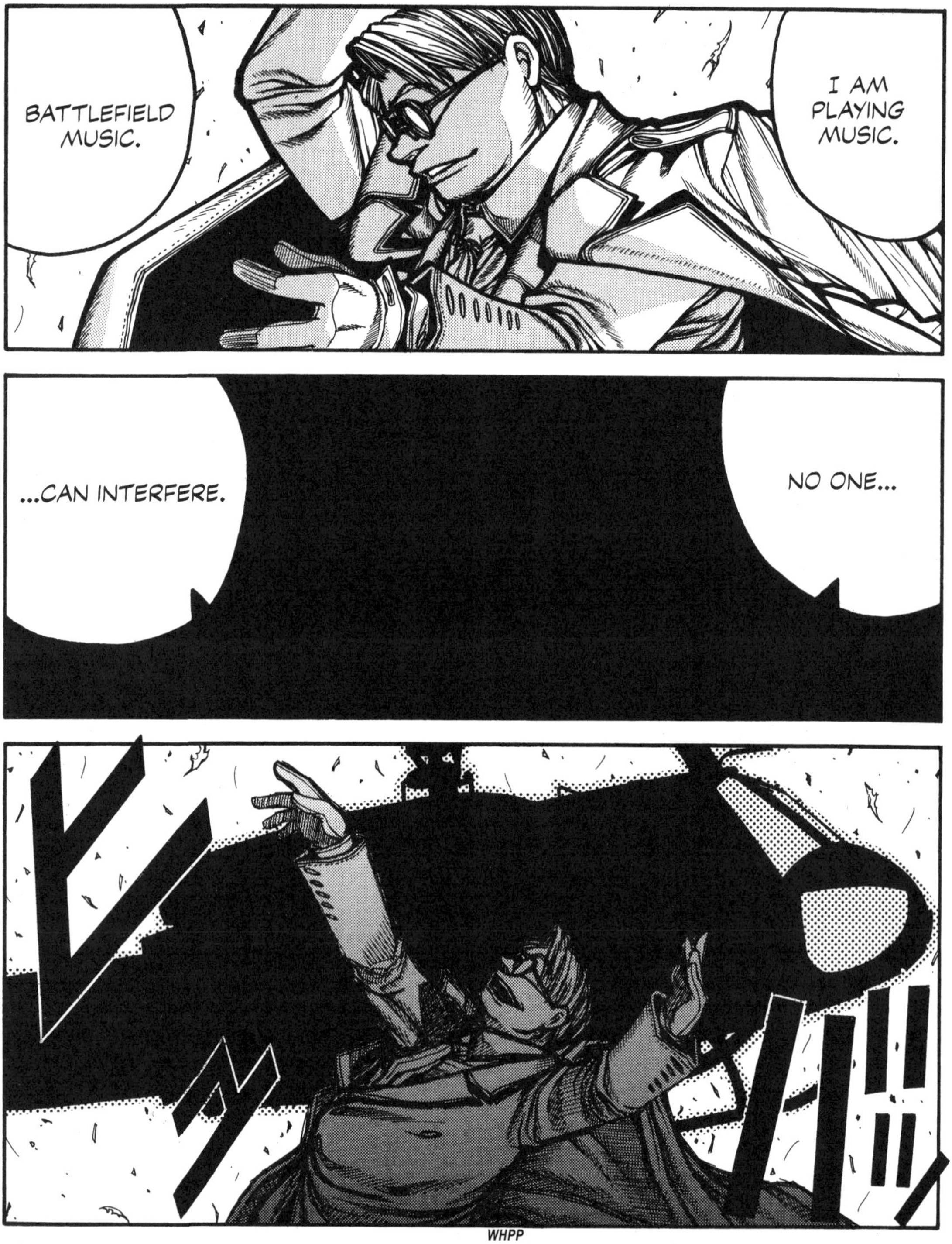
I AM PLAYING MUSIC.
BATTLEFIELD MUSIC.
NO ONE...
...CAN INTERFERE.
WHPP

ORDER 56 / END

ORDER 57
VE ARE INSTRUMENTS!!
HOWLING, CRAWLING INSTRUMENTS **THROWN** INTO THE TIMBRE.
HE IST... DIRECTING IT!!
THE VAR MUSIC...!!
WHUP
WHUP

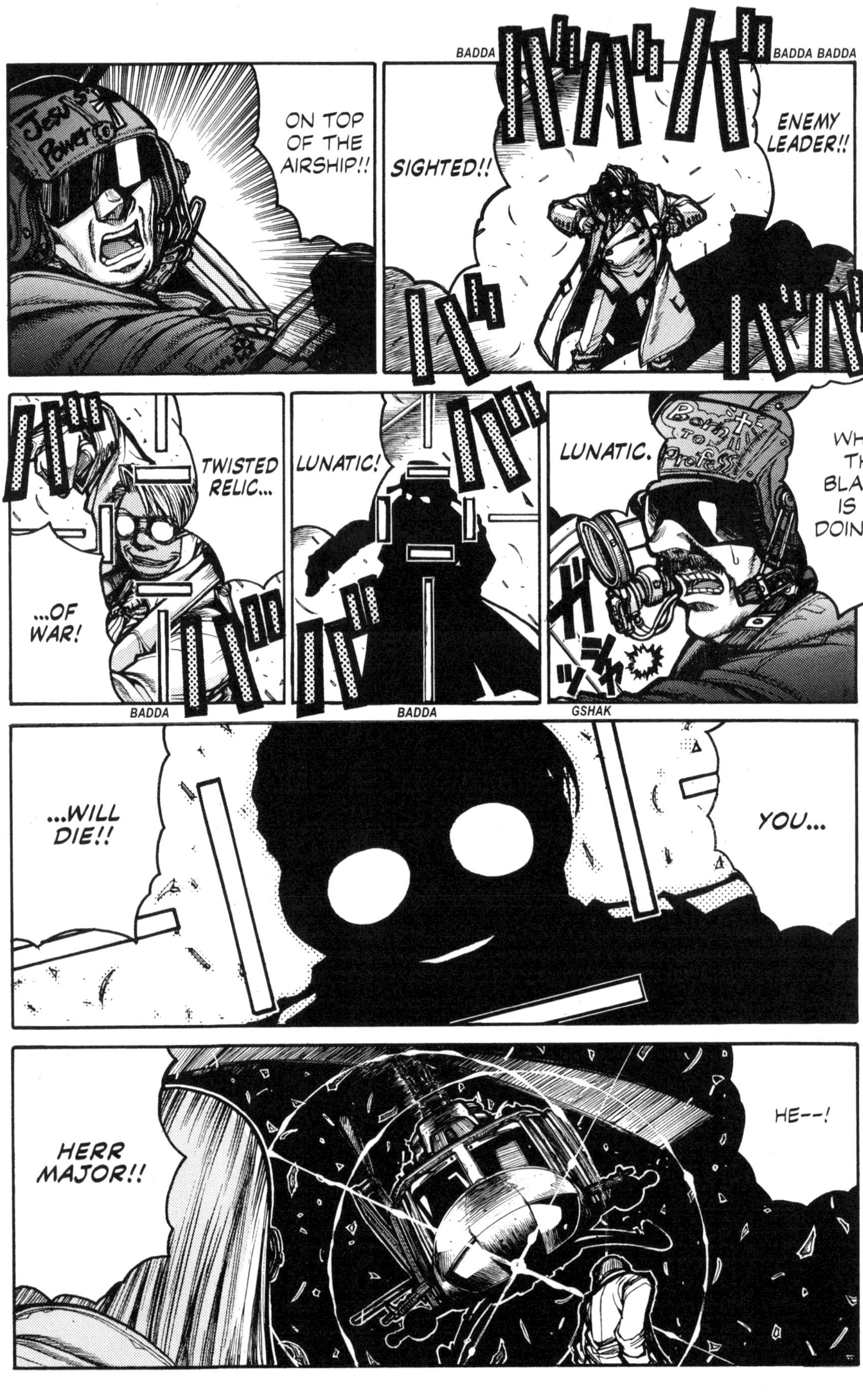
ON TOP OF THE AIRSHIP!!
BADDA
BADDA BADDA
SIGHTED!!
ENEMY LEADER!!
TWISTED RELIC...
...OF WAR!
BADDA
LUNATIC!
BADDA
LUNATIC.
WHAT THE BLAZES IS HE DOING...?!
GSHAK
YOU...
...WILL DIE!!
HE--!
HERR MAJOR!!

ZANNG
KATZ
BUTLER.
GOOD VORK.
AHH!
AH...!!

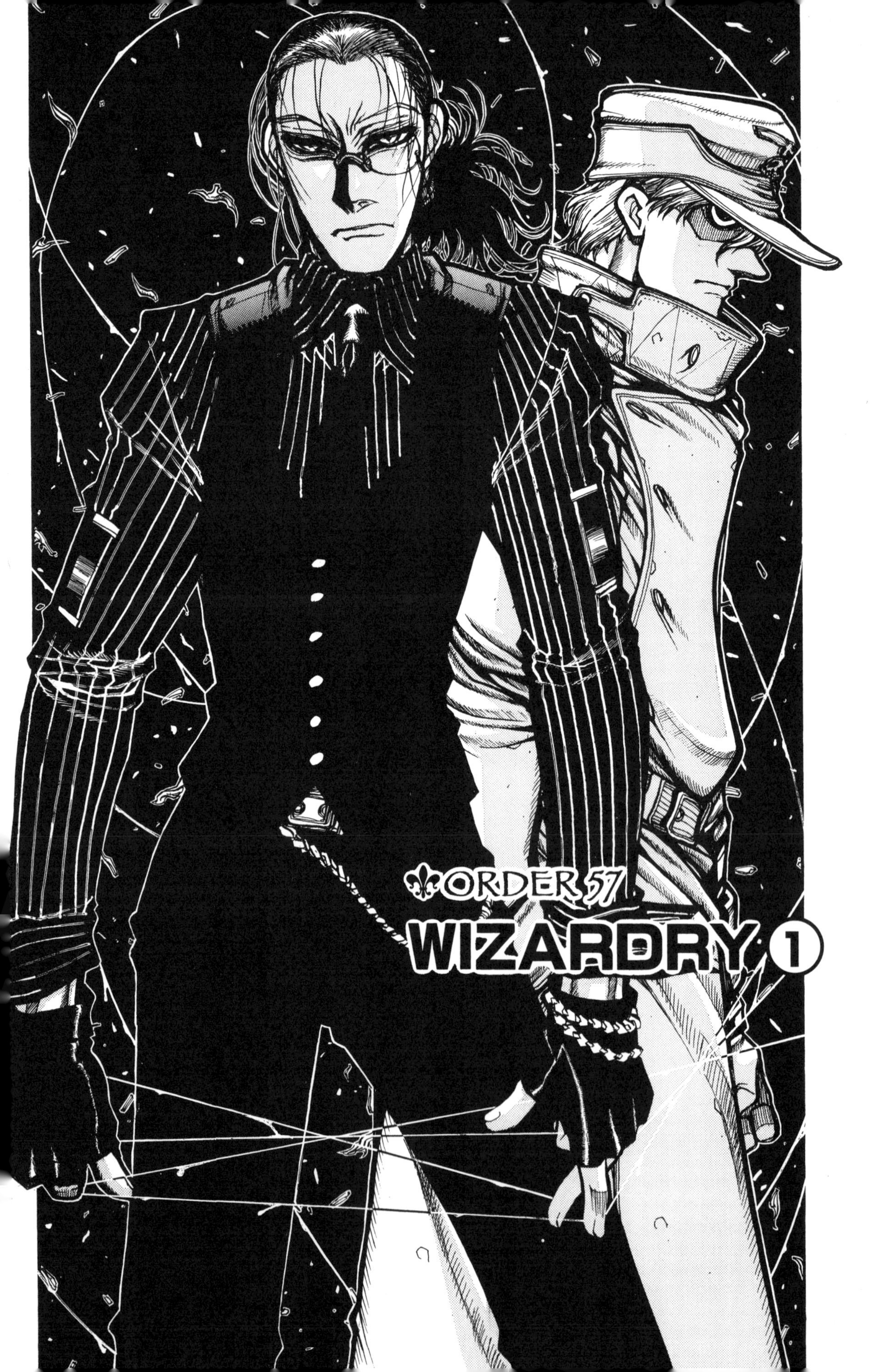
ORDER 57
WIZARDRY 1

I HAD ALREADY DECIDED HALF A CENTURY AGO.
THE DEATH'S HEAD IST A FITTING MATCH FOR THE ANGEL OF DEATH.

BUDDA BUDDA BUDDA BUDDA BUDDA BUDDA
AAH!!
AAH!!
WHA... AH...
AHH?!
BLAM
BLAM
BLAM
TATATATA
DOOM
THEY HAVEN'T... COME TO...
...SAVE US?!

TATATATA
TATATATA
TATATATA
YES! KILL THEM ALL!!
DIE!!
DIE DIE DIE DIE!
TATATATA
THIS IS THE POWER OF THE VATICAN!!
KNOW THIS, INSECTS!
THIS IS OUR POWER!!
FEAST YOUR EYES!!
TATATATATATATA
THE ONLY GOOD PROTESTANT IS A DEAD PROTESTANT!!
HAHAHAHA, LOOK! LOOK AT THOSE MISERABLE PEOPLE!!
BADDA
BADDA
BADDA

OMMMMMM
MAXWELL...!!
YOU DOUBLE-CROSSED ME, MAXWELL!!
DOUBLE-CROSSED?
DINNAE BE STUPID.
SHIFT
ATTACKS O' TREACHERY HAPPEN IN WAR.
ESPECIALLY WHEN IT'S AGAINST HEATHENS.
IN FACT ONE OUGHT TAE BE PRAISED FOR IT.
BUT! BUT!!

BUT HE'S WRONG.
AH DINNAE LIKE IT.
MAXWELL, YER DRUNK. PISS-FACED DRUNK.
ON POWER, AUTHORITY, AND INFLUENCE.
GRIND GRIND GRIND GRIND
ISCARIOT IS SUPPOSED TAE JUST BE AN APPARATUS O' VIOLENCE. AH'M JUST A MAN-KILLING MEAT CLEAVER.
IT'S MA ONLY POWER BY WHICH TAE SERVE GOD.
MAXWELL, NOO YE'VE QUIT SERVING GOD.
A' YE'RE SERVING IS HIS POWER!!
EHH? ISNAE THAT RIGHT? ARCHIEPISCOPUS MAXWELL?
チキッ
チキッ
チキッ
チキッ
チキッ

THIS ORDER IST FROM HIS GRACE BISHOP, NO, ARCHBISHOP MAXVELL.
"IMMEDIATELY RESTRAIN UND APPREHEND HELLSING DIRECTOR INTEGRA!!"
LET US STOP ESCORTING HER.
FATHER ANDERSON.
ジャカ CHAK
ジャカ CHAK
ジャカ CHAK
ジャカッ CHAK
ジャカ CHAK
ジャカ CHAK
ジャカ CHAK
ジャカッ CHAK
AH DINNAE LIKE IT!!
IT'S NOT A QUESTION OF VETHER YOU LIKE IT OR NOT!!
ANDERSON!!
AH DINNAE LIKE IT.

SHOOM
SHOOM
SHOOM
!!
WHP
WHP
WHP
WHP
SHMP
SHMP

SERAS!!
SERAS...!!
SERAS VICTORIA!!
GYRRR
ARE YOU UNHARMED, MISS INTEGRA?!
I'M WELL.
WHAT OF HEAD-QUARTERS?
WE CAME UNDER ATTACK BY AN ENEMY COMPANY.
WE BEAT THEM.
GYRRR
HEAD-QUARTERS... IS WIPED OUT.
ALONG WITH MR. VERNEDEAD...
...SO THAT IS THE WAY OF THINGS.
SERAS, YOU SUCKED VERNEDEAD'S BLOOD.
YOU'VE BECOME A VAMPIRE.

Y--
YES, SIR!!
D--
CHAK
DAMN YOU...!!
CHAK
DINNAE BOTHER, HEINKEL.
YON LASSIE ISNAE LONGER...
...SOMETHING YE CAN HANDLE, EVEN AS AE GROUP.
VAMPIRE SERAS VICTORIA!!
YE'VE MADE YESELF INTAE SOMETHING DREADFUL.
YES, THAT'S RIGHT, FATHER ALEXANDER ANDERSON.
NOW, I DREAD NOTHING.

YER EYES LOOK JUST LIKE THE DEPTHS O' HELL.
SHAME ON YE, STILL TAKING ON AE HUMAN FORM.
GRIN
!!
!!
WHPP

HE IS COMING BACK.
SHAA
SHAA
SHAA
THE BLACK PERIL COMES.
THE BLACK PERIL COMES!!
THIS IS FANTASTIC. IT A' COMES DOWN TAE NOTHIN'.

FORM A BATTLE LINE!!
ZHA
ZHA
ZHA
ZHA
LEGIONE!!
LEGIONE!!
LEGIONE!!
ZHA
ZHA
ZHA
ZHA
ZHA
LEGIONE!!
LEGIONE!!

WHAT IS ANDERSON DOING?!
WHAT ARE THE GUNSHIPS DOING?!
WHERE IS THE ARMED PRIEST VANGUARD?!
ONTINUE TTACKING THE AIRSHIP!!
ROARRRRRR
HOW LONG MUST IT TAKE TO BRING DOWN THAT HUGE THING?!
USE FULL FORCE!!
FULL SCALE ATTACK!!
WE ARE IN THE PROCESS OF LANDING AND FORMING UP TROOPS!!
WE CANNOT YET ATTACK WITH FULL FORCE!!
SHUT UP!!
IF YOUR HEART IS FAITHFUL, DO IT NOW!!
HAS INTEGRA STILL NOT BEEN CAPTURED?!
YOUR GRACE, RCHIEPISCOPUS MAXWELL!!
FURY
ANDERSON!! WHERE IS ANDERSON?!
A REPORT FROM THE CRAFT CARRIER URVEILLANCE CRAFT ABOVE DOVER!!

ZEEZEEZEET
ZEET
ZEEZEEZEET
RIP
FWSS
WHA...?
TH- THEY LOST SIGHT OF IT?!
ZEEZEET
RIDICULOUS! AN ENORMOUS THING LIKE THAT?!
DO YOU MEAN TO SAY IT VANISHED LIKE SOME PHANTOM?!
ZEET
THE ENTIRE AREA OF OCEAN SURFACE WAS SUDDENLY COVERED IN MIST.
THE MIST BECAME MORNING FOG AND COMPLETELY CONCEALED DOVER.
ZEET
ZEET
ARE YOU MAD?! FIND IT!!
THAT IS NOT SIMPLY THE WRECKAGE OF SOME AIRCRAFT CARRIER!!
IT IS ALUCARD!!
ALUCARD IS ONBOARD!!

RMMMMMMBLE
?!!
BRRRRRRNNN
WHAT WAS THAT?!
SOMETHING IS MOVING UPSTREAM ON THE THAMES!!
SOMETHING...!!
A GHOST SHIP?!!
A GHOST SHIP......!!
BOOM

ONCE, A VAMPIRE CAME TO ENGLAND.
ベキベキ
KRAUNCH
ベキ
RAUNCH
ド
BOOSH
ドドド
BOM BOM BOM
...THE VAMPIRE SAILED ABOARD A SCHOONER.
TO GET A WOMAN HE PERSONALLY DESIRED...
オオォオオオォオオォオオオ
WHOOOOOOOO
THE SCHOONER DASHED FROM WAVE TO WAVE THROUGH THE FOG AT UNBELIEVABLE SPEED.
THE ENTIRE CREW WAS KILLED.
WHOOOOOOOOOO

AND SO, THE GHOST SHIP, FULLY LADEN WITH CORPSES AND CASKETS, MADE PORT IN LONDON.

HER NAME IS THE DEMETER.
IN RUSSIAN, THE DEMITRI.

KREE KREE
KREE
KREE

BY KASTER.
"WILANDER, EARL OF WORCESTER, AT THE BATTLE OF MAMON PLAIN."
THOSE WHO GATHERED BEFORE A PAINTING OF RANKS OF SPEARS...
...HAVE NOW MET AGAIN BEFORE THE REAL THING.

*Note: This is a reference to "Walpurgis Night," a part of the "Tragedy of Faust" by Johann Wolfgang von Goethe.

ORDER 57 / END

ORDER 58

TMP TMP TMP TMP TMP TMP
TMP TMP TMP TMP TMP TMP TMP TMP
LEAP

⚜ ORDER 58
WIZARDRY ②

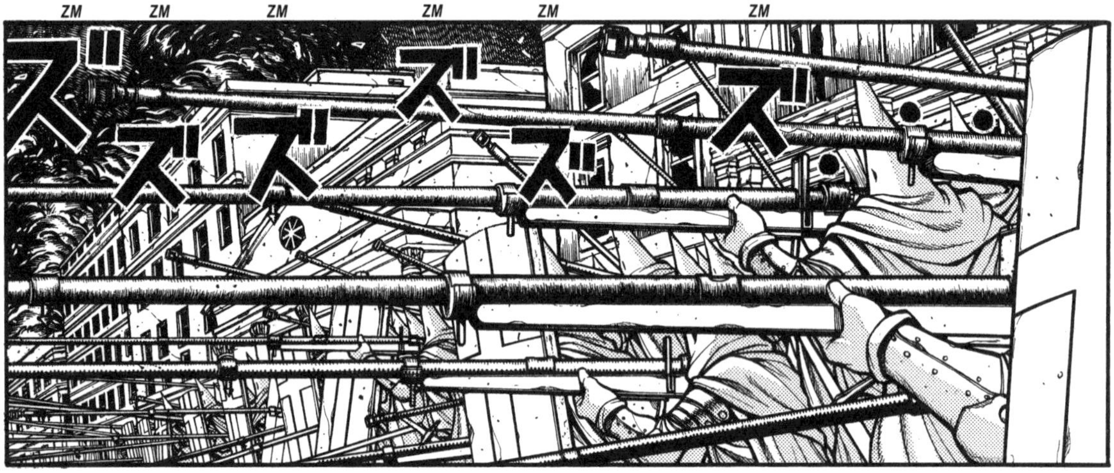
ZM ZM ZM ZM ZM ZM
ズズズズズズ

ズズズズズズ…
ZM ZM ZM ZM ZM ZM

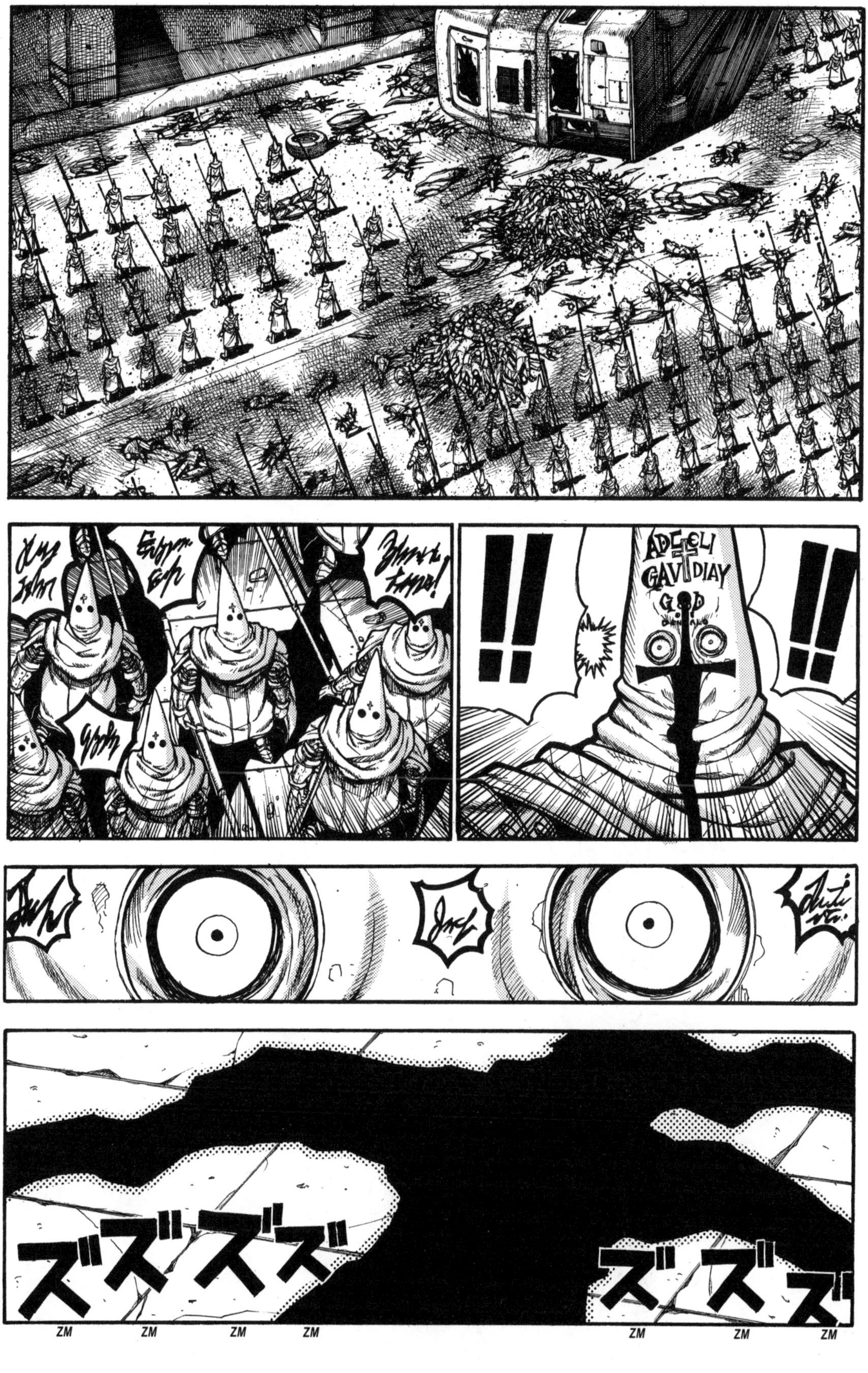
!!
!!
ズズズズ
ZM ZM ZM ZM
ズズズ
ZM ZM ZM

ZOOM
OHH-OH...
OH!
OH!
AHH...

FWASSH
SHKK

WHOO
WHUMP

AH HH HH
ZHAAA
AH
AH HHH HHH H
ZHAAAA

MASTER!!
MY MASTER!!
MY MASTER INTEGRA HELLSING!!
YOUR
RDERS!!
ZSHAAA
ザシャアッ
MY SLAVE.
VAMPIRE ALUCARD!!
I ORDER YOU!!
DESTROY THEM ALL.
DO NOT ALLOW THEM TO GO FROM THIS ISLAND ALIVE.

WITH YOUR SILVER GUN, DYE THE WHITE-ROBED ARMY VERMILION.
WITH YOUR IRON GUN, DYE THE BLACK-ROBED ARMY SCARLET.
DYE EVERY LAST ONE OF OUR FOES THROUGH WITH RED.
KILL ALL ENEMIES!
ALL THAT YOU SEE!!

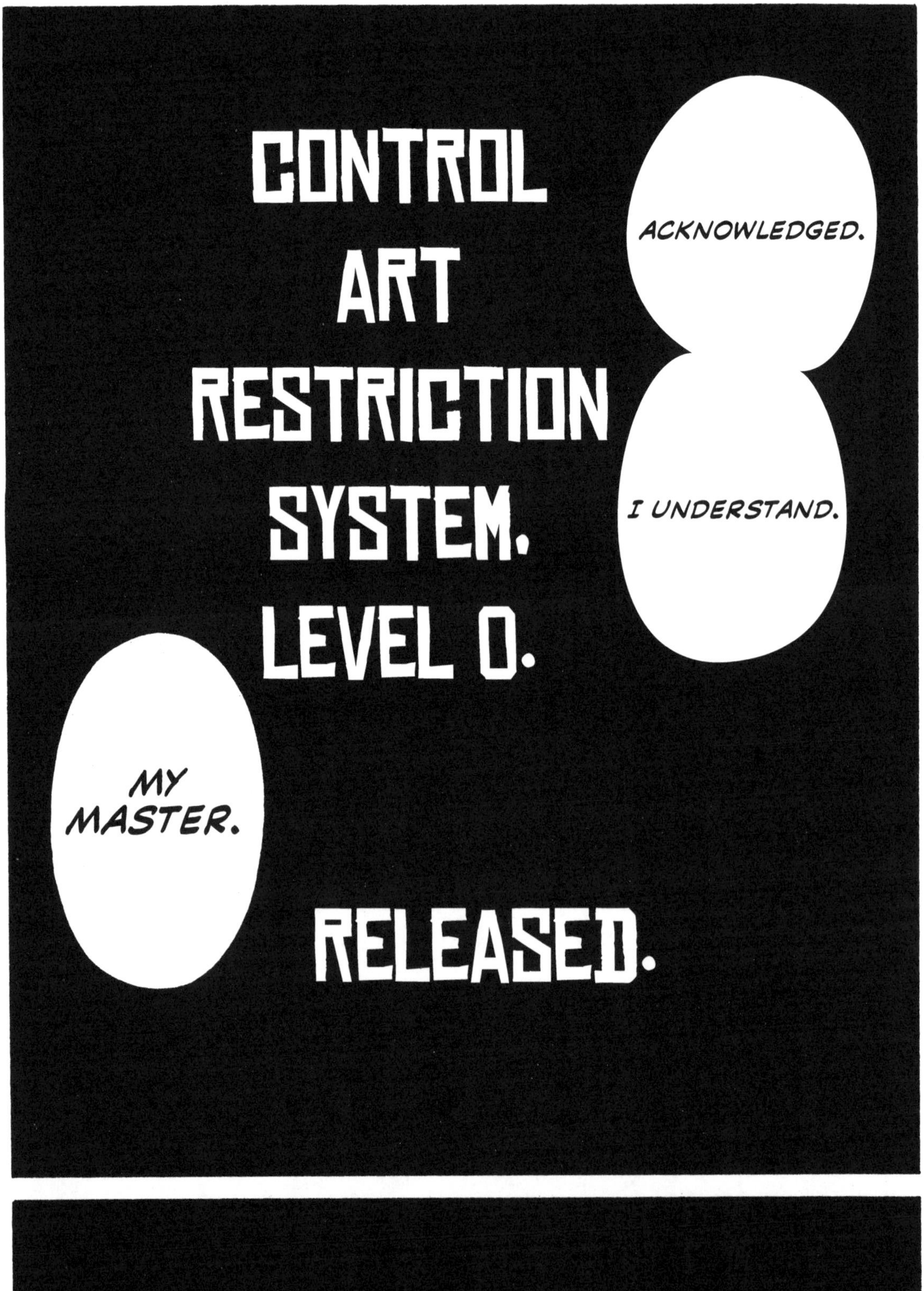
ACKNOWLEDGED.
I UNDERSTAND.
CONTROL ART RESTRICTION SYSTEM. LEVEL 0.
MY MASTER.
RELEASED.
ORDER 58 / END

THE GERMAN THIRD REICH, NAZI PARTY PRIVATE ARMY GROUP WAFFEN SS.
VAMPIRIZED ARMORED GRENADIER KAMPF GRUPPE, "LETZTES BATAILLON."
TOTAL REMAINING FORCES:
572.
ROMAN CATHOLIC VATICAN.
NINTH MOBILIZED AERIAL CRUSADE.
TOTAL REMAINING FORCES:
2875.

UNITED KINGDOM, HELLSING ORDER OF ROYAL PROTESTANT KNIGHTS.
REMAINING FORCES: 3.

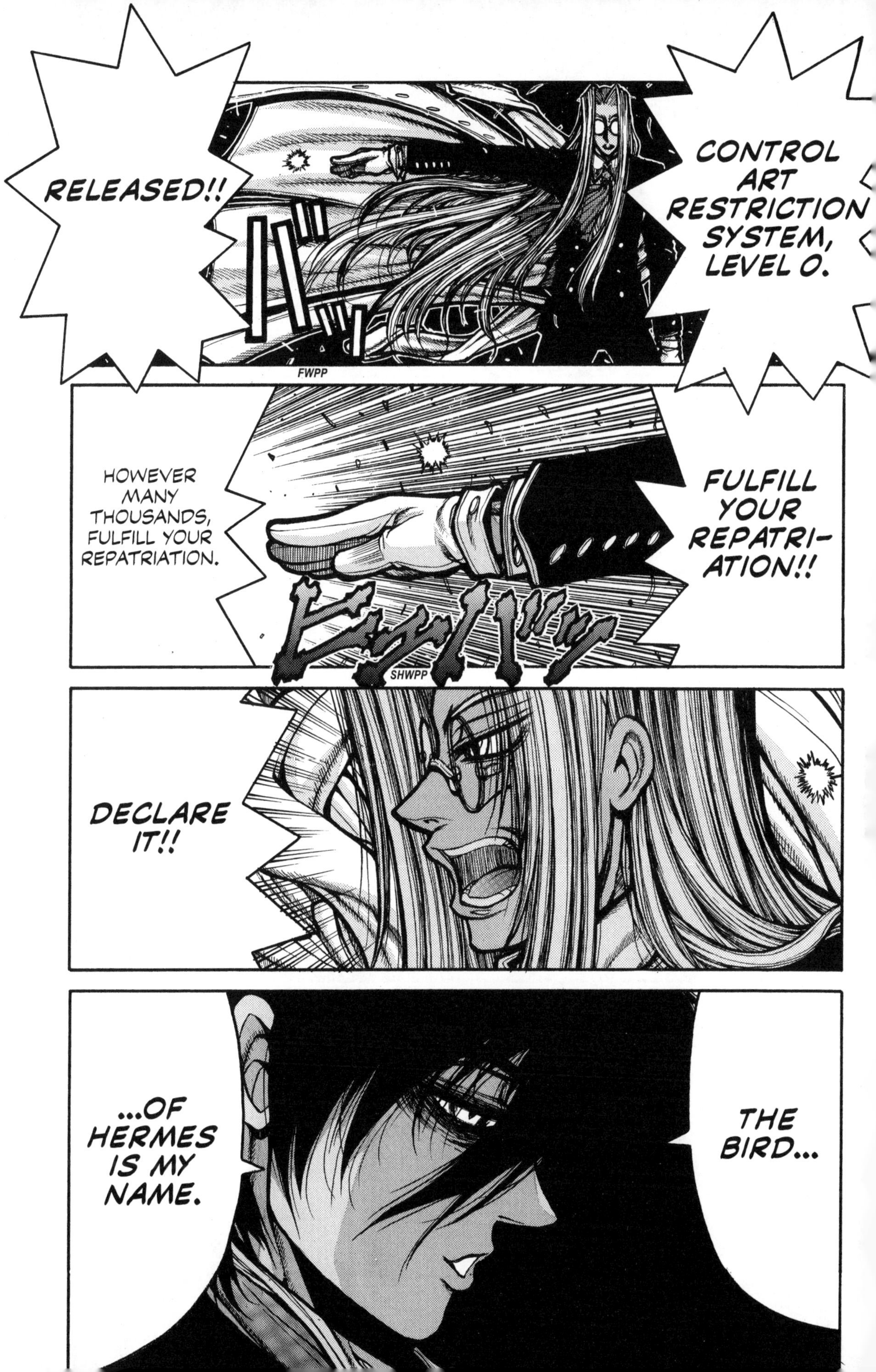
CONTROL ART RESTRICTION SYSTEM, LEVEL 0.
RELEASED!!
FWPP
FULFILL YOUR REPATRI-ATION!!
HOWEVER MANY THOUSANDS, FULFILL YOUR REPATRIATION.
SHWPP
DECLARE IT!!
THE BIRD...
...OF HERMES IS MY NAME.

KRNN...KNN KRNN
KRSSSH
OMMMM
OMMMMMMMM
EATING...
...MY WINGS!!

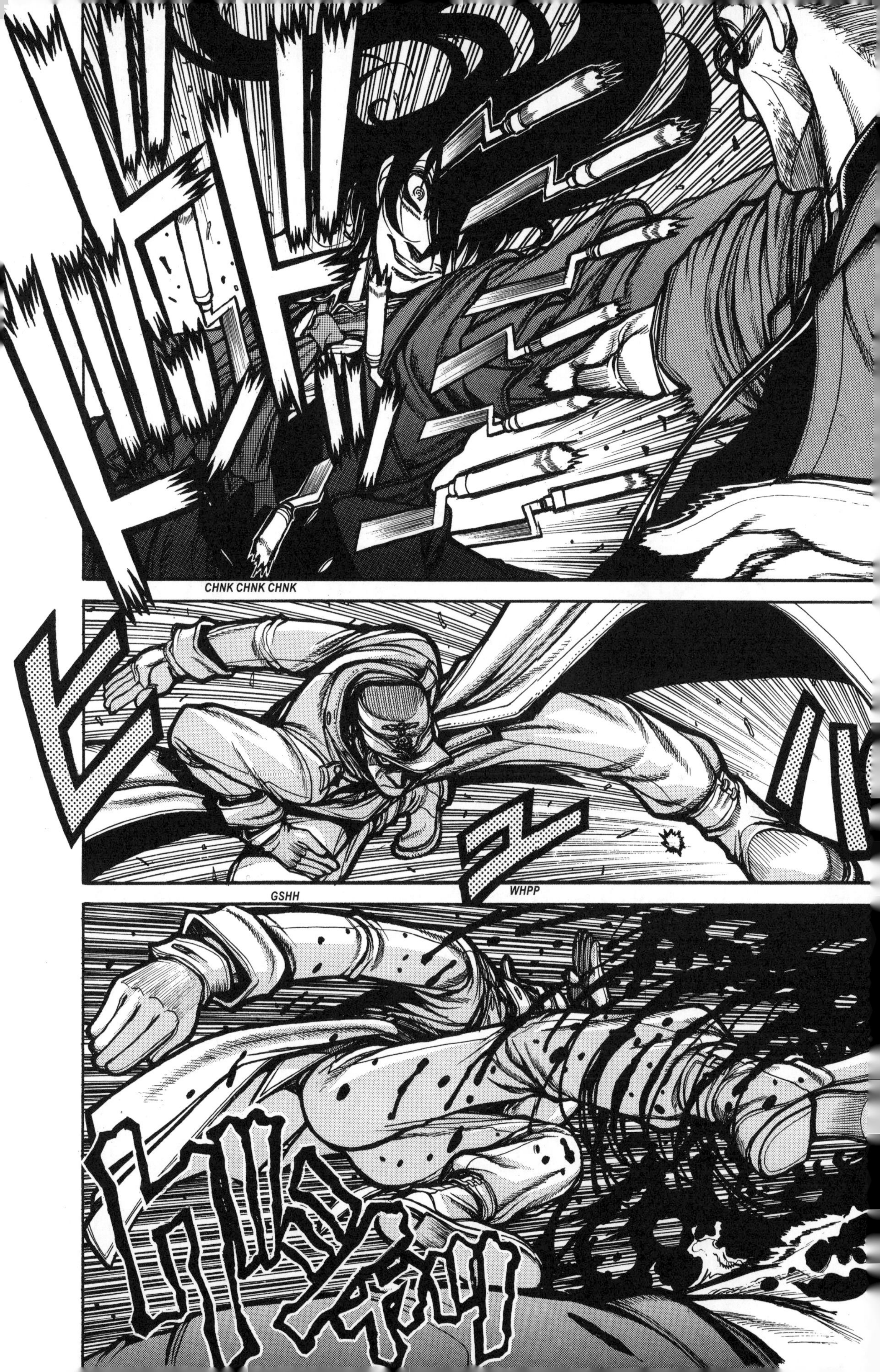

CHNK CHNK CHNK
GSHH
WHPP

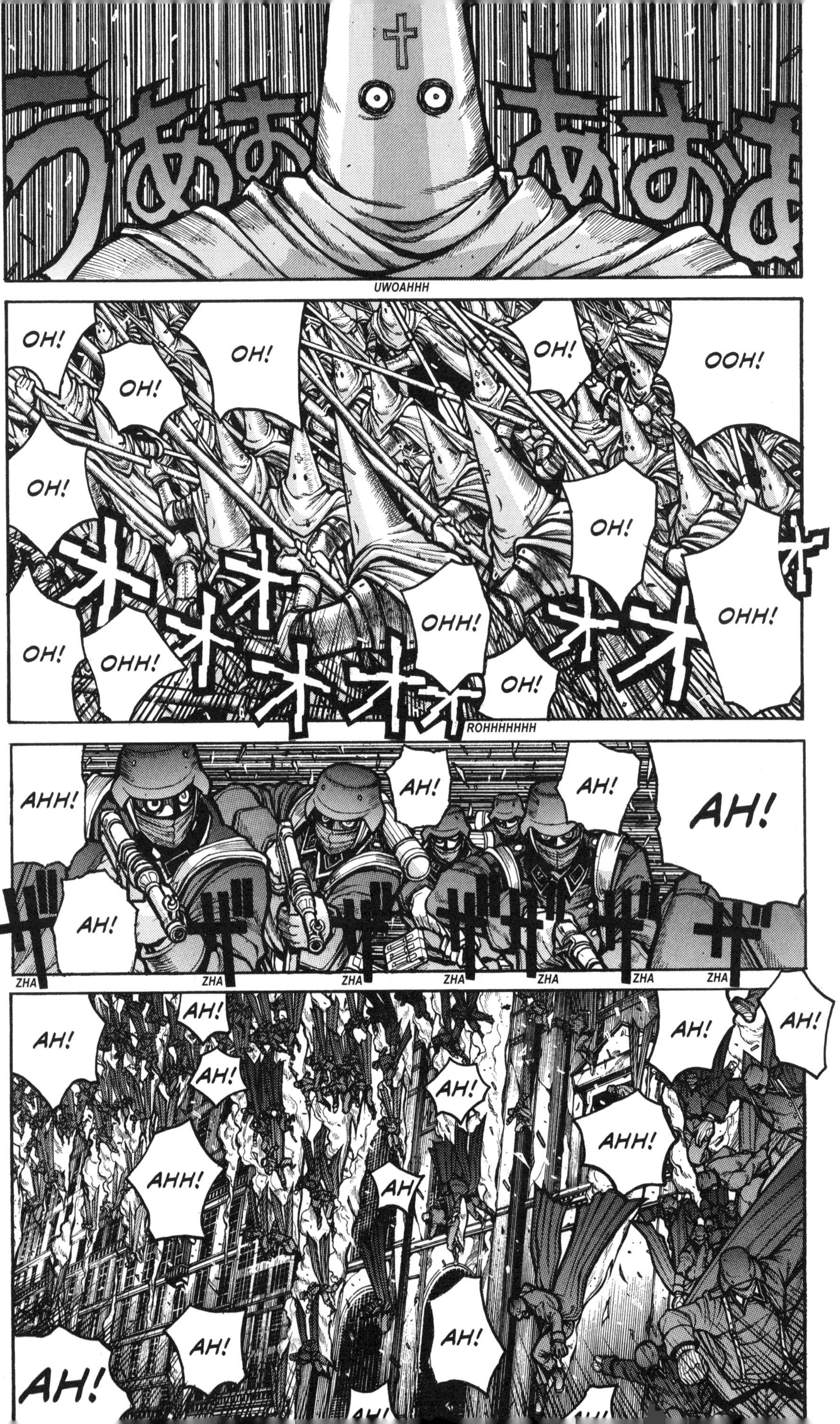
うあああああ
UWOAHHH
OOH!
OH!
OH!
OH!
OH!
OH!
OHH!
OHH!
OH!
OH!
OHH!
オオオ
オオオオオオ
ROHHHHHHH
AH!
AH!
AH!
AHH!
AH!
ザザザザザザザ
ZHA
ZHA
ZHA
ZHA
ZHA
ZHA
ZHA
AH!
AH!
AHH!
AH!
AH
AHH!
AH!
AH!
AH!
AH!
AH!

A' THOSE HERE FELT IT.
IF WE DINNAE DEFEAT THIS MONSTER...
THAT "SOMETHING TERRIBLE IS ABOOT TAE HAPPEN."
SHOOM
...SOMETHING TERRIBLE WILL HAPPEN.
KBLAM
KBLAM
KBLAM
KBLAM
TO MAKE...
...ME TAME.

ZMMMMMM
IT COMES.
RORRRRRR
THE RIVER COMES.
THE RIVER OF DEATH!!
THE DEAD VILL DANCE.
HELL VILL SING.

BOM
BOM
BOM
BOM
BLAM
BLAM
BLAM
BLAM
!!
AH.
VHA...
AH...
AH!!
WHPP
SHSKK

BWOOM
GWEE
GWEE
GWEE
GWEE
BOK
PAK
KYOO
KYOO
KYOO
?!
!!

ズズズズズ
ZM
ZM
ZM
ZM
ZM
MREE
MREE
MREE
めり
めり
めり
ZBOOM

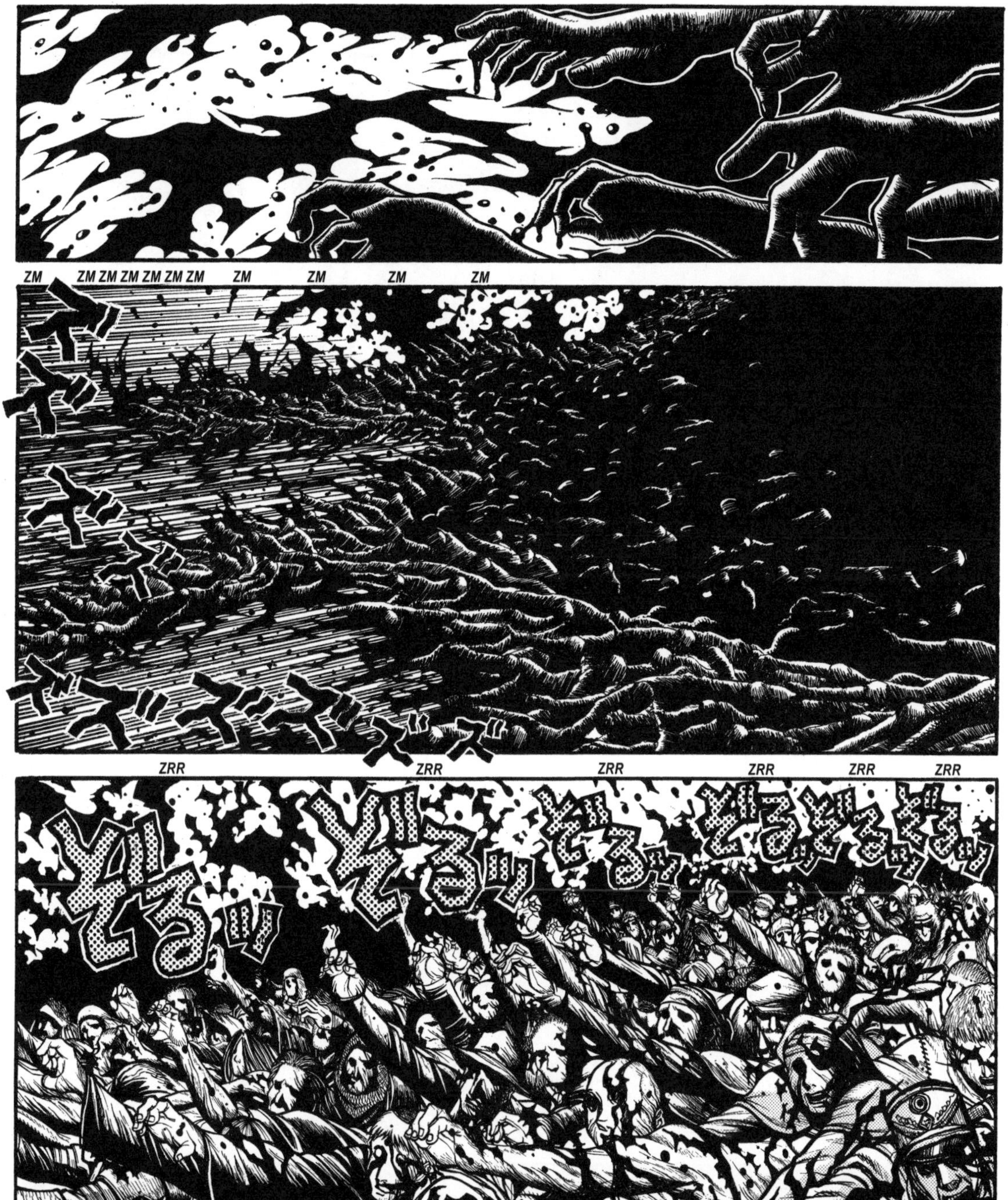
ZM ZM ZM ZM ZM ZM ZM ZM ZM ZM ZM
ZRR ZRR ZRR ZRR ZRR ZRR

OH!
OH!
OH!
OH!
OH!
AH!
OH!
OH!
OH!
AH!
OH!
AH!
LUDICROUS!
RIDICULOUS!
IMPOS-
SIBLE!
HOW COULD SUCH AN ABSURD THING BE?!

THAT IS THE VAMPIRE.
ALUCARD HIMSELF.
ROARRRRR
BLOOD IS THE CURRENCY OF THE SOUL, THE COINAGE OF LIFE.
NO MORE THAN A VEHICLE IN THE TRAFFIC OF LIFE.
TO SUCK BLOOD IS TO MAKE THE WHOLE EXISTENCE OF A LIFE ONE'S OWN.
TWITCH TWITCH TWITCH
WITH YOU AS YOU ARE NOW...
...YOU CAN PROBABLY UNDERSTAND THAT, SERAS VICTORIA.
ビク
ビクッ
YES, SIR!!
ビクッ

KA-
ZANS
...!!
THE
JANIS-
SARY
INFAN-
TRY!!
MREE MREE
MREE
YE BASTARD,
EVEN THEM...
EVEN
SUCH AS
THEM...
...YE DE-
VOORED!!
BKEE
BKEE
BKEE
ベキベキベキ
NAE
WONDER
HE
DINNAE
DIE.
JUST HOO
MANY
LIVES DOES
HE HAVE?!
NAE
WONDER AH
CANNAE
KILL HIM!!
JUST
HOO MANY
HUMAN
LIVES HAS
HE SUCKED?!
ZHAAAAA
MREE
MREE

ZM ZM ZM ZM ZM ZM
BRICHHH BRRIP BRRIP BRRIP BRRIP
ZM ZM
WALLACHIA...
THE PRINCIPALITY'S ARMY...!!

CHARGE

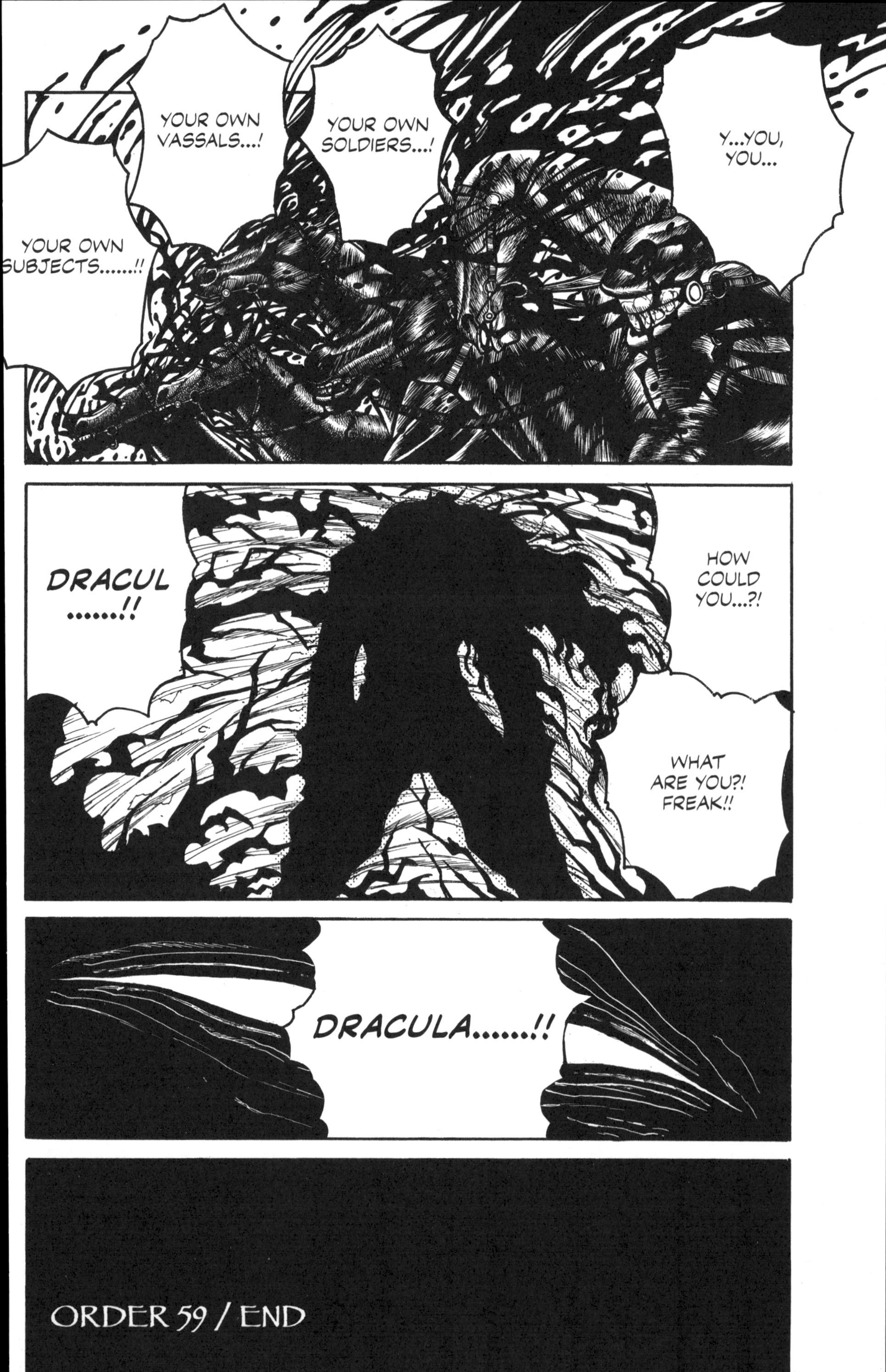
Y...YOU, YOU...
YOUR OWN SOLDIERS...!
YOUR OWN VASSALS...!
YOUR OWN SUBJECTS.......!!
HOW COULD YOU...?!
WHAT ARE YOU?! FREAK!!
DRACUL ....!!
DRACULA.......!!
ORDER 59 / END

ALL SIDES, DEFENSE!! ALL SIDES, DEFENSE!!
PHALANX!! FORM A PHALANX!!
ZHA ZHA ZHA ZHA ZHA ZHA ZHA
WHAT?! WHAT IS...
WHAT IS HAPPEN-ING?!
DEATH!!
DEATH...
...IST HAPPEN-ING!!
ZHA ZHA ZHA ZHA ZHA ZHA ZHA ZHA
OH...
OHHH.
VERY GOOD, JA!!
I VANT IT!! IT'S VONDERFUL!!
OH!
OHH!
OH!
OH!
OHH!

ORDER 60
WIZARDRY④

WHPP
ヒュッ
SHPP
パッ
ZHMM
ZHMM

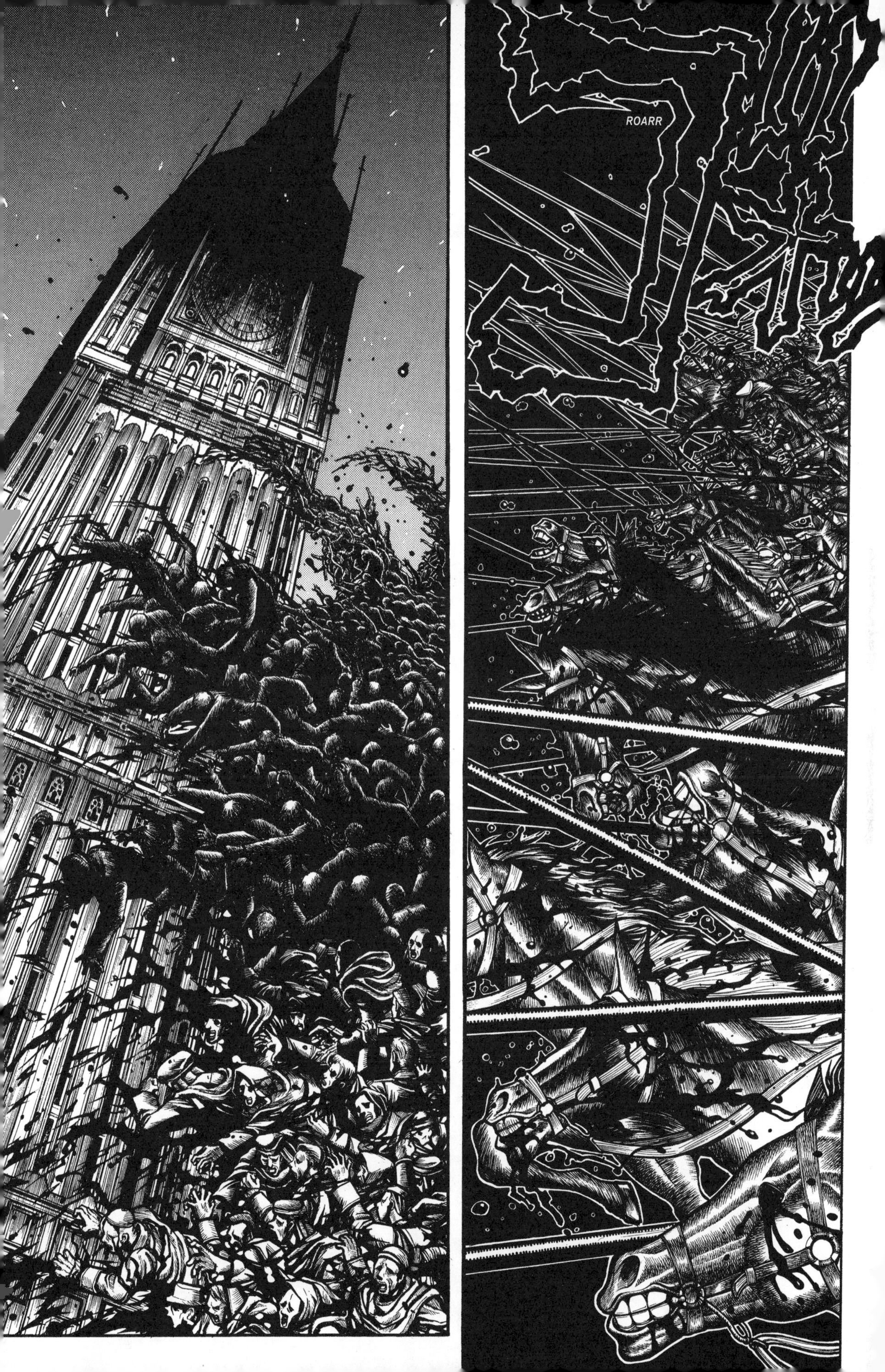
ROARR

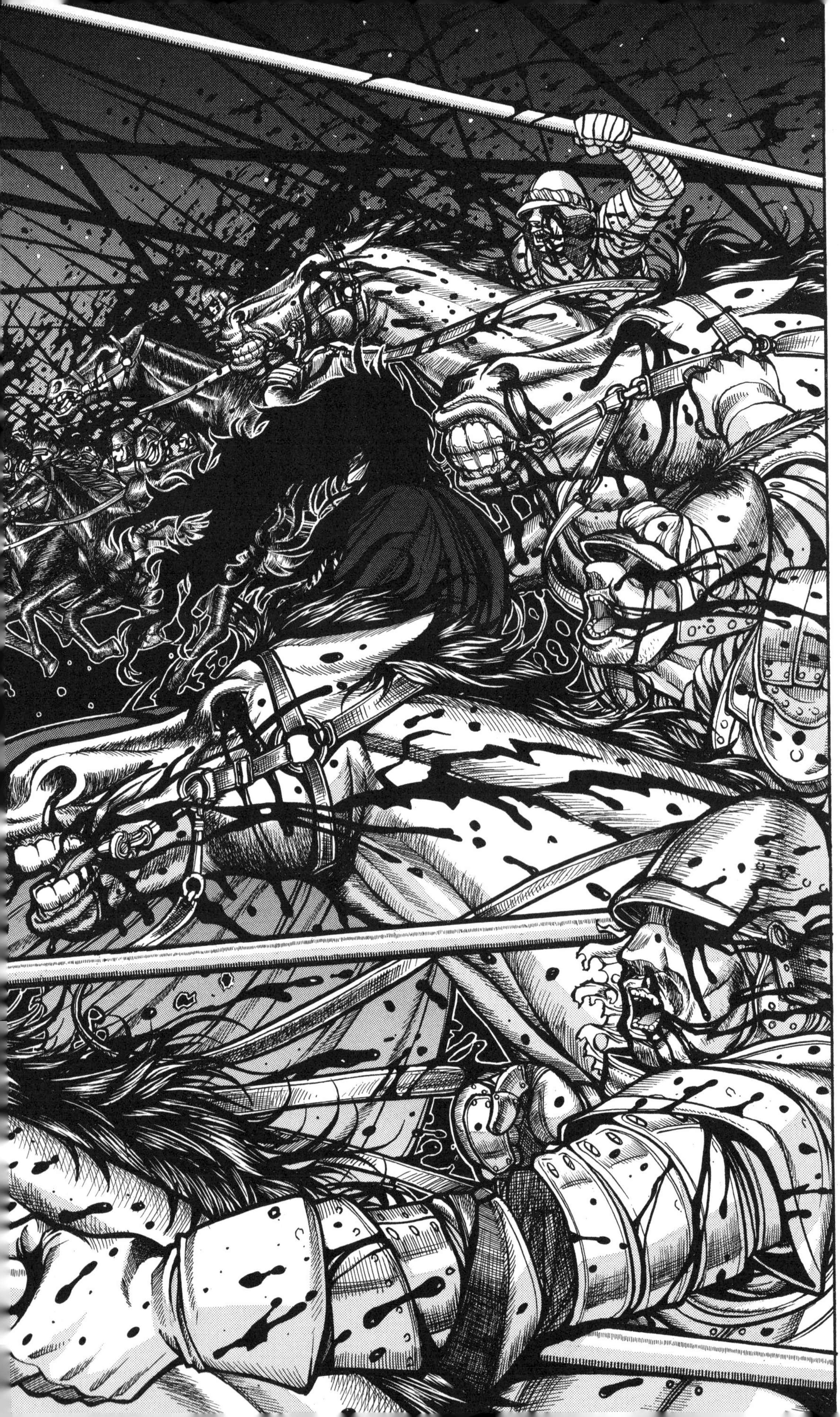

OHHHHHHH!
FIRE AWAY!!
OHHHHHHHH!
FIRE!!
OHH!
OH!
OHH!
OHHH
BAOM!
BAGOH!
ズガガガガガ!
BUDDA
BUDDA
BUDDA
BUDDA
ダダダダダダダダダダダ!
TA
TA
TA
TA
TA
TA
TA
TA
TA
TA

ドドドドドドドド
DM DM DM DM DM DM DM DM

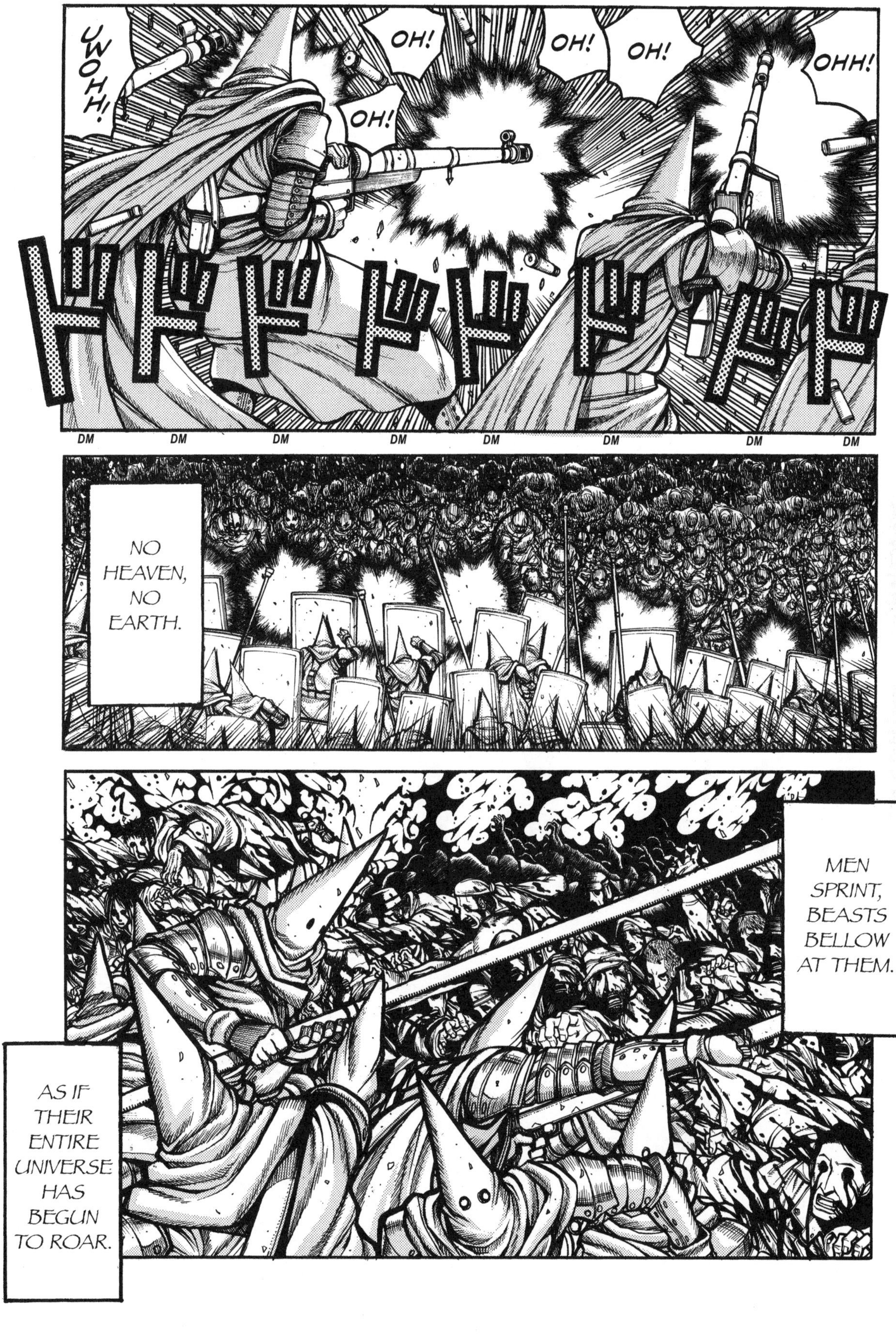
OHH!
OH!
OH!
OH!
OH!
UWOHH!
DM DM DM DM DM DM DM DM
NO HEAVEN, NO EARTH.
MEN SPRINT, BEASTS BELLOW AT THEM.
AS IF THEIR ENTIRE UNIVERSE HAS BEGUN TO ROAR.

FIGHT. DIE. EVERYTHING ELSE IS TRIVIAL.
DIE. DIE. HUMANS ARE NOTHING MORE THAN WALKING SHIMMERS.
GATE
POLICIA

POLICIA
JUST DIE. JUST DISAPPEAR.
SURELY THEY ARE ALL EVIL OUT-SIDERS.
THE WORLD HAS LIFTED UP ITS HEAD TO THIS ABSOLUTE RETRIBU-TION.

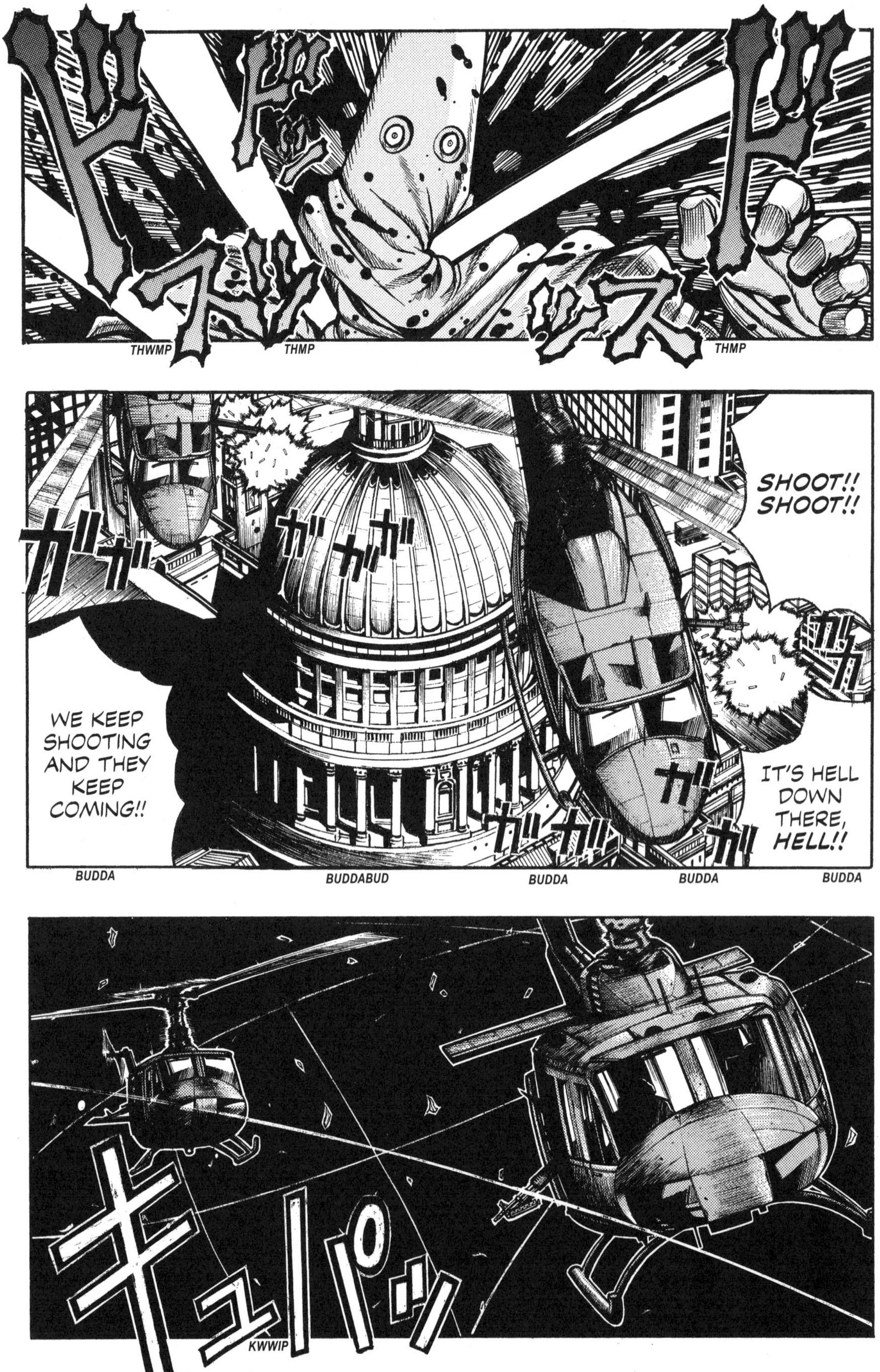
THWMP
THMP
THMP
SHOOT!! SHOOT!!
IT'S HELL DOWN THERE, HELL!!
WE KEEP SHOOTING AND THEY KEEP COMING!!
BUDDA
BUDDABUD
BUDDA
BUDDA
BUDDA
KWWIP

BKOOM
BDOOM
BKOOM

VWADOOM
GSSHH
OH!
OHH!
HHHHH!
BATTLE LINE BROKEN!! BATTLE LINE BROKEN!!
THIS CAN NO LONGER BE CALLED A BATTLE!!
BISHOP!! ORDER RETREAT, YOUR GRACE!!
DON'T TOY WITH ME!!

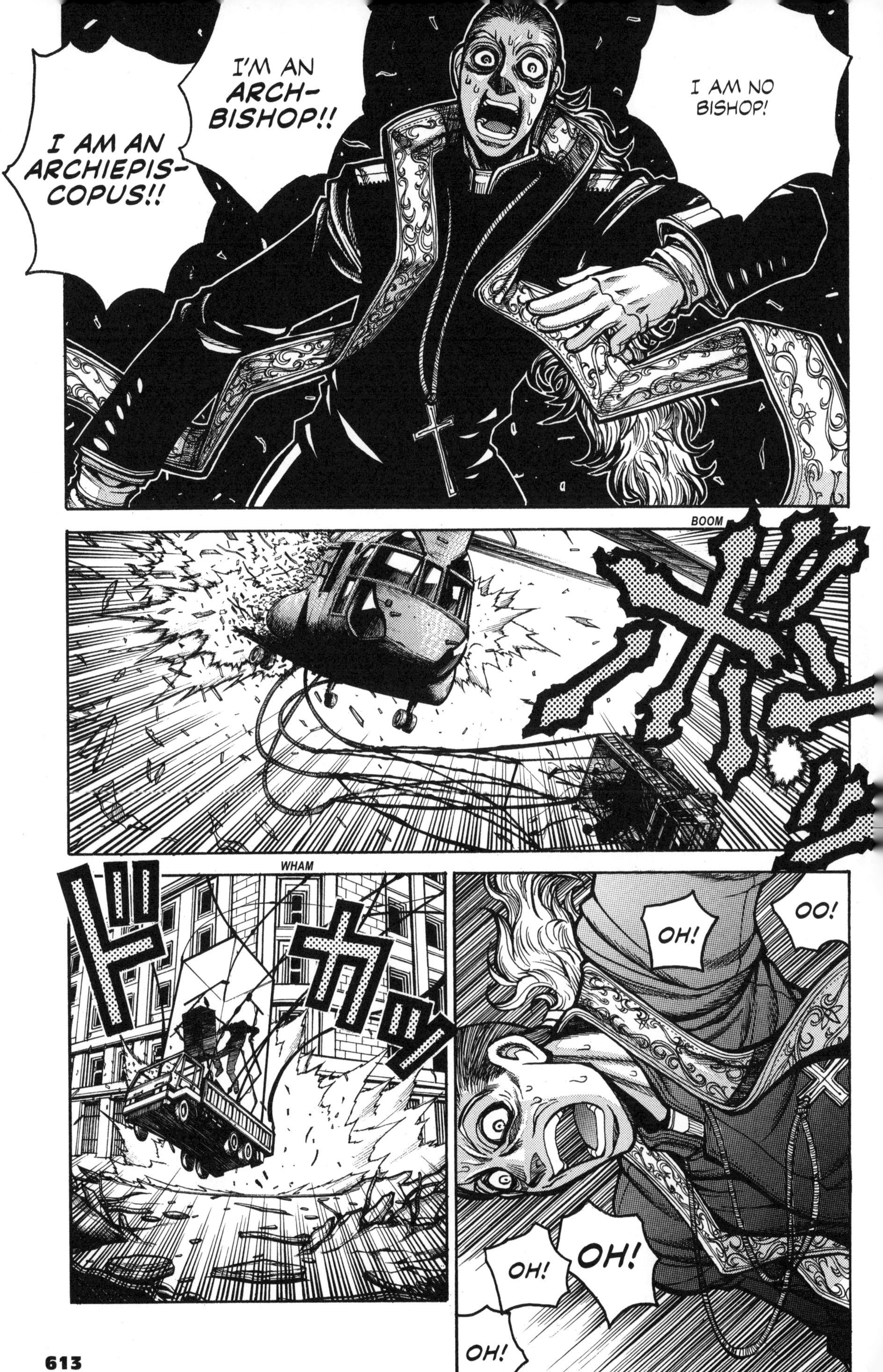
I AM NO BISHOP!
I'M AN ARCH-BISHOP!!
I AM AN ARCHIEPIS-COPUS!!
BOOM
WHAM
OO!
OH!
OH!
OH!
OH!

ROHHHHH
!!
UGH...
GUH...

UGH... AH...
IGH...
UGH...
GREE
BMP BMP
GREE GREEE GREE GREE GREE
BMP
...HA!
...
...
...!
HAHA...!
THE GLASS IS REINFORCED WITH A HARDENED TEKTITE COMPOSITE.
YOU CURSED DEAD WILL NOT EVEN SCRATCH IT!!

SWPP
CHINK CHINK
CHINK
CHINK
CHINK
AH
AH
AH...
AH
!!
SHNNK

ANDER-SON!!
AN...
ANDER-SON!!
KRISSSSSH
AAANN DEER
SSOO NNN
WE ARE SECTION XIII ISCARIOT, EARTHLY AGENTS O' DIVINE PUNISHMENT.
WITHOUT AE SINGLE DISCREPANCY WE WILL SMASH YER DREAM.
FAREWELL!! MA FRIEND!!

ZHMM
OHH
OH
OH
ZWAHHH

ANDERSON!
ANDERSON!!
ANDER-SON!!
HELP ME...
ギ...
ギギ..
REACH
HELP ME...!
TEACHER ...!
TEA-CHER!!

OH...
GUH!
...GAH!
GAHH... AH!
GLB GLB
GLB
IN A PLACE LIKE THIS......! I...!
AM I TO DIE IN A PLACE LIKE THIS?!
GLB
GLB
AM I TO DIE ALONE IN A PLACE LIKE THIS...?!
NO!
NO!
SO I WAS BORN ALONE...
AND I DIE ALONE...?!

ORDER 60 / END

ORDER 61

ZHA
ZHA
ZHA
THIS IS...
...YOUR NEW "HOME."
ZHA
ZHA
ZHA
ZHA
ZHA
ZHA
ZHA
TEACHER, MIGHT THE REASON I AM HERE...
...AND THE REASON FATHER AND MOTHER DO NOT COME GET ME...
...BE BECAUSE...
...I AM THE SON OF A MISTRESS?

I NEED NO FATHER OR MOTHER!!
I NEED NO COMPANIONS.
I NEED NO FRIENDS.
ZHA
ZHA
ZHA
ZHA
I WILL BECOME GREAT AND LOOK DOWN ON ALL OF THEM!!
TEACHER. FATHER ANDERSON.
I WILL BECOME GREAT. I WILL.

ORDER 61
WIZARDRY 5
YE'RE AE FOOL.
AE GREAT DAFT FOOL.

SU...
THIS IS ANDERSON TAE A' ARMED PRIESTS.
THE NINTH CRUSADE EXPEDITION RICONQUISTA IS TOTALLY DESTROYED.
THE MORNING COMES. THE DREAM'S ALREADY UNDONE.
RETURN TAE THE VATICAN.
N-NEIN!! ANDERSON!!
THIS ISNAE YER PLACE TAE DIE!! GO HOME!!
PROTECT THE VATICAN. PROTECT THE POPE.
PROTECT CATHOLICISM FOR A' ETERNITY...
AH WILL DEFEAT HIM.
DEFEAT ALUCARD!!
AH HAVE TAE DO IT.

N-NEIN!! NEIN...!
VHAT VILL COME OF FIGHTING A MAN LIKE HIM?
NAE!! IT HAS TAE BE NOO.
NOO, WHEN ALUCARD'S RESTRICTION SYSTEM IS FULLY RELEASED.
ザアアアアアアアア
ZHAAAAAAA
THAT IS AE SYSTEM THAT LETS HIM RELEASE A' THE LIVES HE HAS AND SEND 'EM INTAE BATTLE.
A' THE SOLDIERS HAVE SALLIED FURTH O' THE CASTLE IN AE COMBINED FORCE.
JUST ONE STANDS INSIDE THE CASTLE, THE LAIRD!!
HE'S ALONE, A' ALONE!!
JUST AE SINGLE VAMPIRE, NOO.
JUST AE SINGLE DRACULA.
PERHAPS THIS AND THIS ALONE WAS YON INSANE BATALLION COMMANDER'S GOAL.
AE SACRIFICE FOR OVER-THROWIN' ALUCARD ALONE.
AE THOUSAND ARMED SS, THREE THOUSAND CRUSADERS, AE MILLION ENGLISH, ENEMIES AND ALLIES ALIKE.

SURELY ALSO THAT...
...AH'D FIGHT TAE THE DEATH.
GRIND
FAREWELL, MEN.
MAXWELL'S CRYING. YON INCORRIGIBLE FOOL.
YON EVER-GUTLESS COWARD.
ZHAAAAAAA
FARE-WELL!!
SEE YE IN LIMBO.
FATHER!!
FATHER!!
FATHER!!
FATHER ANDER-SON!!

KOHHHHHHH

WELCOME BACK.
COUNT.
I RETURN.
COUNT.
U-UH, UHH.
W-WEL-WEL-
WELCOME BACK, MASTER.

YOU HAVE A MOUSTACHE, MASTER.
MOUSTACHE.
REACH
ズ
ウッ
!!
PAT PAT PAT
くしゃ
くしゃ
くしゃ

SERAS.
SERAS VICTORIA.
WHOOOO

GNNN
GNN

SHOO
SHNN

GYANG
HEE! H H H H H HH
MAGNIFI-CENT...
...MY ARCH RIVAL!!

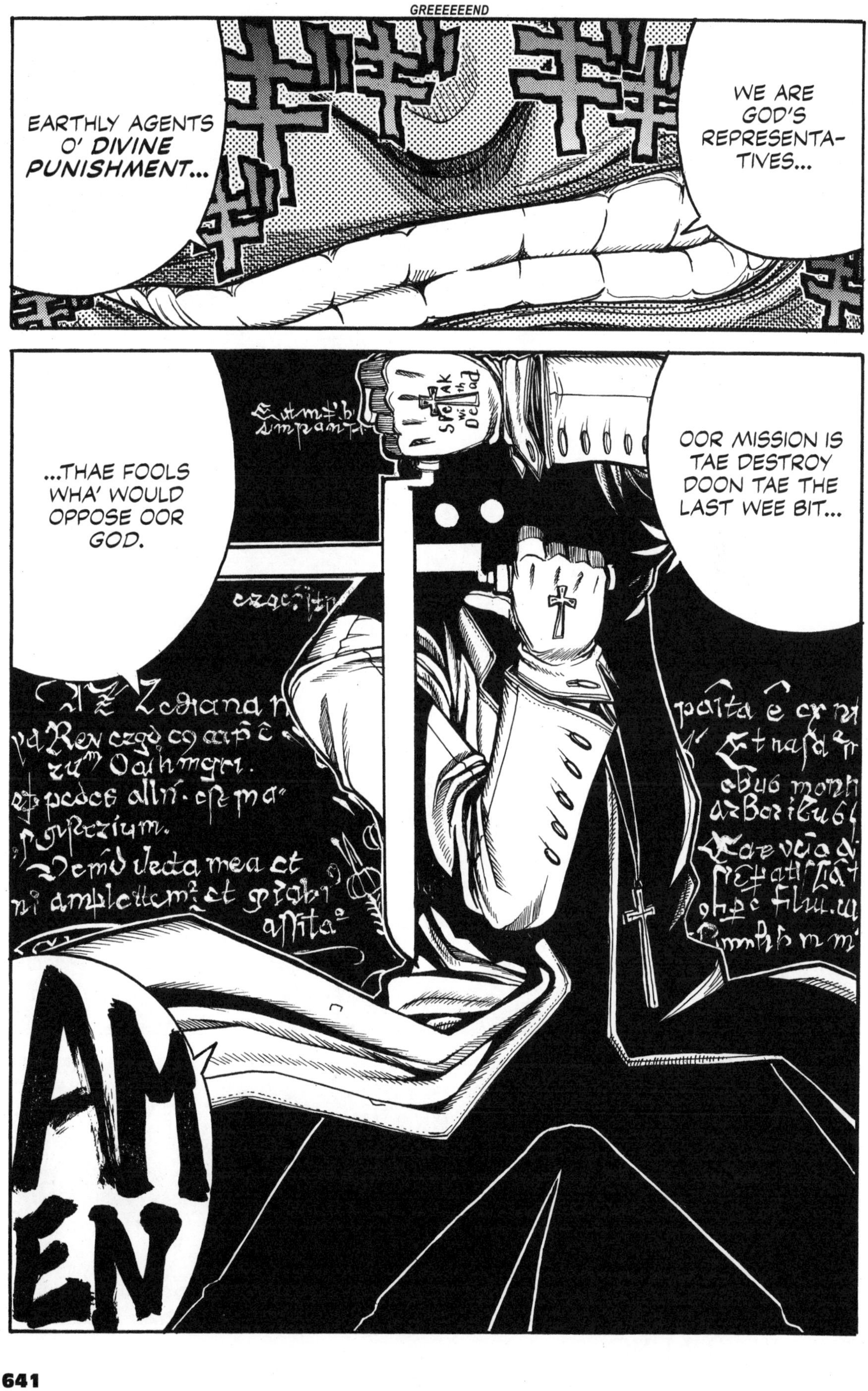
GREEEEEEND
WE ARE GOD'S REPRESENTA-TIVES...
EARTHLY AGENTS O' DIVINE PUNISHMENT...
OOR MISSION IS TAE DESTROY DOON TAE THE LAST WEE BIT...
...THAE FOOLS WHA' WOULD OPPOSE OOR GOD.
AMEN

ORDER 61 / END

ヘルシング

KOHTA HIRANO, born in the Adachi ward of Tokyo in 1973, began his professional manga career as a "horrible" and "lazy" (in Hirano's own words) artist's assistant. Hirano moved on to create a number of relatively obscure manga series, including *Angel Dust*, *Coyote*, *Gun Mania*, and *Hi-Tension*.

In 1996, hentai magazine *Heavenly Pleasure* published Hirano's short story "The Legends of Vampire Hunter," a precursor to what would become his signature creation. In May 1997, *Hellsing* began its run in *Young King OURs* monthly from Shonengahosha, continuing until September 2008. The series ran 95 chapters, plus side stories *Crossfire* and *Hellsing: The Dawn*, which is yet to be completed. While Hirano's early works never reached the level of success of *Hellsing*, many of *Hellsing*'s characters appeared in prototype form in those early series, including Alexander Anderson in *Angel Dust*, Integra Hellsing in *Hi and Low*, and Alucard in "The Legend of Vampire Hunter." A *Hellsing* anime series ran thirteen episodes from October 2001 until January 2002, and ten original video animation (OVA) episodes were released between February 2006 and October 2014.

Since completing *Hellsing*, Hirano has been creating the *Drifters* manga series, a science-fiction/fantasy epic where historical figures from Earth history—including Shimazu Toyohisa, Rasputin, and Adolf Hitler—are thrown into a strange world of clashing fantastical races. The series is currently at 78 chapters and six collected volumes. A twelve-episode *Drifters* anime series ran from October to December 2016, followed by three OVA released in 2017 and 2018.

Kohta Hirano appears as a gun-toting otaku character in the manga/anime series *Highschool of the Dead* by Daisuke Sato and Shouji Sato.

ヘルシング

HELLSING

DELUXE EDITIONS

BY KOHTA HIRANO

AN ENGINEERED ARMY OF VAMPIRES emerges from the darkness under the blood-red banner of the swastika, and the war for the future begins in London. Two groups, the shadowy Hellsing Organization and the Iscariot Agency of the Catholic Church, stand between the undead and the extermination of humanity. But can the forces of the Holy Church ever ally with a group that uses unholy creatures itself, including Alucard, the mightiest vampire of all? Kohta Hirano's manga sensation is now presented in elegant hardcover editions, each collecting over 650 pages of wild action, grisly horror, and savage imagination.

VOLUME 1
ISBN 978-1-50671-553-7 • $49.99

VOLUME 2
ISBN 978-1-50672-001-2 • $49.99

VOLUME 3
ISBN 978-1-50672-002-9 • $49.99

ヘルシング